DEFENDING CONGRESS AND THE CONSTITUTION

DEFENDING CONGRESS AND THE CONSTITUTION

Louis Fisher

University Press of Kansas

Published by the University Press of Kansas (Lawrence, Kansas 66045), which was
organized by the Kansas Board of Regents and is operated and funded by Emporia State
University, Fort Hays State University, Kansas State University, Pittsburg State University,
the University of Kansas, and Wichita State University

Library of Congress Cataloging-in-Publication Data

Fisher, Louis.
  Defending Congress and the Constitution / Louis Fisher.
    p. cm.
  Includes bibliographical references and index.
  ISBN 978-0-7006-1798-2 (cloth : alk. paper)
  ISBN 978-0-7006-1799-9 (pbk. : alk. paper)
  1. United States. Congress—Powers and duties. 2. Separation of powers—United States.
3. United States. Constitution. I. Title.
  KF4935.F57 2011
  342.7302—dc22
                              2011015101

British Library Cataloguing-in-Publication Data is available.

Printed in the United States of America

10 9 8 7 6 5 4 3 2 1

To Senator Robert C. Byrd

CONTENTS

PREFACE

There are two broad messages to this book. The first is to members of Congress. In order to protect your independence and the system of checks and balances, do not defer to the Supreme Court or to Presidents because of their presumed competence. Accept their judgments only when they convince on evidence. Go on reason, not faith. The executive and judicial branches are capable of great errors. The second message is to the public: understand the importance of Congress in protecting and defending your rights and liberties. Without a strong Congress, we cannot speak of democracy. Safeguarding individual rights is often assumed to reside almost wholly with the judiciary, but history offers scant support for that position. Congress frequently takes the lead in defending personal rights and minorities that are not protected in the courts. During my four decades as a staff member of Congress, I testified frequently before committees and wrote committee reports and floor statements. I worked closely on many constitutional and interbranch issues and will talk about those experiences.

A book complimentary to Congress is a rarity, especially in recent decades when public venom is once again aimed at the legislative branch. Some of the criticism is merited. Much is not. I hope this book will give a deeper appreciation of not only the capacity of Congress but also its achievements. Anyone reading this book understands how difficult it is to maintain marriages and friendships, even when the initial attraction is positive. Imagine what it is like to maintain a healthy relationship in a branch that has 535 members, each with a legitimate stake as an elected official from far-flung districts and states. Add to that the tensions that come from a legislative branch divided into two chambers, the competition of rival political parties with conflicting agendas, powerful and well-financed interest groups, almost nonstop political campaigns, media scrutiny, and constant rivalry with the executive and judicial branches. In that light, it is remarkable that anything gets done in Congress. Much that Congress accomplishes merits acclaim, but let the reader reserve judgment until the end of this book.

It was my good fortune to work closely with Senator Sam Ervin in the early 1970s on budgetary issues that posed fundamental constitutional questions. That relationship is explained in Chapter 8. Over the years I worked with other lawmakers who understood and defended their institution. I grew close to Senator Robert C. Byrd and admired his efforts to protect constitutional values. On occasion his staff would call and ask: "Can you speak with the Senator?" Senator Byrd would come on the phone and ask what I was doing. After I described a current project he would say: "Can you come over and talk to me about that?" He was always a wonderful host, eager to explore and learn. I met with him in his spacious quarters in the Appropriations Committee in the Capitol, in the tiny area across the hall he inhabited while in the minority (office space he called Elba), and the magnificent room in the Capitol he occupied as president pro tempore.

At the height of his powers Senator Byrd remained humble and always curious. He delighted in sharing time, trading ideas, and discovering something new. I am happy to dedicate this book to a remarkable public servant. His death was a loss to the nation and to those who knew him, but his principles and values remain with us. He attracted an exceptionally able and dedicated staff and it was my pleasure to work with them: Chief of Staff Barbara Videnieks, Caryn Compton, Dave Corbin, Jim English, Kathleen Hatfield, Dave McMaster, Erik Raven, and Jim Tuite.

Throughout the course of writing this book I received valued advice and feedback from friends and colleagues. Several read the entire manuscript: Reb Brownell, Jeff Crouch, Lee Fisher, Mort Rosenberg, and Mitch Sollenberger. Amsie Hecht, intern for the Constitution Project, offered thoughtful comments on the first four chapters. Valuable feedback on individual chapters came from Dave Adler, Dean Alfange, Nancy Baker, Henry Cohen, Ron Collins, Curtis Copeland, Mike Davidson, Moe Davis, Sandy Davis, John Dean, Neal Devins, Chris Edelson, Mickey Edwards, Jasmine Farrier, Herb Fenster, Gene Fidell, Morgan Frankel, Mike Glennon, Joel Grossman, Katy Harriger, Ryan Hendrickson, Henry Hogue, Phil Joyce, Fred Kaiser, Tom Karako, Nancy Kassop, Chris Kelley, Kevin Kosar, Mel Laracey, Daniel McAdams, Adam Miles, Ron Moe, Irv Nathan, Jim Nathan, Walter Oleszek, Rob Pallitto, Dick Pious, Harold Relyea, Mark Rozell, Mark Rush, Issam Saliba, Jim Saturno, Bob Spitzer, Bill Weaver, and Don Wolfensberger. My deep appreciation to all.

We tend to think of "checks and balances" arising from the three branches of government, but many effective checks come from private individuals and outside groups. It has been my pleasure to work closely with several over the decades: Steve Aftergood of the Federation of American Scientists, the American Civil Liberties Union, the Brennan Center, The Cato Institute, Center for Constitutional Rights, the Constitution Project, Government Accountability Project, and Project on Government Oversight.

I was fortunate to have the completed manuscript reviewed by Robert Spitzer, who has developed a distinguished record in the fields of presidential power and constitutional law. His thoughtful evaluation clarified and sharpened major themes of the book. As he has in the past, Mike Briggs of the University Press of Kansas encouraged this book from the start and helped guide it to the finish line. I thank Larisa Martin for moving the manuscript through the production stages and Lori D. Kranz for careful proofreading.

NOTE ON CITATIONS

All court citations refer to published volumes whenever available: *United States Reports* (U.S.) for Supreme Court decisions, *Federal Reporter* (F.2d or F.3d) for appellate decisions, and *Federal Supplement* (F.Supp. or F.Supp.2d) for district court decisions. There are also citations to *Opinions of the Attorney General* (Op. Atty Gen.) and *Opinions of the Office of Legal Counsel* (Op. O.L.C.) in the Justice Department. Several standard reference works are abbreviated in the footnotes by using the following system:

Elliot   The Debates in the Several State Conventions, on the Adoption of the Federal Constitution (5 vols., Jonathan Elliot, ed., Washington, D.C., 1836–1845).

Farrand   The Records of the Federal Convention of 1787 (4 vols., Max Farrand, ed., New Haven, Conn.: Yale University Press, 1937).

The Federalist   The Federalist, Benjamin F. Wright, ed. (New York: Metro Books, 2002).

Founders   The Founders Constitution (5 vols., Philip B. Kurland and Ralph
Constitution   Lerner, eds., Chicago: University of Chicago Press, 1987).

Landmark Briefs   Landmark Briefs and Arguments of the Supreme Court of the United States: Constitutional Law (Philip B. Kurland and Gerhard Casper, eds., Washington, D.C.: University Publications of America, 1978–).

Richardson   A Compilation of the Messages and Papers of the Presidents (20 vols., James D. Richardson, ed., New York: Bureau of National Literature, 1897–1925).

Stokes   Anson Phelps Stokes, Church and State in the United States (3 vols., New York: Harper & Bros., 1950).

Swindler   Sources and Documents of United States Constitutions (10 vols., William F. Swindler, ed., Dobbs Ferry, N.Y.: Oceana Publications, 1973–79).

Thorpe   The Federal and States Constitutions, Colonial Charters, and Other Organic Laws (7 vols., Francis Newton Thorpe, ed., Washington, D.C.: Government Printing Office, 1909).

DEFENDING CONGRESS AND THE CONSTITUTION

1

CONSTITUTIONAL VALUES

At the start of each Congress, members of the House and one-third of the Senate take an oath to support and defend the Constitution. The oath is a personal duty placed on each lawmaker, a public act that may not be surrendered and transferred to other officers and branches. It does not matter whether lawmakers possess or lack a law degree. They all raise their hands when taking the oath and say "I do." It is a duty to interpret the Constitution as they individually see it. Taking an oath is a solemn moment; a public official pledges to act in good faith. To fulfill the oath, lawmakers must understand and think about constitutional values and know how to protect them. Often it is a task of balancing one value over another, which Congress can do as capably as the other branches. Congress is a major constitutional arbiter and has played an important role (often unappreciated and misunderstood) since the founding.

Taking the Oath

The Constitution requires U.S. Senators and Representatives, members of state legislatures, and all executive and judicial officers "to support this Constitution; but no religious Test shall ever be required as a Qualification to any Office or public Trust under the United States."[1] As with lawmakers, Presidents and federal judges take the oath. They interpret the Constitution as they see it, not necessarily as others see it. The result is a process called "coordinate construction," with all three branches at liberty to reach separate and different interpretations of the Constitution. Out of this competition and struggle emerge a consensus and public understanding. Taken to an extreme, coordinate construction might yield legal and political chaos. But this broad freedom of interpretation has been exercised in a constructive fashion for over two centuries, helping to keep the constitutional debate open and vibrant.

Coordinate construction often seems weaker today. Many lawmakers acquiesce in constitutional judgments reached by other branches and accept them as authoritative and binding. Especially is that so with decisions issued by the Supreme Court. In 1971, Congressman Abner Mikva expressed concern that his colleagues "look on their oath to support the Constitution more as a patri-

---

1. U.S. Const., art. VI, cl. 3.

otic gesture than as a serious part of their function."[2] When lawmakers defer to constitutional interpretations by other branches, they undermine the vigor of coordinate construction and the system of checks and balances. A submissive attitude weakens the promise and reality of self-government. Popular sovereignty suffers when elected representatives subordinate their judgments about constitutional issues to Presidents, executive officials, and federal judges.

Specific examples of this regrettable trend are discussed in this book. In a recent analysis, political scientist Jasmine Farrier examines the degree to which contemporary members of Congress surrender power to other branches. When they do, they not only weaken their own institution. They also fail to protect the interests of their constituents, the principle of self-government, and the system of checks and balances that is vital in protecting individual rights and liberties. A single surrender, however modest, sets a precedent for the next. Power abdicated is not likely to be recovered.[3]

The first bill enacted by Congress, on June 1, 1789, regulated the time and manner of administering oaths by federal officials. This language was agreed to: "I, A. B. do solemnly swear or affirm (as the case may be) that I will support the Constitution of the United States."[4] The oath for legislative staff omitted the words "support the Constitution": "I, A. B. secretary of the Senate, or clerk of the House of Representatives (as the case may be) of the United States of America, do solemnly swear or affirm, that I will truly and faithfully discharge the duties of my said office, to the best of my knowledge and abilities."[5] The difference in language implies that the duty to support the Constitution falls directly on each lawmaker. Congressional staff offer help in carrying out that core duty.

The oath taken by lawmakers today dates to congressional action in 1966. Except for the President, individuals elected or appointed to an office of honor or profit in the civil service or the uniformed services take the oath to "solemnly swear (or affirm) that I will support and defend the Constitution of the United States against all enemies, foreign and domestic; that I will bear true faith and allegiance to the same; that I take this obligation freely, without any mental reservation or purpose of evasion; and that I will well and faithfully discharge the duties of the office on which I am about to enter. So help me God."[6] Note the qualifier: "without any mental reservation or purpose of evasion." Lawmakers

2. Abner J. Mikva and Joseph R. Lundy, "The 91st Congress and the Constitution," 38 U. Chi. L. Rev. 449, 497 (1971).

3. Jasmine Farrier, Congressional Ambivalence: The Political Burdens of Constitutional Authority (2010); see also Louis Fisher, Congressional Abdication on War and Spending (2000).

4. 1 Stat. 23, sec. 1 (1789).

5. Id. at 24, sec. 5.

6. 80 Stat. 424, sec. 3331.

violate that oath when they say they have not studied an issue, cannot understand it, lack requisite legal knowledge, or offer other excuses. The 1966 statute did not apply to Presidents because their oath appears in the Constitution: "I do solemnly swear (or affirm) that I will faithfully execute the Office of President of the United States, and will to the best of my Ability, preserve, protect and defend the Constitution of the United States."[7]

A Republic with Checks

When a member of Congress pledges to support and defend the Constitution, a key duty is to protect the legislative branch and its capacity to check and balance the other branches. An essential element of that duty is representing constituents and safeguarding popular government. When lawmakers defer to the President or to the Supreme Court, they fail to protect the people who put them in office. To James Madison, writing in Federalist No. 49, "the people are the only legitimate foundation of power."[8] Later, in Federalist No. 51, he emphasized that in republican government "the legislative authority necessarily predominates."[9]

Think of those words: republican government, a republic. How many members of Congress and their constituents understand what they mean? The framers knew the meaning of a republic and were willing to fight and die for it. In a republic, the supreme political power rests with the people exercised through their elected representatives. The word "republic" appears in a sentence that citizens repeat frequently: "I pledge allegiance to the flag of the United States of America and to the Republic for which it stands." The important value here is not the flag. It is the republic. Lose the republic and the flag stands for nothing.

The theory of separation of powers, so closely identified with the American Constitution, is frequently misunderstood. Are the branches actually separate? They must be in order to check each other. If they are too separate and kept at a distance, they cannot check and balance other branches. The framers never embraced a pure theory of separated powers. They understood that powers are separated in order to preserve liberties and that a rigid separation can destroy liberties. The French constitutions of 1791 and 1848, rooted in a pure separation of powers, led to absolutism and reaction.[10] The three branches were unable to work effectively together.

7. U.S. Const., art. II, sec. 1.
8. The Federalist 348.
9. Id. at 356.
10. M. J. C. Vile, Constitutionalism and the Separation of Powers 176–211 (1967).

Those who drafted the U.S. Constitution wanted to avoid political fragmentation and paralysis. Government needs to function. Without government,
citizens revert to a state of nature. Joseph Story explained in the 1830s that a
rigid adherence to separation of powers "in all cases would be subversive of the
efficiency of the government, and result in the destruction of the public liberties."[11] The subtlety and sophistication of the American system were nicely captured by Justice Robert Jackson: "While the Constitution diffuses power the
better to secure liberty, it also contemplates that practice will integrate the dis-
persed powers into a workable government. It enjoins upon its branches sepa-
ratedness but interdependence, autonomy but reciprocity."[12] His formulation
calls for a complex balance that is difficult to achieve but essential for constitutional government.

The Constitution separates the branches but also combines them for various
functions. The overlappings are familiar: the President may veto legislation, subject to a two-thirds override vote by both houses. The President nominates executive officers and judges, but the Senate confirms. The President submits treaties;
the Senate must approve. When the House of Representatives impeaches the
President, its action is subject to a Senate trial presided over by the Chief Justice. Some powers are assigned exclusively to each branch: the President's power
to pardon offenders, the power of each house to discipline and expel lawmakers, and the power of federal courts to decide when a lawsuit presents a "case or
controversy."

After the draft Constitution was sent to the states for ratification, some Anti-
Federalists objected to the overlappings of power. They argued that the presidential veto would encroach upon the legislature. Alexander Hamilton and
James Madison brushed aside protests that the draft Constitution violated the
separation doctrine. In Federalist No. 75, Hamilton defended the combination
of the President and the Senate in the treaty process and bristled at "the trite
topic of the intermixture of powers."[13] By the time of the Philadelphia Convention, the doctrine of separated powers had lost ground to the more important
system of checks and balances. A pamphleteer at that time dismissed the separation doctrine in its pure form, calling it a "hackneyed principle" and a "trite
maxim."[14]

Even so, some delegates at the state ratifying conventions strongly objected
to overlapping powers and drafted language to secure a strict separation. "How

11. 2 Joseph Story, Commentaries on the Constitution of the United States 12 (1991 reissue;
originally published in 1833).
12. Youngstown Co. v. Sawyer, 343 U.S. 579, 635 (1952) (concurring opinion).
13. The Federalist 475.
14. Vile, Constitutionalism and the Separation of Powers, at 153.

is the executive?" demanded one irate delegate at Virginia's ratifying convention. "Contrary to the opinion of all the best writers, blended with the legislative. We have asked for bread, and they have given us a stone."[15] Three states (Virginia, North Carolina, and Pennsylvania) proposed a separation clause as a constitutional amendment to prohibit one branch from exercising the powers vested in the others. Congress rejected this proposal and also a substitute amendment to make the three departments "separate and distinct."[16]

Implied Powers

After taking office in 1789, members of Congress debated a number of complex constitutional issues without any direction from federal judges. District courts had yet to be established by statute; the Senate needed to confirm appointments to the lower courts and the Supreme Court. For several years there were no judicial rulings to guide legislative action. Lawmakers independently interpreted the President's removal power, the scope of the Commerce Clause, congressional access to executive branch documents, the legislative power to investigate executive agencies, warrantless searches and seizures at the border, and statutory procedures to limit the President's power to use the militia to put down insurrections in the states. Those and other issues were settled solely by the elected branches without the involvement of the courts.

An early dispute concerned the President's authority to remove executive officials. The Constitution did not expressly vest that power in the President, but lawmakers explored the President's duty under Article II to "take Care that the Laws be faithfully executed." If a department head interfered with the execution of law, the President needed to remove the individual. This implied power preoccupied the House of Representatives from May 19 through June 24, 1789, occupying almost 200 pages of the legislative record. James Madison led the debate. Many of his colleagues participated actively in exploring the source and limits of presidential authority.[17] In the end, both houses agreed that the President possesses an implied power to remove department heads.

---

15. 3 Elliot 280.
16. 3 Elliot 280; 4 Elliot 116, 121. See John Bach McMaster and Frederick D. Stone, eds., Pennsylvania and the Federal Constitution 475–77 (1888). Amendment language: Edward Dumbault, The Bill of Rights and What It Means Today 174–75, 183, 199 (1957). Rejection: 1 Annals of Cong. 435–36 (June 8, 1789) and 789–90 (August 18, 1789); 1 Senate Journals 64, 73–74 (1820).
17. Louis Fisher, Constitutional Conflicts Between Congress and the President 48–52 (5th ed., 2007).

It would be a mistake from this debate to conclude that the President has plenary power to remove all executive officials. Law professor and former Justice Department official John Yoo has argued, "From the time of George Washington, presidents have understood Article II to grant them the authority to hire and fire all subordinate officers of the United States, and hence command their activities, even though the Constitution mentions only the power to appoint, not to remove."[18] That is far too sweeping a claim. When Madison turned his attention to the position of Comptroller in the Treasury Department, he refused to treat that official as a purely executive officer. He said it was necessary "to consider the nature of this office." Its properties, Madison concluded, were not "purely of an Executive nature." Instead, they "partake of a Judiciary quality as well as Executive; perhaps the latter obtains in the greatest degree." Because of the mixed nature of the Comptroller's duties, "there may be strong reasons why an officer of this kind should not hold his office at the pleasure of the Executive branch of the Government."[19]

It may seem odd for Madison to speak with such confidence about the nature of an office that was just being created. How did he know, in looking forward, that the Comptroller would be exercising quasi-judicial duties? The answer: he needed only recall the actions of the Continental Congress in 1781 when it took steps to shift financial duties to new administrative officers: a Superintendent of Finance, auditors, and the Comptroller. Technically they were not executive officers because they served as agents of Congress. They had no independent or separate existence, but the Comptroller of 1781 was expected to settle all public accounts. On all appeals, he "shall openly and publicly hear the parties, and his decision shall be conclusive."[20]

Madison in 1789 wanted to protect that independence, even from the President. Legislation in 1795 provided that in all cases where the Comptroller decides a case against a claimant involving debts to the United States, his determination "shall be final and conclusive to all concerned."[21] The precedent for the Comptroller's office would later be extended to cover other types of adjudicatory work performed in federal agencies, including decisions by administrative law judges and executive officials who handle individual claims and benefits.

In their study of the "unitary executive," Steven Calabresi and Christopher

18. John Yoo, "An Executive Without Much Privilege," New York Times, May 26, 2010, at A23.

19. 1 Annals of Cong. 611–12 (1789).

20. Louis Fisher, "The Administrative World of *Chadha* and *Bowsher*," 47 Pub. Adm. Rev. 213, 215 (1987).

21. 1 Stat. 441–42, sec. 4 (1795).

Yoo conclude that all employees in the executive branch are subordinate to the President and answerable to him. On the basis of this model, they advocate plenary removal power for the President: "[A]ll forty-three presidents, from George Washington to George W. Bush, have insisted on the view that the Constitution gives them the power to remove and direct subordinates as to law execution. All forty-three presidents have refused to acquiesce in repeated congressional efforts to sabotage the unitary executive bequeathed to us by the framers."[22] No such power was "bequeathed." To Madison and his colleagues in the First Congress, the Comptroller was immune from the removal power, either by the President or the department head, unless the Comptroller's action prevented the law from being faithfully carried out. Otherwise, he was independent and not subject to presidential influence or control.

To Calabresi and Yoo, the Constitution "gives presidents the power to control their subordinates by vesting all of the executive power in one, and only one, person: the president of the United States."[23] The President does control subordinates to the extent of ensuring that they faithfully carry out the law. If they do, there is no reason to interfere and no authority to ask department heads or White House staff to intervene. The superior force is the law, not the President. Agency employees handling social security payments and veterans' claims, among other administrative tasks, should not have their professional judgments second-guessed and overridden by executive officials who not only lack technical skills but who probably also have a political and partisan agenda. Any administration that functioned in that manner would be justifiably condemned. The distinction between executive officials who carry out political duties (subject to full presidential control) and those who discharge "ministerial" and legal duties (where presidential control is restricted) is discussed at the end of Chapter 2.

Other issues tackled by Congress in 1789 (the scope of the commerce power and the legislative power to investigate) are explored in subsequent chapters. Here I briefly give three examples of Congress settling constitutional issues without the assistance of judicial rulings: warrantless searches at the border, congressional access to executive branch documents, and statutory procedures designed to limit the President's use of the militia when putting down domestic insurrections.

Long before the Supreme Court discovered exceptions to the warrant requirement under the Fourth Amendment, Congress and the executive branch decided that warrants were not necessary for border searches. A statute in 1789 autho-

22. Steven G. Calabresi and Christopher S. Yoo, The Unitary Executive: Presidential Power from Washington to Bush 418 (2008) (hereafter "Calabresi and Yoo").
    23. Id. at 4.

rized federal officials to enter any ship or vessel suspected of having concealed goods or merchandise and to search and seize such goods.[24] Many years later, in 1985, the Supreme Court acknowledged: "Since the founding of our Republic, Congress has granted the Executive plenary authority to conduct routine searches and seizures at the border, without probable cause or a warrant, in order to regulate the collection of duties and to prevent the introduction of contraband into the country."[25]

In 1790, Congress experienced its first taste of trying to get documents from the executive branch. Treasury Secretary Alexander Hamilton asked Congress to provide financial compensation to Baron von Steuben for his service during the Revolutionary War. The House and the Senate appointed committees to draft and report legislation to provide this assistance. As part of the investigation, Senator William Maclay discovered that the Continental Congress had already given Steuben $7,000. Maclay obtained some documents from the Treasury Department but not everything he asked for.

Hamilton refused Maclay access to some documents because he saw no grounds for opening "any Gentlemen's Papers." Maclay disagreed, insisting that the papers "belonged to the public & to no private Gentleman" and that Hamilton lacked any authority "to refuse information to a Committee of Congress."[26] Congress clearly had the upper hand. If Hamilton chose to stonewall, Maclay and his committee members could simply put the bill on the shelf and take no further action. Hamilton had to settle. His haughty attitude prompted Maclay to refer to him as "his Holiness" and to offer this judgment about Hamilton's explanations: "A School Boy should be Whipped for such pitiful Evasions."[27] Instead of the lump sum of $7,394.74 recommended by Hamilton, plus an annuity for life and "a moderate grant of land," Congress provided less: an annuity of $2,500 for life.[28]

In 1792, Congress debated a bill to establish a uniform militia drawn from the various states. Some members of the House expressed concern about the power of the militia not only to suppress insurrections and repel invasions but also to turn itself against the community. To curb military abuses, Representative Abraham Baldwin offered an amendment to provide that information of any insurrection shall be communicated to the President by either a Justice of

24. 1 Stat. 43, sec. 24 (1789).
25. United States v. Montoya de Hernandez, 473 U.S. 531, 535 (1985).
26. Kenneth R. Bowling and Helen Veit, eds., The Diary of William Maclay 266 (1988).
27. Id. at 270.
28. 6 Stat. 2 (1790); 1 Annals of Cong. 978–80. For further details on the Steuben investigation and bill, see Louis Fisher, The Politics of Executive Privilege 7–10 (2004).

the Supreme Court or a district judge. The clear objective: add a judicial check on executive decisions to use military force. The enacted bill included the judicial limitation on the power of Commander in Chief.[29] When President George Washington used the militia to put down the Whiskey Rebellion, he complied fully with these statutory restrictions.[30] Three years later, Congress removed the judicial check.[31]

A Government of "Enumerated Powers"?

Members of Congress, executive officials, and federal courts often refer to the U.S. Constitution as one of "enumerated powers," as though every power granted to the national government is expressly stated in the Constitution. Some powers are enumerated, but the federal government is more than that. This chapter has already identified executive and legislative powers that are not enumerated or expressly given: the President's removal power and the power of Congress to investigate and obtain executive documents. Those "implied powers" can be reasonably drawn from express powers. The President has the express power to see that the laws are faithfully executed, and from that power he has broad power to remove executive officials who are not executing the law. Congress has the express power to legislate. From that power, it has an implied power to investigate and obtain documents so that it can legislate in an informed manner and ensure that statutes are being properly implemented.

In 1995, while striking down a congressional effort to regulate guns in schoolyards, the Supreme Court announced: "We start with first principles. The Constitution creates a Federal Government of enumerated powers."[32] Two years later, when invalidating the Religious Freedom Restoration Act, the Court again stated: "Under our Constitution, the Federal Government is one of enumerated powers."[33] Those statements are highly misleading. If the U.S. Constitution were limited to enumerated or express powers, the Court would have no power to strike down congressional or executive actions. Nowhere does the Constitution expressly grant the Court the power of judicial review. It is an implied power, as explained more fully in the next chapter.

---

29. 1 Stat. 264 (1792).

30. Details on this statute and the Whiskey Rebellion appear in Louis Fisher, "Domestic Commander in Chief: Early Checks by Other Branches," 29 Cardozo L. Rev. 961, 975–79 (2008), available at http://www.loufisher.org/docs/wp/418.pdf.

31. 1 Stat. 424 (1795).

32. United States v. Lopez, 514 U.S. 549, 552 (1995).

33. Boerne v. Flores, 521 U.S. 507, 516 (1997).

The Constitution specifically provides that each house of Congress "may determine the Rules of its Proceedings" and may "punish its Members for disorderly Behaviour."[34] Under the Constitution, the President "may require the Opinion, in writing, of the principal Officer in each of the executive Departments."[35] Would anyone doubt that Congress and the President could exercise those powers even if not enumerated? Why should the Court suggest that government consists only of enumerated powers? Is the purpose to emphasize that the federal government is subject to limits and that the Court exists to monitor the boundaries? Then why not speak plainly: the federal government is one of limited powers. Surely that is the case. Why mislead the public with simplistic statements about enumerated powers?

The framers understood the need for implied powers. Madison explained in Federalist No. 44: "No axiom is more clearly established in law, or in reason, than that wherever the end is required, the means are authorized; wherever a general power to do a thing is given, every particular power necessary for doing it is included."[36] During the First Congress, Madison had to beat back an effort to limit the national government to powers expressly granted. The Articles of Confederation, which guided the United States after its break with England in 1776, gave broad protection to the states. They retained all powers except those "expressly delegated" to the national government.

When the members of the First Congress debated the Bill of Rights, it was proposed that the Tenth Amendment include the language "expressly delegated." Madison objected to "expressly" because the functions and responsibilities of the federal government could not be delineated with such precision. It was impossible to confine a government to the exercise of express or enumerated powers, for there "must necessarily be admitted powers by implication, unless the Constitution descended to recount every minutiae."[37] Madison prevailed. Congress refused to include "expressly" in the Tenth Amendment, which states: "The powers not delegated to the United States by the Constitution, nor prohibited by it to the States, are reserved to the States respectively, or to the people."

Despite this clear history against the doctrine of enumerated powers, members of Congress continue to advocate it. On June 22, 2009, Senator Tom Coburn introduced a bill to require Congress "to specify the source of authority under the United States Constitution for the enactment of laws, and for other purposes."[38] Called the Enumerated Powers Act, it is actually something else.

34. U.S. Const., art. I, sec. 5.
35. U.S. Const., art. II, sec. 2.
36. The Federalist 322.
37. 1 Annals of Cong. 761 (Aug. 18, 1789).
38. S. 1319, 111th Cong., 1st Sess. (2009).

The bill merely requires that each statute of Congress "shall contain a concise explanation of the specific constitutional authority relied upon for the enactment of each portion of that Act."[39] The bill language is not confined to express or enumerated authority but rather to "specific constitutional authority." That phrase would include a range of implied powers, such as the implied power to investigate, issue subpoenas, and hold witnesses in contempt.

Floor debate on the bill, however, emphasized the word "enumeration." Senator Coburn asked how the federal government accumulated budget deficits in the trillions of dollars: "How did we get to where we can put our children and grandchildren in such dire straits in their future? We got to it by ignoring the enumerated powers of the Constitution."[40] However, the deficits were caused by exercising ordinary enumerated powers: cutting taxes at the same time that the government increased military spending, continued growth in domestic spending, enactment of new entitlements (prescription drug benefits), and engaging in unpaid military commitments in Iraq and Afghanistan. Of course there are much larger entitlements, including social security, Medicare, and Medicaid. Those programs were enacted with the understanding that they fit within the federal government's enumerated powers.

In supporting Coburn's bill, Senator Orrin Hatch denied that the Constitution granted Congress "all legislative authority. Article I gives Congress only 'legislative powers herein granted.' Those powers are listed, or enumerated, in article I, section 8." The herein-granted phrase is analyzed in the next section, but congressional powers are not merely those that are enumerated. They can be implied. Hatch continued: "The 10th amendment affirms that the Federal Government has only powers that are affirmatively delegated to it. James Madison agreed in Federalist No. 45 that the powers delegated to the Federal Government are 'few and defined.'"[41] In using those words, Madison never meant that Congress was restricted to enumerated powers. His position is clear in other Federalist Papers and in his position on the Tenth Amendment, where he successfully deleted "expressly."

Hatch offered another argument to support the Enumerated Powers Act. He drew attention to language by Chief Justice John Marshall in *McCulloch v. Maryland* (1819): "This government is acknowledged by all, to be one of enumerated powers. The principle, that it can exercise only the powers granted to it . . . is now universally admitted."[42] It is curious that Marshall in this case would

---

39. Id., sec. 2 (§102a).
40. 155 Cong. Rec. S6933 (daily ed. June 23, 2009).
41. Id. at S9548 (daily ed. September 17, 2009).
42. 17 U.S. (4 Wheat.) 316, 404 (1819), cited by Senator Hatch at 155 Cong. Rec. S9548.

encourage a belief in enumerated powers. The issue in *McCulloch* was whether the national government possessed authority to create a U.S. Bank. Marshall was not dogmatic about enumerated powers. He acknowledged: "Among the enumerated powers, we do not find that of establishing a bank or creating a corporation."[43] One need not be a learned Justice to look at the text of the Constitution and realize that it says nothing about national banks or corporations.

Marshall did not decide the case on the basis of enumerated powers. He wrote: "But there is no phrase in the instrument which, like the articles of confederation, excludes incidental or implied powers; and which requires that everything granted shall be expressly and minutely described."[44] Marshall upheld the bank on the basis of implied powers and by interpreting in broad fashion the Necessary and Proper Clause: "Let the end be legitimate, let it be within the scope of the constitution, and all means which are appropriate, which are plainly adapted to that end, which are not prohibited, but consist with the letter and spirit of the constitution, are constitutional."[45] Obviously that is far afield from enumerated powers.[46] The U.S. Bank issue is covered more thoroughly in Chapter 4.

Legislative Powers "Herein Granted"

Advocates of broad executive and presidential power try to limit Congress to express and enumerated powers while extending to the President a full array of plenary, implied, emergency, and inherent powers. One of the first efforts to limit the powers of Congress under Article I and to expand presidential power under Article II was by Alexander Hamilton. Writing under the name Pacificus in 1793, he vigorously defended a proclamation of neutrality issued by President George Washington, who directed Americans to be neutral in the war between England and France. Critics protested that Washington had overstepped his constitutional authority.

Hamilton disagreed, pointing to this language in Article II: "The executive power shall be vested in a President of the United States of America." Although Article II proceeds to identify various presidential powers (including the func-

---

43. 17 U.S. (4 Wheat.) at 404.

44. Id.

45. Id. at 421.

46. For further details on the Enumerated Powers Act, see 156 Cong. Rec. S2795–97 (daily ed. April 29, 2010).

tions as Commander in Chief, the power to nominate, and to grant pardons), he said it "would not consist with the rules of sound construction, to consider this enumeration of particular authorities as derogating from the more comprehensive grant in the general clause, further than as it may be coupled with express restrictions or limitations."[47] In short, Article II vests in the President the full "executive power" subject to certain express limits. Hamilton compared this general grant of executive power to his claim of a more narrow grant of authority to Congress: "In the article which gives the legislative powers of the government, the expressions are: 'All legislative powers herein granted shall be vested in a Congress of the United States.'"[48] To Hamilton, the words "herein granted" were intended to limit Congress to the powers enumerated in Article I.

Hamilton's line of argument has been followed by some public officials and legal scholars, including John Yoo, Steven Calabresi, and Christopher Yoo. (John Yoo and Christopher Yoo are not related.) During his service in the Justice Department from 2001 to 2003, John Yoo wrote a series of memos to provide legal justification for harsh methods of interrogation and other broad interpretations of presidential power in the field of war-making and foreign affairs. In a memo on September 25, 2001, he concluded that any unenumerated executive powers must be placed with the President because of the Vesting Clause in Article II, which states that "the executive power shall be vested in a President of the United States of America." Article I, Yoo reasoned, "gives Congress only the powers 'herein granted,'" while the President's powers "include inherent executive powers that are unenumerated in the Constitution."[49] Yoo relied on Hamilton for his analysis.[50] In their writings on the "unitary executive," law professors Steven Calabresi and Christopher Yoo similarly read Article II expansively while pointing to the supposedly more restrictive "herein granted" language in Article I.[51]

The interpretations by Hamilton, John Yoo, Steven Calabresi, and Christopher Yoo are not persuasive. First, Congress is not limited to the express and enumerated powers of Article I. The legislative branch (along with other branches)

47. 4 The Works of Alexander Hamilton 438 (Henry Cabot Lodge, ed., G. P. Putnam's, 1904).
48. Id. at 438–39.
49. Memorandum opinion from John C. Yoo, Deputy Assistant Attorney General, to Timothy Flanagan, Deputy Counsel to the President, September 25, 2001, reprinted in The Torture Papers: The Road to Abu Ghraib 8 (Karen J. Greenberg and Joshua L. Dratel, eds., 2005) (hereafter Greenberg and Dratel).
50. For a critique of Yoo's analysis of Hamilton, see David Gray Adler, "Presidential Power and Foreign Affairs in the Bush Administration: The Use and Abuse of Alexander Hamilton," 40 Pres. Stud. Q. 531 (2010). A more general critique: Louis Fisher, "John Yoo and the Republic," 41 Pres. Stud. Q. 177 (2011), available at http://www.loufisher.org/docs/wp/Yoo_psq_2011.pdf.
51. Calabresi and Yoo, at 55.

has access to a broad array of implied powers that radiate from express powers. Second, "express" powers in Article I are hardly limited to narrow areas. Consider the vast scope attached to the power to tax, borrow money, and regulate commerce. Third, in addition to these legislative powers expressly stated and implied, Article I vests in Congress this authority: "To make all Laws which shall be necessary and proper for carrying into Execution the foregoing Powers, and all other Powers vested by this Constitution in the Government of the United States, or in any Department or Officer thereof."[52] The Necessary and Proper Clause reinforces not only the capacity of Congress to implement its powers over national policy but also its authority over executive departments and executive officials.

Inherent Powers

In analyzing presidential power, John Yoo supported "inherent executive powers that are unenumerated in the Constitution."[53] Some scholars treat "implied powers" and "inherent powers" as the same.[54] They are fundamentally different. Implied powers, which must be drawn reasonably from express powers, are anchored in the Constitution. Inherent powers, by definition, are not drawn from express powers. They "inhere" in the person or the office. *Black's Law Dictionary* has defined inherent power in this manner: "An authority possessed without its being derived from another. . . . [P]owers over and beyond those explicitly granted in the Constitution or reasonably to be implied from express grants."[55] It is clearly set apart from express and implied powers.

The Constitution is protected when Presidents act under express and implied powers. It is endangered when they act under inherent powers because they claim the freedom to act outside the Constitution. John Yoo consistently argues that inherent powers are so central to presidential power that they cannot be limited by statutes or treaties: "[T]he constitutional structure requires that any ambiguities in the allocation of a power that is executive in nature—such as the power to conduct military hostilities—must be resolved in favor of the executive branch."[56] The President, he argues, possesses "complete discretion in exercising the Commander-in-Chief power."[57]

52. U.S. Const., art. I, sec. 8, cl. 18.
53. Memo of September 25, 2001, reprinted in Greenberg and Dratal, at 8.
54. E.g., Calabresi and Yoo, at 20, 430.
55. Black's Law Dictionary 703 (5th ed. 1979).
56. Greenberg and Dratel, at 8.
57. Id. at 5.

A constitution protects individual rights and liberties by specifying and limiting government. Express and implied powers serve that purpose. Inherent powers do not. They open the door to claims of power that have no limits. What inheres in the President? Inherent is sometimes cross-referenced to "intrinsic," which can be something "belonging to the essential nature or constitution of a thing."[58] What is in the "nature" of an office? Nebulous words and concepts invite political abuse and endanger individual liberties. Presidents who assert inherent powers move the nation from one of limited powers to boundless and ill-defined authority, undermining the doctrine of separation of powers and the system of checks and balances.[59]

Congressional Competence

In 1983, Abner Mikva (by now a federal judge) wrote critically of the capacity of Congress to engage in effective constitutional deliberation. No doubt he is correct that Congress will often pass "the hard questions to the courts."[60] The same, however, can be said of Presidents and federal courts when they sidestep difficult questions and push them elsewhere for resolution.

Presidents frequently sign bills into law while at the same time expressing deep misgivings about unconstitutional features of the legislation. As the Court has noted, "it is not uncommon for Presidents to approve legislation containing parts which are objectionable on constitutional grounds."[61] When President Ronald Reagan received a bill in 1987 to reauthorize the independent counsel, he raised strong constitutional objections to some of its provisions.[62] Yet he decided to sign it. Public confidence in government had eroded, he said, and there was a need to assure citizens that procedures were available to uncover and punish corruption and illegality within the executive branch. If he objected to the unconstitutionality of the bill, he should have vetoed it and asked Congress to fix the constitutional problems. It is not the responsibility of Presidents to simply kick an unconstitutional bill out the door to see what courts (or Congress) might do.

58. Merriam-Webster's Collegiate Dictionary 614 (10th ed. 1965).

59. Louis Fisher, "The Unitary Executive and Inherent Executive Power," 12 U. Pa. J. Const. L. 569, 586–90 (2010), available at http://www.loufisher.org/docs/pip/unitaryexecutive2010.pdf.

60. Abner J. Mikva, "How Well Does Congress Support and Defend the Constitution?," 61 N.C. L. Rev. 587, 588–89 (1983).

61. INS v. Chadha, 462 U.S. 919, 942 n.13 (1983).

62. Public Papers of the Presidents, 1987, II, at 1524.

For their part, courts have a history of receiving "hard questions" and quickly pushing them away. They do this by relying on various threshold questions to prevent judicial resolution: the person or group bringing the case lacks standing to sue, the case is not ripe, it is so ripe it is moot, it is a political question, and so forth. Judicial tactics for avoiding difficult constitutional questions (like covert spending) are covered in Chapter 3. When courts duck a constitutional issue, it is left to the executive and legislative branches.

Mikva offered three examples of Congress engaging in constitutional interpretation over the previous decade, concluding that lawmakers failed each time to conduct their deliberations with adequate care. In a separate article, I looked at the same examples and found that Congress was reasonably informed and careful in its deliberations. Its judgments compared favorably to those announced by the courts.[63]

In one example, Mikva points out that the Court in *National League of Cities v. Usery* (1976) struck down a provision in the Fair Labor Standards Amendments of 1974 that extended the minimum wage level to employees of state and local governments. Quite true. But Congress concluded that its action in 1974 was strongly supported by *Maryland v. Wirtz* (1968), issued by an 8-to-1 Court. By contrast, *National League* split the Court 5 to 4. Not only was it impossible to anticipate *National League*, but its reasoning was so strained and unpersuasive that it seemed guaranteed to have a short shelf life, which is what happened. In *Garcia v. San Antonio Metropolitan Transit Authority* (1985), the Court swung around and reversed itself, again 5 to 4.[64] The constitutional judgment of Congress in 1974 was as sound as the Court's in 1976. The tortured journey from *National League* to *Garcia* is discussed in Chapter 4.

Mikva criticized lawmakers who think their task is to behave like federal judges in lower courts, "reading and interpreting Supreme Court precedent."[65] Congress should reach its own decisions about constitutionality, he said, "rather than having to predict what the Supreme Court would do—a function that is presumably already being performed by the judicial system."[66] Congress needs to provide "a different viewpoint on the Constitution and become an innovative force."[67] I fully agree with that analysis.

63. Louis Fisher, "Constitutional Interpretation by Members of Congress," 63 N.C. L. Rev. 707 (1985), available at http://www.loufisher.org/docs/ci/461.pdf.
64. Id. at 732–34; Maryland v. Wirtz, 392 U.S. 183 (1968); National League of Cities v. Usery, 426 U.S. 833 (1976); Garcia v. San Antonio Metropolitan Transit Authority, 469 U.S. 528 (1985).
65. Mikva, "How Well Does Congress Support and Defend the Constitution?," at 607.
66. Id.
67. Id. at 608.

Yet at the end of his article, Mikva advised members of Congress to "remember that the system was designed to give the courts the final say."[68] I know of no evidence to support that. The constitutional and political system was never designed to give the courts that power. Even Mikva, I am sure, would agree that if the Court interprets a statute to mean A, not B, Congress is fully empowered to pass another statute that says it means B, not A. This type of "statutory reversal" happens regularly. Did Mikva mean that courts have the final say not on statutory questions but only on constitutional interpretation? As the next section explains, and indeed the entire book will drive home, that claim is far too broad and finds no support in U.S. history, law, or practice.

Claims of Judicial Supremacy

During debate on March 23, 1982, Senator Harrison Schmitt told his colleagues: "The final word on the meaning of the Constitution is concededly that of the Supreme Court but until that tribunal has spoken in a definitive manner, we cannot deem ourselves shackled and mute." Later he explained: "Congress, not less than the judiciary, is bound by the Constitution and is obligated to assess the constitutionality of its actions. The notion that the judiciary has a monopoly on constitutional decisionmaking has never held sway in our history."[69] According to this view, lawmakers may participate in constitutional interpretation until the Court decides the matter, after which lawmakers must accept the result. More than two centuries of experience offer no support for this automatic deference to the judiciary. Often lawmakers and the public have refused to accept a Supreme Court decision. We are better off (democratically and constitutionally) when elected officials decide to press their political agenda, with or without judicial support.

Many academics treat the Court as the final word. A 1975 article by Professor Paul Brest offered lawmakers guidance on how to conscientiously interpret the Constitution. He hesitated to accept the Court's claim in *Powell v. McCormack* (1969) that the Court is "the ultimate interpreter of the Constitution." Nonetheless, without providing any evidence, Brest described the judiciary as "its most skilled, disinterested, and articulate interpreter."[70] That gives far too much credit to the courts. Few people who read judicial opinions, including

68. Id. at 610–11.
69. 128 Cong. Rec. 5091 (1982).
70. Paul Brest, "The Conscientious Legislator's Guide to Constitutional Interpretation," 27 Stan. L. Rev. 585, 588 (1975); Powell v. McCormack, 395 U.S. 486 (1969).

those of the Supreme Court, could describe them as invariably skilled, disinterested, or articulate. Subsequent chapters discuss these judicial limitations.

Toward the end of his article, Brest focused on "the practical problems that confront a legislator whose constitutional obligations conflict with the political demands of his office. Perhaps it is naïve to assume that the Constitution will often prevail when political interests are threatened."[71] There is no necessary tension between the Constitution and political interests. As this book explains, the Constitution is often protected when political interests triumph. Political interests have successfully prevailed over judicial opinions in such areas as commerce, race, women's rights, child labor, religion, and privacy. Brest urged lawmakers "to analyze the opinions of courts—the most systematic and best qualified constitutional interpreters."[72] Courts are the best qualified? On what grounds? What evidence can be assembled? The examples provided in this book argue against this judicial idolatry.

In 1975, Professor Henry Monaghan explained how "constitutional common law" offers a coordinate role to Congress. Congressional debate in committee and on the floor may provide the Supreme Court useful feedback about constitutional issues. But this coordinate role, he cautioned, was necessarily subordinate to judicial supremacy: "After a history of far more struggle than is generally remembered, it is now settled that (absent a constitutional amendment) the Court has the last say, and in that sense its constitutional interpretations are both authoritative and final."[73] Erroneous Supreme Court decisions are typically repudiated not by constitutional amendments but by the regular political process. Monaghan's phrase "it is now settled" is a mere claim. It is not an argument substantiated with evidence.

Some scholars insist that judicial finality is needed to settle political disputes and put them to rest.[74] That is sometimes true, as with the Little Rock desegregation crisis in 1957. Also, individuals need to go about their activities with the assurance that legal rules will not be constantly changing. Uncertainty undermines personal and business decisions. But settling something is successful only when the outcome receives public understanding and support. In the nineteenth century, a President in his inaugural address told the country that a particular issue was before the Supreme Court, "where it will be speedily and finally decided." The

71. Id. at 601.

72. Id.

73. Henry P. Monaghan, "Foreword: Constitutional Common Law," 89 Harv. L. Rev. 1, 2 (1975).

74. Larry Alexander and Frederick Schauer, "On Extrajudicial Constitutional Interpretation," 110 Harv. L. Rev. 1359 (1997). For a rebuttal, see Neal Devins and Louis Fisher, "Judicial Exclusivity and Political Instability," 84 Va. L. Rev. 83 (1998).

President was James Buchanan. The case about to be decided: *Dred Scott v. Sandford* (1857). The decision was certainly speedy but hardly final. Within four years the country lurched into a bloody and costly civil war. Settling a dispute in court is not enough. It must be settled properly. The Court's record in *Dred Scott* and other racial issues after the Civil War is examined in Chapter 5.

Many examples in this book illustrate how courts attempted to settle a constitutional issue only to have it fester for years, breeding anger and resentment. Eventually the political process forced the courts to rethink the issue and accommodate society's judgment. A prominent example is the congressional effort to regulate child labor. Twice the Supreme Court declared federal legislation unconstitutional, the first time on grounds of the commerce power and the second on the taxing power. Congress and the country continued to press for legislation. Two decades later the Court not only capitulated but acknowledged that its earlier decisions were indefensible. Child labor legislation is discussed in Chapter 4.

Even when the Court decides a case 8 to 1, as it did in 1940 in upholding a compulsory flag salute, there is no inevitable finality. Protests against the decision were so powerful (in the press, law reviews, Congress, and the public) that within three years the Court reversed itself and struck down the flag salute as an offense against religious liberty. The full story appears in Chapter 6.

Ducking and Balancing Constitutional Issues

Members of Congress many times refuse to debate and decide a constitutional issue. As a substitute, they include language in a bill to authorize "expedited review" in the courts. Typically the bill anticipates that parties who object on constitutional grounds may take their case to a three-judge court (combining district and appellate judges) and from there directly to the Supreme Court. For example, the Gramm-Rudman deficit control statute of 1985 provided that any member of Congress "may bring an action, in the United States District Court for the District of Columbia, for declaratory judgment and injunctive relief on the ground that any order that might be issued [under the statute] violates the Constitution." It is then the duty of the district court and the Supreme Court "to advance on the docket and to expedite to the greatest possible extent the disposition of any matter" brought under the statute.[75] Gramm-Rudman is discussed in Chapter 8. Members of Congress who vote on bills with this language do so with their fingers crossed and their eyes closed.

75. 99 Stat. 1098–99, sec. 274 (1985).

Congress turned to expedited review four times from 1985 to 1996. On all four occasions either a section of a bill or the entire bill was declared unconstitutional. Examples include the Gramm-Rudman statute, the Flag Protection Act of 1989, the Line Item Veto Act of 1996, and the Communications Decency Act of 1996. When lawmakers choose expedited review they violate their oaths to support and defend the Constitution, discredit their capacity and willingness to debate and understand constitutional issues, and send the unfortunate (and erroneous) signal that true expertise and authority to interpret constitutional matters reside solely in the courts.

Self-government is protected when lawmakers form independent judgments and do not genuflect to judicial and presidential positions. Constitutional issues considered by Congress are within the capability of its members, whether they have legal training or not. Those issues generally turn not so much on highly technical legal points about a particular dispute but rather on a balancing of competing values. For example, how does one resolve disputes between congressional investigations and executive privilege, or between a free press and a fair trial? There is no ready answer in the Constitution.

It is not true, as Justice Robert Jackson once remarked, that Justices of the Supreme Court "are not final because we are infallible, but we are infallible because we are final"[76]—a cleverly constructed sentence, perhaps, but politically and legally shallow. Much of constitutional law depends on fact-finding and the balancing of competing values, areas in which Congress justifiably can claim substantial expertise and competence. Certainly there are no grounds to conclude that the judiciary has a superior edge in balancing constitutional, political, and social values. The political process handles those as well as, or better than, the courts.

Courts do not have a good record of rethinking what they have done. They need to be pushed and prodded. Something decided in some manner many years back does not necessarily have contemporary value and acceptance (or even value and acceptance when first decided). Constitutional government requires an open public dialogue and continued debate. Just because the Court decides an issue does not mean, as Burt Neuborne has said, that everyone must "roll over" and accept the ruling. "Criticism and attempts to change and foster re-litigation are part of the system and should be encouraged."[77] Amen to that.

A 1962 article by Chief Justice Earl Warren offers a refreshing and modest position on judicial capacity to correctly decide constitutional questions. He

76. Brown v. Allen, 344 U.S. 443, 540 (1953) (Jackson, J., concurring).
77. Burt Neuborne, "The Role of the Legislative and Executive Branches in Interpreting the Constitution," 73 Corn. L. Rev. 375, 376–77 (1988).

spoke in the context of the wretched Court decisions in 1943 and 1944 that upheld the exclusion and detention of 110,000 Japanese Americans during World War II. They were punished not because of illegal or criminal conduct but because of their race. Here is extraordinary language from a Chief Justice. The fact that the Court announces that "a given program is constitutional, does not necessarily answer the question whether, in a broader sense, it actually is."[78]

Read that several times. How instructive it would be to place those words over the entrance to the Supreme Court. Warren advised his readers not to seek constitutional answers always from the courts. In a democratic society, the legislative and executive branches still have "the primary responsibility for fashioning and executing policy consistent with the Constitution."[79] He correctly cautioned against excessive reliance even on the political branches: "[T]he day-to-day job of upholding the Constitution really lies elsewhere. It rests, realistically, on the shoulders of every citizen."[80] Well said. The obligation to defend constitutional government also rests, realistically, on the elected lawmakers who represent the citizens.

78. Earl Warren, "The Bill of Rights and the Military," 37 N.Y.U. L. Rev. 181, 193 (1962).
79. Id. at 202.
80. Id.

2

UNPACKING *MARBURY*

Much nonsense has been written about *Marbury v. Madison* (1803), especially in recent decades by the Supreme Court. Yes, it represents the first time the Court held a statutory provision of Congress to be unconstitutional. Other extravagant claims, including judicial supremacy, were disowned by its author, Chief Justice John Marshall. By placing a public stamp of approval on judicial review in 1803, the Court formally announced what was obvious: the elected branches of government are subject to the constraints of the Constitution. Often forgotten: so is the Supreme Court. The more interesting and complex issue is who gets to decide what is unconstitutional and whether that decision is in any sense final. In our democracy, no branch is final on constitutional questions.

The *Marbury* Drill

During hearings by the Senate Judiciary Committee in the 1980s, nominees to the Supreme Court were regularly asked if they thought *Marbury v. Madison* gave the Court the last word on constitutional law. In 1986, Senator Arlen Specter spoke about the "binding precedent" of *Marbury*. He asked William H. Rehnquist, nominee for Chief Justice, if he believed the Court "is the final arbiter, the final decisionmaker of what the Constitution means." Possibly wanting to dispose of the issue quickly, Rehnquist responded with one word: "Unquestionably." Specter pursued the issue: "So that if the Supreme Court has ruled on a legal issue, the executive branch, the legislative branch, have a responsibility to observe the decisions of the Supreme Court of the United States on a constitutional matter." Rehnquist replied: "Yes, I think they do."[1]

The following week, committee chairman Strom Thurmond put the same question to Antonin Scalia, nominee for Associate Justice: "Do you agree that *Marbury* requires the President and the Congress to always adhere to the Court's interpretation of the Constitution?" Scalia, finding the question too complex to be dismissed with one word, called *Marbury* "one of the great pillars to American law" but added: "I hesitate to answer, and indeed think I should not answer the precise question you ask—do I agree that *Marbury v. Madison* means that

---

1. "Nomination of Justice William Hubbs Rehnquist," hearings before the Senate Committee on the Judiciary, 99th Cong., 2d Sess. 187 (1986).

in no instance can either of the other branches call into question the action of the Supreme Court." Admitting that if a nominee to the Court were "so foolish, or so extreme as to kick over one of the pillars of the Constitution, you should not confirm him," he nevertheless did not think he should answer questions "regarding any specific Supreme Court opinion, even one so fundamental as *Marbury v. Madison.*"[2] Later in the hearing, Specter asked if *Marbury* "is a settled issue as far as you are concerned?" Scalia refused to say that "anything is a settled issue as far as I am concerned. If somebody wants to come in and challenge *Marbury v. Madison,* I will listen to that person." He did not want to be in the position "of saying as to any case that I would not overrule it."[3]

A year later, Senator Specter explored the finality of Court decisions with Anthony M. Kennedy, nominee for Associate Justice. Specter expressed concern about something Kennedy said in a speech in 1982: "As I have pointed out, the Constitution, in some of its most critical aspects, is what the political branches of the government have made it, whether the judiciary approves or not." Specter inquired: "By making that statement, you didn't intend to undercut, to any extent at all, your conviction that the Supreme Court of the United States has the final word on the interpretation of the Constitution?"[4] Kennedy declined to give a simple yes or no. In such areas as separation of powers, the growth in the office of the presidency, and in "the shape of federalism," Kennedy regarded Congress as far more powerful and authoritative than the Court.[5] Kennedy engaged in a thoughtful discussion about the reach of *Marbury* and the scope of the Court's authority to decide constitutional meaning, telling Specter: "I am somewhat reluctant to say that in all circumstances each legislator is immediately bound by the full consequences of a Supreme Court decree." Specter pressed forward: "Why not?"[6]

Kennedy could "think of instances, or I can accept the proposition that a chief executive or a Congress might not accept as doctrine the law of the Supreme Court." Specter: "Well, how can that be if the Supreme Court is to have the final word?" Kennedy presented a hypothetical. Suppose the Court were to overrule its decision in *New York Times v. Sullivan,* removing from newspapers the immunity they had enjoyed from libel lawsuits. To Kennedy, lawmakers could say the

2. "Nomination of Judge Antonin Scalia," hearings before the Senate Committee on the Judiciary, 99th Cong., 2d Sess. 33 (1986).

3. Id. at 83, 84.

4. "Nomination of Anthony M. Kennedy to be Associate Justice of the Supreme Court of the United States," hearings before the Senate Committee on the Judiciary, 100th Cong., 1st Sess. 221 (1987).

5. Id. at 222.

6. Id.

decision was "constitutionally wrong" and decide to pass legislation to restore immunity and protect the freedom of the press. Kennedy advised: "I think you could stand up on the floor of the U.S. Senate and say I am introducing this legislation because in my view the Supreme Court of the United States is 180 degrees wrong under the Constitution. And I think you would be fulfilling your duty if you said that."[7] Specter found that line of argument troubling: "[I]f *Marbury v. Madison* is to have any substance, then it seems to me that we do have to recognize the Supreme Court as the final arbiter of the Constitution, just as rockbed."[8]

Kennedy disagreed, insisting on an independent capacity of the elected branches to interpret the Constitution and not automatically defer to judicial rulings. There "just may be instances in which I think it is consistent with constitutional morality to challenge those views." He spoke in favor of the elected branches voicing their independent judgments about the meaning of the Constitution, even if it produced confrontations with the Court: "I point out that having to rely on the courts may infer, or may imply an institutional weakness on the part of the Congress that is ultimately debilitating. It seems to me that in some instances Congress is better off standing on its own feet and making its position known, and then its strength in the federal system will be greater than if it had relied on the assistance of the courts."[9]

Sources of Judicial Review

Judicial review is a legitimate part of American constitutional history. However, it is not the same as judicial supremacy. An early example of judicial review dates to the Dr. Bonham case of 1610. Justice Coke announced that when an act of Parliament was "against common right and reason, or repugnant, or impossible to be performed, the common law will controul it, and adjudge such Act to be void."[10] Read literally, his language seems to invite courts to invalidate statutes whenever they find a problem with common right or reason, feel repugnance, or discover something impossible to perform. The circumstances of the case explain why he did not entrust such broad authority to the judiciary. He did not grant courts open season to control the legislative branch.

Dr. Thomas Bonham brought a lawsuit against the Royal College of Physi-

---

7. Id. at 222–23 (New York Times v. Sullivan, 376 U.S. 254 (1964)).
8. Id. at 223.
9. Id. at 225.
10. Dr. Bonham's Case, 77 Eng. Rep. 646, 652 (1610).

cians, charging that it had falsely imprisoned him. Initially, he was fined by the college. When he refused to pay, the college prevailed in having him imprisoned. Justice Coke decided that the college possessed no authority to levy a fine. Under the law, imposition of fines belonged solely to the king.[11] Coke also identified a serious conflict of interest: the college received money from the fine. He ruled that "one cannot be Judge and attorney for any of the parties."[12] Under the statute, any fines levied went to the king, not to a party to the case.[13] The defect was not in the law but in the college's misapplication of it. Coke did not announce a new claim of judicial supremacy. He merely interpreted a statute.

After Bonham's case, a few British judges in the seventeenth and eighteenth centuries cited Coke's argument, but the principle of judicial review never took root on English soil.[14] In 1884, the U.S. Supreme Court noted: "[N]otwithstanding what was attributed to Lord Coke in *Bonham's Case* . . . the omnipotence of Parliament over the common law was absolute, even against common right and reason."[15] For their understanding of British law, the American framers relied heavily on William Blackstone's *Commentaries,* which rejected the theory that parliamentary statutes contrary to reason were void. He wrote: "[I]f the Parliament will positively enact a thing to be done which is unreasonable, I know of no power that can control it; . . . for that were to set the judicial power above that of the legislature, which would be subversive of all government."[16]

Blackstone seemed influenced by Bonham's case because he accepted the need for *temporary* judicial review. Acts of Parliament "impossible to be performed are of no validity; and if there arise out of them collaterally any absurd consequences, manifestly contradictory to common reason, they are, with regard to those collateral consequences, void."[17] This form of judicial action, however, could be quickly overturned by Parliament simply by stating that the "unreasonable" result is exactly what it intended. In this second effort, Parliament necessarily prevailed: "[T]here is no court that has power to defeat the intent of the legislature."[18]

British efforts in the 1760s to exercise control over America provoked colonists to argue that the laws of Parliament had violated the "common law"

---

11. Id. at 646.

12. Id.

13. Id. at 655.

14. Day v. Savadge, 80 Eng. Rep. 235, 237 (1614); The City of London v. Wood, 88 Eng. Rep. 1592, 1602 (1702).

15. Hurtado v. California, 110 U.S. 516, 531 (1884).

16. 1 William Blackstone, Commentaries §3, at 91 (Oxford 1775).

17. 1 Blackstone's Commentaries 90–91 (Philadelphia 1803).

18. Id. at 91.

and the "law of reason" and were therefore void. In the writs of assistance case in Boston, in 1761, James Otis claimed that British customs officials were not empowered by Parliament to use general search warrants. Even if Parliament had authorized writs of assistance, the statute would be "against the Constitution" and "against natural equity," and therefore void.[19] On the eve of the Declaration of Independence in 1776, a Massachusetts judge instructed the jury to treat acts of Parliament that violated fundamental law as "void" and "inoperative."[20]

Those political arguments were used to justify the break from England. They did not automatically deliver the power of judicial review to American courts, and certainly not any doctrine that elevated the Supreme Court over Congress and the President. From independence to the drafting of the U.S. Constitution, state judges occasionally challenged the acts of their legislatures. Scholars disagree on the strength of those precedents, but judges in Virginia, New Jersey, New York, Connecticut, Rhode Island, and North Carolina spoke the language of judicial review. Results were often less than rhetorical flourishes, and those actions were at *the state*, not the national, level.[21]

By the time of the constitutional convention at Philadelphia, some of the framers expected judicial review to be part of the new national government, but they did not have a clear or fully developed understanding. Instead of the legislative supremacy that existed during the Articles of Confederation, the new Congress would be one of three coordinate and coequal branches. Initially, the framers saw the need for the U.S. Supreme Court to exercise control not over Congress or the President but over the 13 states. In Federalist No. 80, Alexander Hamilton warned that independent state courts of final jurisdiction "over the same causes, arising upon the same laws, is a hydra in government from which nothing but contradiction and confusion can proceed."[22] Part of the remedy is the Supremacy Clause: "This Constitution, and the Laws of the United States which shall be made in Pursuance thereof; and all Treaties made, or which shall be made, under the Authority of the United States, shall be the supreme Law of the Land; and the Judges in every State shall be found thereby, any Thing in the Constitution or Laws of any State to the Contrary notwithstanding."[23]

Did the framers expect the U.S. Supreme Court to invalidate actions by Congress and the President? Testifying in 1937 at the time of the court-packing plan, constitutional scholar Edward Corwin offered this intriguing advice: "These

19. 2 The Works of John Adams 521–22, 523–25 (Charles Francis Adams, ed., 1856).
20. Edward S. Corwin, The Doctrine of Judicial Review 32 (1914).
21. Charles Grove Haines, The American Doctrine of Judicial Supremacy 88–121 (1932).
22. The Federalist 500.
23. U.S. Const., art. VI, cl. 2.

people who say the framers intended [judicial review] are talking nonsense; and the people who say they did not intend it are talking nonsense. There is evidence on both sides."[24] One clue comes from the proposal at the convention to create a Council of Revision consisting of the "Executive and a convenient number of the National Judiciary . . . with authority to examine every act of the National Legislature before it shall operate . . . and that the dissent of the said Council shall amount to a rejection, unless the Act of the National Legislature be again passed."[25] This second bite of the apple sounds like Blackstone's position. The proposal failed, in part because delegates wanted the judiciary fully independent to decide a case brought before it, and not compromised by participating earlier in the legislative process.[26]

Judicial review attracted support at the Philadelphia Convention, but only over state—not national—legislation. State courts should exercise judicial review to control legislative excesses or errors. Those courts "would not consider as valid any law contravening the Authority of the Union," and if such laws were not set aside by the state judiciary they "may be repealed by a National law."[27] Referring to judicial review at the state level, Madison said that a law "violating a constitution established by the people themselves, would be considered by the Judges as null & void."[28] At the ratification conventions, James Wilson, Oliver Ellsworth, Samuel Adams, and John Marshall defended judicial review, including by the federal judiciary, but the context of their remarks suggests that they were attempting to assure the states that national power would be held in check.[29]

Constitutional Text

Article III, section 1, of the Constitution states that the "judicial Power of the United States, shall be vested in one Supreme Court, and in such inferior Courts as the Congress may from time to time ordain and establish." Section 2 extends the judicial power to various "cases and controversies," but there is no specific

24. Senate Committee on the Judiciary, "Reorganization of the Federal Judiciary" (Part 2), 75th Cong., 1st Sess. 176 (1937).
25. 1 Farrand 21.
26. Id. at 97 (Elbridge Gerry objecting that the judiciary should not be part of the Council of Revision, "as they will have a sufficient check agst. encroachments on their own department by their exposition of the laws, which involved a power of deciding on their Constitutionality").
27. 2 Farrand 27–28 (Roger Sherman, James Madison, and Gouverneur Morris).
28. Id. at 93.
29. Louis Fisher and Katy Harriger, American Constitutional Law 37–38 (9th ed., 2011).

grant of authority to declare congressional or presidential actions unconstitutional. The absence of an explicit grant of judicial review is not conclusive. An implied power might exist, as it does for the other branches. There are other possible sources of judicial review.

One is Article III, section 2, which extends the judicial power to all cases "arising under the Constitution, the Laws of the United States, and Treaties made." What is meant by "arising under"? In most of the early drafts at the constitutional convention, those two words extended to congressional statutes.[30] On August 27, 1787, during debate on the language "arising under the Laws of the United States," William Samuel Johnson moved to insert the word "this Constitution and the" before the word "Laws." Objecting, Madison thought it was "going too far" to provide jurisdiction to the Court over all cases arising under the Constitution. Courts should be limited to cases of "a judiciary nature."[31] Johnson's motion was agreed to without further discussion, "it being generally supposed that the jurisdiction was constructively limited to cases of a judiciary nature."[32]

What is meant by "judiciary nature"? Whatever it might be, it was something less than a full-scale power of judicial review. It was a subset. At the Virginia ratifying convention on June 20, 1788, Madison interpreted "arising under" to justify judicial review only against the states.[33] Hamilton made the same point in Federalist No. 80.[34] Under those readings, the purpose of judicial review was to control the states and protect national power. It was not intended to control Congress and the President. There is a major difference between federal courts monitoring states under the Supremacy Clause and controlling the coequal branches of Congress and the President. Justice Oliver Wendell Holmes once remarked: "I do not think the United States would come to an end if [the Supreme Court] lost [its] power to declare an act of Congress void. I do think the Union would be imperiled if we could not make that declaration as to the laws of the several States."[35]

In Federalist No. 78, Hamilton promoted a broad definition of judicial review. Many of his arguments would reappear in *Marbury*. Constitutional limits on Congress, he reasoned, could only be preserved by the power of judicial review "to declare all acts contrary to the manifest tenor of the Constitution

---

30. 2 Farrand 132–33, 146, 172, 186.
31. Id. at 430.
32. Id.
33. 3 Elliot 523.
34. The Federalist 503–04.
35. Oliver Wendell Holmes Jr., Collected Legal Papers 295–96 (1920).

void. Without this, all the reservations of particular rights or privileges would amount to nothing."[36] Quite an overstatement! Without judicial review, rights and privileges would amount to nothing? Other democratic countries, including the Netherlands, preserve constitutional systems without judicial review. Hamilton denied that judicial review would "imply a superiority of the judiciary to the legislative power."[37] What else, under his reading, could it possibly imply? If he objected that Congress should not be the judge of its own powers, what would limit the judiciary (other than its own sense of self-restraint)? Why should federal courts be the sole judge of *their* powers?

Hamilton insisted that courts "may truly be said to have neither FORCE nor WILL, but merely judgment."[38] His argument was not credible in 1788; it is not credible now. Judges clearly exercise both force and will. An Anti-Federalist, "Brutus," spoke more realistically than Hamilton about judicial power: "The opinions of the supreme court, whatever they may be, will have the force of law; because there is no power provided in the constitution, that can correct their errors, or control their adjudications."[39]

Setting the Stage for *Marbury*

From 1789 to *Marbury,* members of Congress often discussed the availability of judicial review. When Madison introduced the Bill of Rights in the House of Representatives in 1789, he predicted that once they were incorporated into the Constitution, "independent tribunals of justice will consider themselves in a peculiar manner the guardians of those rights; they will be an impenetrable bulwark against every assumption of power in the Legislative or Executive."[40] One can only smile at his reasoning when we think of his attitude in 1803 while serving as Secretary of State. There is little doubt that if Chief Justice Marshall ordered Madison to deliver Marbury's commission, he would have ignored the court order.

Moreover, nine days after speaking about the Bill of Rights, Madison offered his thoughts on whether the President had an implied power to remove certain executive officials. He denied that Congress should defer to the judiciary on this constitutional issue. On what principle, he begged to know, could it be contended "that any one department draws from the Constitution greater powers

36. The Federalist 491.
37. Id.
38. Id. at 490.
39. The Anti-Federalist Papers 295 (Ralph Ketcham, ed., 2003).
40. 1 Annals of Cong. 439 (June 8, 1789).

than another, in marking out the limits of the powers of the several departments?" If questions emerged on the boundaries between the branches, he did
not see "that any one of these independent departments has more right than
another to declare their sentiments on that point."[41] Under this reading, the
elected branches should not be subordinate to the Supreme Court.

In 1792, three federal circuit courts objected to a congressional statute that
appointed federal judges to serve as commissioners for claims settlement. Their
judgments could be set aside by the Secretary of War. Why should federal judges
perform nonjudicial duties, and how could their conclusions be overridden by
an executive officer? Before the Supreme Court could get a chance to consider
the constitutionality of this process, Congress repealed the offending sections
and removed the Secretary's authority to veto decisions rendered by judges.[42] In
1794, a year after Congress fixed the statute, the Supreme Court observed that
the original statute would have been unconstitutional if it attempted to place
nonjudicial powers on the circuit courts.[43] This latter case (not published until
1851) is hardly evidence of judicial review. The Court was referring to a statute
that had been repealed.

Between 1791 and 1799, federal courts struck down a number of state laws.[44]
At the national level, the Supreme Court in 1796 *upheld* a congressional statute
that imposed a tax on carriages.[45] If it possessed authority to sustain a congressional law, presumably it could strike one down. However, Justice Chase said it
was unnecessary "*at this time*, for me to determine, whether this court, *constitutionally* possesses the power to declare an act of Congress *void*, on the ground
of its being made contrary to, and in violation of, the Constitution; but if the
court have such power, I am free to declare, that I will never exercise it, *but in a
very clear case.*"[46] The Court was inching up to judicial review over Congress,
but not yet ready to announce it. Two years later, the Court upheld the constitutionality of a congressional action, this time involving the process of constitutional amendment.[47] In other cases on the eve of *Marbury,* Supreme Court
Justices tiptoed around the existence of their authority to invalidate congressional statutes.[48]

41. Id. at 500 (June 17, 1789).
42. Hayburn's Case, 2 Dall. 409 (1792); 1 Stat. 243 (1792); 1 Stat. 324 (1793).
43. United States v. Yale Todd, 13 How. 52 (1794).
44. 1 Charles Warren, The Supreme Court in United States History 65–69 (1937).
45. Hylton v. United States, 3 Dall. 171 (1796).
46. Id. at 175 (emphases in original).
47. Hollingsworth v. Virginia, 3 Dall. 378 (1798).
48. E.g., see the remarks of Justices Chase and Iredell in Calder v. Bull, 3 Dall. 386, 392, 395,
399 (1798), and Justice Chase in Cooper v. Telfair, 4 Dall. 14, 19 (1800).

Although these Justices spoke guardedly about judicial review, members of Congress had no such qualms. They understood that the Constitution imposed limits on the elected branches and courts existed to monitor the boundaries. Representative James Bayard remarked in 1802: "To maintain, therefore, the Constitution, the judges are a check upon the Legislature. The doctrine I know is denied, and it is therefore incumbent upon me to show that it is sound."[49] Like Justice Chase, Bayard anticipated judicial review only in very clear cases. For example, the Constitution prohibits Congress from passing a bill of attainder (legislative punishment without judicial trial). If Congress passed such a bill the courts "are bound to decide."[50] Another clear illustration: the Constitution empowers Congress to suspend the privilege of habeas corpus in times of rebellion or invasion. Bayard asked: "Suppose a law prohibited the issuing of the writ at a moment of profound peace."[51] Judges would be required to take a case challenging the suspension and decide it.

Thomas Jefferson hoped that federal courts would strike down the repressive Alien and Sedition Acts of 1798. He appealed to the courts to protect basic rights: "[T]he laws of the land, administered by upright judges, would protect you from any exercise of power unauthorized by the Constitution of the United States."[52] To his disappointment, no upright judges were willing to challenge and invalidate the Alien and Sedition Acts. A Federalist Congress and Federalist President (John Adams) enacted them; Federalist judges would not void them.

The national elections of 1800 marked a critical turning point in U.S. history. The Jeffersonians swept the elections, taking both Congress and the White House. The only branch left with Federalists was the judiciary. How would the nation manage this transfer of power? In February 1801, with a few weeks remaining in the lame-duck Congress, the Federalists passed two bills to create a number of new federal judges. One statute created 16 lifetime judges to serve in newly created circuits, relieving Justices of the Supreme Court of the need to travel outside Washington, D.C., to perform "circuit riding."[53] The second statute created new justices of the peace for the District of Columbia, each with a five-year term.[54] President Adams began nominating Federalists to those positions, and the Federalist Senate moved quickly to confirm them. Just one day

49. 11 Annals of Cong. 645 (1802).
50. Id.
51. Id. at 647.
52. 10 Writings of Thomas Jefferson 61 (Albert Ellery Bergh, ed., 1903).
53. 1 Stat. 89 (1801).
54. 1 Stat. 103, 107, sec. 11 (1801).

before Jefferson took power, the Senate confirmed 42 justices of the peace.[55] At that point, John Marshall was serving as Secretary of State, even though he had already been appointed to the Supreme Court for the next term. After the Senate's action, Marshall was supposed to deliver the commissions to the new office-holders. Because of last-minute pressures and distractions, some were never delivered, including one for William Marbury to be justice of the peace in the District of Columbia.

Marbury Entitled to a Job?

Upon entering the White House, Jefferson ordered that the judicial nominations confirmed by the Federalist Senate and signed and sealed by President Adams, but not yet delivered, be withheld. He also urged Congress to repeal the Circuit Court Act (with its additional judgeships) and to cancel the anticipated 1802 term for the Supreme Court. The Republican Congress passed both measures.[56] The Justices, to their dismay, had to return to circuit riding. The House of Representatives impeached District Judge John Pickering (a Federalist), and the Senate removed him. The impeachment machinery was cranked up for others, including Justice Samuel Chase. Chief Justice John Marshall had every reason to believe he could be next. One thing he appreciated in full: any attempt on his part to compel Jefferson or Madison to deliver the commissions would be futile. Chief Justice Warren Burger reflected: "The court could stand hard blows, but not ridicule, and the ale houses would rock with hilarious laughter" if Jefferson ignored Marshall's order.[57]

Law professor Barry Friedman states that *Marbury* "is revered today both at home and abroad for establishing the Supreme Court's power of judicial review."[58] We need to distinguish between features of the decision that should and should not be revered. First, Marshall should not have participated in the case. His previous position as Secretary of State and failure to deliver the commission to Marbury disqualified him. He should have recused himself. The conflict of interest was so overwhelming he could not possibly claim impartiality, a

55. William W. Van Alstyne, "A Critical Guide to Marbury v. Madison," 1969 Duke L. J. 1, 4 (1969).

56. 2 Stat. 132, 156 (1802).

57. Warren E. Burger, "The Doctrine of Judicial Review: Mr. Marshall, Mr. Jefferson, and Mr. Marbury," in Judges on Judging: Views from the Bench 14 (David M. O'Brien, ed., 2004).

58. Barry Friedman, The Will of the People: How Public Opinion Has Influenced the Supreme Court and Shaped the Meaning of the Constitution 44 (2009).

quality essential for those who judge. Writing in 1929, one scholar concluded that "it would have been more in keeping with sound legal ethics had Marshall, who had a personal interest in the case, withdrawn from the court during its consideration."[59] More recently, law professor Jeffrey Rosen offered his judgment about Marshall: "By modern standards, he should never have agreed to hear the case in the first place."[60] One could say the same about standards in place in 1803.

As a second point, once Marshall decided that the Court had no jurisdiction to decide the case, nothing else need be said. Yet he devoted considerable time (and space) in finding fault with Jefferson: "To withhold his commission, therefore, is an act deemed by the court not warranted by law, but violative of a vested legal right."[61] Barry Friedman concluded: this "gratuitous tongue-lashing of Jefferson and Madison for failing to deliver Marbury's commission was entirely unwarranted."[62] Jefferson wrote in 1807: "Because the judges, at the outset, disclaimed all cognizance of the case, although they then went on to say what would have been their opinion, had they had cognizance of it. This, then, was confessedly an extrajudicial opinion, and, as such, of no authority."[63]

Edward Corwin made a similar observation in 1914: "The court was bent on reading the President a lecture on his legal and moral duty to recent Federalist appointees to judicial offices."[64] A few years later, Corwin praised Marshall for sidestepping a collision with the executive branch he could not possibly have won. At the same time, "he stigmatized his enemy Jefferson as a violator of the laws which as President he was sworn to support."[65] In 1928, a critic of *Marbury* observed: "[W]e must come to the conclusion that everything said by Marshall concerning Marbury's title was distinctly unauthoritative and in no sense constituted a decision. It was legally valueless. If there is anything fundamental in law, I should say it is that the acts of a court wanting jurisdiction are void."[66]

59. J. A. C. Grant, "Marbury v. Madison Today," 23 Am. Pol. Sci. Rev. 673, 678 (1929).

60. Jeffrey Rosen, The Most Democratic Branch: How the Courts Serve America 22 (2006). Writing in 1950, Justice Harold Burton noted that had Marshall disqualified himself "there would not have been the required quorum of four present." Harold H. Burton, "The Cornerstone of Constitutional Law: The Extraordinary Case of Marbury v. Madison," 36 Am. Bar Ass'n J. 805, 807 (1950).

61. Marbury v. Madison, 5 U.S. (1 Cr.) 137, 162 (1803).

62. Friedman, The Will of the People, at 63.

63. 11 The Writings of Thomas Jefferson 213 (Bergh ed. 1904).

64. Edward S. Corwin, "Marbury v. Madison and the Doctrine of Judicial Review," 12 Mich. L. Rev. 538, 543 (1914).

65. Edward S. Corwin, John Marshall and the Constitution 66 (1919).

66. Andrew C. McLaughlin, "Marbury v. Madison Again," 14 Am. Bar Ass'n J. 155, 156 (1928).

Third, Marshall spoke disingenuously about Marbury's "right" to have his job. Marshall claimed that because Jefferson and Madison refused to take required steps, Marbury "has a consequent right to the commission."[67] To Friedman, Marshall "cut right to the chase. William Marbury was entitled to his commission."[68] Yet given the manner in which Marshall decided the case, Marbury walked away empty-handed. Why speak loftily about rights and entitlements that do not exist?

Original and Appellate

As a fourth point, few scholars are satisfied with Marshall's explanation why the Court lacked jurisdiction to do what Congress had authorized in section 13 of the Judiciary Act of 1789: issue a writ of mandamus to compel Jefferson or Madison to deliver the commissions.[69] We know that the writ would have been ignored, but Marshall engaged in a highly artificial legal analysis to conclude that section 13 expanded the original jurisdiction of the Court and thereby violated the Constitution. As a result, the Court lacked jurisdiction to decide the case. To one legal scholar: "The learned Justice really manufactured an opportunity to declare an act void."[70]

Marbury and other plaintiffs brought their case directly to the Supreme Court rather than starting out in district court. In this manner they asked the Court to exercise original jurisdiction. The Constitution distinguishes between original and appellate jurisdiction. In all cases "affecting Ambassadors, other public Ministers and Consuls, and those in which a State shall be Party, the supreme Court shall have original jurisdiction."[71] In all other cases, the Court "shall have appellate Jurisdiction, both as to Law and Fact, with such Exceptions and under such Regulations as the Congress shall make." The language about exceptions and regulations appears to give Congress a certain amount of discretion in legislating on the two types of jurisdiction.

To Marshall, section 13 was unconstitutional because it expanded the original jurisdiction of the Court. Congress, he said, could alter the boundaries only of appellate jurisdiction. The word "original" might appear to imply exclusivity, suggesting that what is granted by the Constitution may not be abridged or

---

67. Marbury v. Madison, 5 U.S. (1 Cr.) at 168.
68. Friedman, The Will of the People, at 60.
69. 1 Stat. 81, sec. 13 (1789).
70. McLaughlin, "Marbury v. Madison Again," 14 Am. Bar. Ass'n J., at 157.
71. U.S. Const., art. III, sec. 2.

altered by Congress. But Congress divided original jurisdiction into two types: (1) original and exclusive, and (2) original but not exclusive.[72] The Judiciary Act of 1789 expressly spoke of "original but not exclusive jurisdiction."[73] The two categories, original and exclusive, are not as distinct as Marshall argued. A close analysis of *Marbury* by constitutional scholar William Van Alstyne found no persuasive reasoning by Marshall on this question of jurisdiction. It can be argued that Congress may not *reduce* the Court's original jurisdiction but what prohibits Congress from increasing original jurisdiction?[74] An article by law professor Michael McConnell concluded that Marshall's analysis of original and appellate jurisdiction amounted to "strained reading."[75]

If the constitutional meaning of original jurisdiction was as clear as Marshall argued, he should have disposed of the case by informing Marbury and the other plaintiffs: "Gentlemen, the Constitution plainly prohibits you from bringing this dispute directly to the Supreme Court. You must initiate your action in district court. Case dismissed."

In *Cohens v. Virginia* (1821), Marshall returned to the issue of original and appellate jurisdiction and handled the topic with deeper understanding. The Constitution provides that in all cases involving ambassadors, other public ministers, and consuls, the Supreme Court shall have original jurisdiction. He asked what would happen if an individual were to sue a foreign minister in a state court, and the court held against the minister. Would the Supreme Court be incapable of taking the case and revising the lower court's judgment, "because the constitution had given it original jurisdiction in the case?"[76] Marshall rejected that construction. The Court would be able to accept this "original" case as part of its appellate jurisdiction.

In *Cohens,* Marshall objected to litigants who read *Marbury* carelessly, failing to separate what was at its core from "some *dicta* of the Court."[77] When it appeared that litigants were rummaging around *Marbury* to find nuggets favorable to their case, Marshall insisted that general expressions in a case "are to be taken in connection with the case in which those expressions are used." If those expressions "go beyond the case, they may be respected, but ought not to control the judgment in a subsequent suit when the very point is presented for deci-

---

72. 28 U.S.C. §1251 (2006).

73. 1 Stat. 80, sec. 13 (1789).

74. Van Alstyne, "A Critical Guide to *Marbury v. Madison*," 1969 Duke L. J. at 15–16, 30–33.

75. Michael W. McConnell, "The Story of *Marbury v. Madison*," in Constitutional Law Stories 29 (Michael C. Dorf, ed., 2004).

76. Cohens v. Virginia, 19 U.S. (6 Wheat.) 264, 397 (1821).

77. Id. at 399 (emphasis in original).

sion."[78] A question before a court must be "investigated with care, and considered to its full extent."[79] In *Marbury,* the "single question" before the Court was "whether the legislature could give this Court original jurisdiction in a case in which the constitution had clearly not given it."[80] That was the core holding. Everything else, including possible claims of judicial supremacy, amounted to dicta. Some of the language in *Marbury* was not only too broad, Marshall said, "but in some instances contradictory to its principle."[81] We are left to wonder about the reach of *Marbury.* The constitutional authority to find a statutory provision invalid is far short of judicial supremacy.

"Emphatically the Province"

Fifth, federal courts and constitutional scholars often cite a sentence in *Marbury* as evidence that the Supreme Court possesses authority not merely to strike down congressional legislation but to do so permanently. Here is Marshall's sentence: "It is emphatically the province and duty of the judicial department to say what the law is."[82] Think about the essence of that sentence, first by removing the frills up front to produce: "It is the duty of the judicial department to say what the law is." Next, eliminate the archaic "the judicial department" and substitute "courts," reducing the sentence to: "It is the duty of courts to say what the law is." Even briefer: "Courts decide the law." We all know that. That is why we have courts. Consider this modest rewrite: "It is emphatically the province and duty of Congress to say what the law is." Would anyone dispute its accuracy? Does that make the word of Congress superior or final? Clearly not. Charles Hobson, a scholar of John Marshall, correctly stated that the language "emphatically the province" does not imply "any claim to judicial supremacy in expounding the Constitution or to exclusive guardianship of the fundamental law."[83]

According to a recent study on *Marbury* by Cliff Sloan and David McLean, "the abiding significance" of the case "is that it stands for a system in which independent courts have the last word on the Constitution, and on the requirements of law."[84] In a later passage in the book: "the judiciary is the ultimate authority

---

78. Id.
79. Id.
80. Id. at 400.
81. Id. at 401.
82. Marbury v. Madison, 5 U.S. (1 Cr.) at 177.
83. Charles F. Hobson, The Great Chief Justice: John Marshall and the Rule of Law 67 (1996).
84. Cliff Sloan and David McLean, The Great Decision: Jefferson, Adams, and Marshall and the Battle for the Supreme Court 178 (2009).

on constitutionality."[85] However, the Court's interpretation has never been final on constitutional issues. More than two centuries of Supreme Court jurisprudence provides no support for that position, nor was there anything at the time of Marshall to believe it.

Marshall's reaction to the impeachment of Pickering and Chase suggests that he was quite willing to share constitutional interpretations with the elected branches. He issued *Marbury* on February 24, 1803. The House impeached Pickering a week later, on March 2. The Senate convicted him on March 12, 1804. Congress then turned its guns on Chase, making it clear that Justices were proper targets. Marshall might be next. Under these precarious conditions, Marshall wrote to Chase on January 23, 1805, suggesting that if members of Congress did not like a particular judicial opinion, it was not necessary to impeach a judge. Just pass a statute to reverse objectionable decisions. Here is Marshall's advice to Chase: "I think the modern doctrine of impeachment shoud [*sic*] yield to an appellate jurisdiction in the legislature. A reversal of those legal opinions deemd [*sic*] unsound by the legislature would certainly better comport with the mildness of our character than [would] a removal of the Judge who has renderd [*sic*] them unknowing of his fault."[86] Those sentiments hardly convey judicial supremacy or arrogance. The words are not those of a headstrong Justice determined to impose his will on elected officials.

Sixth, at the end of his opinion Marshall reminds the reader that he was required to strike down the statutory provision because of his oath of office: "Why otherwise does [the Constitution] direct the judges to take an oath to support it? This oath certainly applies in an especial manner, to their conduct in their official character." It would be "immoral" to impose the oath on judges "if they were to be used as the instruments, and the knowing instruments, for violating what they swear to support!"[87] He asked: "Why does a judge swear to discharge his duties in accordance to the constitution of the United States if that constitution forms no rule for his government? [I]f it is closed upon him, and cannot be inspected by him?" If such were the real state of things, "this is worse than solemn mockery. To prescribe, or to take the oath, becomes equally a crime."[88] Marshall goes far afield with his rhetoric. Members of Congress, state

---

85. Id. at 180.

86. 3 Albert J. Beveridge, The Life of John Marshall 177 (1919). Marshall dated the letter January 23, 1804, but modern scholarship fixes the date a year later, to January 23, 1805; 6 The Papers of John Marshall 348 n.1 (Charles F. Hobson, ed., 1990). Like the rest of us, Marshall forgot to switch to the new year.

87. Marbury v. Madison, 5 U.S. (1 Cr.) at 180.

88. Id.

judges, and other public officials take an oath to defend the Constitution. The ceremony of oath taking does not give the Court the final word.

Marshall had the capacity to present a conclusion as though no other alternative could possibly exist. In *Marbury* he wrote: "It is a proposition too plain to be contested, that the constitution controls any legislative act repugnant to it; or, that the legislature may alter the constitution by an ordinary act." Continuing: "The constitution is either a superior paramount law, unchangeable by ordinary means, or it is on a level with ordinary legislative acts, and, like other acts, is alterable when the legislature shall please to alter it."[89] Sounds plausible, but if a statute contrary to the Constitution may not stand, why tolerate a Supreme Court decision that is contrary to the Constitution? Legal scholar Nelson Lund properly asks: "[I]f statutes enacted by the people's representatives are always trumped by the Constitution, it would seem to follow by inexorable logic that mere judicial opinions must also be trumped by the Constitution."[90]

What to Do About *Stuart?*

Marshall faced another possible collision with Jefferson: the lawsuit of *Stuart v. Laird*. It concerned the Circuit Court Act that had been enacted in the remaining days of the Adams administration, creating 16 new judgeships. The lame-duck Federalist Senate quickly confirmed nominations made by President Adams. In taking power, the Jeffersonians repealed the statute. Did Congress have authority to do that? The circuit judges had lifetime appointments. Many Federalists found it repugnant to argue that Congress could not take a judge out of the office (save for impeachment), but could take the office out of the judge.

The constitutionality of the repeal statute came to the Court in the case of *Stuart v. Laird*. Opponents of the repeal statute made this argument: "The words *during good behaviour* can not mean *during the will of Congress*. The people have a right to the services of those judges who have been constitutionally appointed; and who have been unconstitutionally removed from office."[91] If Marshall and the other Justices exercised judicial review against the repeal law and found it invalid, it would greatly intensify congressional efforts to impeach and remove Federalist judges. Although Marshall did not disqualify himself in

89. Id. at 177.
90. Nelson Lund, "Resolved, Presidential Signing Statements Threaten to Undermine the Rule of Law and the Separation of Power" (con), in Richard J. Ellis and Michael Nelson, eds., Debating the Presidency: Conflicting Perspectives on the American Executive 150 (2010).
91. Stuart v. Laird, 5 U.S. (1 Cr.) 299, 304 (1803) (emphasis in original).

the *Marbury* case, as he should have, he stepped aside in *Stuart* because he had tried the case in the court below.[92]

The Court decided *Marbury* on February 24, 1803. *Stuart* came down about a week later, March 2. Would the Court invoke its newfound strength by invalidating what the Jeffersonians had done? Would it declare itself superior to the elected branches? There was no chance of that. The constitutional judgment of Congress would stand. To the Court, the issue of circuit judges had been settled by congressional action in 1789 in creating circuit courts that were a mix of district judges and Supreme Court Justices. From 1789 to the end of the Federalist government, Justices had ridden circuit and no one raised a constitutional objection to it. Said the Court in *Stuart:* "[I]t is sufficient to observe, that practice and acquiescence under it for a period of several years, commencing with the organization of the judicial system, affords an irresistable [*sic*] answer, and has indeed fixed the construction." The congressional judgment represented "a contemporary interpretation of the most forcible nature. This practical exposition is too strong and obstinate to be shaken or controlled."[93] The Court deferred to the constitutional judgment of Congress. The final voice on constitutionality in this case went to the elected branches.

Unfortunately, the attention to *Marbury v. Madison* has greatly eclipsed *Stuart v. Laird.* Chief Justice Marshall and Justice Chase resented the Jeffersonian repeal of the Circuit Court Act and contemplated the possibility of refusing to abide by it, including the requirement of circuit riding. That course of action needed a united Court, but Justices Bushrod Washington and William Paterson declined to join in that strategy. Justices had ridden circuit for the previous decade without constitutional complaint. A solemn protest in 1803 would have lacked any credibility.[94] Marshall might have derived some satisfaction from his lecture to Jefferson in *Marbury,* but the Court's ruling in *Stuart* highlighted the limits of judicial authority to countermand the elected branches. As constitutional scholar Bruce Ackerman has noted:

John Marshall would be obliged to savor his ironical relationship to *Marbury v. Madison* with every lousy meal, lumpy bed, and bumpy road he encountered on the endless ride around his circuit. Each daily indignity could only impress upon him the triumph of Thomas Jefferson's Constitution, as codified by his own Court in *Stuart v. Laird.* And each time the

92. Id. at 308.
93. Id. at 309.
94. Bruce Ackerman, The Failure of the Founding Fathers: Jefferson, Marshall, and the Rise of Presidential Democracy 163–76 (2007 ed.).

great chief justice began a new trial, he was once against establishing that it was the Constitution of 1801, not that of 1787, which served as the foundation of justice in the country.[95]

After *Marbury,* Jefferson wrote to Mrs. John Adams in 1804: "You seem to think it devolved on the judges to decide on the validity of the sedition law. But nothing in the Constitution has given them a right to decide for the Executive, more than to the Executive to decide for them." In articulating the doctrine of coordinate construction, Jefferson said that each branch was "independent in the sphere of action assigned to them." Judges could fine and imprison someone, but the President under his independent power of pardon could then "remit the execution of it." Giving judges the right to decide exclusively a constitutional question "would make the judiciary a despotic branch."[96]

The lesson of *Stuart* would be revisited many times by the Court. The doctrine of "seditious libel" relied on British common law rather than a statute. One case that reached the Supreme Court in 1812 involved editors of a Federalist newspaper in Connecticut who had been prosecuted by the Jefferson administration. The Court noted that it was the first time it had been faced with the question whether federal courts had jurisdiction over seditious libel. Rather than settle the matter unilaterally by the Court as the supreme and final word on the meaning of the Constitution, it concluded that the issue had "been long since settled in public opinion," by which it meant that Congress— after the repeal of the Sedition Act of 1798—had yet to establish by statute that criticism of the national government was a criminal act. In short, constitutional law was decided by the people working through their elected representatives, not by the courts. Whatever the law in England, the exercise of criminal jurisdiction in common law cases was not within the implied power of federal courts.[97]

The Merits of *Marbury*

Marshall's decision in *Marbury* has been described "as a masterful, closely-reasoned document."[98] Masterful, perhaps, but not because it is closely reasoned.

---

95. Id. at 194.

96. 11 The Writings of Thomas Jefferson 51 (Bergh ed., 1904).

97. United States v. Hudson and Goodwin, 11 U.S. (7 Cr.) 32 (1812). See also United States v. Coolidge, 14 U.S. (1 Wheat.) 415 (1816), and Leonard W. Levy, Jefferson and Civil Liberties: The Darker Side 42–69 (1963).

98. Irwin S. Rhodes, "Marbury Versus Madison Revisited," 33 U. Cinc. L. Rev. 23, 25 (1964).

As explained below, the decision deserves praise because it demonstrates the exceptional political and institutional skills of John Marshall. The literature on *Marbury* is generally critical of Marshall's reasoning, but he has many defenders.[99] Why has there been such unstinting praise for a decision with so many flaws? Consider what the Court said about *Marbury* in 1958 when it responded to opposition by the Arkansas legislature and Governor Orval Faubus to efforts to integrate public schools in Little Rock. The Court stated:

> In 1803, Chief Justice Marshall, speaking for a unanimous Court, referring to the Constitution as "the fundamental and paramount law of the nation," declared in the notable case of *Marbury* v. *Madison,* 1 Cranch 137, 177, that "It is emphatically the province and duty of the judicial department to say what the law is." This decision declared the basic principle that the federal judiciary is supreme in the exposition of the law of the Constitution, and that principle has ever since been respected by this Court and the Country as a permanent and indispensable feature of our constitutional system.[100]

Of course that is not true. The Court has not respected that principle, nor has the country. If that principle had any substance the nation would have accepted *Dred Scott, Plessy's* "separate but equal doctrine," the child labor cases, the first flag-salute case of 1940, the Japanese-American cases of 1943 and 1944, the trimester framework of *Roe v. Wade,* and many other decisions that the public and Congress (and eventually the Court) have repudiated.

In 1962, the Court in *Baker v. Carr* referred to itself as the "ultimate interpreter of the Constitution."[101] That is a self-serving claim by an interested party, nothing more. Assertions by one branch about its powers are appropriately suspect. The Court in 1969 repeated the claim about being ultimate interpreter.[102] Repetition can help drive home a point, provided there is a point. No one with

---

99. For a lengthy defense of Marbury, see Louise Weinberg, "Our *Marbury*," 89 Va. L. Rev. 1235 (2003). Generally critical evaluations include Sanford Levinson, "Why I Do Not Teach *Marbury* (Except to Eastern Europeans) and Why You Shouldn't Either," 38 Wake Forest L. Rev. 553 (2003); James M. O'Fallon, "*Marbury*," 44 Stan. L. 219 (1992); Jerry I. Phillips, "Marbury v. Madison and Section 13 of the 1789 Judiciary Act," 60 Tenn. L. Rev. 51 (1992); Susan Low Bloch and Maeva Marcus, "John Marshall's Selective Use of History in *Marbury v. Madison*," 1986 Wis. L. Rev. 301 (1986); Akhil Reed Amar, "*Marbury*, Section 13, and the Original Jurisdiction of the Supreme Court," 56 U. Chi. L. Rev. 443 (1985).

100. Cooper v. Aaron, 358 U.S. 1, 18 (1958).

101. Baker v. Carr, 369 U.S. 186, 211 (1962).

102. Powell v. McCormack, 395 U.S. 486, 521 (1969).

a straight face can look at the last two centuries and call the Court the ultimate interpreter.

In 1997, the Court spoke arrogantly about being the last word: "Our national experience teaches that the Constitution is preserved best when each part of the Government respects both the Constitution and the proper actions and determinations of the other branches. When the Court has interpreted the Constitution, it has acted within the province of the Judiciary Branch, which embraces the duty to say what the law is. *Marbury v. Madison,* 1 Cranch, at 177." According to that decision, when there is a conflict between a Court decision and a congressional statute, the Court's precedent "must control."[103] Besides being self-serving, that statement poorly understands "our national experience." The Court's decision in 1997, on religious liberty, is explored more fully in Chapter 6.

Marbury deserves praise not because of Marshall's command of constitutional principles in 1803 but for his political skills. By this I mean nothing derogatory. Political judgment is essential for all three branches. Courts are part of government and must be politically sensitive. Probably nothing is more dangerous in a constitutional system than a judge who lacks political understanding. At the time of *Marbury,* the national judiciary was an endangered branch. Marshall's genius lay in his political sophistication of what a Court may and may not do. Constitutional scholar Michael McConnell put it well: "*Marbury* was brilliant, then, not for its effective assertion of judicial power, but for its effective avoidance of judicial humiliation."[104] The Aaron Burr trial of 1807 posed another dangerous collision between Marshall and Jefferson. Marshall played it perfectly, issuing one ruling after another until there was little left of the administration's effort to find Burr guilty of treason.[105]

Marshall's political judgment included his knowledge of what his Court could do after the Federalist Party had been severely weakened by the John Adams administration and the Alien and Sedition Acts. The party lost power until it passed out of existence. We need to remind ourselves that *Marbury* marked the only time that Marshall found a congressional statute unconstitutional. He did not try to use *Marbury* to elevate himself above the other branches—quite the contrary. Judicial review became a mechanism to affirm, not invalidate, the constitutional judgments of elected officials. As noted by Jean Edward Smith in his biographical study, Marshall in *Marbury* "was neither embarking on a crusade

103. Boerne v. Flores, 521 U.S. 507, 535–36 (1997).

104. McConnell, "The Story of *Marbury v. Madison*," supra note 75, at 31.

105. Louis Fisher, In the Name of National Security: Unchecked Presidential Power and the *Reynolds* Case 212–20 (2006).

for judicial supremacy, nor was he charting new territory. . . . Read in its entirety, *Marbury* v. *Madison* is an essay on the necessity for moderation."[106]

The driving force in establishing new constitutional doctrines during the era of the Marshall Court was Congress and the President, not the Court. Marshall found ways to bestow a judicial blessing to what the elected branches wanted to do with the commerce power and in creating a national bank. Constitutional grounds existed in 1819 to declare the bank unconstitutional, but Marshall discovered and developed doctrines to uphold it (Chapter 4). In a series of cases, he fortified national power over the states. His decisions were as much political as legal. Writing in 1911, Louis B. Boudin concluded that Marshall's "great place in the history of our country" is due not to his decision in *Marbury,* which over the years produced many claims of "doubtful warrant," but "to the liberal spirit in which he interpreted, and thus help to develop, the legislative powers of Congress."[107]

One section of *Marbury* that receives little attention is Marshall's treatment of "ministerial duties" by executive officials. The heads of executive departments function in part as political agents of the President. They also receive legal duties assigned to them by Congress. That dual role was discussed by Marshall in *Marbury.* The Secretary of State exercises two types of duties: ministerial and discretionary. The first duty extends to the nation and its citizens. Through statutory language, Congress may direct executive officials to carry out certain activities. The discretionary duty is to the President alone. When a Secretary of State performs "as an officer of the United States," he or she is "bound to obey the laws." In that capacity, the Secretary acts "under the authority of law, and not by the instructions of the president. It is a ministerial act which the law enjoins on a particular officer for a particular purpose."[108]

The distinction between ministerial/legal and discretionary/political has been treated in many court cases and opinions issued by Attorneys General. In one dispute, Postmaster General Amos Kendall in the Jackson administration refused to pay the claim of an individual who had contracted to carry the mail and wanted compensation for his services. Congress directed that the amount be paid, as did the circuit court for the District of Columbia. The Supreme Court agreed that Kendall could not refuse a payment authorized by law. Payment constituted a "purely ministerial" act for which there was no discretion. The legal obligation was to the statute, "not to the direction of the President."[109]

---

106. Jean Edward Smith, John Marshall: Definer of a Nation 326 (1998).
107. L. B. Boudin, "Government by Judiciary," 26 Pol. Sci. Q. 238, 256 (1911).
108. Marbury v. Madison, 5 U.S. (1 Cr.) at 157.
109. Kendall v. United States, 12 Pet. (37 U.S.) 524, 610 (1838). For other ministerial duties,

Attorneys General have interpreted ministerial duties in the same manner. In 1854, Attorney General Caleb Cushing concluded that when laws "define what is to be done by a given head of department, and how he is to do it, there the President's discretion stops; but if the law require an executive act to be performed, without saying how or by whom, it must be for him to supply the direction."[110] Other Attorneys General provided similar advice to Presidents, explaining when they can and cannot intervene in the action of a subordinate executive official.[111] President James Monroe asked whether he could alter a decision made by auditors and comptrollers in the Treasury Department. Attorney General William Wirt advised him to stay out: "It appears to me that you have no power to interfere. . . . If the laws, then, require a particular officer by name to perform a duty, not only is that officer bound to perform it, but no other officer can perform it without a violation of the law; and were the President to perform it, he would not only be not taking care that the laws were faithfully executed, but he would be violating them himself."[112]

An Open, Public Dialogue

Toward the end of his life, Jefferson continued to endorse coordinate construction. In a letter in 1820 he wrote to a correspondent: "You seem . . . to consider the judges as the ultimate arbiters of all constitutional questions; a very dangerous doctrine indeed, and one which would place us under the despotism of an oligarchy." Jefferson regarded judges "as honest as other men, but not more so." They have "the same passions for party, for power, and the privilege of their corps." They represented a danger because they were not responsible to the people as the elected branches. The Constitution "has more wisely made all the departments coequal and co-sovereign within themselves."[113] He knew of no "safe depository" for the power of society other than "the people."[114] To

---

see United States v. Schurz, 102 U.S. 378 (1880); Butterworth v. Hoe, 112 U.S. 50 (1884); United States v. Price, 116 U.S. 43 (1885); United States v. Louisville, 169 U.S. 249 (1898); Clackamus County, Ore. v. McKay, 219 F.2d 479, 496 (D.C. Cir. 1954), vacated as moot, 349 U.S. 909 (1955).

110. 6 Op. Att'y Gen. 326, 341 (1854).

111. 10 Op. Att'y Gen. 527 (1863).

112. 1 Op. Att'y Gen. 624, 625 (1823). For further details on ministerial duties, see Louis Fisher, "The Unitary Executive: Ideology Versus the Constitution," in The Unitary Executive and the Modern Presidency 21–26 (Ryan J. Barilleaux and Christopher S. Kelley, eds., 2010).

113. 15 The Writings of Thomas Jefferson 277 (Bergh ed., 1904).

114. Id. at 278.

those who insisted "there must be an ultimate arbiter somewhere," Jefferson agreed, but selected as the ultimate arbiter "the people of the Union, assembled by their deputies in convention, at the call of Congress, or of two-thirds of the States."[115]

The framers never intended to vest in the Court final authority over the meaning of the Constitution, nor has the Court ever succeeded in exercising that authority. Edward Corwin wrote in 1938: "The juristic conception of judicial review invokes a miracle. It supposes a kind of transubstantiation whereby the Court's opinion of the Constitution, if pertinent to the decision of the case properly before the Court, becomes the very blood and body of the Constitution."[116] A majority of five Justices lacks both the legitimacy and the competence to claim an exclusive voice. Justice Byron White put the matter crisply in 1970 when he said that "this Court is not alone in being obliged to construe the Constitution in the course of its work; nor does it even approach having a monopoly on the wisdom and insight appropriate to the task."[117]

On the issue of judicial supremacy, it is useful to recall that we have not one constitution but 51. Just because the Court issues a ruling in a particular case does not mean that all of the states must march to it. In many cases, state interpretations of their own constitutions will provide broader protection to individual rights than those decided by the U.S. Supreme Court. When state courts base their decisions on "bona fide, separate, adequate, and independent grounds," the Court will not interfere with state efforts to interpret their constitutions.[118] In those conflicts, the last word on state constitutional law rests with the states. Each state, the Court acknowledges, has the "sovereign right to adopt in its own constitution individual liberties more expansive than those conferred by the Federal Constitution."[119]

If the Court decides that it is constitutionally permissible to provide public funds to religious schools for transportation and textbooks, states have every right to say: "Not under our constitution." The U.S. Constitution says nothing about education. State constitutions are often quite specific in prohibiting the use of public funds for religious or private schools. The Court adopted the "child benefit" theory to argue that public funds do not benefit a church but rather the child. States are free to reject that doctrine when they invalidate public assis-

---

115. Id. at 451 (letter to Judge William Johnson, June 12, 1823).

116. Edward S. Corwin, "What Kind of Judicial Review Did the Framers Have in Mind?," 86 Pittsburgh L. J. 4, 15 (1938). The published version incorrectly used the first name "Edwin."

117. Welsh v. United States, 398 U.S. 333, 370 (1970) (White, J., dissenting).

118. Michigan v. Long, 463 U.S. 1032 (1983).

119. PruneYard Shopping Center v. Robins, 447 U.S. 74, 81 (1980).

tance to religious schools.[120] Chapter 4 includes many examples of states trumping U.S. Supreme Court jurisprudence.

Proponents of judicial supremacy place great value on the importance of finality and the settlement of disputes, preferring that outcome over the often disorderly process of self-government. According to legal scholar Ronald Dworkin: "Our legal culture insists that judges—and finally the justices of the Supreme Court—have the last word about the proper interpretation of the Constitution."[121] Nothing in U.S. legal culture requires that result or value. Dworkin reached his judgment not because of unbounded admiration for the Court's performance. Instead, judges "must answer intractable, controversial, and profound questions of political morality that philosophers, statesmen, and citizens have debated for many centuries, with no prospect of agreement." If the questions are intractable, what makes the Court particularly gifted or wise in resolving them?

Dworkin prefers that legal matters be settled even if the results are very far from ideal: "It means that the rest of us must accept deliverances of a majority of the justices, whose insight into these great issues is not spectacularly special."[122] An interesting argument. The insight of a majority of the Court is not demonstrably reliable or one to inspire confidence or support, but we should defer to their judgment, however deficient in reasoning and persuasive power. Dworkin, in fact, does not hesitate to attack the Court, as seen recently in his vigorous critique of the campaign finance decision of 2010, *Citizens United v. FEC.*[123]

In her book *The Majesty of the Law,* Justice Sandra Day O'Connor sent conflicting signals about the conclusive effect of Court rulings. At times she referred to the judiciary as "the final arbiters of the constitutionality of all acts of government," even repeating the "emphatically the province" rhetoric of *Marbury.*[124] Elsewhere, however, she showed a deeper appreciation for the mix of judicial and nonjudicial forces that shape the Constitution. She supports the "dynamic dialogue between the Court and the American public" and correctly states that no one could consider the Supreme Court abortion decision in *Roe v. Wade*

120. Louis Fisher and Katy J. Harriger, American Constitutional Law 596 (9th ed., 2011).

121. Ronald Dworkin, Freedom's Law: The Moral Reading of the American Constitution 74 (1996).

122. Id.

123. Ronald Dworkin, "The 'Devastating' Decision," New York Review of Books, February 25, 2010, at 39; "The 'Devastating' Decision: An Exchange," New York Review of Books, April 29, 2010, at 65; Ronald Dworkin, "The Decision That Threatens Democracy," New York Review of Books, May 13, 2010, at 63–64, 66–67; Citizens United v. FEC, 558 U.S. ___ (2010).

124. Sandra Day O'Connor, The Majesty of the Law: Reflections of a Supreme Court Justice 243 (2003).

(1973) "to have settled the issue for all time."[125] Under fire, the Court retreated in 1992 by jettisoning the trimester framework that attempted to define the rights of women and government over the nine months of pregnancy.[126] O'Connor said that a nation "that docilely and unthinkingly approved every Supreme Court decision as infallible and immutable would, I believe, have severely disappointed our founders."[127]

No matter how often scholars and courts cite *Marbury* as evidence of judicial supremacy, the argument fails. If one wanted to select a case where the Supreme Court attempted to make itself superior over the elected branches, a more apt citation would be *Dred Scott,* which fortunately the nation repudiated in its entirety. Robert Clinton, author of a study on *Marbury,* rejected the belief that Chief Justice Marshall and his colleagues had any intent to claim for themselves the final word on constitutional meaning. Clinton encouraged "maximum participation in constitutional decision by all agencies of government. Constitutional interpretation is a subtle but critical process. It should not be the special province of a small group of persons who happen to occupy the Supreme Court bench."[128] The following chapters offer specific examples to reinforce that point.

125. Id. at 45; Roe v. Wade, 410 U.S. 113 (1973).

126. Planned Parenthood v. Casey, 505 U.S. 833 (1992).

127. O'Connor, The Majesty of the Law, at 45. On the complex dialogue on abortion by all three branches and the states, see Neal Devins, Shaping Constitutional Values: Elected Government, the Supreme Court, and the Abortion Debate (1996).

128. Robert Lowry Clinton, Marbury v. Madison and Judicial Review 231 (1989).

3

ELECTED BRANCH INTERPRETATIONS

Questions of constitutional law do not always come to the courts. Often they are settled by the elected branches without litigation. Imagine that. When constitutional disputes do reach the judiciary, the Supreme Court may prefer to push them back to the elected branches for settlement. Or the Court may take the case and decide it, guided largely if not exclusively by what the elected branches had already agreed to. On many constitutional matters the dominant interpreter is not the judiciary but elected officials. Scholarly journals, including law reviews, pay scant attention to these statutory and interbranch accommodations, treating them as political rather than constitutional.[1] They are both.

Deferring to Elected Officials

During his visit to America in the 1830s, Alexis de Tocqueville marveled at the power of judicial review. At the same time, he understood that courts operate at risk when they stray beyond what is politically acceptable. Judges must exercise pragmatism and statesmanship to guard against the release of legal opinions that damage their institution and the country. The power of the Supreme Court, he

---

1. For efforts to understand constitutional law in a political context, see William G. Andrews, Coordinate Magistrates: Constitutional Law by Congress and President (1969); John Agresto, The Supreme Court and Constitutional Democracy (1984); Louis Fisher, Constitutional Dialogues: Interpretation as Political Process (1988); Edward Keynes, with Randolph K. Miller, The Court vs. Congress: Prayer, Busing, and Abortion (1989); Robert A. Licht, ed., Is the Supreme Court the Guardian of the Constitution? (1993); Neal Devins, ed., "Elected Branch Influences in Constitutional Decisionmaking," 56 Law & Contemp. Prob. 1 (Autumn 1993); Neal Devins, Shaping Constitutional Values: Elected Government, the Supreme Court, and the Abortion Debate (1996); Colton C. Campbell and John H. Stack Jr., Congress Confronts the Court: The Struggle for Legitimacy and Authority in Lawmaking (2001); Neal Devins and Louis Fisher, The Democratic Constitution (2004); Mark C. Miller and Jeb Barnes, eds., Making Policy, Making Law: An Interbranch Perspective (2004); J. Mitchell Pickerill, Constitutional Deliberation in Congress: The Impact of Judicial Review in a Separated System (2004); Neal Devins and Keith E. Whittington, eds., Congress and the Constitution (2005); Charles Gardner Geyh, When Courts and Congress Collide: The Struggle for Control of America's Judicial System (2006); Mark C. Miller, The View of the Courts from the Hill: Interaction Between Congress and the Federal Judiciary (2009); Louis Fisher, The Supreme Court and Congress: Rival Interpretations (2009); Louis Fisher and Neal Devins, Political Dynamics of Constitutional Law (5th ed., 2011); Louis Fisher and Katy J. Harriger, American Constitutional Law (9th ed., 2011).

wrote, "is enormous, but it is the power of public opinion. They are all-powerful as long as the people respect the law; but they would be impotent against popular neglect or contempt of the law." Federal judges, he warned, "must be statesmen, wise to discern the signs of the times, not afraid to brave the obstacles that can be subdued, nor slow to turn away from the current when it threatens to sweep them off."[2] With remarkable prescience, he warned: "if the Supreme Court is ever composed of imprudent or bad men, the Union may be plunged into anarchy or civil war."[3] Within two decades, in 1857, the Court released its slavery opinion in *Dred Scott.*

J. Clifford Wallace, while serving as a federal judge on the Ninth Circuit in 1981, urged courts to respect the need for judicial restraint. He concluded that legislatures, "with their committees, staffs, and deliberative processes, are institutionally better-equipped to investigate the consequences of policy decisions than are courts."[4] Many legal disputes "are better resolved in a nonjudicial setting." Courts are "cost-effective, for the most part, in settling disputes. They become cost-ineffective when asked to re-engineer social structures and reorganize social priorities."[5] Further: "Doing good by creating rights is not a judicial responsibility—it rests with the separate legislative branch."[6] For those and other reasons, members of Congress should not sit and wait for judicial solutions. It is their duty to independently debate and decide national policy.

In 1987, in the midst of the bicentennial celebration of the U.S. Constitution, polls revealed an unsurprising lack of public knowledge about the founding document. Nearly half of respondents believed the Constitution contains the Marxist declaration, "From each according to his ability, to each according to his need."[7] Six in ten, according to a newspaper account, "said correctly that the Supreme Court is the final authority on constitutional change."[8] Of course the six in ten were incorrect. Constitutional change can come in ways that have nothing to do with the judiciary: constitutional amendments, constitutional decisions by the elected branches that are never litigated, and constitutional settlements by elected officials that receive judicial blessing.

In a weak rhetorical slip in 1953, Justice Jackson made this claim: "We are

---

2. 1 Alexis de Tocqueville, Democracy in American 157 (Phillips Bradley, ed., 1945).

3. Id.

4. J. Clifford Wallace, "The Jurisprudence of Judicial Restraint: A Return to the Moorings," 50 G.W. L. Rev. 1, 6 (1981).

5. Id. at 7.

6. Id. at 11.

7. Ruth Marcus, "Constitution Confuses Most Americans," Washington Post, February 15, 1987, at A13.

8. Id.

not final because we are infallible, but we are infallible only because we are final."[9] He knew better than that. In the same year he uttered this unfortunate bromide, he delivered a more searching and thoughtful speech to the American Bar Association, recognizing that in the contest between judicial power and public opinion, the latter is often the most powerful force:

> [L]et us not deceive ourselves; long-sustained public opinion does influence the process of constitutional interpretation. Each new member of the ever-changing personnel of our courts brings to his task the assumptions and accustomed thought of a later period. The practical play of the forces of politics is such that judicial power has often delayed but never permanently defeated the persistent will of a substantial majority.[10]

Journalists often promote the belief in judicial supremacy. In an article for the *Washington Post* in 1996, Joan Biskupic remarked that the Court's importance is not in the number of cases it decides but rather "in the court having the last word. The justices are the final arbiter of what is in the Constitution."[11] She offered several cases to support her argument, but in none did the Court have the last word: *Dred Scott v. Sandford* (1857), overridden initially by congressional statute and an opinion from Attorney General Bates in 1862 and later by constitutional amendment; *Brown v. Board of Education* (1954), which had such limited impact that legislation was needed in 1964 to move the country toward desegregation; and *Roe v. Wade* (1973), an abortion decision of such unacceptable breadth that in *Planned Parenthood v. Casey* (1992) the Court beat a partial retreat by discarding its trimester framework.[12]

A year later, Biskupic treated the Court more as coequal than superior. Referring to litigation on affirmative action, she described the Court as "at the center not merely because it has the last word on legal cases" but because the Court, "for better or worse, is articulating principles that elected politicians on both sides of the debate studiously avoid." She explained that Presidents and Con-

9. Brown v. Allen, 344 U.S. 443, 540 (1953) (Jackson, J., concurring). The issue in this case was exceptionally narrow: whether anything can be read into the Court's decision not to take a case (by denying certiorari). The Court said no.

10. Robert H. Jackson, "Maintaining Our Freedoms: The Role of the Judiciary," delivered to the American Bar Association, Boston, Mass., August 24, 1953, reprinted in Vital Speeches, No. 24, vol. XIX, at 761 (October 1, 1953).

11. Joan Biskupic, "The Shrinking Docket," Washington Post, March 18, 1996, at A15.

12. Dred Scott v. Sandford, 60 U.S. (19 How.) 393 (1857); Brown v. Board of Education, 347 U.S. 483 (1954); Roe v. Wade, 410 U.S. 113 (1973); Planned Parenthood v. Casey, 505 U.S. 833 (1992).

gress had opposed judicial doctrines on affirmative action and that the Court itself was in the process of disowning doctrines it had earlier announced. The Court was now just one of many players: "The ultimate question is whether the Supreme Court, in its departure from precedent on affirmative action, is in sync with a national consensus. If it is not, experience teaches, society and other institutions of government will force it into step."[13] Here the Court is not the last word but an institution sharing the interpretive function with other branches. The latter model has governed the nation.

The constructive work of the elected branches in constitutional interpretation is at times overshadowed by claims of judicial finality. Writing in 2000, Linda Greenhouse of the *New York Times* described the Court's authority in very broad terms. Her opening sentence: "It was a Supreme Court term of surpassing interest, rich in symbol and substance, a vivid reminder of the court's power to scramble settled expectations, put old questions to rest and, ultimately, to have the last word."[14] Her summaries of individual decisions seemed to give the Court the upper hand over the elected branches.

Quite a different message emerged in her last article written in 2008 as Supreme Court reporter for the *New York Times*. Having covered the Court for 30 years, she now saw an institution that did not exercise an exclusive and final word on constitutional law. Instead, the Justices participated "in the ceaseless American dialogue about constitutional values." A judicial ruling was not necessarily the "final voice" on a dispute. Elected national leaders and the states were at liberty to respond with less than full acquiescence, deciding to do indirectly what the Court said they could not do directly, yielding what Greenhouse called a "constitutional Ping-Pong match." She concluded that the court "can only do so much. It can lead, but the country does not necessarily follow." At times it is the Court that follows. The historical pattern shows that it "ratifies or consolidates change rather than propelling it." Justices "live in constant dialogue with other institutions, formal and informal." When the Court collides with the policies of the elected branches, "it is often the court that eventually retreats when it finds itself out of sync with the prevailing mood."[15]

The Supreme Court continues to boast an independent and exclusive power, but occasionally Justices in unaccustomed modesty will concede they share the stage with other political institutions. In public comments in 2006, Chief Jus-

13. Joan Biskupic, "On Race, a Court Transformed," Washington Post, December 15, 1997, at A1.

14. Linda Greenhouse, "The Court Rules, America Changes," New York Times, July 2, 2000, at WK1.

15. Linda Greenhouse, "2,691 Decisions," New York Times, July 13, 2008, at WK1, WK4.

tice John Roberts and Justice Samuel Alito agreed that constitutional interpretation is not a judicial monopoly. Alito said that "all public servants, not just judicial officers, play a role in shaping our law, interpreting our Constitution." It would be a mistake for "any public officials to ignore questions about the bounds of their authority in our constitutional system and simply say that the courts will sort that out for them." Roberts sounded a similar theme: "The great gift of the founding generation was the right of self-government. We shouldn't give it up so easily to think that all the important issues are going to be decided by the Supreme Court."[16] These observations are welcome, but frequently Justices (and their abettors) bang the drum for judicial supremacy.

In *Cohens v. Virginia* (1821), Chief Justice Marshall declared: "It is most true that this Court will not take jurisdiction if it should not: but it is equally true, that it must take jurisdiction if it should. . . . With whatever doubts, with whatever difficulties, a case may be attended, we must decide it, if it be brought before us."[17] Questions may occur, he said, "which we would gladly avoid; but we cannot avoid them."[18] That statement is flatly wrong. The Court has many methods of not taking and ruling on a particular case, even when it has jurisdiction.

Judicial self-restraint is one technique for pushing constitutional disputes back to the elected branches. A variety of thresholds (also called "gatekeeping rules") are useful in avoiding judicial involvement in politically sensitive areas. What the Supreme Court decides to do is largely a matter of discretion. To Justice Louis Brandeis, the "most important thing we do is not doing."[19] Although thresholds are frequently couched in complex legal jargon, they represent key political and institutional judgments by the judiciary. The question of who gains access to the courts has a lot to do with preserving public support and avoiding needless and damaging collisions with elected officials.

Article III of the Constitution limits the jurisdiction of federal courts to "cases" and "controversies." Congress can attempt by statute to bring issues before the courts, but it is left always to the judiciary to decide what is a case or controversy. Lawsuits that fail to satisfy that test are called "nonjusticiable." Plaintiffs must then look elsewhere for relief, including the elected branches and the 50 states. Among the thresholds used to sidestep cases are standing, mootness, ripeness, and political questions. All of them rely on prudential considerations.

To demonstrate standing, parties must show injury to a legally protected

16. Robert Barnes, "New Justices Take the Podium, Putting Personalities on Display," Washington Post, November 20, 2006, at A15.
17. 19 U.S. (6 Wheat.) 264, 404 (1821).
18. Id.
19. Alexander M. Bickel, The Unpublished Opinions of Mr. Justice Brandeis 17 (1957).

interest, an injury that is real rather than abstract or hypothetical.[20] Courts recognize that Congress can, by statute, confer standing on an individual or group. When appropriate, courts will defer to Congress, but Congress cannot compel the courts to grant standing. Judges always retain the authority to decide that a given suit lacks the necessary ingredients to be a case or controversy. Lowering the barrier for standing not only means more work for the courts, but also an increased risk that the judiciary will expose itself to unwise dangers. Failure to exercise judicial self-restraint can provoke retaliation by the elected branches and the general public.

Ripeness applies to cases brought too early. Premature consideration by the courts does more than bring judges unnecessary work. It deprives them of information needed for informed adjudication, forcing courts to deal at an abstract, speculative, and hypothetical level. A case is moot when it appears that whatever legitimate issue initially existed no longer does. The mootness doctrine avoids the useless expenditure of judicial resources and ensures that the courts will not intrude into policies better left to the elected branches.[21] The meaning of the political question doctrine has been mired in great confusion, but generally it is a handy tool to either avoid or postpone deciding something that seems inappropriate for the judiciary.[22]

The President's Veto

The President's veto power has precipitated many constitutional clashes between the elected branches. Disputes have been largely resolved by the President and Congress. The Constitution states that if the President vetoes a bill he must return it "with his Objections to the House in which it shall have originated, who shall enter the Objections at large on their Journal, and proceed to reconsider it."[23] This language provokes an initial question: must Congress immediately "proceed" to reconsider a veto? Under the early Presidents, when vetoes were rare, that was the practice. Later, Congress decided to delay an override vote by referring the veto message to a select committee. Delays could stretch to weeks and months. In some cases, lawmakers decided to dispense with an override vote. The veto simply went unchallenged. Today it is established that when

20. O'Shea v. Littleton, 414 U.S. 488, 494 (1974).
21. For more on ripeness and mootness, see Louis Fisher and Katy J. Harriger, American Constitutional Law 95–101 (9th ed., 2011).
22. Id. at 102–11.
23. U.S. Const., art. I, sec. 7, cl. 2.

a President vetoes a bill, members of Congress may schedule an override vote at any time during the two years of a Congress. This constitutional question has been left exclusively to the rules, procedures, and political judgments of members of Congress. On that constitutional issue the courts are nonplayers.[24]

What is meant by the constitutional language that "two thirds of that House" is needed for an override vote? Two-thirds of the total membership of each chamber, or two-thirds of those present? The House of Representatives early decided that the answer was two-thirds of the members present, provided they formed a quorum. Later, lawmakers changed the margin to members present and voting. In 1919, the Court deferred to these precedents and decided that two-thirds of a quorum sufficed for an override.[25] The practice of Congress has been to accept two-thirds of the members present and voting.

Here is another veto dispute: may a President sign a bill after Congress has recessed? The issue arose because some executive officials believed that presidential approval of a bill was not strictly an executive function. By their theory, it was legislative in nature and needed to be done when both houses were actually sitting. The Court in 1899 refused to accept that argument, reasoning that if a President decides to sign a bill, no further action by Congress is required, and there is no need for lawmakers to be in session.[26]

This dispute invited a related issue: may a President sign a bill after the final adjournment of a Congress? Consistent with the belief that Presidents were a constituent part of Congress regarding the lawmaking process, Presidents would travel to a special room in the Capitol to sign hundreds of bills in the final days of a Congress. President Grover Cleveland decided to challenge this practice. After refusing to go to the Capitol, he relented a year later on the advice of his Attorney General.[27] In 1920 and again in 1931, two Attorneys General concluded that the President possesses constitutional authority to sign a bill after the final adjournment of Congress.[28] In 1932, the Court agreed with that analysis.[29] In all these disputes the Court accepted the constitutional judgments of the elected branches.

In signing a bill, Presidents often make statements about the contents of the legislation, including concerns about the constitutionality of certain provisions.

24. Louis Fisher, "Separation of Powers: Interpretation Outside the Courts," 18 Pepp. L. Rev. 57, 65–67 (1990), available at http://www.loufisher.org/docs/ci/460.pdf.
25. Missouri Pac. Ry. v. Kansas, 248 U.S. 276, 280–81 (1919).
26. La Abra Silver Mining Co. v. United States, 175 U.S. 423, 453–54 (1899).
27. E. I. Renick, "The Power of the President to Sign Bills After the Adjournment of Congress," 32 Am. U. L. Rev. 208 (1898).
28. 32 Op. Att'y Gen. 225 (1920); 36 Op. Att'y Gen. 403, 406 (1931).
29. Edwards v. United States, 286 U.S. 482 (1932).

In 1830, President Andrew Jackson signed a bill and simultaneously sent to Congress a message that restricted the reach of the statute.[30] A House report objected that his message constituted, in effect, an item veto of one of the bill's provisions.[31] President John Tyler provoked a similar outcry in 1842 when he signed a bill but deposited with the Secretary of State "an exposition of my reasons for giving to it my sanction." The document included misgivings about the constitutionality and policy of the entire statute.[32] A House committee insisted that the President is limited to three choices when receiving a bill: sign it, veto it, or issue a pocket veto in the event that a congressional recess prevents the return of a veto. To sign a bill and add extraneous matter in a separate document could be regarded "in no other light than a defacement of the public records and archives."[33]

The constitutionality of these "signing statements" is handled almost exclusively outside the courts. A rare case when a federal court decided such a case was in 1972. President Richard Nixon, while signing a military authorization bill, stated that a section called the Mansfield Amendment, dealing with the military commitment to Southeast Asia, did not represent the policy of his administration. He regarded that section as "without binding force or effect."[34] A district court disagreed: "No executive statement denying efficacy to the legislation could have either validity or effect."[35] The court advised Nixon that the Mansfield Amendment became the policy of his administration when he signed the bill into law.

Earlier, in 1943, President Franklin D. Roosevelt found it necessary to sign an emergency appropriation bill for military needs in World War II, even though in his signing statement he objected that a provision was unconstitutional because it represented a bill of attainder (a legislative act that inflicts punishment without judicial proceeding). The Constitution provides, regarding the powers of Congress: "No Bill of Attainder ... shall be passed."[36] The same restriction applies to the states: "No State shall ... pass any Bill of Attainder."[37] Congress in 1943 decided to deny the use of appropriations to pay the salaries of three officials in the executive branch, concluding that their "subversive" views

30. 3 Richardson 1046 (May 30, 1830).
31. H. Rept. No. 909, 27th Cong., 2d Sess. 5–6 (1842).
32. 5 Richardson 2012 (June 25, 1842).
33. H. Rept. No. 909, 27th Cong., 2d Sess. 2 (1842).
34. Public Papers of the Presidents, 1971, at 1114.
35. DaCosta v. Nixon, 55 F.R.D. 145, 146 (E.D.N.Y. 1972).
36. U.S. Const., art. I, sec. 9, cl. 3.
37. U.S. Const., art. I, sec. 10, cl. 1.

disqualified them from receiving federal funds.[38] Three years later, when the Supreme Court decided that the legislative language constituted a prohibited bill of attainder, it referred to Roosevelt's signing statement.[39]

Other than these two examples that involved the courts, the constitutionality of signing statements is basically up to the two elected branches. Congress needs to monitor the statements to ensure that its statutory policy is carried out. Failure to implement a law can take many forms. The executive branch may decide to prepared a memo that directs agency officials not to carry out a particular section of a statute. An example comes from 1984 when Attorney General William French Smith and OMB Director David Stockman instructed agencies not to comply with a provision of the Competition in Contracting Act. Extensive litigation upheld the constitutionality of the provision and forced the administration to implement it.[40]

Signing statements attracted public attention in 2005 when Congress passed a bill containing language against torture. Press reports had described the abuse of detainees at Abu Ghraib in Iraq and in CIA "black sites" abroad. The bill provided that no one in the custody of the U.S. government, "regardless of nationality or physical location, shall be subject to cruel, inhuman, or degrading treatment or punishment."[41] That policy had supposedly been settled earlier by statute and treaty. In signing the bill, President Bush said he would interpret it "in a manner consistent with the constitutional authority of the President to supervise the unitary executive branch and as Commander in Chief and consistent with the constitutional limitations on the judicial power."[42] In other words, Congress can pass what it likes but the President may decide the extent to which he will carry out the law, even if the Constitution plainly directs the President to "take Care that the Laws be faithfully executed."[43]

This type of signing statement is offensive not merely because it attempts to nullify statutory policy but because of its broad-brush nature. President Roosevelt's signing statement in 1943 singled out a specific provision that violated express language in the Constitution: the Bill of Attainder Clause. The statement by President Bush relied on vague and ill-defined concepts: the unitary

38. Louis Fisher, The Constitution and 9/11: Recurring Threats to America's Freedoms 138–43 (2008).

39. United States v. Lovett, 328 U.S. 303 (1946).

40. Lear Siegler, Inc., Energy Products Div. v. Lehman, 842 F.2d 1102, 1124 (9th Cir. 1988). See also the Ameron rulings at 607 F.Supp. 962 (D. N.J. 1985), 610 F.Supp. 750 (D. N.J. 1985), 787 F.2d 875 (3d Cir. 1986), and 809 F.2d 979 (3d Cir. 1986).

41. 119 Stat. 2739, sec. 1003(a) (2005).

42. 41 Weekly Comp. Pres. Doc. 1919 (2005).

43. U.S. Const., art. II, sec. 3.

executive branch, the Commander in Chief Clause, and supposed constitutional limits that restrain judicial control. As explained in Chapter 1, claims of a "unitary executive" embrace many misconceptions. The Commander in Chief Clause is not a source of limitless presidential power. Federal courts have been involved in war power cases from 1800 forward (covered in Chapter 9). Furthermore, with most signing statements it is possible to observe whether the administration does or does not carry out the law as written. With interrogation of detainees, no one knows unless they are present in the room.

Other types of signing statements are largely hortatory with no discernible impact. What matters is not what a President says in signing a bill but what the administration does afterward. If the bill is faithfully carried out, what he said in a signing statement carries little interest. For example, about one-fourth of signing statements object to committee vetoes on the ground that they are invalid under the Court's 1983 decision of *INS v. Chadha*. As explained in Chapter 7, executive agencies regularly and dutifully comply with committee and subcommittee vetoes.

The Pocket Veto

The Constitution provides that any bill returned by the President "within ten Days (Sundays excepted)" shall become law "unless the Congress by their Adjournment prevent its Return, in which Case it shall not be a Law."[44] In 1787, the framers understood that Congress would be in adjournment for many months. They wanted to ensure that legislation would not sit in limbo for long periods waiting for legislators to return to session. Several issues emerge with the pocket veto. First, may it be used only during an adjournment at the end of a Congress or also in the middle of a Congress? The scope of the pocket veto has bedeviled the elected branches for more than two centuries, with no final resolution yet. On several occasions this issue seemed to be ripe for a final word from the Supreme Court, but each time the Court returned the matter to the elected branches in search of a satisfactory accommodation.

At times, the Supreme Court supplies some guidance. In 1929, it held that a five-month adjournment at the end of a first session prevented a bill's return and justified the President's pocket veto.[45] A decade later it decided that a recess by the Senate for three days was so brief that the Senate could act with "reasonable

---

44. U.S. Const., art. I, sec. 7, cl. 2.
45. The Pocket Veto Case, 279 U.S. 655 (1929).

promptitude" in taking an override vote.[46] To demonstrate that the President was not prevented from returning a bill, the Senate authorized the Secretary of the Senate to receive bills during a recess.[47]

Additional direction came from litigation over a pocket veto during a Christmas adjournment in 1970. The Senate was absent for four days and the House for five. Although the recess was brief and the Senate had designated an officer to receive messages from the White House, President Nixon pocket vetoed a bill. Unlike the 1929 ruling, his initiative involved a short adjournment during a session rather than a lengthy adjournment at the end of a session. A district court held that the adjournment did not prevent Nixon from returning the bill to Congress as a regular veto.[48] After that decision was upheld the next year by an appellate court, it appeared that pocket vetoes during any intrasession adjournment (no matter how long) would be unconstitutional, unless Congress failed to make appropriate arrangement for the receipt of presidential messages during the adjournment.[49]

Judicial clarity on the pocket veto seemed on the horizon, but no such luck. The Nixon administration decided not to appeal the case to the Supreme Court.[50] In 1975, the Ford administration reached a political accommodation with Congress by promising not to use a pocket veto during a session.[51] It even agreed a year later to eliminate the pocket veto during both intrasession and intersession adjournments.[52] The pocket veto would be available only at the end of a Congress. President Carter honored that accommodation, but President Reagan provoked further litigation by using the pocket veto between the first and second sessions. A district court upheld his action; an appellate court reversed.[53]

With the case heading toward the Supreme Court, would clear rules finally emerge for the pocket veto? Not this time either. The Court held that the dispute between Congress and Reagan was moot because the bill had expired by

---

46. Wright v. United States, 302 U.S. 583, 590 (1938).

47. Id. at 589–90.

48. Kennedy v. Sampson, 364 F.Supp. 1075, 1086–87 (D.D.C. 1973).

49. Kennedy v. Sampson, 511 F.2d 430, 442 (D.C. Cir. 1974).

50. Arthur John Keeffe, with John Harry Jorgenson, "Solicitor General Pocket Vetoes the Pocket Veto," 61 Am. Bar. Assn. J. 755 (1975).

51. 121 Cong. Rec. 41884 (1975) (statement by Rep. Rhodes).

52. 122 Cong. Rec. 11202 (1976); Kennedy v. Jones, 412 F.Supp. 353 (D.D.C. 1976).

53. Barnes v. Carmen, 582 F.Supp. 163 (D.D.C. 1984); rev'd sub nom. Barnes v. Kline, 759 F.2d 21 (D.C. Cir. 1985).

its own terms.[54] Very likely the Court used the mootness argument to avoid an issue even more troublesome: whether the member of Congress bringing the case had standing to sue in court.[55] In any event, the Court's action returned the issue to the elected branches for possible resolution. In 1990, the House Rules Committee reported legislation to restrict the pocket veto to the end of a Congress (adjournment sine die). The bill was referred to the House Judiciary Committee, which reported the bill favorably, but the House never took a final vote.[56] I testified on the pocket veto in 1989 and 1990, before both House Rules and House Judiciary, and worked with lawmakers and their staff on bill language that might resolve the matter.[57]

The scope of the pocket veto remains unsettled. A new twist popped up during the administrations of Bill Clinton and George W. Bush. They decided to pocket veto a bill but return it to Congress, inviting a possible override. This type of hybrid veto (part pocket, part return) created confusion on how to count it. Congress treated the hybrid veto as a regular veto, capable of being overridden. The Senate Library records the hybrid veto as a regular veto.[58] When President Barack Obama used this same approach on December 30, 2009, claiming to exercise a pocket veto while at the same time returning the bill to Congress, he received a bipartisan rebuke from Speaker Nancy Pelosi and House Majority Leader John Boehner. They said his return of the bill was "absolutely inconsistent with this most essential characteristic of a pocket veto, to wit: retention of the parchment by the President for lack of a legislative body to whom he might return it with his objections." They said the House would treat his veto message "as a return veto," not a pocket veto.[59] In October 2010, Obama released another hybrid veto.[60]

54. Burke v. Barnes, 479 U.S. 361, 363 (1987).

55. Id. at 366 (Stevens, J., dissenting).

56. H. Rept. No. 417, Part 1, 101st Cong., 2d Sess. (1990); H. Rept. No. 417, Part 2, 101st Cong., 2d Sess. (1990).

57. "H.R. 849," hearing before the House Committee on Rules, 101st Cong., 1st Sess. 32–54 (1989); "Pocket Veto Legislation," hearing before the House Committee on the Judiciary, 101st Cong., 2d Sess. 71–84, 91–92, 95–114 (1990).

58. Presidential Vetoes, 1989–1996, S. Pub. 105-22, at 2. For additional details on the strange hybrid veto, see Louis Fisher, Constitutional Conflicts Between Congress and the President 129–130 (5th ed., 2007), and Robert J. Spitzer, "The 'Protective Return' Pocket Veto: Presidential Aggrandizement of Constitutional Power," 31 Pres. Stud. Q. 720 (2001).

59. 156 Cong. Rec. E941 (daily ed., May 26, 2010).

60. Jackie Calmes, "Much Ado over . . . Notarization," New York Times, October 16, 2010, available at http://www.nytimes.com/2010/10/17/us/politics/17veto.html.

Federal Appointments

The Appointments Clause of the Constitution seems fairly straightforward. The President "shall nominate, and by and with the Advice and Consent of the Senate, shall appoint Ambassadors, other public Ministers and Consuls, Judges of the supreme Court, and all other Officers of the United States, whose Appointments are not herein otherwise provided for, and which shall be established by Law." Congress may also by statute "vest the Appointment of such inferior Officers, as they think proper, in the President alone, in the Courts of Law, or in the Heads of Departments."[61]

When the President submits a nomination, must the Senate always take action, either by agreeing to the President's choice or voting it down? There is no obligation on the part of the Senate to act. In 2003, after the Senate delayed taking a vote on the nomination of Miguel Estrada to the D.C. Circuit, President George W. Bush stated that the Senate "has a constitutional responsibility to hold an up-or-down vote on all judicial nominees within a reasonable time."[62] Although the Senate generally takes floor votes on nominees for the Supreme Court, that custom does not apply to the lower courts. Nominees to a district or circuit court need not be reported from committee, much less receive a floor vote.[63]

What of the language "he shall nominate"? Does it give the President an exclusive voice in selecting the nominee? President Washington decided that he did not have to be personally involved in all federal appointments. In responding to a request for a postal appointment, he wrote: "I can only observe, that I have uniformly avoided interfering with any appointments which do not require my official agency, and the Resolutions and Ordinances establishing the Post Office under the former Congress, and which have been recognized by the present Government, giving power to the Postmaster General to appoint his own Deputies, and making him accountable for their conduct, is an insuperable objection to my taking any part in this matter."[64]

With regard to judicial appointments, Justice O'Connor has written that when the framers inserted "advice and consent" for the Senate regarding the

---

61. U.S. Const., art. II, sec. 2, cl. 2.

62. Public Papers of the Presidents, 2003, I, at 263.

63. Mitchel A. Sollenberger, "Must the Senate Take a Floor Vote on a Presidential Judicial Nominee?," 34 Pres. Stud. Q. 420 (2004).

64. Mitchel A. Sollenberger, The President Shall Nominate: How Congress Trumps Executive Power 31 (2008).

making of appointments, "the practice almost always has been that the President selects a nominee for the [Supreme] Court without any 'advice' from the Senate, and merely forwards the nomination for the confirmation process."[65] Practice has been quite different. A few Presidents tried to exercise exclusive control over nominations, but invariably gave ground to allow not only Senators but other nonexecutive actors to decide who gets nominated.

Research by political scientist Mitchel Sollenberger demonstrates that the republican form of government necessarily opens the door wide during the pre-nomination stage. Any effort by a President to monopolize the choice of nominees would result in Senate retaliation, not just against nominees but against other presidential objectives and priorities. Sollenberger notes that Presidents must be "mindful of the democratic values that dominate the exercise of the Appointments Clause."[66] To protect republican government, the Senate has armed itself with formidable tools to safeguard its institutional interest in the nomination process, including committee investigations, blue slips, filibusters, and holds.[67]

Another constitutional issue that might have been settled by the Supreme Court but was not: presidential use of the recess appointment power. The framers realized that the Senate would not always be in session to give its advice and consent to presidential nominations. To cover periods of absence, the President "shall have Power to fill up all Vacancies that may happen during the Recess of the Senate, by granting Commissions which shall expire at the End of their next Session."[68] Heavy use of recess appointments threatens the Senate's constitutional power over confirmations and provokes intense confrontations between the branches.

What is the constitutional meaning of "happen"? Does it mean only vacancies that "happen to take place" during a recess, or the much broader meaning of a vacancy that may *happen to exist* at the time of a recess? A long list of opinions by Attorneys General supports the latter (and broader) interpretation.[69] To

65. Sandra Day O'Connor, The Majesty of the Law, at 20.
66. Mitchel A. Sollenberger, The President Shall Nominate, at 190.
67. Mitchel A. Sollenberger, Judicial Appointments and Democratic Controls (Carolina Academic Press, 2011).
68. U.S. Const., art. II, sec. 2, cl. 3.
69. 1 Op. Att'y Gen. 631 (1823); 2 Op. Att'y Gen. 525 (1832); 4 Op. Att'y Gen. 523 (1846); 10 Op. Att'y Gen. 356 (1862); 12 Op. Att'y Gen. 32, 38 (1866); 12 Op. Att'y Gen. 455, 457 (1868); 16 Op. Att'y Gen. 522, 524 (1880); 18 Op. Att'y Gen. 29 (1884); 19 Op. Att'y Gen. 261, 262 (1889); 30 Op. Att'y Gen. 314, 315 (1914); 33 Op. Att'y Gen. 20, 23 (1921); 41 Op. Att'y Gen, 463, 465–66 (1960). See also In re Farrow 3 F. 112, 113–15 (C.C.N.D. Ga. 1880) (concurring with the opinions of the Attorneys General from 1823 to 1880).

protect its institutional interests, Congress retaliated with statutory restrictions. A report by the Senate Judiciary Committee in 1863 rejected the Attorney General position that a recess appointee may fill any vacancy. Interpreting the language "may happen during the Recess of the Senate" to include what happened before a recess seemed to the committee "a perversion of language."[70] Unless Congress placed limits on recess appointments, an "ambitious, corrupt, or tyrannical executive" could nullify the Senate's constitutional role.[71]

Congress invoked its power of the purse. Legislation in 1863 prohibited the use of federal funds to pay the salary of anyone appointed during a Senate recess to fill a vacancy that existed "while the Senate was in session and is by law required to be filled by and with the advice and consent of the Senate, until such appointee shall have been confirmed by the Senate."[72] The statutory remedy proved far too rigid, forcing some federal officials to serve without pay and rely on personal savings and loans. At times Congress found it necessary, as it did in 1916, to pass legislation to compensate officials who served for long periods without a salary.[73] By 1939, Congress understood it needed to pass legislation to permit several exceptions to the 1863 statute, allowing payment of salaries to officials covered by those exceptions. That bill became law in 1940 and remains part of permanent law today.[74]

The constitutionality of this funding restriction has never been settled in the courts. In dicta in a 1979 decision, a federal judge remarked: "It might be noted that if any and all restrictions on the President's appointment power, however limited, are prohibited by the Constitution, 5 U.S.C. §5503 [the 1940 statute] . . . might also be invalid. That question, however, is not before the court in this case."[75] Not only was it not before the court, the judge's hypothetical included the all-important "if." The statutory remedy has not eliminated disputes between the executive and legislative branches. Statutes are not self-executing. Senators must be willing to monitor recess appointments and use appropriate tools of retaliation.[76]

The use of recess appointments to place men and women on federal courts is especially serious. They remain on the bench for a year or more and must face confirmation after their recess appointment ends. Without the independence

70. S. Rept. No. 80, 37th Cong., 3d Sess. 5 (1863).
71. Id. at 6.
72. 12 Stat. 642, 646 (1863).
73. E.g., 39 Stat. 801 (1916).
74. 54 Stat. 751 (1950), presently codified at 5 U.S.C. §5503 (2006).
75. Staebler v. Carter, 464 F.Supp. 585, 596 n.24 (D.D.C. 1979).
76. Fisher, "Separation of Powers: Interpretation Outside the Courts," supra note 24, at 72–73.

of a judge with a lifetime appointment, recess judges may decide to reshape a decision to avoid alienating the White House when it comes time to nominate the judge to a lifetime appointment. They might want to alter language in an opinion to ensure that their decisions do not cost them votes in the Senate. The use of the recess appointment power to place individuals on the federal bench has been upheld in a number of decisions, most recently in 2004 regarding the placement of William H. Pryor Jr. on the Eleventh Circuit during an eleven-day President's Day recess by the Senate.[77]

If Congress wants to exercise greater control over recess appointments to federal courts, remedies are available. The Senate can ask a colleague to attend every three days during a recess to hold a pro forma session. It can pass a resolution stating that any individual who accepts a recess appointment to a federal court will not receive any Senate action if the President later submits the name for a lifetime position. But Senate resolutions are nonbinding and can be ignored in a future Congress. A stronger message would be the Senate's adoption of this language: "When someone who has served as a recess appointee comes before us for a lifetime appointment, we will not waste time with a hearing. Instead, we will bring the name to the Senate floor and defeat it 100 to zero, sending an unmistakable signal to Presidents and nominees that we will not tolerate recess appointments to federal courts."[78]

Incompatibility and Ineligibility

Although the framers rejected a pure separation of powers, they added two provisions to the Constitution to preserve some distance between the branches. The Constitution prohibits members of either house from simultaneously holding any other civil office (the Incompatibility Clause). It also prohibits members of Congress from being appointed to any federal position whose salary has been increased during their term of office (the Ineligibility Clause).[79] Sporadic efforts over the years have attempted to litigate these clauses, but their meaning has been developed and clarified almost entirely by the elected branches.

77. Evans v. Stephens, 387 F.3d 1220 (11th Cir. 2004), cert. denied, 544 U.S. 942 (2005). See also United States v. Woodley, 751 F.2d 1008 (9th Cir. 1985) (en banc); United States v. Allocco, 305 F.2d 704 (2d Cir. 1962).

78. For further details on recess appointments of federal judges, see Fisher, "Separation of Powers: Interpretation Outside the Court," supra note 24, at 73–74, and Fisher, Constitutional Conflicts Between Congress and the President, at 42–45.

79. U.S. Const., art. I, sec. 6, cl. 2.

The framers adopted the Incompatibility and Ineligibility Clauses to prevent the Executive from using the appointment power to corrupt legislators.[80] They recalled that the English king used appointments to undermine the independence of Parliament.[81] The Incompatibility Clause reached a district court in 1971, involving the authority of members of Congress to hold a commission in the armed forces reserves. The judge understood that the "meaning and effect of this constitutional provision have never before been determined by a court."[82]

By the time the case reached the Supreme Court three years later, it held that the plaintiffs lacked standing to bring the case.[83] To the objection that if courts fail to clarify the constitutional meaning of the Incompatibility Clause, as a practical matter no one can, the Court answered: "Our system of government leaves many crucial decisions to the political processes."[84] In 1977, the Justice Department examined whether members of Congress may hold commissions as officers in the armed forces reserves. It concluded that the "exclusive responsibility for interpreting and enforcing the Incompatibility Clause rests with Congress."[85] The department saw no clear basis for interpreting the clause and decided to defer to Congress.

Experience with the Ineligibility Clause yields a similar lesson: its meaning is left essentially to the elected branches. Opinions by Attorneys General from 1882 to 1895 held that certain members of Congress were ineligible under the Constitution to accept appointment to an executive position.[86] In several instances the executive branch displayed a willingness to nominate a member of Congress to an executive office even though the individual was ineligible under a plain reading of the Constitution. For example, President William Howard Taft wanted Senator Philander Knox to serve as his Secretary of State. However, the salary for that office had been increased during Knox's term in the Senate, making him ineligible to serve. To resolve this constitutional issue, the Senate passed legislation to reduce the compensation of the Secretary of State to the previous level.[87] That initiative did not satisfy the literal meaning of the Ineligibility Clause, but it did remove the appearance of gain and corruption. Several

80. 1 Farrand 379–82, 386–90; 2 Farrand 283–84, 489–92.
81. Reservists Comm. to Stop the War v. Laird, 323 F.Supp. 833, 835–37 (D.D.C. 1971), aff'd, 495 F.2d 1075 (D.C. Cir. 1972), rev'd, 418 U.S. 208 (1974).
82. Reservists Comm. to Stop the War v. Laird, 323 F.Supp. at 834.
83. Schlesinger v. Reservists to Stop the War, 418 U.S. 208–09 (1974).
84. Id. at 227.
85. 1 Op. O.L.C. 242 (1977).
86. 17 Op. Att'y Gen. 365 (1882); 17 Op. Att'y Gen. 522 (1883); 21 Op. Att'y Gen. 211 (1895).
87. 43 Cong. Rec. 2205 (1909).

members of the House objected to this effort to circumvent the constitutional prohibition, but the bill passed the House and became law.[88]

This congressional remedy has been used many times. It allowed Senator William Saxbe to be Secretary of State in 1973, Senator Ed Muskie to be Secretary of State in 1980, Senator Lloyd Bentsen to be Secretary of the Treasury in 1993, and Senator Hillary Clinton to serve as Secretary of State in 2009.[89] No litigation emerged from these statutory actions from 1973 to 1993, but a foreign service officer went to court to challenge Clinton's appointment as a violation of the Ineligibility Clause. The case was dismissed for lack of standing.[90]

Several cases tested the boundaries of the Ineligibility Clause. When Senator Hugo Black was nominated to the Supreme Court in 1937, his appointment ended up in court because Congress had enacted a retirement system for Justices while he served in the Senate. The Court held that the plaintiff lacked standing to bring the suit.[91] Similarly, the appointment of Representative Abner Mikva to the D.C. Circuit led to litigation in 1981 because the salaries of federal judges had been increased during his term in Congress. The courts held that the plaintiff lacked standing.[92] In this way it decided to leave with Congress (and in this case with the Senate) the duty to police the Ineligibility Clause.

Covert Spending

To provide citizens with information about how the federal government spends money, the Constitution requires that "a regular Statement and Account of the Receipts and Expenditures of all public Money shall be published from time to time."[93] Yet the spending of tens of billions of dollars by the intelligence community, including the CIA and the National Security Agency, had been withheld from the public. Efforts to have federal judges decide the constitutionality of covert spending have been unsuccessful. The decision to make these expenditures public was left to the elected branches.

88. 35 Stat. 626; for further details, see Fisher, "Separation of Powers: Interpretation Outside the Courts," supra note 24, at 76–77.

89. 87 Stat. 697 (1973); 94 Stat. 343 (1980); 107 Stat. 4 (1993); 122 Stat. 5036 (2008).

90. Rodearmel v. Clinton, 666 F.Supp.2d 123 (D.D.C. 2009), dismissed by the Supreme Court on June 7, 2010, for want of jurisdiction.

91. Ex parte Levitt, 302 U.S. 633 (1937).

92. McClure v. Carter, 513 F.Supp. 265 (D. Idaho 1981), aff'd sub nom. McClure v. Reagan, 454 U.S. 1025 (1981).

93. U.S. Const., art. I, sec. 9, cl. 7.

At the Philadelphia Convention, George Mason proposed that "an Account of the public expenditures should be annually published." Gouverneur Morris objected that publication would be "impossible in many cases."[94] He may have had in mind some element of secrecy and confidentiality.[95] Rufus King flagged other problems: "The term expenditures went to every minute shilling. This would be impracticable. Congs. might indeed make a monthly publication, but it would be in such general Statements as would afford no satisfactory information." King seemed to put the emphasis not on secrecy but excessive and meaningless details. Madison proposed that "annually" be replaced with "from time to time." The convention accepted his amendment without a dissenting vote.[96]

When this constitutional provision was discussed at the Virginia ratifying convention in 1788, Mason explained that he added the phrase "from time to time" because there "might be some matters which might require secrecy." Madison's language protected both secrecy and the public's right to know: "In matters relative to military operations, and foreign negotiations, secrecy was necessary sometimes. But he did not conceive that the receipts and expenditures of the public money ought ever to be concealed. The people, he affirmed, had a right to know the expenditures of their money."[97] The debate offers conflicting values, but at some point, after some delay, the public was entitled to know how the government spent money, including for secret operations.

In 1790, Congress provided the President with a $40,000 account to be used for foreign intercourse. The statute left to the President the degree to which expenditures would be made public. Three years later, Congress passed legislation authorizing the President to make a certificate of the amount of expenditures in foreign intercourse "he may think it advisable not to specify." The President's certificate balanced two values by stating publicly that funds had been spent without necessarily giving any details. The President's certificate represented a sufficient voucher for the sums expended.[98]

Only once in the nineteenth century did Congress authorize resort to unvouchered funds. The contingency account for foreign intercourse grew to $63,000 by 1899. Marking a second deviation from the Statement and Account Clause, Congress passed a secret statute in 1811, providing President Madison with $63,000 to take temporary possession of territory south of Georgia. The

94. 2 Farrand 618.
95. Fisher, Constitutional Conflicts Between Congress and the President, at 207.
96. 2 Farrand 619.
97. 3 Farrand 326; 3 Elliot 459.
98. 1 Stat. 129 (1790); 1 Stat. 300 (1793), codified at 31 U.S.C. §3526(e) (2006).

law was not published until 1818.[99] Another unvouchered account appeared in 1916, just before the United States entered World War I, authorizing the Secretary of the Navy to make a certificate of expenses for "obtaining information from abroad and at home." Congress created a third unvouchered account in 1935: a confidential fund of $20,000 for the FBI.[100] For a period of 146 years, from 1789 to 1935, Congress created only three unvouchered accounts and they involved relatively small amounts of money.

Initiatives during World War II prompted dramatic departures from democratic budgeting. The Roosevelt administration used lump-sum amounts to fund the Manhattan Project, which developed and produced the atomic bomb. The bulk of the money (over $2 billion) came from two appropriation accounts: (1) Engineer, Service, and (2) Army and Expedited Production.[101] No one in the public could have imagined how those funds would be spent. When the administration needed $1.6 billion to manufacture the bomb, it contacted three leaders of the House of Representatives: Speaker Sam Rayburn, Majority Leader John McCormack, and Minority Leader Joe Martin. The executive branch wanted the money made available "without a trace of evidence as to how it would be spent."[102] Clarence Cannon, chairman of the House Appropriations Committee, and John Taber, ranking member of that committee, agreed to provide an inscrutable appropriation. They moved the funds through both chambers without breaking secrecy.[103] During that same period, Congress authorized unvouchered funds for many new agencies and executive officials: the White House, the Defense Department, the District of Columbia, the Attorney General, the Bureau of Narcotics and Dangerous Drugs, the Secret Service, the Coast Guard, the Bureau of Customs, and the Immigration and Naturalization Service.[104]

Overshadowing even those examples of confidential spending are funds allocated to the U.S. intelligence community, consisting of the Central Intelligence Agency, the National Security Agency, the Defense Intelligence Agency, and other federal units. Beginning with the Central Intelligence Act of 1949, the CIA and other agencies did not receive a direct appropriation from Congress. Instead, funds were tucked into various appropriation accounts. After those bills

---

99. 3 Stat. 471–72 (1818). See David Hunter Miller, Secrets Statutes of the United States (1918).

100. 39 Stat. 557 (1916), 10 U.S.C. §7231 (2006); 49 Stat. 78 (1935), 28 U.S.C. §537 (2006).

101. Leslie R. Groves, Now It Can Be Told: The Story of the Manhattan Project 360–61 (1962).

102. Joe Martin, My First Fifty Years in Politics 100–01 (1960).

103. Id.

104. Louis Fisher, "Confidential Spending and Governmental Accountability," 47 G.W. L. Rev. 347 (1979).

were signed into law, the Office of Management and Budget transferred the funds to the CIA and other agencies in the intelligence community. That process has two main drawbacks: the public does not know what is being appropriated, and appropriation accounts are artificially inflated to make room for hidden funds.

William B. Richardson, a resident of Greensburg, Pennsylvania, filed a lawsuit asking federal courts to declare the Central Intelligence Act a violation of the Statement and Account Clause. The litigation continued for five years, from 1969 to 1974. In the end, the Supreme Court decided that Richardson lacked standing to bring his suit.[105] Lower courts credited him with drawing attention to a vital principle of democratic government:

> A responsible and intelligent taxpayer and citizen, of course, wants to know how his tax money is being spent. Without this information he cannot intelligently follow the actions of the Congress or the Executive. Nor can he properly fulfill his obligations as a member of the electorate. The Framers of the Constitution deemed fiscal information essential if the electorate was to exercise any control over its representatives and meet their new responsibilities as citizens of the Republic.[106]

Justice William O. Douglas, one of four members dissenting from the standing argument, denied that Congress by statute is at liberty to suspend a constitutional provision. The idea that Congress is empowered to read the Statement and Account Clause out of the Constitution seemed to him "astounding."[107] Subsequent efforts by members of Congress and the general public to seek relief from federal courts on this issue were regularly turned aside on the ground of standing.[108] Over the years, Congress held frequent hearings on the advisability of publishing the aggregate budget for the intelligence community. I testified before the House Intelligence Committee in 1994, urging disclosure of the aggregate amount for two reasons: to comply with the Statement and Account Clause, and to avoid the deception that occurs when funds for the intelligence community are placed undisclosed in appropriation accounts.[109] Sometimes the

---

105. United States v. Richardson, 418 U.S. 166 (1974).

106. Richardson v. United States, 465 F.2d 844, 853 (3d Cir. 1972).

107. United States v. Richardson, 418 U.S. at 200–01.

108. In 1977 an appellate court decided that Rep. Michael J. Richardson lacked standing to bring suit against the use of public funds for illegal CIA activities; Harrington v. Bush, 553 F.2d 190 (D.C. Cir. 1977).

109. "Public Disclosure of the Aggregate Intelligence Budget Figure," hearings before the House Permanent Select Committee on Intelligence, 103d Cong., 2d Sess. 109–21 (1994).

House took the lead in wanting to disclose the totals; at other times, it was the Senate. Bills never made it through both chambers.

Steven Aftergood, a private citizen, filed a series of Freedom of Information Act (FOIA) requests and lawsuits to uncover the aggregate budget of the intelligence community. His persistence bore fruit in 1997 when the CIA voluntarily released a figure of $26.6 billion, with CIA accounting for about $3 billion of that total. It released a figure of $26.7 billion the following year, at which point the agency resorted to its previous policy of nondisclosure. Other Aftergood lawsuits were repeatedly dismissed by federal courts.[110] In one of those cases I filed a declaration to support his efforts. In 2005, a top U.S. intelligence official inadvertently revealed at a public meeting what she thought to be the annual intelligence budget: $44 billion.[111]

In 2004, the 9/11 Commission recommended that the aggregate budget of the intelligence community be made public. Three years later Congress passed legislation to implement that proposal. The statute required the Director of National Intelligence (DNI) to disclose the aggregate budget, but by fiscal 2009 the President would be authorized to waive the disclosure requirement.[112] On October 30, 2007, DNI Mike McConnell released the aggregate amount of $43.5 billion for fiscal 2007.[113] His figure understated the total. News reports pointed out that his aggregate excluded funds for the military services on intelligence operations. Including those amounts pushed the total substantially beyond $50 billion.[114] An estimate in July 2010 put the total at approximately $75 billion.[115] In October 2010, the government announced that it had spent $80.1 billion for intelligence activities.[116]

---

110. E.g., Aftergood v. C.I.A., 355 F.Supp.2d 557 (D.D.C. 2005); Aftergood v. C.I.A., 2004 WL 3262743 (D.D.C. 2004); Aftergood v. C.I.A., 225 F.Supp.2d 27 (D.D.C. 2002); Aftergood v. C.I.A., Civ. No. 8-2107 (TFH) (D.D.C. 1999).

111. Scott Shane, "Official Reveals Budget for U.S. Intelligence," New York Times, November 11, 2005, at A24.

112. 121 Stat. 335 (2007).

113. Office of the Director of National Intelligence, Public Affairs Office, News Release, "DNI Releases Budget Figure for National Intelligence Program," October 30, 2007.

114. Mark Mazzetti, "$43.5 Billion Spying Budget for Year, Not Including Military," New York Times, October 31, 2007, at A16; Walter Pincus, "2007 Spying Said to Cost $50 Billion," Washington Post, October 30, 2007, at A4.

115. "Clapper: Military Intel Budget to be Disclosed," included in the July 21, 2010, issue (vol. 2010, no. 59) of "Secrecy News," available at http://www.fas.org/blog/secrecy.

116. Walter Pincus, "Intelligence Spending at Record $80.1 Billion Overall," Washington Post, October 29, 2010, at A2.

Foreign Affairs and War

From the early 1790s to the present, the elected branches have independently decided constitutional questions of foreign affairs and military force without waiting for judicial guidance, or even receiving it later. Some judgments by Congress and the President found acceptance in the courts. Chapter 2 reviewed how Congress passed a militia statute in 1792, requiring the President to receive judicial validation before using troops to put down a domestic insurrection. That procedure was removed three years later, but clearly Congress has substantial constitutional authority to place conditions on the use of troops. In the Quasi-War of 1798, Congress chose to pass authorization bills to prepare for military action rather than adopt a formal declaration of war against France, stipulating that it would be a naval war, not a land war. The Supreme Court in 1800 and 1801 agreed that Congress has the option of either declaring or authorizing war and deciding its scope.[117]

The treaty power has been substantially defined by the elected branches. There are many ambiguities in the Treaty Clause, which states that the President "shall have Power, by and with the Advice and Consent of the Senate, to make Treaties, provided two-thirds of the Senators present shall concur." Does that exclude the House from the treaty power? It might appear to, given misconceptions about President Washington and the Jay Treaty in 1795. He told the House it had no right to documents because the Senate alone is constitutionally responsible for legislative action on treaties. Members of the House understood what was constitutionally obvious: treaties are made by the President and the Senate. But the House wanted documents to decide whether to *authorize and fund the treaty*. It fell short a few votes on requesting documents. Even without the votes it could have told the administration it would not consider legislation to implement the Jay Treaty unless it received the documents. A few years earlier, on the Algerine Treaty, Washington treated the House and the Senate equally on access to documents. These constitutional disputes (discussed in detail in Chapter 7) are resolved solely by the elected branches.

Second, how are treaties to be negotiated: by the President alone or with Senate participation? In the famous 1936 *Curtiss-Wright* case, Justice George Sutherland, writing for the Supreme Court, claimed that the President "*makes* treaties with the advice and consent of the Senate; but he alone negotiates. In the field of negotiation the Senate cannot intrude; and Congress itself is powerless to invade

---

117. Bas v. Tingy, 4 U.S. (4 Dall.) 36 (1800); Talbot v. Seeman, 5 U.S. (1 Cr.) 1 (1801).

it."[118] That is demonstrably false. Even Sutherland, in a book published earlier when he was a U.S. Senator from Utah, recognized that Senators do in fact participate in the negotiation phase and that Presidents often acceded to this "practical construction."[119]

It is true that President George Washington was disappointed with the results of meeting personally with Senators to receive their thoughts on a treaty "*to be negotiated* with the Southern Indians."[120] The experience proved to be sufficiently unpleasant that he never again met with Senators to obtain their advice on a draft treaty. But he continued to seek Senate advice by written communications rather than personal visits. He asked Senators to approve not only the appointment of treaty negotiators but also their negotiating instructions.[121]

Other Presidents included Senators in the negotiation of treaties. President James K. Polk sought Senate advice on the negotiation of a treaty because it was prudent to consult lawmakers in advance of "important measures of foreign policy which may ultimately come before them for their consideration." By acting jointly with the Senate in the negotiation of treaties, he was able to secure "harmony of action between that body and himself."[122] Presidents include both Senators and members of the House of Representatives in the negotiation of treaties. Both chambers of Congress may be called on to pass authorizing and funding legislation to implement a treaty.

Of the eight members of Congress invited to participate in the negotiation and passage of the United Nations Charter, half came from Congress: two from the Senate and two from the House. Senators were closely involved in the negotiation of the North Atlantic Treaty Organization (NATO).[123] In 1991, U.S. Trade Representative Carla A. Hills told the Senate Finance Committee that the procedure for negotiating trade agreements "is a genuine partnership between the two branches." Appreciating that Congress has the power to defeat a bill needed to implement a trade agreement, she emphasized that lawmakers have "a full role throughout the entire process in formulating the negotiating objectives in close consultation as the negotiations proceed."[124]

118. United States v. Curtiss-Wright Export Corp., 299 U.S. 304, 319 (1936) (emphasis in original).

119. George Sutherland, Constitutional Power and World Affairs 123 (1919).

120. 1 Annals of Cong. 67 (1789) (emphasis added).

121. Fisher, Constitutional Conflicts Between Congress and the President, at 222.

122. 5 Richardson 2299.

123. Fisher, Constitutional Conflicts Between Congress and the President, at 224–25. See also Louis Fisher, "Congressional Participation in the Treaty Process," 137 U. Pa. L. Rev. 1511 (1989), available at http://www.loufisher.org/docs/pip/442.pdf.

124. "Extension of Fast Track Legislative Procedures," hearings before the Senate Committee on Finance, 102d Cong., 1st Sess. 9 (1991).

Third, what is meant by this constitutional language: "two thirds of the Senators present" must consent to a treaty? Two-thirds of a quorum? Two-thirds without a quorum? Merely two Senators out of three? In 1952, with only two Senators on the floor, the Senate gave its advice and consent to the ratification of three treaties. One of the Senators did not even vote. The presiding officer, casting an "aye" vote, stated that "two-thirds of the Senators present concurring therein, the resolution of ratification is agreed to, and the convention is ratified." A year later, Senate Majority Leader William Knowland announced that future treaties would be preceded by a quorum call and subjected to "a yea-and-nay vote, at least on the first of a series of treaties." That remains the general practice.[125]

A fourth issue left unresolved in the constitutional text is how to terminate treaties. Is that done by the President alone, or through congressional action, or by courts? The issue of treaty termination was not discussed at the Philadelphia Convention; the Constitution is silent on the question. Under Article VI, treaties are vested with the same domestic status as federal statutes. One option is therefore to terminate treaties through the regular legislative process. Some of the early treaties were abrogated or terminated by statute. To the extent that a new statute conflicts with an existing treaty, it cancels or amends those portions of the treaty.[126] Other treaties have been terminated by presidential action without any prior congressional authorization, by Senate resolutions, and by new treaties.[127]

In 1978, President Carter simultaneously recognized the People's Republic of China (PRC) and terminated the U.S. defense treaty with Taiwan. The Senate considered several steps to block his initiative but never took final action.[128] Without oral argument and within days of the scheduled treaty termination, the Supreme Court dismissed a complaint brought by Senator Barry Goldwater, who opposed Carter's action. The Justices split along so many lines that no common theme emerges, other than letting this particular termination stand. Justice Powell said the issue was not ripe for adjudication. Chief Justice Burger and Justices Rehnquist, Stewart, and Stevens viewed the matter as a nonjusticiable political question. Justices Blackmun and White believed the Court

125. 99 Cong. Rec. 9231 (1953); 98 Cong. Rec. 7217–23 (1952). See Carl Marcy, "A Note on Treaty Ratification," 47 Am. Pol. Sci. Rev. 1130 (1953).

126. The Chinese Exclusion Case, 130 U.S. 581, 600–02 (1889). See also Whitney v. Robertson, 124 U.S. 190, 193–94 (1888); The Head Money Cases, 112 U.S. 580, 597–99 (1884).

127. Digest of United States Practice in International Law, 1978, at 734–65. The convenient section here on treaty termination does not appear in current issues of the Digest.

128. Fisher, Constitutional Conflicts Between Congress and the President, at 236–38.

should have held oral argument and given the case plenary consideration. Justice Brennan concluded that the President's power to recognize foreign governments carried with it an implied power to terminate treaties. Justice Marshall concurred in dismissing Goldwater's complaint.[129]

Goldwater introduced legislation in 1981 to require a two-thirds affirmative vote in the Senate to terminate defense treaties. His measure was never enacted. As a result, the question of treaty termination remains where it has always been: full of uncertainty and left very much to decisions by the elected branches.

Finally, may the President submit a treaty to the Senate, have it approved, and later "reinterpret" it in a manner that Senators could not have anticipated? Treaty reinterpretation ripened into a serious dispute during the Reagan administration. It wanted to build a sophisticated antimissile defense shield consisting of satellites armed with laser weapons. The administration called it the Strategic Defense Initiative (SDI); the press preferred "Star Wars." Some lawmakers believed that deployment or even testing of SDI would violate the Antiballistic Missile (ABM) Treaty with Russia. A restrictive interpretation of the treaty allowed only research and development. The administration wanted a broader interpretation to permit development, testing, and deployment.

This interbranch conflict became more intense when proponents of the broader interpretation decided to rely on the treaty negotiation records, which were classified and not shared with the Senate.[130] Also objectionable to many Senators was the administration's position that the Senate gives advice and consent to a treaty, not to explanations of the treaty offered by executive officials. Under this theory, executive officials could offer explanations to the Senate about the meaning and intent of a treaty but not be bound by their statements. Those and other questions were carefully explored in a joint hearing held by two Senate committees: Foreign Relations and the Judiciary.[131]

Treaty reinterpretation is exquisitely complex in terms of rival constitutional theories, but the legislative remedy was a simple one. Congress passed legislation with language stating that the Secretary of Defense "may not deploy any anti-ballistic missile system unless such deployment is specifically authorized by law after the date of the enactment of this Act."[132] Ambitious constitutional the-

129. Goldwater v. Carter, 444 U.S. 996 (1979).

130. Abram Chayes and Antonia Handler Chayes, "Testing and Development of 'Exotic' Systems Under the ABM Treaty: The Great Reinterpretation Caper," 99 Harv. L. Rev. 1956 (1986); Abraham D. Sofaer, "The ABM Treaty and the Strategic Defense Initiative," 99 Harv. L. Rev. 1972 (1986).

131. "The ABM Treaty and the Constitution," joint hearings before the Senate Committee on Foreign Relations and the Judiciary, 100th Cong., 1st Sess. 122–23, 130, 143 (1987).

132. 101 Stat. 1057, sec. 226 (1987).

ories pursued by the executive branch were run aground by a statute. Judicial interpretations were not needed.

Broad themes of Congress and the Constitution have been explored in these first three chapters. More detailed examples of coordinate construction appear later in the book, starting with the next chapter on federalism. The purpose is to appreciate constitutional interpretations that are not centered in the judiciary, much less in the Supreme Court. All three branches of the national government and all 50 states are continuously involved in debating and shaping the U.S. Constitution. In a democracy, there could be no other process.

4

FEDERALISM

By relying on the Commerce Clause, taxing powers, federal spending, and other constitutional authorities, members of Congress play a pivotal role in defining federalism and the distribution of political power between the national government and the states. At times the Supreme Court has checked and reversed legislative initiatives, but both the doctrine and practice of federalism have been shaped far more by the elected branches than the judiciary. A prominent struggle pitted the Court against Congress on the issue of regulating child labor. Lawmakers pursued their effort over several decades, eventually prevailing in 1941 when a unanimous Court not only upheld the legislative judgment but apologized for deficient judicial reasoning in earlier rulings. The national dialogue over federalism cannot be settled or dictated by judicial decisions.

Bank of the United States

In 1791, Congress passed legislation to create a national bank. Assisted by constitutional analysis prepared by executive officers, lawmakers concluded that Article I provided sufficient powers to justify the statute. The elected branches tackled this question at the start of the national government, deciding on their own initiative the constitutional principles without looking to the judiciary for guidance. Not until 1819 did the Supreme Court join the debate with its ruling in *McCulloch v. Maryland*. As explained in this chapter, it reviewed the constitutional judgment reached by the elected branches and added its endorsement, illustrating how judicial review can be a positive force in ratifying and legitimating policies already adopted by the elected branches.

The Continental Congress had created a national bank in 1781 to deal with the crisis of the Revolutionary War, but six years later, delegates at the Philadelphia Convention gave little attention to the issue of a national bank.[1] In debating language in Article I that granted Congress authority to establish post offices and post roads, the delegates considered giving the legislative branch the power "to grant charters of incorporation where the interest of the U.S. might require & the legislative provisions of individual States may be incompetent." On September 14, 1787, Rufus King of Massachusetts expressed concern that Congress

---

1. 20 Journals of the Continental Congress 519, 530–31, 545–48.

might use the power to establish a national bank, triggering new tensions between Philadelphia and New York about the authority of Congress to charter a competing national institution. The delegates decided against the language on incorporation.[2]

In 1790, the House of Representatives asked Secretary of the Treasury Alexander Hamilton to prepare a report on creating a national bank. Hamilton produced a lengthy study, explaining the benefits of a bank and attempting to rebut arguments against it. At this stage he did not address constitutional concerns.[3] The following year, House members debated legislative authority to establish a bank. Madison objected that the power of creating a national bank was not among the authorities enumerated in Article I and the bank would interfere with the rights of the states.[4] Colleagues pointed to his inconsistent constitutional analysis. In 1789, he had defended the President's power to remove department heads even though the removal power is not expressly stated in Article II.[5] Why recognize implied powers for the President but not for Congress? Also, during debate on the Bill of Rights, Madison denied that powers had to be "expressly" delegated to the national government. It was necessary, he argued, to have not only enumerated powers but implied powers.[6]

The bill for a national bank passed the House handily, 39 to 20.[7] The Senate had already supported the measure, making it ready to be signed into law. President George Washington asked his cabinet to advise him on the bill's constitutionality. Attorney General Edmund Randolph and Secretary of State Thomas Jefferson concluded that Congress lacked authority to create a bank.[8] Toward the end of his legal analysis, Jefferson hedged a bit, suggesting that congressional judgment could temper strict legal reasoning. He advised Washington that if "the pro and the con hang so even as to balance his judgment, a just respect for the wisdom of the legislature would naturally decide the balance in favour of their opinion."[9] Jefferson did not urge total deference to legislative judgment, but rather a considered measure of respect. His attitude found a place within the judiciary, as with *McCulloch*.

2. 2 Farrand 615–16.
3. 2 Annals of Cong. 2082–112 (December 13, 1790).
4. Id. at 1945–1952 (1791).
5. Id. at 1960 (remarks of Rep. Sedgwick).
6. Discussed in Chapter 1, at 10.
7. 2 Annals of Cong. 2012.
8. Walter Dellinger and H. Jefferson Powell, "The Constitutionality of the Bank Bill: The Attorney General's First Constitutional Law Opinions," 44 Duke L. J. 110 (1994).
9. 19 The Papers of Thomas Jefferson 280 (Julian P. Boyd, ed., 1974). For Randolph's evaluation, see 31 The Writings of George Washington 215–16 (John C. Fitzpatrick, ed., 1939).

Hamilton strongly defended the constitutionality of a national bank.[10] His analysis later guided John Marshall's decision in *McCulloch*. Faced with conflicting advice, Washington decided to sign the bill.[11] Over the years the bank experienced several cycles, with Congress willing to recharter it at times and later refusing to renew it. Economic difficulties after the War of 1812 prompted Congress to restore the bank in 1816.[12] Two years later Maryland passed legislation to impose a tax on all banks or branches of banks in the state not chartered by the state legislature. James W. McCulloch, cashier of the U.S. Bank in Baltimore, refused to pay the tax. The dispute invited the Supreme Court to explore several constitutional issues: the reach of the Necessary and Proper Clause, the extent of state sovereignty, and the validity of a state tax on a federal instrumentality.

During oral argument, Daniel Webster defended the bank in large part by deferring to the judgment of elected officials: "When all branches of the government have thus been acting on the existence of this power nearly thirty years, it would seem almost too late to call it into question, unless its repugnancy with the constitution were plain and manifest."[13] He meant deference to the elected branches, not total acquiescence. Every "settled" constitutional issue may be reopened and reversed in later years by all three branches of government.

When Chief Justice Marshall upheld the bank in *McCulloch*, he relied heavily on the analysis that Hamilton submitted to Washington in 1791. Like Hamilton, Marshall read the Necessary and Proper Clause broadly. Consider this parallel language. In determining the constitutionality of a bill, Hamilton offered this standard: "If the end be clearly comprehended within any of the specified powers, & if the measure have an obvious relation to that end, and is not forbidden by any particular provision of the constitution—it may safely be deemed to come within the compass of the national authority."[14] Marshall's version: "Let the end be legitimate, let it be within the scope of the constitution, and all means which are appropriate, which are plainly adapted to that end, which are not prohibited, but consist with the letter and spirit of the constitution, are constitutional."[15]

Although Marshall shied away from a claim of judicial supremacy in *Marbury*, he seemed to promote that doctrine in *McCulloch*. If a constitutional dis-

10. 8 The Papers of Alexander Hamilton 46–49, 63–135 (Harold C. Syrett, ed., 1965).
11. 1 Stat. 191 (1791).
12. 3 Stat. 266 (1816).
13. 1 Landmark Briefs 323; printed also in McCulloch v. State of Maryland, 4 Wheat. (17 U.S.) 316, 323 (1819).
14. 8 The Papers of Alexander Hamilton 107 (Syrett ed.).
15. McCulloch v. State of Maryland, 4 Wheat. (17 U.S.) at 421.

pute must be decided, "by this tribunal alone can the decision be made. On the supreme court of the United States has the constitution of our country devolved this important duty."[16] *By this tribunal alone?* Whatever judicial insecurity existed in 1803, Marshall seemed more assured when writing *McCulloch.* Having donned the mantle of "final interpreter," he immediately injured his cause by stating: "This government is acknowledged by all to be one of enumerated powers."[17] The national government does not depend solely on enumerated powers. No power of "judicial review" is enumerated in the Constitution. If the three branches depended on enumerated powers, Marshall would have had to concede, at the very outset of his decision in *McCulloch,* that Congress lacked express authority to create a national bank because there is no enumerated power to do so. As he acknowledged a page later: "Among the enumerated powers, we do not find that of establishing a bank or creating a corporation."[18]

Two paragraphs after announcing the false constitutional doctrine of enumerated powers, Marshall spoke with greater care: the national government is "limited in its powers."[19] He moved from the rigid principle of enumerated powers to the defensible position of implied powers. There was no language in the U.S. Constitution, "which, like the articles of confederation, excludes incidental or implied powers; and which requires that every thing granted shall be expressly and minutely described." Recalling the history of the Tenth Amendment, he said it "omits the word 'expressly,' and declares only that the powers 'not delegated to the United States, nor prohibited to the States, are reserved to the States or to the people.'"[20]

Marshall developed this point. If it were necessary for a constitution to contain "an accurate detail of all the subdivisions of which its great powers will admit, and of the means by which they may be carried into execution," it would necessarily "partake of the prolixity of a legal code, and could scarcely be embraced by the human mind. It would probably never be understood by the public." No statement could more strongly repudiate the idea of enumerated powers. Marshall explained that the nature of a constitution only requires that "its great outlines should be marked, its important objects designated, and the minor ingredients which compose those objects be deduced from the nature of the objects themselves." The constitution described here is not one of enumerated powers but one of express powers plus implied powers. Marshall concluded

16. Id. at 401.
17. Id. at 405.
18. Id. at 406.
19. Id. at 405.
20. Id. at 406.

with his famous statement: "In considering this question, then, we must never forget, that it is *a constitution* we are expounding."[21] He meant a constitution that is not restricted to enumerated powers and has the capacity to respond to unanticipated crises.

Marshall escaped the box of enumerated powers by pointing to constitutional language that empowers Congress to make "all laws which are necessary and proper, for carrying into execution the foregoing powers, and all other powers vested by this constitution, in the government of the United States, or in any department thereof."[22] He interpreted the Necessary and Proper Clause as enlarging, not diminishing, the powers vested in Congress.[23] He did more than fully embrace implied powers. He deferred to the judgment of lawmakers: "But we think the sound construction of the constitution must allow to the national legislature that discretion, with respect to the means by which the powers it confers are to be carried into execution, which will enable that body to perform the high duties assigned to it, in the manner most beneficial to the people."[24]

Having reached that judgment, Marshall had to retreat from his initial claim of judicial supremacy. He now reasoned that "where the law is not prohibited, and is really calculated to effect any of the objects entrusted to the government, to undertake here to inquire into the degree of its necessity, would be to pass the line which circumscribes the judicial department, and to tread on legislative ground. This court disclaims all pretensions to such a power."[25] In this realm of public policy, where a law is not specifically prohibited by the Constitution, the final word is not the Court but the elected branches. When statutes are challenged in court, the role of the judiciary is simply to inquire whether Congress possessed the power to exercise its authority.

The breadth of national power defended by Marshall in *McCulloch* sparked a remarkable debate in the newspapers, not merely because of the quality of legal analysis but because the prominent advocates on each side used pseudonyms. The Court released *McCulloch* on March 6, 1819. Before the end of the month, the *Richmond Enquirer,* a strong proponent of states' rights, published two essays signed by "Amphictyon." Probably written by Judge William Brockenbrough, they were sharply critical of *McCulloch.* A sophisticated rebuttal, appearing in the Philadelphia *Union* a month later, was signed "A Friend of the Union." The author: John Marshall. Within a few weeks the *Richmond Enquirer* printed four

21. Id. at 407 (emphasis in original).
22. Id. at 411–12.
23. Id. at 420.
24. Id. at 421.
25. Id. at 423.

essays signed "Hampden," written by Judge Spencer Roane of the Virginia Court of Appeals. Marshall, writing this time as "A Friend of the Constitution," responded with a sophisticated nine-part rebuttal in the Alexandria *Gazette.*[26]

Under the leadership of John Marshall, the Court greatly shaped federalism by extending national control over the states, including *United States v. Peters* (1809) and *Fletcher v. Peck* (1810). In the first, the Court established that state legislatures cannot interfere with the operation of the federal judicial process.[27] In the second, the Court struck down an act of a state legislature as unconstitutional.[28] In these cases and others, the Court extended its control over the states, not over Congress.

Andrew Jackson Insists on Autonomy

In some cases the authority on the meaning of the Constitution is not the Court or Congress but the President. Congress passed legislation once again in 1832 to create a national bank. When the bill reached President Andrew Jackson, he understood that the bank had been enacted many times and had been upheld by the Court in *McCulloch.* Recognizing that a national bank "is in many respects convenient for the Government and useful for the people," he vetoed the bill.[29] He had been advised by many advocates of the bank that "its constitutionality in all its features ought to be considered as settled by precedent and by the decisions of the Supreme Court." To that conclusion, he said, "I can not assent." He considered "mere precedent" a "dangerous source of authority, and should not be regarded as deciding questions of constitutional power except where the acquiescence of the people and the States can be considered as well settled."[30] Jackson pointed to the ebbs and flows of congressional action: favoring a national bank in 1791, deciding against it in 1811 and 1815, and returning its support in 1816. Up to the time of Jackson's veto, "the precedents drawn from that source were equal."[31] At the state level, legislative, judicial, and executive opinions against the bank were mixed. He found nothing in precedent persuasive or decisive to him.

To Jackson, even if *McCulloch* "covered the whole ground of this act, it ought

26. Gerald Gunther, ed., John Marshall's Defense of McCulloch v. Maryland (1969).
27. United States v. Peters, 9 U.S. (5 Cr.) 115 (1809).
28. Fletcher v. Peck, 10 U.S. (6 Cr.) 87 (1810).
29. 3 Richardson 1139.
30. Id. at 1144–45.
31. Id. at 1145.

not to control the coordinate authorities of this Government." All three branches "must each for itself be guided by its own opinion of the Constitution." Each public official takes an oath to support the Constitution, "as he understands it, and not as it is understood by others." It is as much the duty of lawmakers in the House and the Senate and the President "to decide upon the constitutionality of any bill or resolution which may be presented to them for passage or approval as it is of the supreme judges when it might be brought them for judicial decision." A judicial opinion "has no more authority over Congress than the opinion of Congress has over the judges, and on that point the President is independent of both." The Supreme Court must not be permitted "to control the Congress or the Executive when acting in their legislative capacities, but to have only such influence as the force of their reasoning may deserve."[32] A valuable insight. We defer to the Court not because it decides a case but because its reasoning is persuasive.

Jackson examined Marshall's reasoning at the end of *McCulloch* that if a law is not prohibited by the Constitution, it is inappropriate for the Court "to tread on legislative ground." Under those conditions, the Court should defer to Congress. But it would also have to defer, Jackson reasoned, to the President and to his exercise of the veto power. He disagreed fundamentally that the Necessary and Proper Clause authorized Congress to shift its Article I powers to a private bank and to grant foreigners an exemption from all state and national taxation.[33] To Jackson, the national bank showered benefits on the rich and powerful at the expense of the "humble members of society—the farmers, mechanics, and laborers—who have neither the time nor the means of securing like favors to themselves."[34] Congress sustained Jackson's veto.[35]

Webster Against Jackson

In a passionate speech, Senator Daniel Webster condemned Jackson's veto message. As a general matter he conceded the existence of the veto power but disagreed with its application against the bank bill: "It is not to be doubted, that the Constitution gives the President the power which he has now exercised; but

32. Id.
33. Id. at 1146–47.
34. Id. at 1153.
35. See Lynn L. Marshall, "The Authorship of Jackson's Bank Veto Message," 50 Miss. Valley Hist. Rev. 466 (1965); Richard P. Longaker, "Andrew Jackson and the Judiciary," 71 Pol. Sci. Q. 341 (1956).

while the power is admitted, the grounds upon which it has been exerted become fit subjects of examination."[36] He agreed that "each branch of the legislature has an undoubted right, in the exercise of its functions, to consider the constitutionality of a law proposed to be passed."[37] That duty fell equally on lawmakers and Presidents. But "when a law has been passed by Congress, and approved by the President, it is now no longer in the power, either of the same President, or his successors, to say whether the law is constitutional or not." At that point the question of constitutionality "becomes a judicial question, and a judicial question alone."

For Webster, the very nature of *McCulloch* required that the Court's judgment be "final, and from which there is no appeal, be conclusive." Otherwise, "there would be no government of laws; but we should all live under the government, the rule, the caprices, of individuals." Tolerate Jackson's veto, he warned, and "the executive power becomes at once purely despotic."[38] Wouldn't it be similarly despotic to live under judicial edicts, regardless of their merit?

Objections against presidential vetoes were frequent during this period, especially from Whigs who believed in legislative primacy and trust in representative government.[39] During the first 28 years, covering four Presidents and seven administrations, there were only seven regular vetoes, five resting on constitutional grounds. Sensitivity to vetoes reached absurd levels under President John Tyler when his opponents introduced a resolution to impeach him, in part for "withholding his assent to laws undispensable [*sic*] to the just operations of government, which involved no constitutional difficulty on his part."[40] It would be rare today to hear such arguments.

Webster seemed to conclude that once national policy is established by statute, it may never be altered or discontinued in the future. Lawmakers, Presidents, and courts could not reconsider a policy in light of new developments unanticipated when the statute was first adopted. Elected officials and judges would have to leave an original decision untouched, even if it became obvious that the policy rested on deficient reasoning or facts, or expressed a priority that contemporary policy makers no longer shared or valued.

Webster could have been advancing a more narrow position. He particularly

36. Edwin P. Whipple, The Great Speeches and Orations of Daniel Webster 320 (1879).

37. Id. at 330.

38. Id.

39. Robert J. Spitzer, The Presidential Veto: Touchstone of the American Presidency 33–53 (1988).

40. Cong. Globe, 27th Cong., 3d Sess. 144 (1843). For the veto record in the early years, see Louis Fisher, Constitutional Conflicts Between Congress and the President 115–20 (5th ed., 2005).

opposed Jackson's claim that on constitutional matters he was coequal to the other branches, enabling him to reach an independent judgment. Webster readily conceded that Jackson could have vetoed the bank bill on purely policy grounds. If the President "sees fit to negative a bill, on the ground of its being inexpedient or impolitic, he has a right to do so."[41] But the line between constitutional and policy objections is not always a bright one. Different Congresses, Presidents, and the Court had held the bank bill to be necessary and proper. At times Congress found it was not necessary and proper. What is the difference between a bill being necessary and proper ("constitutional") and inexpedient or impolitic ("policy")?

Webster found it difficult to sort out policy and constitutional arguments. If a President exercised a veto that identified only policy reasons, the bank would be just as lifeless as if struck dead on constitutional grounds. Those who counted on the stability of the law in the past would have a revered policy discredited and discontinued. On either constitutional or policy grounds, Webster found it necessary to condemn Jackson's veto of the bank bill: "If that which Congress has enacted, and the Supreme Court has sanctioned, be not the law of the land, then the reign of law has ceased, and the reign of individual opinion has already begun."[42] Why is it lawless for a President to exercise an independent judgment when vetoing a bill?

The choice between vetoing a bill on policy or constitutional grounds came to my attention during the Clinton years. Invited to give a luncheon talk at the Office of Legal Counsel (OLC) in the Justice Department, I decided to begin with something we could agree on and then move to more contentious issues. My initial choice, however, caused us to divide at once. I said that although the Supreme Court in *Morrison v. Olson* (1988) had upheld the constitutionality of the office of independent counsel, with only Justice Scalia in dissent, any President could use constitutional grounds to veto a bill that reauthorized the independent counsel. I suggested that the President's veto message could give due recognition to *Morrison,* but insist that whatever grounds the Court found persuasive did not bind a future President or Congress.

The Court in *Morrison* offered several grounds for upholding the independent counsel. It treated the office as "inferior" and "temporary" for purposes of the Appointments Clause. It was therefore permissible, said the Court, for Congress to place the power to appoint the independent counsel in an officer outside the executive branch, subject to the direction of a special panel of federal judges. Taken as a whole, the Court said, the statute did not "unduly interfere"

41. Whipple, supra note 36, at 332.
42. Id. at 334.

with the President's role.[43] Unduly? Why couldn't a President challenge the impact of a bill on his constitutional powers? To the Court, the statute did not work "any *judicial* usurpation of properly executive functions."[44] Suppose it worked a *legislative* usurpation? I told the OLC attorneys that a President could announce in his veto message: "A decade ago the Court decided there was no significant interference with my constitutional authorities. First, we have learned since the Court's decision much about the operation and potential abuses of the independent counsel statute. There is legitimate cause for concern in placing prosecutorial authority in a single person outside the regular procedures of the Justice Department. Second, the branch responsible for protecting the duties and powers of the President is not the judiciary or Congress. That duty belongs to me. I must decide when a statute impermissibly interferes with my constitutional responsibilities. I so find and veto the bill for that reason."

I was surprised when most attorneys in the room strongly objected to my analysis. They insisted that the constitutionality of the independent counsel had already been litigated and definitively decided by the Court in *Morrison*. No President could later conclude otherwise. The constitutional issue was settled. They acknowledged that a President could veto an independent counsel bill on policy (but not constitutional) grounds. I raised some practical questions. If a President vetoed a bill on constitutional grounds and Congress failed to override, that was the end of it. Who would have standing in court to challenge the President's independent judgment? To me: no one.

In my opinion, *Morrison* merely announced that if the two elected branches wanted to create an independent counsel, the Court could find no constitutional objection. If lawmakers and Presidents later concluded that the manner in which these counsels exercised their powers created substantial concerns, including constitutional, the two branches were free to change their minds.

Beyond the President's independence to exercise the veto power, I asked what would happen if lawmakers concluded that the independent counsel statute, however noble its original intent, created so many unintended and harmful consequences (including constitutional) that Congress saw no reason to reauthorize it. Would not that congressional decision be the "final voice" on a constitutional question, or at least until a subsequent Congress reconsidered the matter?

That is what happened in 1999. The statute authorizing the independent counsel expired, and lawmakers decided not to continue it. Members of Congress did not feel bound by *Morrison*. They found the office to be indefensible (on either policy or constitutional grounds). A President might veto a bill and

43. Morrison v. Olson, 487 U.S. 654, 693 (1988).
44. Id. at 695 (emphasis in original).

Congress could not override. Lawmakers could decide it was time to kill the office. The *Morrison* decision provided judicial permission, not compulsion. It did not take from the elected branches their independent duty to interpret and decide constitutional questions.

As the discussion with OLC attorneys continued, I began to look around the room more closely. I realized that many seemed to be in their late 20s or early 30s. Their professional life had been in law school and clerking for a federal judge or Supreme Court Justice. During that time, they accepted that when the Supreme Court decides a constitutional matter it is settled, with no opportunity for Presidents or members of Congress to independently challenge the judicial result. As employees in the Justice Department, I thought they might feel a special loyalty to safeguard presidential power and the independence of the executive branch. When former OLC head Jay Bybee appeared before the House Judiciary Committee on May 26, 2010, he said his responsibility in that position "was to be a vigorous defender of the President's prerogative."[45] At least on the question we discussed at the luncheon, the commitment of the OLC attorneys seemed to be to the Court.

In December 2010, I was invited to give another luncheon talk at OLC. There were three points on my agenda. First were the experiences I had over a period of four decades at the Library of Congress on constitutional questions. Second: some of the themes that would appear in this book. Third: a continuation of the discussion I had with OLC attorneys at the earlier luncheon. I wanted to see if the attorneys in the room would respond the same way as during the Clinton years. Perhaps because of that introduction, or preparation, the response in the room was not as critical of a President exercising independent judgment on a matter previously decided by the Court, as in *Morrison*. I'm not saying I drew anyone to my position, but the discussion was much more open, thoughtful, and constructive. The unintentional bomb I had earlier dropped on the table did not seem as menacing this time.

Dialogue over a Bridge

A series of judicial and legislative actions in the 1850s highlighted (once again) that the Court does not have the final word on constitutional issues. In the great case of *Gibbons v. Ogden* (1824), the Court decided that the power of Congress over commerce includes navigation. Chief Justice Marshall for the Court

---

45. "Transcript of May 26, 2010, House Judiciary Committee Interview of Former Assistant Attorney General Jay Bybee," at 264.

explained that commerce is more than discrete transactions. It is intercourse. Congress had the power to regulate economic life and promote the free flow of interstate business activities, including actions within state borders that interfered with that flow.[46]

In 1852, the Court ruled that the height of the Wheeling Bridge over the Ohio River (constructed under Virginia state law) was a "nuisance" because the structure was so low it obstructed navigation.[47] Several months before the Court decided the case, Justice John Catron confided in a letter that the "question then and now, was political, & not of judicial cognizance."[48] The Supreme Court appointed a commissioner to determine the facts about the bridge. By measuring its height, the water level, and the height of chimneys on approaching boats, the commissioner concluded that the bridge was an obstruction over a navigable stream.

The objectivity of the commissioner, R. Hyde Walworth, was in doubt. The engineer selected to take the measurements was a brother-in-law of one of the counsels for the complainant, the Commonwealth of Pennsylvania.[49] Some newspapers described Justice Robert Grier, from Pennsylvania, as "the Pittsburgh judge of the Supreme Court."[50] Although ships had hinges and machinery to lower their chimneys, the Court accepted Walworth's judgment on several particulars. Navigation on the river needed to be made free by either eliminating the bridge or elevating it to permit passage of "the largest class of steam-vessels now navigating the Ohio River." The bridge had to be elevated to the height of at least 111 feet above the low-water mark and maintained at 300 feet "on a level headway over the channel of the said river."[51] For a judicial ruling, particularly on constitutional matters, it read more like a congressional statute.

Congress made short work of the Court's decision, which was released on February 6, 1852, and in amended form in May. On August 12, 1852, the House debated a bill to make the Wheeling Bridge "a lawful structure."[52] A sponsor of the legislation insisted that the "ultimate right" to decide this issue "was in Congress," pursuant to its power to regulate commerce and preserve the intercourse

46. 22 U.S. (9 Wheat.) 1 (1824).

47. Pennsylvania v. Wheeling &c. Bridge Co., 54 U.S. (13 How.) 518 (1852). For earlier litigation on this issue, see Pennsylvania v. Wheeling and Belmont Bridge Co., 50 U.S. (9 How.) 647 (1850).

48. 5 History of the Supreme Court of the United States: The Taney Period, 1836–1864, at 412 (Carl B. Swisher, 2010). Catron's letter was to James Buchanan.

49. Id. at 411; Pennsylvania v. Wheeling &c. Bridge Co., 54 U.S. (13 How.), at 556.

50. 5 History of the Supreme Court, supra note 48, at 415.

51. Pennsylvania v. Wheeling &c. Bridge Co., 54 U.S. (13 How.), at 626–27.

52. Cong. Globe, 32d Cong., 1st Sess. 2195 (1852).

between states.[53] Representative Carlton B. Curtis asked: "Should Congress sit as a court of errors and appeals over the decision and adjudication of the Supreme Court of the United States, and consider matters which, without a doubt, properly belonged to that tribunal, and review them in a manner entirely unknown to law?"[54]

Senator George Edmund Badger denied that Congress was seeking "some revising power over the adjudications of the Supreme Court." Instead, Congress was exercising "our legislative functions, as the court discharged its judicial function." The bill required vessels navigating the Ohio River "to conform the elevation of their chimneys to the height of the bridge, in the exercise of our undoubted right to regulate and control the commerce of the river."[55] Instead of altering the bridge to accommodate vessels, ships should adjust to the bridge. To Badger, it was a "question of expediency" best left to the legislative branch: "Shall seven steamboats, out of the three hundred and fifty navigating the Ohio, be put to the trouble of reducing their smoke-pipes five or six feet, so as to be able to pass under the bridge?"[56]

A colleague in the Senate, James Murray Mason, objected that the dispute was deliberately provoked by Pittsburgh steamboats that elevated their smoke chimneys so they would not clear the bridge.[57] What was at issue, then, was not a purely legal or constitutional issue but one of fact. Who should decide a factual issue, members of Congress or a commissioner appointed by the Supreme Court? Senator Walker Brooke remarked: "In all legal questions, I am willing, and more than willing, to yield to the authority of the Supreme Court; but, in questions of fact, I conceive, that, as a member of the Congress of the United States, I have the same right of judgment, humble as I am, as the Supreme Court has." In his opinion, some of the steamboats navigating the Ohio River had intentionally elevated their chimneys "to an unnecessary height, for the purpose of destroying this structure." Under those conditions, he would do "everything I can, as a legislator, to nullify, if I may use the expression, the decision of the Supreme Court."[58] Senator John B. Weller pursued that point. Suppose a bridge

53. Id. at 2196 (Rep. Joseph Addison Woodward). See also 2206 (Rep. Woodward), 2216 (Rep. Thomas M. Howe and Rep. John Singleton Millson), 2227 (the Speaker calling up the Wheeling bill), 2228, 2235, 2256, 2310, 2439–42.
54. Id. at 2240. Curtis's full speech appears at 967–68. Other speeches on the Wheeling Bridge appear at 967–68, 972–74, 974–77, 1037–41, 1041–44, 1044–47, 1047–49, 1065–68, 1068–71.
55. Id. at 2310.
56. Id at 2440.
57. Id.
58. Id.

had been constructed over the Ohio River at an elevation of only 20 feet and the Supreme Court decided it was "a constitutional bridge." Should not Congress be able to entertain the opinion that the river was "a great national highway" and order that the obstruction be removed?[59]

Legislative language on the Wheeling Bridge dispute was inserted in the appropriations bill for the Post Office Department, enacted on August 31, 1852, three months after the Court's amended decision. Section 6 of the bill provided: "*And be it further enacted,* That the bridges across the Ohio River at Wheeling, in the State of Virginia, and at Bridgeport, in the State of Ohio, abutting on Zane's Island, in said river, are hereby declared to be lawful structures in their present position and elevation, and shall be so held and taken to be, any thing in any law or laws of the United States to the contrary notwithstanding." Section 7 authorized the Wheeling and Belmont Bridge Company to "have and maintain their said bridges at their present site and elevation" and required vessels navigating the Ohio River to ensure that any pipes or chimneys shall not "interfere with the elevation and construction of said bridges."[60]

Less than two years later the story took a bizarre turn. In May 1854, a violent windstorm hurled the bridge into the river. The company immediately began to rebuild.[61] The dispute returned to the Supreme Court when Pennsylvania insisted that the congressional statute was "unconstitutional and void."[62] Writing for the majority, Justice Samuel Nelson explained that the Court in 1852 concluded that the bridge was inconsistent with the power of Congress to regulate commerce. The new statute now removed that objection.[63] What of the argument that Congress lacked authority to "annul the judgment of the court already rendered, or the right determined thereby in favor of the plaintiff"? As a general rule, Justice Nelson affirmed that Congress could not annul "adjudication upon the private rights of parties," but he distinguished the Wheeling case.[64] Because of the new statute, "the bridge is no longer an unlawful obstruction" and "it is quite plain the decree of the court cannot be enforced."[65]

Three members of the Court were appalled by the decision. Justice John McLean objected in one of the dissents: "It was said by Chief Justice Marshall, many years ago, that congress could do many things, but that it would not alter

59. Id. at 2441.
60. 10 Stat. 112 (1852).
61. 5 History of the Supreme Court, supra note 48, at 415.
62. Pennsylvania v. Wheeling and Belmont Bridge Co., 18 How. 421, 429 (1856).
63. Id. at 430.
64. Id. at 431.
65. Id. at 432.

a fact. This it has attempted to do in the above act."[66] For McLean, the statute declaring the bridge to be a legal structure, "being the exercise of a judicial and appellate power, is unconstitutional, and consequently inoperative."[67] Justice Robert Grier agreed: "I concur with my brother McLean, that congress cannot annul or vacate any decree of this court; that the assumption of such a power is without precedent, and, as a precedent for the future, it is of dangerous example."[68] Justice James Wayne wrote the third dissent: "Whatever congress may have intended by the act of August, 1852, I do not think it admits of the interpretation given to it by the majority of the court; and if it does, then my opinion is that the act would be unconstitutional."[69]

Their views have remained a minority position. No clear line divides what is "legislative" in Congress and "judicial" in the courts. States lacking authority over commerce at one point may have their powers strengthened by an act of Congress. As the Court noted in 1946, "whenever Congress' judgment has been uttered affirmatively to contradict the Court's previously expressed view that specific action taken by the states in Congress' silence was forbidden by the commerce clause, this body has accommodated its previous judgment to Congress' expressed approval."[70] In 1985, the Court said that when Congress "so chooses, state actions which it plainly authorizes are invulnerable to constitutional attack under the Commerce Clause."[71]

State Controls on Intoxicating Liquors

The dialogue between Congress and the Court on the Wheeling Bridge is not unusual. In other areas of constitutional law, it is often the case that the Court will find that a state lacks authority to regulate an activity, only to reverse itself when Congress enacts legislation that supports the state. In an effort to distinguish between national and state regulatory authorities, Chief Justice Marshall in 1827 developed the "original package" concept. The Court struck down a Maryland statute because it violated two constitutional provisions: the prohibition on states to lay a duty on imports, and the power of Congress to regulate

66. Id. at 439.
67. Id. at 443.
68. Id. at 449.
69. Id. at 450.
70. Prudential Ins. Co. v. Benjamin, 326 U.S. 408, 425 (1946).
71. Northeast Bancorp v. Board of Governors, FRS, 472 U.S. 159, 174 (1985). In a concurrence in 1995, Justices Kennedy and O'Connor conceded that "if we invalidate a state law, Congress can in effect overturn our judgment." United States v. Lopez, 514 U.S. 549, 580 (1995).

interstate commerce. Under the original-package concept, states could not tax an import in its original form or package, but after the imported article became "incorporated and mixed up with the mass of property in the country," states could tax it.[72]

After the Civil War, federal courts developed the doctrine of "dual federalism," making some powers exclusively national and others exclusively state. The intent was to remove friction between the two political systems but the concept proved difficult to apply. The Court tried to preserve the doctrine of exclusive jurisdictions over commerce: whatever fell under national control was excluded from state control, and vice versa. The Court insisted in 1876: "The powers which one possesses, the other does not."[73] Economic and commercial transactions could not be hermetically sealed within state boundaries. In 1886, the Supreme Court struck down an Illinois railroad statute because it affected commerce among the states and invaded congressional powers, even if part of the train's journey was within the state.[74] In 1905, a unanimous Court upheld a congressional statute that prevented a meatpacking company from controlling trade. Although the company's cattle came to rest within a stockyard of a particular state, the movement of cattle from state to state created a "current of commerce" that only Congress could regulate.[75] In 1922, the Court described stockyards as a temporary resting place for cattle moving interstate: "a throat through which the current of commerce flows."[76]

Judicial efforts to uphold mutually exclusive powers led to a collision between Congress and the Court in 1890. The Court ruled that a state's prohibition of intoxicating liquors from outside its borders could not be applied to original packages or kegs. The firm of Leisy & Company transported sealed kegs of beer from Peoria, Illinois, to Keokuk, Iowa, where a state official seized the property and took it into custody because Iowa prohibited the sale of intoxicating liquors. The Court held that only after the original package entered Iowa and was broken into smaller packages could the state regulate the product. To the Court, the power of Congress over interstate commerce necessarily trumped the police powers of the state "unless placed there by congressional act."[77] The Court's ruling deliberately lacked finality. The judicial doctrine of "exclusive jurisdictions" depended on what Congress would do: "The conclusion follows that, as the

---

72. Brown v. Maryland, 25 U.S. (12 Wheat.) 419, 441 (1827).
73. United States v. Cruikshank, 92 U.S. 542, 550 (1876).
74. Wabash, &c., Railway Co. v. Illinois, 118 U.S. 557 (1886).
75. Swift & Co. v. United States, 196 U.S. 375, 399 (1905).
76. Stafford v. Wallace, 258 U.S. 495, 516 (1922).
77. Leisy v. Hardin, 135 U.S. 100, 108 (1890).

grant of the power to regulate commerce among the States, so far as one system is required, is exclusive, the States cannot exercise that power without the assent of Congress."[78] States could not exclude incoming articles "without congressional permission."[79]

As with the Wheeling case, members of Congress quickly went to work on remedial legislation, this time by providing states with independent authority to regulate incoming liquor. The Court issued its opinion on April 28, 1890. By May 14, the Senate had reported a bill.[80] Imaginative entrepreneurs responded to the Court's decision by opening up "original-package saloons" to prevent states from exercising any control. Brewers and distillers from outside the state decided to package their goods "even in the shape of a vial containing a single drink."[81] Congressional debate underscored the hazards of courts attempting to speak about abstract doctrines that proved clumsy and unworkable in practice.

The irreverent attitude of some lawmakers toward the Court's theoretical pronouncements about original packages is captured in remarks by Senator George Edmunds of Vermont. He described the Court as "an independent and co-ordinate branch of the Government." Its mission is to decide cases, but "as it regards the Congress of the United States, its opinions are of no more value to us than ours are to it. We are just as independent of the Supreme Court of the United States as it is of us, and every judge will admit it." If members of Congress concluded that the Court made an error with its constitutional reasoning, "are we to stop and say that is the end of the law and the mission of civilization in the United States for that reason? I take it not." Courts had a record of deciding things one way and then another way. Edmunds added: "[A]s they have often done, it may be their mission next year to change their opinion and say that the rule ought to be the other way."[82] Faced with vague and fluctuating judicial doctrines, lawmakers needed to think independently about the kind of legislation needed to reasonably and constitutionally regulate commerce.

Congress enacted remedial legislation on August 8, 1890, slightly more than three months after the Court's decision. The statute made intoxicating liquors, upon their arrival in a state or territory, subject to the police powers of a state "to the same extent and in the same manner as though such liquids or liquors had been produced in such State or Territory, and shall not be exempt therefrom by reason of being introduced therein in original packages or otherwise."[83] The

78. Id. at 119.
79. Id. at 125.
80. 21 Cong. Rec. 4642 (1890).
81. Id. at 4954.
82. Id. at 4964.
83. 20 Stat. 313 (1890).

constitutionality of this statute returned to the Court. A unanimous opinion upheld the judgment of Congress.[84]

Regulating Child Labor

By the turn of the twentieth century, private organizations began to lobby Congress to eliminate the harsh and unhealthy conditions of child labor. In 1904, Progressives organized the National Committee on Child Labor to advocate legislative remedies by Congress. The initial effort was at the state level until it became clear that this type of legislation lacked uniformity. Also, resistance to regulation was especially strong in the South.[85] Two years later, Senator Albert Beveridge placed in the *Congressional Record* details on the kinds of working conditions inflicted on children.[86] Writing in 1913 as a professor of law at Yale University, William Howard Taft regarded any congressional legislation that attempted to suppress the use of child labor in the process of shipment as "a clear usurpation of that State's rights."[87]

Party platforms of 1916 came down squarely in favor of Congress regulating child labor. Democrats backed "speedy enactment of an effective Federal Child Labor Law," while Republicans supported "enactment and rigid enforcement of a Federal child labor law."[88] Writing in 1908 in his role as university professor, Woodrow Wilson opposed child labor legislation. He warned that if the congressional power to regulate commerce between the states "can be stretched to include the regulation of labor in mills and factories, it can be made to embrace every particular of the industrial organization and action of the country."[89] By 1916, after serving four years as President and preparing to campaign for reelection, he was advised that support for the bill would attract the women's vote and failure to pass legislation would be politically costly for the Democrats. Rethinking the issue, he urged immediate passage of the child labor bill.[90]

84. In re Rahrer, 140 U.S. 545 (1891).

85. John R. Vile, Encyclopedia of Constitutional Amendments, Proposed Amendments, and Amending Issues, 1789–2002, at 61 (2d ed., 2003).

86. Richard B. Bernstein, Amending America 179 (1993).

87. William Howard Taft, Popular Government: Its Essence, Its Permanence, and Its Perils 143 (1913).

88. 1 National Party Platforms, vol. 1, 1840–1956, at 199, 207 (Donald Bruce Johnson, comp., 1978).

89. Woodrow Wilson, Constitutional Government in the United States 179 (1964 paper ed., originally published in 1908).

90. 37 The Papers of Woodrow Wilson 428–29, 431, 436, 447–48, 451, 463, 469, 522–23

The House Labor Committee concluded that "the entire problem has become an interstate problem rather than a problem of isolated States and is a problem which must be faced and solved only by a power stronger than any State."[91] The bill became law on September 1, 1916. Based on the national power to regulate commerce, it prohibited the products of child labor from being shipped interstate. No producer, manufacturer, or dealer could ship or deliver for shipment in interstate or foreign commerce any article produced by children within specified age ranges: under the age of 16 for products from a mine or quarry, or under the age of 14 from any mill, cannery, workshop, factory, or manufacturing establishment.[92]

Within two years, a closely divided Supreme Court struck down the statute as unconstitutional. A 5-to-4 ruling concluded that the "production" and "manufacture" of goods were local in origin and therefore not part of "commerce" subject to regulation by Congress.[93] Earlier cases had upheld congressional regulation over goods or activities deemed harmful: lottery schemes, impure foods and drugs, prostitution, and intoxicating liquors.[94] The majority recognized that child labor required regulation and that every state had a law on the subject. However, the goods shipped as a product of child labor "are of themselves harmless."[95] The grant of power to Congress over interstate commerce "was to enable it to regulate such commerce, and not to give it authority to control the States in their exercise of the police power over local trade and manufacture."[96] To the majority, the congressional statute invaded state authority.

Justice Oliver Wendell Holmes, in a dissent joined by three colleagues, reviewed earlier decisions that had read broadly the authority of Congress to regulate economic conditions within states: "It does not matter whether the supposed evil precedes or follows the transportation. It is enough that in the opinion of Congress the transportation encourages the evil."[97] Congress, not the Court, possessed the constitutional authority to determine these policy ques-

(Arthur S. Link, ed., 1981); 38 The Papers of Woodrow Wilson 14, 61, 63, 123–24, 264–85, 469, 471, 586 (Link ed., 1982).

91. H. Rept. No. 46, 64th Cong., 1st Sess. 7 (1916).

92. 39 Stat. 675, sec. 1 (1916).

93. Hammer v. Dagenhart, 247 U.S. 251 (1918).

94. Id. at 270–71, citing Champion v. Ames, 188 U.S. 321 (1903), Hipolite Egg Co. v. United States , 220 U.S. 45 (1911), Hoke v. United States, 227 U.S. 308 (1913), Caminetti v. United States, 242 U.S. 470 (1917), and Clark Distilling Co. v. Western Maryland Ry. Co., 242 U.S. 311 (1917).

95. Id. at 272.

96. Id. at 273–74.

97. Id. at 279–80.

tions: "It is not for this Court to pronounce when prohibition is necessary to regulation if it ever may be necessary—to say that it is permissible as against strong drink but not as against the product of ruined lives."[98]

Within a matter of days, members of Congress offered legislation to regulate child labor through the taxing power. An excise tax would be levied on the net profits of persons employing child labor within prohibited ages.[99] Senator Robert L. Owen reintroduced the identical bill the Court had invalidated, adding this plainspoken language: "Any executive or judicial officer who in his official capacity denies the constitutionality of this act shall ipso facto vacate his office."[100] Owen denied that the Court enjoyed a supreme or exclusive role in interpreting the Constitution:

> It is said by some that the judges are much more learned and wiser than Congress in construing the Constitution. I can not concede this whimsical notion. They are not more learned; they are not wiser; they are not more patriotic; and what is the fatal weakness if they make their mistakes there is no adequate means of correcting their judicial errors, while if Congress should err the people have an immediate redress; they can change the House of Representatives almost immediately and can change two-thirds of the Senate within four years, while the judges are appointed for life and are removable only by impeachment.[101]

The new effort to regulate child labor through the taxing power found ready support in the Senate, 50 to 12. The bill passed the House, 312 to 11, and became law.[102] A federal district court in North Carolina declared the excise tax unconstitutional. When the issue returned to the Supreme Court, Solicitor General James M. Beck advised the Justices to exercise political prudence when reviewing legislation that has been adopted by the elected branches. He said the Philadelphia Convention "voted down any proposition that the judiciary should have an absolute revisionary power over the legislature, which as the representative of the people was regarded as the most direct organ of their will."[103] Only when a case presents an *"invincible, irreconcilable, and indubitable repugnancy"*

98. Id. at 280.

99. 56 Cong. Rec. 8341, 11560 (1918).

100. Id. at 7432.

101. Id. at 7433.

102. 57 Cong. Rec. 609–21, 3029–35 (1918–19); 40 Stat. 1138 (1919).

103. "Brief on Behalf of Appellants and Plaintiff in Error," Bailey v. George and Bailey v. Drexel Furniture Co., Supreme Court of the United States, October Term, 1921, Nos. 590, 657, February 1922, reprinted at 21 Landmark Briefs 45 (using number at top of page).

between a congressional statute and the Constitution should the Court nullify the statute.[104]

Beck rejected the idea that federal courts have "an unlimited power to nullify a law if its incidental effect is in excess of the governmental sphere of the enacting body." There exists a large field of political activity "into which the judiciary may not enter."[105] He reminded the Justices of the consequences of *Dred Scott,* "possibly the principal cause, next to slavery itself, in precipitating the greatest civil war in history."[106] The belief that the Court is fully empowered to judge the motives or objectives of the elected branches "is a mischievous one, in that it so lowers the sense of constitutional morality among the people that neither in the legislative branch of the Government nor among the people is there as strong a purpose as formerly to maintain their constitutional form of Government."[107] The idea that the Court "is the sole guardian and protector of our constitutional form of government has inevitably led to an impairment, both with the people and with their representatives, of what may be called the constitutional conscience."[108]

The Court had no patience for his argument or the new legislation from Congress. A majority of 8 to 1 struck down the child labor tax. Chief Justice William Howard Taft wrote for the majority, agreeing that courts are generally reluctant to speculate about legislative motives but it "must be blind not to see that the so-called tax is imposed to stop the employment of children within the age limits prescribed. Its prohibitory and regulatory effect and purpose are palpable."[109] Allowing this use of the taxing power "would be to break down all constitutional limitation of the powers of Congress and completely wipe out the sovereignty of the States."[110] Justice Clarke dissented without giving his reasons.

Once again Congress refused to accept the Court's decision as final. It passed a constitutional amendment in 1924 to give it the power to regulate child labor. By 1937 only 28 of the necessary 36 states had ratified it.[111] However, constitutional doctrines issued by the judiciary by 1937 indicated that Congress would

104. Id. at 46 (emphases in original).
105. Id. at 47.
106. Id. at 48.
107. Id. at 54.
108. Id.
109. Child Labor Tax Case (Bailey v. Drexel Furniture Co.), 259 U.S. 20, 37 (1922).
110. Id. at 38.
111. John R. Vile, Encyclopedia of Constitutional Amendments, Proposed Amendments, and Amending Issues, 1789–2002, at 61–63 (2003); David E. Kyvig, Explicit and Authentic Acts: Amending the U.S. Constitution, 1776–1995 (1996); Richard B. Bernstein, Amending America 179–81 (1993); Alan P. Grimes, Democracy and the Amendments to the Constitution 101–04 (1978).

be acting within its authority if it prohibited the products of child labor from being shipped in interstate commerce.[112] Congress in 1938 passed legislation to regulate child labor, returning to its original reliance on the commerce power.[113] Two years later a district court in Georgia held the statute to be unconstitutional because the activity within the state was not "interstate commerce" subject to the control of Congress. The court accepted the Supreme Court's earlier position that the "manufacture" of goods is not commerce.[114]

In 1941, a reconstituted (and chastened) Supreme Court reversed the district court and not only upheld the child labor provision, but did so unanimously. A brief opinion by Justice Harlan Fiske Stone noted that "[w]hile manufacture is not of itself interstate commerce, the shipment of manufactured goods interstate is such commerce and the prohibition of such shipment by Congress is indubitably a regulation of the commerce."[115] Drawing language from *Gibbons v. Ogden,* he said that the power of Congress over interstate commerce "is complete in itself, may be exercised to the utmost extent, and acknowledges no limitations other than are prescribed in the Constitution."[116] Congress, "following its own conception of public policy," may exclude from interstate commerce whatever goods it conceives to be injurious to the public health, morals or welfare, "even though the state has not sought to regulate their use."[117] Stone deferred fully to the constitutional judgment of members of Congress:

> The motive and purpose of a regulation of interstate commerce are matters for the legislative judgment upon the exercise of which the Constitution places no restriction and over which the courts are given no control. ... Whatever their motive and purpose, regulations of commerce which do not infringe some constitutional prohibition are within the plenary power conferred on Congress by the Commerce Clause. Subject only to that limitation, presently to be considered, we conclude that the prohibition of the shipment interstate of goods produced under the forbidden substandard labor conditions is within the constitutional authority of Congress.[118]

---

112. 83 Cong. Rec. 7400–01, 7407 (1938).

113. For constitutional analysis supporting the child labor provision in the Fair Labor Standards Act of 1938, see H. Rept. No. 2738, 75th Cong., 3d Sess. (1938).

114. United States v. F. W. Darby Lumber Co., 32 F.Supp. 734 (S.D. Ga. 1940).

115. United States v. Darby, 312 U.S. 100, 113 (1941).

116. Id. at 114.

117. Id.

118. Id. at 115.

Stone explained that this broad reading of the commerce power, in place since *Gibbons v. Ogden,* was upended "by a bare majority of the Court" in *Hammer v. Dagenhart.*[119] The reasoning advanced in *Dagenhart* "was novel when made and unsupported by any provision of the Constitution" and has "long since been abandoned."[120] Quite an indictment: a 5–4 decision by the Court, striking down a statute enacted by the elected branches, could find no support from any provision in the Constitution. Five years after Stone's opinion, the Court admitted that "the history of judicial limitation of congressional power over commerce, when exercised affirmatively, had been more largely one of retreat than of ultimate victory."[121]

A Failed Judicial Experiment

After retreating in the child labor cases, the Supreme Court tried other doctrines to monitor federal–state powers. A collision in the 1970s between Congress and the Court involved the extension of federal minimum-wage and overtime provisions to the states. In 1966, Congress imposed federal minimum wages and overtime pay to state-operated hospitals and schools. In *Maryland v. Wirtz* (1968), the Court upheld the statute as rationally based, concluding that Congress had properly taken into account the effect on interstate competition and the promotion of labor peace.[122] The Court split 6 to 2, with only Justices Douglas and Stewart objecting that the statute represented "a serious invasion of state sovereignty protected by the Tenth Amendment."[123]

Six years later, Congress relied in part on *Wirtz* when extending minimum-wage and maximum-hour provisions to cover almost all employees of states and their political divisions. In *National League of Cities v. Usery* (1976), a 5-to-4 Court struck down the statute, overruled *Wirtz,* and unveiled a new theory of federalism. To reach its decision, the Court identified two abstract categories of governmental functions: "traditional" and "nontraditional." The idea was to prohibit Congress from displacing state powers in such "traditional" governmental functions as fire prevention, police protection, sanitation, public health, and parks and recreation. For the first time in four decades, the Court had invalidated a statute passed by Congress based on the commerce power.[124]

119. Id.
120. Id.
121. Prudential Ins. Co. v. Benjamin, 328 U.S. 408, 415 (1946).
122. 392 U.S. 183 (1968).
123. Id. at 201.
124. National League of Cities v. Usery, 426 U.S. 833 (1976).

To create the five-man majority, Justice Blackmun contributed a brief concurrence. Admitting that he was "not untroubled by certain implications of the Court's opinion," he decided to go along. Although he might "misinterpret the Court's opinion," it seemed to him that "it adopts a balancing approach, and does not outlaw federal power in areas such as environmental protection, where the federal interest is demonstrably greater and where state facility compliance with imposed federal standards would be essential."[125] It was a shaky fifth vote, with little to anchor it in constitutional text or the framers' intent. Blackmun looked principally to contemporary federal and state competence.

Who would define what is "traditional" and "nontraditional"? The Supreme Court decided not to try, transferring that chore to a three-judge district court. Would that court explain the difference between the two categories? Not a chance. It asked the Labor Department to identify nontraditional state functions. It did so, providing a list of traditional state functions as well. Included within the Labor Department's list of nontraditional functions was "local mass transit systems," a decision that prompted new litigation and a challenge to *National League.*[126]

In the meantime, federal courts had little success in distinguishing between traditional and nontraditional. Various district and circuit courts tried their best to identify traditional governmental functions, only to have their decisions shot down regularly by the Supreme Court. During this period, Blackmun's position appeared to shift, suggesting that his tentative vote in *National League* was about to switch to the other side, forming a new majority.[127] In 1983, Linda Greenhouse of the *New York Times* predicted that little life remained in the *National League* doctrine: "If there is a lesson here, it is not one to comfort those who cherish the illusion of the Constitution as a revealed truth. For it reveals constitutional adjudication as a fitful, fragile, human process."[128]

The Court overturned *National League* in 1985, with Blackmun finally deciding to abandon the position he took nine years earlier. Initially voting in conference to affirm *National League,* he reversed course because he "ha[d] been able to find no principled way in which to affirm."[129] Writing for a new 5–4 majority, he concluded that the essential safeguard for federalism was not the judiciary but rather the political dynamics operating within Congress. The doc-

125. Id. at 856.

126. Neal Devins and Louis Fisher, The Democratic Constitution 67–68 (2004).

127. Fisher and Harriger, American Constitutional Law 349 (box) (9th ed., 2011).

128. Linda Greenhouse, "Court Takes the Glow off the 10th Amendment," New York Times, March 13, 1983, at E9.

129. Mark Tushnet, "Why the Supreme Court Overruled National League of Cities," 47 Vand. L. Rev. 1623, 1628 (1994).

trine of *National League* he now rejected "as unsound in principle and unworkable in practice."[130]

In a dissent, Justice O'Connor (joined by Powell and Rehnquist) expressed dismay: "The Court today surveys the battle scene of federalism and sounds a retreat. Like JUSTICE POWELL, I would prefer to hold the field and, at the very least, render a little aid to the wounded.... With the abandonment of *National League of Cities,* all that stands between the remaining essentials of state sovereignty and Congress is the latter's underdeveloped capacity for self-restraint."[131] The Court would soon decide to be more active in policing federalism and congressional power.

Returning to the Battlefield

In 1991, the Court reviewed a provision in Missouri's constitution that required most state judges to retire at age 70. It concluded that the provision did not violate the federal Age Discrimination and Employment Act (ADEA). Missouri, as an independent state, retained a range of autonomy safeguarded by the Tenth Amendment and the Guarantee Clause of Article IV, Section 4.[132] The next year the Court rejected, 6 to 3, a congressional statute that compelled states to either find a way to dispose of low-level radioactive waste by 1996 or take possession of it. To the Court, the legislative policy amounted to "commandeering" state governments to serve federal regulatory purposes and violated the Tenth Amendment.[133]

The Court's opinion suggested that Congress was acting in a heavy-handed manner to invade state sovereignty. In fact, the bill had been drafted by the National Governors' Association.[134] In defending the statute, Solicitor General Kenneth Starr advised the Court: "In light of the origin of the problem as a dispute among the States, the requests of the States for a state-oriented solution and the assiduous care Congress displayed in attending to the interests and concerns of the several States, the Act is a constitutionally permissible example of cooperative federalism designed to preserve, rather than preempt, state author-

130. Garcia v. San Antonio Metropolitan Transit Authority, 469 U.S. 528, 546 (1985).
131. Id. at 580, 588.
132. Gregory v. Ashcroft, 501 U.S. 452 (1991). Article IV, section 4: "The United States shall guarantee to every State in this Union a Republican Form of Government, and shall protect each of them against Invasion; and on Application of the Legislature, or of the Executive (when the Legislature cannot be convened) against domestic Violence."
133. New York v. United States, 505 U.S. 144, 175–77 (1992).
134. Id. at 190–92 (White, J., dissenting).

ity."[135] Instead of trying to draft another statute that might satisfy the Court, Congress chose to rely on existing compacts that states had already formed to dispose of radioactive waste.

In *United States v. Lopez* (1995), the Court struck down a federal statute that banned guns within 1,000 feet of a school. Sharply divided, 5 to 4, the Court ruled that Congress had exceeded its authority under the commerce power. It specifically rejected the administration's argument that Congress had "ample basis" to conclude that the presence of guns on schoolyard property posed an unacceptable threat to primary and secondary education, and that "disruption of the educational process would have substantial deleterious effects on the national economy."[136] To the Court, the statute had nothing to do with commerce or any sort of economic enterprise, and intruded into areas traditionally reserved to states: schools and crime.[137]

Within two months of the decision, Congress held hearings to explain why the statute rested on valid constitutional grounds. At a Senate subcommittee hearing, Senator Herbert Kohl testified: "Almost every gun is made from raw material from one State, assembled in a second State, and transported to the schoolyards of yet another State." Walter Dellinger, head of the Office of Legal Counsel, presented a similar analysis during his testimony.[138] Undeterred by *Lopez,* Congress passed new legislation in 1996. It found that crime at the local level "is exacerbated by the interstate movement of drugs, guns, and criminal gangs," violent crime in school zones resulted in a decline in the quality of education, and it had authority under the Commerce Clause to enact the new bill. That statute provided that "[i]t shall be unlawful for any individual knowingly to possess a firearm that has moved in or that otherwise affects interstate or foreign commerce at a place that the individual knows, or has reasonable cause to believe, is a school zone."[139] No litigation challenged this second statute.

Another judicial challenge to congressional authority came in 2000. Guided largely by *Lopez,* the Supreme Court in *United States v. Morrison* held that a provision in the Violence Against Women Act (VAWA) of 1994 could not be sustained either under the Commerce Clause or Section 5 of the Fourteenth

135. "Brief for the United States," State of New York v. United States, No. 91-543, U.S. Supreme Court, at 20–21; 213 Landmark Briefs 314–15.

136. "Brief for the United States," United States v. Lopez, No. 93-1260, at 9; 242 Landmark Briefs 471.

137. United States v. Lopez, 514 U.S. 549 (1995).

138. "Guns in Schools: A Federal Role?," hearing before the Subcommittee on Youth Violence, Senate Committee on the Judiciary, 104th Cong., 1st Sess. 4, 10 (1995).

139. 110 Stat. 3009–3370, sec. 657 (1996).

Amendment.[140] The provision permitted victims of rape, domestic violence, and other crimes "motivated by gender" to sue their attackers in federal court. In one dissent in Morrison, Justice Souter referred to "the mountain of data assembled by Congress" that demonstrated the effects of violence against women on interstate commerce.[141] Passage of the legislation followed four years of hearings and testimony from physicians, law professors, survivors of rape and domestic violence, and representatives of state law enforcement and private business. The legislative record included reports on gender bias from task forces in 21 states.[142] Far from Congress intruding on state sovereignty, the National Association of Attorneys General supported the statute unanimously.[143] The Court was unpersuaded by this evidence.

Mixed Signals After *Lopez*

A decision by the Court in 2005 might have added some clarity to its position on federalism. The case involved a California law that authorized limited marijuana use for medicinal purposes. Federal Drug Enforcement Agency (DEA) agents seized and destroyed the cannabis plants of the plaintiffs. The Ninth Circuit, following the reasoning in *Lopez* and *Morrison,* decided that federal law (the Controlled Substances Act) violated the Commerce Clause by attempting to regulate intrastate activities.[144] In *Gonzales v. Raich* (2005), the Supreme Court reversed, holding that the Commerce Clause empowers Congress to prohibit the local cultivation and use of marijuana, even when in compliance with state law.[145]

The Court struggled unsuccessfully to offer a clear and persuasive ruling on federalism. Five Justices formed a majority, Scalia added a concurrence, and O'Connor dissented (joined by Rehnquist and Thomas). Thomas wrote a separate dissent. A reader looks in vain for some doctrinal threads that might provide guidance for future disputes over federalism. It is understandably difficult for 535 members of Congress to reach agreement on constitutional principles. Five Justices should have an easier time to produce a coherent opinion, but little evidence for that assumption is available when reading decisions like this one.

140. United States v. Morrison, 529 U.S. 598 (2000).
141. Id. at 628–29.
142. Id. at 629–30.
143. Id. at 653.
144. Raich v. Ashcroft, 352 F.3d 1222 (9th Cir. 2003).
145. Gonzales v. Raich, 545 U.S. 1 (2005).

In a study called "Just Blowing Smoke?," one scholar reviewed the Court's hand-
iwork on federalism and politely concluded that "it is unlikely that *Raich* spells
the end of the conversation."[146]

At the time of *Raich,* California and eight other states legalized medical marijuana. In the face of the Court's decision, additional states continued to pass
similar legislation, pushing the number of states that support medical marijuana
up to 15. Political changes also occurred at the national level. The administration of George W. Bush decided to prosecute individuals who used medical marijuana. After Barack Obama took office in January 2009, U.S. attorneys were
instructed not to prosecute medical marijuana uses. State and local officials,
declining to accept the reasoning in *Raich,* refused to use enforcement officials
to police medical marijuana. In addition to spawning confusion about the principles of federalism, the Court's decision in *Raich* had practically no impact on
the nation's policy toward medical marijuana. Private citizens and public officials, at both national and state levels, were reaching independent judgments
about the appropriate policy toward medical marijuana.[147]

Federalism has changed fundamentally over the past two centuries. Areas in
which state and local government once operated virtually supreme (agriculture,
mining, manufacturing, labor) slowly gave way to national controls. Railroads
and highways helped ensure that what had been purely intrastate was now mixed
with interstate. Issues long identified with local government (education, health,
welfare, law enforcement) became a matter of federal–state cooperation. Especially is that so with billions of dollars in federal grants allocated to the states,
often with conditions. If states object to the conditions, an option is to forgo
federal funds.

In the 1990s, Congress clashed with the Court over the scope of religious liberty. It passed the Religious Freedom Restoration Act (RFRA) of 1993, only to
have the Court strike it down four years later, largely on grounds of federalism.
The Court's rhetoric implied it had the last and final word on constitutional
meaning, but its claim had no basis in history or even in the text of the Court's
decision. In 2000, Congress managed to enact a scaled-down version of a religious restoration act. That story is told in Chapter 6.

146. Ernest A. Young, "Just Blowing Smoke? Politics, Doctrine, and the Federalist Revival
After Gonzales v. Raich," 2005 The Supreme Court Review, 1–50.
147. Louis Fisher and Neal Devins, Political Dynamics of Constitutional Law 98–107 (5th
ed., 2011).

5

INDIVIDUAL RIGHTS

Although federal courts are praised as guardians of constitutional rights, Congress frequently takes the lead in protecting individual and minority liberties. After the Civil War, lawmakers recognized broad rights for newly freed slaves, including equal access to public accommodations. The Supreme Court struck down that initiative, postponing by nearly a century a fundamental right of citizens. Congress in the 1870s passed legislation to secure the right of women to practice law, a professional opportunity that had been regularly denied by state and federal judges. Legislative advances on behalf of individual rights continued into the twentieth and twenty-first centuries, often having to overcome judicial roadblocks.

Who Protects Minority Rights?

We are generally taught that courts, not the political process, are far better structured to protect individual rights. Constitutional scholar Laurence Tribe has written that the Supreme Court "often stands alone as the guardian of minority groups. The democratic political process, by its very nature, leaves political minorities vulnerable to the will of the majority." He conceded that the Court's record "in championing the cause of oppressed minorities is hardly unstained."[1] Some of those black marks are analyzed in this chapter and others. Legal scholars argue that it is necessary to place political power in an unelected Court to protect minorities "from democratic excess."[2]

It may seem logical to defer to the judiciary for the protection of minorities. Because Congress operates by majority vote, how can it be trusted to protect politically weak minorities? History and political practice need not follow logic. Contrary to popular belief, over the past two centuries American legislatures have performed quite well in protecting minority rights; courts for most of that period were insensitive and unreliable. From 1789 up to World War II, it is difficult to find federal court decisions in any area that upheld and championed

1. Laurence H. Tribe, God Save This Honorable Court 20 (1985).
2. William Mishler and Reginald S. Sheehan, "The Supreme Court as a Countermajoritarian Institution? The Impact of Public Opinion on Supreme Court Decisions," 87 Am. Pol. Sci. Rev. 87, 87 (1993).

individual rights. Blacks, women, and other minorities found it necessary to turn to the legislative and executive branches for support.

When James Madison argued in favor of the Bill of Rights in 1789, he hoped that "independent tribunals of justice will consider themselves in a peculiar manner the guardians of those rights."[3] Exactly what he meant by "peculiar" manner is worth pondering. During the court-packing battle of 1937, the Senate Judiciary Committee praised the courts as guardians of individual and minority rights: "Minority political groups, no less than religious and racial groups, have never failed, when forced to appeal to the Supreme Court of the United States, to find in its opinions the reassurance and protection of their constitutional rights."[4] It is one thing for minority groups to appeal to the courts; to actually prevail in a lawsuit is something else. In 1938, in the famous Carolene Products case, Justice Harlan Fiske Stone concluded that a "more searching judicial inquiry" may be required to protect "discrete and insular minorities" left unprotected by the regular political process.[5]

At that same time, an article by Henry W. Edgerton (later a federal judge) punched a hole through these assertions. After studying Supreme Court opinions from 1789 to the 1930s, he concluded that judicial rulings "give small support to the theory that Congress had attacked, and judicial supremacy defended, 'the citizen's liberty.'" Far from defending individual and minority rights, the courts "sided uniformly with the interests of government and corporations."[6] In 1943, historian Henry Steele Commager reached a similar understanding. The Court had "intervened again and again to defeat congressional efforts to free slaves, guarantee civil rights to Negroes, to protect workingmen, outlaw child labor, assist hard-pressed farmers, and to democratize the tax system."[7]

A prominent study by constitutional scholar Jesse Choper recognized that while judicial review is incompatible with a basic precept of American democracy (majority rule), "the Court must exercise this power in order to protect minority rights, which are not adequately represented in the political process."[8] Whatever evidence might be assembled to demonstrate that federal courts safeguard minority and religious rights, the judicial rulings that merit praise are largely from the past half century. Even over that period—representing only a quarter of the nation's history—the judicial record inspires little confidence or

3. 1 Annals of Cong. 439 (1789).

4. S. Rept. No. 711, 75th Cong., 1st Sess. 20 (1937).

5. United States v. Carolene Products Co., 304 U.S. 144, 153 n.4 (1938).

6. Henry W. Edgerton, "The Incidence of Judicial Control over Congress," 22 Corn. L. Q. 299 (1937).

7. Henry Steele Commager, Majority Rule and Minority Rights 55 (1943).

8. Jesse H. Choper, Judicial Review and the National Political Process 2 (1980).

praise. There remains (always) a need for an open political process that responds to constitutional rights. The judicial process is far too closed, limited, and unreliable.

Ending Slavery

All three branches of the federal government after 1789 failed to take steps to liberate black slaves and avoid the onrushing civil war. Although the word "slavery" does not appear in the U.S. Constitution, it is implied in various sections. Article V states that no amendment to the Constitution prior to 1808 "shall in any Manner affect the first and fourth Clauses in the Ninth Section of the first Article." The first clause in Section 9 of Article I provides: "The Migration or Importation of such Persons as any of the States now existing shall think proper to admit" shall not be prohibited by Congress before 1808. Allowing the slave trade to continue over that period of time provoked Madison to say: "Twenty years will produce all the mischief that can be apprehended from the liberty to import slaves. So long a term will be more dishonorable to the National character than to say nothing about it in the Constitution."[9] The first clause in Section 9 permitted a tax or duty on imported slaves, not exceeding $10 for each person, treating them as incoming articles of merchandise. Madison found it offensive "to admit in the Constitution the idea that there could be property in men."[10]

The existence of slavery required calculations on how to apportion taxes and representatives among the states. The fourth clause of Section 9 prohibited a capitation tax (a uniform tax placed on each person) or other direct tax unless in proportion to population. The delegates at the Philadelphia Convention had to decide how to count slaves. Article I, Section 2, of the Constitution of 1787 counted "the whole Number of free Persons, including those bound to Service for a Term of Years, and excluding Indians not taxed, three fifths of all other Persons." That language is frequently misunderstood to mean that black slaves were "three-fifths" of a person, or subhuman. If the objective had been to place maximum value on human dignity, slaves would have been counted not as a fraction but as zero. Counting them a larger number would have given slave states greater representation. Southern states wanted to count slaves as a whole person for the purpose of the census because it added to their seats in the House. The delegates at Philadelphia compromised at three-fifths.

Another reference to slavery appears in Section 3 of Article IV. Persons "held

9. 2 Farrand 415.
10. Id. at 417.

to Service or Labour" in a state shall be delivered back to that state in cases of escape. Madison spoke openly about that provision at the Virginia ratifying convention. The language was included to "enable owners of slaves to reclaim them."[11] This provision in the Constitution led to the fugitive slave laws later passed by Congress. The 1790 census reported 757,363 blacks in the United States, or 19.3 percent of the population. Only 59,466 were free. Several states had more than 20 percent slaves, including Delaware, Georgia, Maryland, North Carolina, South Carolina, and Virginia. A statute enacted in 1807 appeared to stop the slave trade as of January 1, 1808, but slaves continued to enter the country illegally, requiring additional legislation.[12]

Congress attempted to maintain a balance between free states and slave states. When extensive property acquired by the Louisiana Purchase threatened to upset the balance, lawmakers passed the Missouri Compromise Act of 1820. In admitting Missouri as a slave state, Congress prohibited slavery in future states north of the 36°30' line. Land acquired from the Mexican War of 1846–1848 was further destabilizing. In his memoirs, Ulysses S. Grant described the war as "one of the most unjust ever waged by a stronger against a weaker nation." Nations, he said, like individuals, are "punished for their transgressions. We got ours in the most sanguinary and expensive war of modern times"—the Civil War.[13] The Kansas–Nebraska Act of 1854 repealed the Missouri Compromise and left the issue of slavery to new territories and states, a policy referred to as "popular sovereignty." It became increasingly difficult to prevent secession or civil war.

Throughout this period the moral force opposing slavery originated not from Congress, Presidents, or the Supreme Court. It came from members of the public. Large numbers of Americans viewed slavery as repugnant to the principles embedded in the Declaration of Independence. The essential antislavery documents were not judicial rulings, presidential statements, or legislative statutes but private writings and speeches.[14] Americans of the mid-nineteenth century "were not inclined to leave to private lawyers any more than to public men the conception, execution, and interpretation of public law. The conviction was generally that no aristocracy existed with respect to the Constitution. Like politics, with which it was inextricably joined, the Constitution was everyone's business."[15] That attitude should prevail today.

Churches had long led the fight against slavery. The first published protest

11. 3 Farrand 325.

12. 2 Stat. 426 (1807); 3 Stat. 450 (1818); 3 Stat. 532 (1819); 3 Stat. 600, secs. 4, 5 (1820).

13. Ulysses S. Grant, Memoirs and Selected Letters 41–42 (1990).

14. William M. Wiecek, The Sources of Antislavery Constitutionalism in America, 1760–1846 (1977).

15. Harold M. Hyman, A More Perfect Union 6 (1975).

against slavery in America came from a Quaker in 1688.[16] Quakers expelled slave-owning Friends in 1776.[17] The Pennsylvania Abolition Society was founded in 1794, and in 1800 the Methodist Conference advocated the gradual emancipation of slaves.[18] In 1818, the General Assembly of the undivided Presbyterian Church unanimously adopted a manifesto declaring slavery to be "utterly inconsistent with the law of God," although counseling against "hasty emancipation."[19] Other members of the clergy defended slavery as "clearly established in the Holy Scriptures, both by precept and example."[20] England abolished slavery in 1833.[21] The American Anti-Slavery Society was created that year to keep slavery out of the territories. One study concluded: "No other groups pushed for abolition as persistently and passionately over so many years or over so broad a spectrum of citizens as did the churches and the antislavery associations they founded."[22]

Deciding *Dred Scott*

As elected officials responsible for national policy, it was the duty of members of Congress and the President to resolve the issue of slavery and prevent the headlong rush to secession and war. Instead, many public officials preferred to treat it as a legal matter to be resolved by the courts. After his election in 1856 as President, James Buchanan wanted to mention the issue of slavery in his inaugural address. He was uncertain how the Supreme Court would rule on the pending case of *Dred Scott v. Sandford*. Justices John Catron and Robert Grier informed Buchanan that the Court was very close to deciding the case and encouraged him to mention it at the inauguration. Catron suggested to Buchanan that because of the "high and independent character" of the Court, "it will decide & settle a controversy which has so long and seriously agitated the country, and which *must* ultimately be decided by the Supreme Court."[23] A sep-

---

16. Luke Eugene Ebersole, Church Lobbying in the Nation's Capital 2 (1951).

17. Robert Booth Fowler and Allen D. Hertzke, Religion and Politics in America: Faith, Culture, and Strategic Choices 18 (1995).

18. Ebersole, Church Lobbying in the Nation's Capital, at 3.

19. Sydney E. Ahlstrom, A Religious History of the American People 648 (1972).

20. Michael Corbett and Julia Mitchell Corbett, Politics and Religion in the United States 95 (1999).

21. Abolition Act, 1833, 3 and 4 Will. 4, ch. 73.

22. Paul J. Weber and W. Landis Jones, U.S. Religious Interest Groups: Institutional Profiles xviii (1994).

23. 10 The Works of James Buchanan 106 (John Bassett Moore, ed., 1910) (emphasis in original).

arate letter from Grier supplied details on how the Justices would split and along what lines.[24]

In his inaugural address of March 4, 1857, Buchanan naively told the nation that the explosive issue of slavery was before the Court, where it would be safely resolved. He admitted that people differed on whether to admit a territory as a free or slave state and whether the doctrine of "popular sovereignty" (leaving the issue of slavery to citizens within a state) was the proper course. He assured citizens, "[t]his is, happily, a matter of but little practical importance. Besides, it is a judicial question, which legitimately belongs to the Supreme Court of the United States, before whom it is now pending, and will, it is understood, be speedily and finally settled." To the Court's decision, "in common with all good citizens, I shall cheerfully submit, whatever this may be."[25]

No doubt the Court's decision was speedy. Two days after Buchanan's inauguration the Court attempted to "settle" the issue. Many citizens refused to follow Buchanan's advice to cheerfully accept the decision, whatever it might be. They broke into irreconcilable camps. Dred Scott, a slave from Missouri, insisted that he became free by following his master to a free state (Illinois) and to a free territory (Upper Louisiana). The Court ruled he was not a citizen of the United States and could not sue in federal court. It also held that Congress lacked authority to prohibit slavery in the territories.[26] Large sections of the country rejected both conclusions. Within five years, Congress and the executive branch repudiated each plank of the Court's decision.

Predictably, the press divided sharply on the merits of the ruling. To the *New York Tribune:* "The decision, we need hardly say, is entitled to just as much moral weight as would be the judgment of a majority of those congregated in any Washington bar-room."[27] To the *Louisville Democrat,* the decision "is right, and the argument unanswerable, we presume, but whether or not, what this tribunal decides the Constitution to be, that it is; and all patriotic men will acquiesce."[28] The *Mercury* of Charleston, South Carolina, acknowledged that "everybody in the South is disposed to unite in the chorus of congratulation." However, the substance and tone of the Court's decision gave the newspaper pause. In the collision between slavery and abolitionism, the ruling "will precipitate rather than retard." It was far too early, the newspaper cautioned, to

24. Id. at 106–08.
25. 7 Richardson 2962.
26. Dred Scott v. Sandford, 60 U.S. (19 How.) 393 (1857).
27. Stanley I. Kutler, The Dred Scott Decision: Law or Politics? 47 (1967).
28. Don E. Fehrenbacher, The Dred Scott Case: Its Significance in American Law and Politics 418 (1978).

"abandon ourselves to the delirium of a premature triumph." The Court's decision might add "as much to the material strength of the North as it deducts from its moral power." A final warning: "Another such success as was achieved in the Kansas–Nebraska Act, and the South would have been undone."[29]

Shortly after *Dred Scott,* a speech by Frederick Douglass reminded the audience that the Court's author, Roger Taney, "cannot perform impossibilities." There were limits on what the Court could do. Taney "cannot bale [*sic*] out the ocean, annihilate this firm old earth, or pluck the silvery star of liberty from our Northern sky. He may decide, and decide again; but he cannot reverse the decision of the Most High. He cannot change the essential nature of things—making evil good, and good, evil."[30] Writing in 1928, Charles Evans Hughes identified three decisions of the Supreme Court as "self-inflicted wounds."[31] The list included *Dred Scott,* a case that erred not just in substance but for failing to judge politically and institutionally what the Court could and could not do.

After the Civil War

Dred Scott accelerated the tragic move toward civil war. Out of a population of about 30 million, more than 600,000 died and another 400,000 were wounded. In his inaugural address of March 4, 1861, President Abraham Lincoln told the nation that the Court's constitutional decisions bound the parties to the particular case. Beyond that he would not go. The "candid citizen must confess" that if government policy "upon vital questions affecting the whole people is to be irrevocably fixed" by the Court, whenever made in the course of litigation, "the people will have ceased to be their own rulers, having to that extent practically resigned their Government into the hands of that eminent tribunal."[32]

Five years after *Dred Scott,* the elected branches rejected its two principal constitutional positions. On November 29, 1862, an opinion by Attorney General Edward Bates concluded that men of color, if born in America, are citizens of the United States. To those who claimed that "persons of color," though born in the United States, are incapable of being citizens of the United States, he called it a "naked assumption" because the Constitution "contains not one word upon the subject." To the "new-found idea" that citizenship depends on color, other

29. Paul Finkelman, Dred Scott v. Sandford 131 (1997).
30. Id. at 174.
31. Charles Evans Hughes, The Supreme Court of the United States 54 (1928).
32. 7 Richardson 3210.

nations would react "with incredulity, if not disgust."[33] The Constitution is "silent about *race* as it is about *color*."[34] Bates repudiated Taney's remarks about citizenship as pure dicta and "of no authority as a legal decision."[35] Also in 1862, Congress passed legislation prohibiting slavery in the territories.[36] During debate on the bill, not a single lawmaker referred to the Court's decision. Congress never doubted its independent constitutional authority to prohibit slavery in the territories, with or without the Court.

Congress passed the Thirteenth Amendment to abolish the institution of slavery. It was quickly ratified in 1865. It passed the Fourteenth Amendment to provide for the equality of whites and blacks before the law. Ratification came in 1868. The Fifteenth Amendment, effective in 1870, gave blacks the right to vote. The express language of those amendments empowered Congress to enforce them "by appropriate legislation." It would not be long before the Court would decide that some congressional enactments were not "appropriate."

The Fourteenth Amendment had been foreshadowed by the Civil Rights Act of 1866. After passage of the Thirteenth Amendment, some Southern states enacted "black codes" to keep newly freed slaves in a subordinate status: economically, politically, culturally. The congressional statute declared that all persons born in the United States, excluding Indians not taxed, are citizens of the United States. Citizens "of every race and color" have the same right in every state and territory "to make and enforce contracts, to sue, be parties, and give evidence, to inherit, purchase, lease, sell, hold, and convey real and personal property, and to full and equal benefit of all laws and proceedings for the security of person and property, as is enjoyed by white citizens." President Andrew Johnson vetoed the bill, claiming that it invaded state authority. Congress quickly overrode him.[37]

In 1870 and 1871, Congress passed what are called the force acts. The purpose of the first one was to enforce the rights of citizens to vote in the states, "without distinction of race, color, or previous condition of servitude; any constitution, law, custom, usage, or regulation of any State or Territory, or by or under its authority, to the contrary notwithstanding."[38] To administer the statute, Congress extended jurisdiction to federal courts assisted by federal district attorneys and marshals.[39] Congress authorized the President "to employ such part of the

33. 10 Op. Att'y Gen. 382, 397 (1862).
34. Id. at 398 (emphasis in original).
35. Id. at 412.
36. 12 Stat. 432 (1862).
37. 14 Stat. 27, sec. 1 (1866).
38. 16 Stat. 140, sec. 1 (1870).
39. Id. at 142, sec. 8.

land or naval forces of the United States, or of the militia, as shall be necessary to aid in the execution of judicial process issued under this act."[40]

The second force act, known as the Ku Klux Klan Act, marked an effort by Congress to enforce the provisions of the Fourteenth Amendment. The statute provided criminal penalties to individuals who conspired to act against the national government "by force, intimidation, or threat to prevent, hinder, or delay the execution of any law of the United States."[41] As with the 1870 statute, Congress authorized the President to use military force to carry out the statutory objectives and prosecute violators in federal courts. The statute authorized the President to suspend the privilege of the writ of habeas corpus to act against rebellion.[42] President Ulysses S. Grant invoked that authority to suppress a rebellion in South Carolina.[43]

Public Accommodations

Another legislative step toward racial justice came in 1875 when members of Congress passed legislation to close the gap between the Declaration of Independence and the Constitution. The preamble to the statute read: "Whereas, it is essential to just government we recognize the equality of all men before the law. . . ."[44] Although the Civil War amendments officially elevated blacks to the status of citizen, in many states they were denied access to public facilities. Under the 1875 statute, all persons in the United States were entitled to the "full and equal enjoyment of the accommodations, advantages, facilities, and privileges of inns, public conveyances [transportation] on land and water, theaters, and other places of public amusement."[45]

The statute did not identify the provision in the Constitution on which Congress relied. Because the Thirteenth Amendment abolished slavery, it could be argued that denying blacks access to public accommodations represented a "badge of slavery." The Fourteenth Amendment was another possible source of authority. It provides that no state "shall make or enforce any law which shall abridge the privileges or immunities of citizens of the United States; nor shall any State deprive any person of life, liberty, or property, without due process of law; nor deny to any person within its jurisdiction the equal protection of the laws."

40. Id. at 143, sec. 13.
41. 17 Stat. 13, sec. 2 (1871).
42. Id. at 15, sec. 4.
43. 9 Richardson 4090.
44. 18 Stat. 335 (1875).
45. Id. at 336.

In the House, Benjamin Butler of Massachusetts insisted that Congress possessed full authority to safeguard constitutional rights left unprotected by some of the states. As chairman of the Judiciary Committee and Republican floor leader, he denied that Congress was attempting to impose a national standard of "social equality" among blacks and whites. The issue was one of law: "The colored men are either American citizens or they are not. The Constitution, for good or for evil, for right or for wrong, has made them American citizens; and the moment they were clothed with that attribute of citizenship, they stood on a political and legal equality with every other citizen, be he whom he may."[46]

Social equality, Butler explained, has nothing to do with law. Everyone has a right to pick his own associates and friends. Those choices had nothing to do with access to public accommodations or who someone sits next to at a theater, a restaurant, or a train. He insisted that the men and women riding in the cars "are not my associates." Many white men and white women he preferred not to associate with, but they "have a right to ride in the cars." It was not an issue "of society at all; it is a question of a common right to a public conveyance." Butler applied that same reasoning to other public accommodations: "I do not understand that a theater is a social gathering. I do not understand that men gather there for society, except the society they choose to make each for himself." The same principle covered inns and taverns: "[E]very man, high and low, rich and poor, learned or ignorant, clean or dirty, has a right to go into an inn and have such accommodations exactly as he will pay for." Butler felt no obligation to speak to anyone at a restaurant table or in a room in a railroad car serving refreshments.[47] The bill was necessary "because there is an illogical, unjust, ungentlemanly, and foolish prejudice upon this matter." It was not an issue of whites refusing to associate with blacks:

> There is not a white man at the South that would not associate with the negro—all that is required by this bill—if that negro were his servant. He would eat with him, suckle from her, play with her or him as children, be together with them in every way, provided they were slaves. There never has been an objection to such association. But the moment that you elevate this black man to citizenship from a slave, then immediately he becomes offensive. That is why I say that this prejudice is foolish, unjust, illogical, and ungentlemanly.[48]

46. 3 Cong. Rec. 939–40 (1875).
47. Id. at 940.
48. Id.

The bill passed the House 161 to 79 and the Senate 38 to 26.[49] There was some question whether President Ulysses S. Grant would veto the measure, but he signed it into law.[50] Passage of the bill became easier after it was stripped of language providing equal access to schools.[51]

Judicial Retreat

In the *Slaughter-House Cases* of 1873, the Court expressed its support for independent state powers. It upheld a Louisiana law that granted an exclusive right to a corporation to supervise slaughterhouses in the community of New Orleans. The Court agreed that the statute, granting the corporation an exclusive privilege for a period of 25 years, did not violate the Thirteenth and Fourteenth Amendments. The majority rejected interpretations of the Civil War Amendments that would "fetter and degrade the State governments by subjecting them to the control of Congress."[52] Notwithstanding those amendments, states retained authority within their territories to regulate domestic government and civil rights.[53] A dissent by Justice Field objected that the Louisiana statute conflicted with federal law, including the provision in the Civil Rights Act of 1866 giving citizens the right to make and enforce contracts.[54]

On Easter Sunday, April 13, 1873, armed white men attacked blacks who had assembled at a courthouse in Colfax, Louisiana. More than a hundred blacks were murdered. Federal prosecution under the 1870 statute signaled an effort to protect freedmen after the Civil War. The Supreme Court, in *United States v. Cruikshank* (1876), decided that the counts in the indictments against the defendants were too vague and general. They lacked the specificity needed under the Sixth Amendment, which requires that in all criminal prosecutions the accused "be informed of the nature and cause of the accusation." *Cruikshank* announced something more sweeping about the meaning and application of the Civil War Amendments. The Court promoted the doctrine of dual federalism, establishing a pure separation between federal and state powers: "The powers which one possesses, the other does not."[55] Under that theory, enforcement of

---

49. Id. at 991, 1870.
50. Bertram Wyatt-Brown, "The Civil Rights Act of 1875," 18 West. Pol. Q. 763 (1965).
51. Id. at 765, 767, 769, 773. See also Stephen W. Stathis, "Civil Rights Act of 1875," in Landmark Debates in Congress 193–202, 487 (2009).
52. 83 U.S. (16 Wall) 36, 78 (1873).
53. Id. at 82.
54. Id. at 91.
55. United States v. Cruikshank, 92 U.S. (2 Otto), 542, 550 (1876).

the Civil War Amendments had to respect state sovereignty. The protection of due process and equal protection would be left to the states.[56]

Part of the Civil Rights Act of 1875 granted rights to jurors in federal and state courts. No citizen qualified to serve could be disqualified "on account of race, color, or previous condition of servitude."[57] A state judge in Virginia, who violated the provision, was prosecuted in federal court. That statutory provision was upheld by the Court in *Ex parte Virginia* (1880), providing a broad reading to the Thirteenth and Fourteenth Amendments. The objective of each was to "raise the colored race from that condition of inferiority and servitude in which most of them had previously stood, into perfect equality of civil rights with all other persons within the jurisdiction of the States."[58] The amendments were intended "to take away all possibility of oppression by law because of race or color. They were intended to be, what they really are, limitations of the power of the States and enlargements of the power of Congress."[59]

To the Court, the amendments worked a fundamental change in the relationship between the national government and the states. It did not matter that congressional legislation was "restrictive of what the State might have done before the constitutional amendment was adopted." Enforcement by congressional statute was "no invasion of State sovereignty."[60] A state "cannot disregard the limitations which the Federal Constitution has applied to her power." Every addition to national power "involves a corresponding diminution of the governmental powers of the States. It is carved out of them."[61]

Within three years, however, the Court would swing in the other direction to read the Fourteenth Amendment narrowly to apply strictly to state action, not private action. What is "state action"? *Ex parte Virginia* interpreted state action to be more than what the state does directly. A state functions in part by the legislative, executive, and judicial authorities, but it is more than that. The Fourteenth Amendment "must mean that no agency of the State, or of the officers or agents by whom its powers are exerted, shall deny to any person within its jurisdiction the equal protection of the laws." Some state actions are done by those who decide "by virtue of public position." State actions also include those of someone who acts "in the name and for the State, and is clothed with the State's power." Such an interpretation "must be so, or the constitutional prohi-

56. Id. at 554–55.
57. 18 Stat. 336, sec. 4 (1875).
58. 100 U.S. 339, 344–45 (1880).
59. Id. at 345.
60. Id. at 346.
61. Id.

bition has no meaning. Then the State has clothed one of its agents with power to annul or to evade it."[62]

This opinion seemed to support congressional legislation needed to carry out the intent of the Civil War Amendments. However, the issue in *Ex parte Virginia* of racial discrimination in the selection of jurors was of a different character than the more emotional requirement that ensured equal access by blacks to public accommodations.

The Court Says No

The public accommodations provision, challenged in five states (California, Kansas, Missouri, New York, and Tennessee), did not reach the Supreme Court until 1882. The following year, in the *Civil Rights Cases*, the Court struck down this section of the statute, treating it as a federal encroachment on the states and an interference with private relationships. It found no basis in the Fourteenth Amendment for Congress to act as it did. The amendment empowers Congress to enact "by appropriate legislation" but the Court held that Congress could regulate only "state action," not discrimination by private parties. The amendment reads: "No State shall make or enforce . . . ; nor shall any State deprive . . . ; nor deny to any person." Focusing solely on this language, the Court ruled it is "State action of a particular character that is prohibited. Individual invasion of individual rights is not the subject-matter of the amendment."[63] It was necessary to direct the amendment against "State laws and State proceedings."[64] Any broader reading would allow Congress to establish "a code of municipal law regulative of all private rights between man and man in society," permitting Congress to "take the place of the State legislatures and to supersede them."[65]

The Court suggested that Congress might have acted under its commerce power, especially in regulating "public conveyances passing from one State to another." But Congress did not invoke that authority and the question was not before the Court.[66] As to the Thirteenth Amendment and its prohibition of slavery, the Court rejected the argument that denying persons access to public accommodations amounted to "servitude" or a "badge of slavery."[67]

62. Id. at 347.
63. Civil Rights Cases, 109 U.S. 8, 11 (1883).
64. Id.
65. Id. at 13.
66. Id. at 19.
67. Id. at 20–25.

Only one Justice dissented: John Marshall Harlan, who regarded the majority's position as "entirely too narrow and artificial." When interpreting a law or a constitutional provision, it was not enough to examine only the words. It was necessary to understand "the internal sense" of the legislative product and the intent of those who drafted and debated the law. For Harlan, the purpose of the first section of the 1875 law "was to prevent *race* discrimination in respect of the accommodations and facilities of inns, public conveyances, and places of public amusement."[68]

Applying this analysis to the Thirteenth Amendment, Harlan said it did "something more than to prohibit slavery as an *institution*."[69] Congress could not have intended to destroy slavery "and then remit the race, theretofore held in bondage, to the several States for such protection, in their civil rights, necessarily growing out of freedom, as those States, in their discretion, might choose to protect." States that had previously accepted slavery and fought a civil war to preserve it should not be "left free, so far as national interference was concerned, to make or allow discriminations against that race, as such, in the enjoyment of those fundamental rights which by universal concession, inhere in a state of freedom."[70] Harlan believed that burdens and "badges of slavery and servitude" survived the Civil War and required congressional remedies, including the Civil Rights Act of 1866. The Thirteenth Amendment "established freedom" but it was necessary for Congress to determine whether certain burdens and disabilities continued after the war and needed legislative relief.[71]

In analyzing the difference between state action and private discrimination, Harlan carefully reviewed the history of public conveyances on land and water. Railroads became public highways established by the state for public use. Even if controlled and owned by private corporations, they were nonetheless public highways to be operated and maintained for the convenience of the public. Railroads frequently extended their territory after the state seized land through the right of eminent domain. States regulated railroads by prescribing speed and safety standards. To Harlan, it was artificial to now regard the railroads as purely private operations. Blacks had every right to use those public highways without being subjected to discrimination.[72]

What of the right of blacks to inns? Private owners built the inns and taverns without the level of state assistance given to railroads. Did that permit the own-

68. Id. at 26 (emphasis in original).
69. Id. at 34 (emphasis in original).
70. Id.
71. Id. at 35.
72. Id. at 38–39.

ers to discriminate on the basis of race and previous condition of servitude? Harlan explained that inns were not the same as a boardinghouse. An innkeeper offered lodging to travelers and wayfarers seeking shelter for the night. Under law existing for centuries, it was the duty of an innkeeper to take all travelers and provide them with both room and food. The innkeeper had no legal right to accept one traveler and exclude another. To that extent an innkeeper was a public servant. The traveler's only qualification was ability to pay.[73]

Another issue: access to places of public amusement. No question of state assistance (as with railroads) arose, and there was no question of needing shelter or food for the night, as with an inn. Could owners of a place of public amusement therefore discriminate on the basis of race? Harlan pointed out that places of public amusement are established and licensed under the law. The authority to maintain them comes from the public. A license from the public "imports, in law, equality of right, at such places, among all the members of that public."[74] The fundamental question: what type of court would someone turn to in cases of discrimination? State or federal? The 1875 statute required federal courts. Without exploring that issue in any detail, Harlan concluded that discrimination by corporations and individuals in places of public accommodations constituted a badge of servitude that Congress could regulate through the Thirteenth Amendment.[75]

For Harlan, the language giving Congress the power to enforce the Civil War Amendments by "appropriate legislation" gave to the legislative branch the broadest possible authority. It was for Congress, "not the judiciary, to say that legislation is appropriate—that is—best adapted to the end to be attained." Attempts by the Court to dictate to Congress how to use its granted powers "would be sheer usurpation of the functions of a co-ordinate department." Harlan cited the expansive language of Chief Justice Marshall in *McCulloch:* "Let the end be legitimate, let it be within the scope of the Constitution, and all means which are appropriate, which are plainly adapted to that end, which are not prohibited, but consist with the letter and spirit of the Constitution, are constitutional."[76]

Harlan clearly differed with his colleagues on the scope of the Constitution. To the majority, the provision on equal accommodations violated state sovereignty and the Tenth Amendment. They assumed that the intent of the Tenth Amendment retained full force after the Civil War and adoption of Civil War

73. Id. at 40–41.
74. Id. at 41.
75. Id. at 43.
76. Id. at 51.

Amendments. The majority fixed its attention on specific language in those amendments, especially the words "no state" in the Fourteenth. Harlan concluded that the sovereign powers of the states had been significantly reduced by the Civil War Amendments. His analysis would later gain strength, but only after many costly years of a Court embracing judicial supremacy as the highest possible value, trumping all others. That attitude continues to resurface.

At the end of his dissent, Harlan reminded the Court that *Ex parte Virginia* held that the Fourteenth Amendment was aimed not merely at "States" in a limited sense but any "agency of the State" and anyone who acted under the name and for the state and "is clothed with the State's power."[77] Harlan took that a step further to include "railroad corporations, keepers of inns, and managers of places of public amusement," individuals he called "agents or instrumentalities of the State, because they are charged with duties to the public, and are amenable, in respect to their duties and functions, to governmental regulation."[78] Court decisions during the Reconstruction period undermined the capacity of Congress to protect blacks in Southern states. The cumulative effect was to make black Americans "second-class citizens."[79]

The Civil Rights Act of 1964

The Court's desegregation decision in 1954 probably represents, in the minds of many, a dramatic example of the judiciary protecting minority rights. *Brown v. Board of Education* did indeed arouse the public conscience and help articulate constitutional values.[80] Yet it is also true that the Court, in *Plessy v. Ferguson* (1896), had upheld the "separate but equal" doctrine, keeping blacks and whites segregated in trains and other public facilities. The Court eventually reversed *Plessy,* but the principal force for social and legal change was not the Court. As political scientist John Denvir points out: "It was overturned because a group of citizens refused to accept the Supreme Court's interpretation of the Fourteenth Amendment and engaged in a long, arduous and ultimately successful struggle to have the Court correct its error."[81]

77. Ex parte Virginia, 100 U.S. at 346–47 (cited by Harlan at 109 U.S. at 58).

78. 109 U.S. at 58–59.

79. Robert J. Kaczorowski, The Politics of Judicial Interpretation: The Federal Courts, Department of Justice, and Civil Rights, 1866–1876, at xviii (2005).

80. 347 U.S. 483 (1954).

81. John Denvir, Democracy's Constitution: Claiming the Privileges of American Citizenship 16 (2001).

The desegregation decision of 1954 did little to integrate public schools. Part of the reason is that a year later the Court announced *Brown II,* explaining how its policy would be implemented. The Court chose to rely on local school authorities and invited obstruction and procrastination with such phrases as "practical flexibility," "as soon as possible," "a prompt and reasonable start," and "all deliberate speed."[82] The remarkable unanimity of the 1954 ruling was made possible by the Court's decision to encourage weak implementation.[83] A decade later the Court complained that there "has been entirely too much deliberation and not enough speed."[84] A federal appeals court spoke directly to that point in 1966, making it clear that it was a mistake to think that the judiciary by itself could desegregate schools: "A national effort, bringing together Congress, the executive and the judiciary may be able to make meaningful the right of Negro children to equal educational opportunities. *The courts acting alone have failed.*"[85]

What Congress attempted to do in 1875 with respect to public accommodations, only to be turned back by the Court in 1883, finally prevailed almost a century later, in 1961. Harlan's understanding of the relationship between "state action" and private parties now found acceptance in the federal judiciary. A restaurant in a building owned by Delaware refused to serve blacks. The building, constructed with public funds for public purposes, was owned and operated by the state. Part of the building was leased to a privately owned restaurant. To the Court, the state was therefore a joint participant in operating the restaurant, and the Fourteenth Amendment applied to the establishment.[86]

After his inauguration in 1961, President John F. Kennedy did little to advocate equal access for blacks to public accommodations. Early in his first year he issued Executive Order 10925, to establish the Committee on Equal Opportunity, but decided against any civil rights initiatives with respect to housing or other issues. For two years he bided his time. Prompted by outside pressures, by 1963 he was ready to urge legislation on equal accommodations.[87]

The administration recognized the hurdle of the *Civil Rights Cases,* which had never been overturned. It chose to rely both on the Fourteenth Amendment and the commerce power. American society, Kennedy argued, had become more

82. Brown v. Board of Education, 349 U.S. 294 (1955).
83. Louis Fisher and Katy J. Harriger, American Constitutional Law 780–82 (9th ed., 2011).
84. Griffin v. School Bd., 377 U.S. 218, 229 (1964).
85. United States v. Jefferson County Board of Education, 372 F.2d 836, 847 (5th Cir. 1966) (emphasis in original).
86. Burton v. Wilmington Pkg. Auth., 365 U.S. 715 (1961).
87. Ted Sorensen, Counselor: A Life at the Edge of History 273–74, 282 (2008).

mobile and economic life increasingly interdependent: "Business establishments which serve the public—such as hotels, restaurants, theatres, stores and others— serve not only the members of their immediate communities but travelers from other States and visitors from abroad."[88] During testimony before the Senate Commerce Committee, Attorney General Robert F. Kennedy explained that "much of the force" of the *Civil Rights Cases* no longer existed but it was prudent to defend the legislation on both grounds, including the commerce power.[89]

In reporting the bill, the Senate Commerce Committee concluded that the commerce power provided sufficient constitutional authority.[90] The House Judiciary Committee justified the public accommodations provision on both "state action" (Fourteenth Amendment) and the commerce power.[91] Congressional action attracted top-heavy majorities of 289–126 in the House and 73–27 in the Senate. Private groups lobbied for the bill, creating a political base that was essential to educate citizens and build public support. The rights of blacks were secured far better through the majoritarian process than through a Court decision. In two unanimous opinions, the Supreme Court relied on the commerce power to uphold the public accommodations title.[92] Eventually, over time, the congressional judgment on a constitutional question triumphed through the regular legislative process.

Any thought of judicial supremacy in desegregating public schools is dispelled by the poor judgment of the Court in ordering school busing, a policy widely condemned throughout the country by both whites and blacks. Having deferred to the Southern states in *Brown II*, the Court decided after 1964 to accelerate desegregation by court-ordered busing within cities and between cities and suburbs. As Jeffrey Rosen accurately notes, this decision was "judicial unilateralism of the most aggressive kind." In the face of presidential, congressional, and public opposition, federal judges "proved unable to and ultimately unwilling to impose an unpopular and destabilizing social reform on their own."[93] A judicial final voice? Hardly.

88. Public Papers of the Presidents, 1963, at 485–87.

89. "Civil Rights—Public Accommodations (Part 1)," hearings before the Senate Committee on Commerce, 88th Cong., 1st Sess. 23 (1963).

90. S. Rept. No. 872, 88th Cong., 2d Sess. 12–14 (1964).

91. H. Rept. No. 914, 88th Cong., 1st Sess. 2–3, 20–22, 98–101 (1963); H. Rept. No. 914 (Part 2), 88th Cong., 1st Sess. 1–2, 7–9 (1963).

92. Heart of Atlanta Motel v. United States, 379 U.S. 241, 250 (1964); Katzenbach v. McClung, 379 U.S. 294 (1964).

93. Jeffrey Rosen, The Most Democratic Branch: How the Court Serves America 69 (2006).

Women Practicing Law

Building on the rights promised black Americans, women pressed for recognition of their political and professional needs. They found success in legislative bodies but rarely in the courts. Legal doctrines dating back to William Blackstone placed women in a subordinate state. In 1783 he wrote about the doctrine of coverture, which in marriage made husband and wife "one person in law: that is, the very being or legal existence of the woman is suspended during the marriage, or at least is incorporated and consolidated into that of the husband: under whose wing, protection, and *cover*, she performs every thing."[94] It is true that many women never marry and should not be subject to that doctrine, but courts typically treated unmarried women as the exception, not the rule.

After the Civil War, Myra Bradwell gained a law degree but needed the approval of a panel of judges (all men, of course) to practice law in Illinois. They turned down her application solely because she was a woman. In her appeal to the Supreme Court of Illinois, she lost. Of her qualifications, the state court in 1869 said "we have no doubt."[95] British law and custom entered heavily into its analysis. Female attorneys "were unknown in England, and a proposition that a woman should enter the courts of Westminster Hall in that capacity, or as a barrister, would have created hardly less astonishment than one that she should ascend the bench of Bishops, or be elected to a seat in the House of Commons."[96] For the Illinois court, it was enough to look back centuries for constitutional guidance and rely on a nation from which America had declared its independence a mere nine decades before.

If British practice seemed inadequate to decide the case, the court looked to much higher authority: "That God designed the sexes to occupy different spheres of action, and that it belonged to men to make, apply and execute the laws, was regarded as an almost axiomatic truth."[97] Axiomatic. No further thinking required. This type of analysis is frequently followed by courts. Judges are often satisfied that if something was decided at some point in the past, for whatever reason, it is enough to cite the precedent and rely on it again. Lawmakers are more likely to take into account changes in social and political attitudes.

For a society in the midst of change, hope is better placed on legislative bodies, not on courts. The Illinois court concluded that if changes were needed, "let

94. 2 William Blackstone, Commentaries on the Laws of England *442 (London: 1783) (emphasis in original).

95. In re Bradwell, 55 Ill. 535, 536 (1869).

96. Id. at 539.

97. Id.

it be made by that department of the government to which the constitution has entrusted the power of changing the laws."[98] The legislature could decide if permitting women to "engage in the hot strifes of the bar, in the presence of the public, and with momentous verdicts the prizes of the struggle, would not tend to destroy the deference and delicacy with which it is the pride of our ruder sex to treat her."[99] Bradwell's appeal to the legislative branch proved successful. Three years later, the Illinois legislature passed a bill stating that no person "shall be precluded or debarred from any occupation, profession or employment (except military) on account of sex." The statute qualified that nothing in it was to be construed "as requiring any female to work on streets or roads, or serve on juries."[100]

After prevailing in Illinois, Bradwell took the issue to the U.S. Supreme Court, hoping to establish the right of women to practice law to be among the *national* rights established under the Privileges and Immunities Clause of the Fourteenth Amendment. The attorney who handled her case, Matthew H. Carpenter, had served as a U.S. Senator from Wisconsin. He assured the Court that he was only trying to secure a woman's right to practice law, not to vote. The latter issue, he explained, was highly emotional if not irrational: "The great problem of female suffrage, the solution of which lies in our immediate future, naturally enough, from its transcendent importance, draws to itself, in prejudiced minds, every question relating to the civil rights of women; and its seems to be feared that doing justice to women's rights in any particular would probably be followed by the establishment of female suffrage, which, it is assumed, would overthrow Christianity, defeat the ends of modern civilization, and upturn the world."[101]

Generally a court hears a case argued by opposing parties. The procedure permits the court to better understand a dispute after professional advocates square off. A clash between rival parties, each with a sufficient stake in the outcome, helps illuminate the issue for the court. In Bradwell's case, after Carpenter presented his argument in her defense, the court record simply states: "No opposing counsel."[102] In a brief opinion, the Court agreed that certain privileges and immunities belong to citizens of the United States, but "the right to admission to practice in the courts of a State is not one of them."[103] The Court acknowl-

98. Id. at 540.
99. Id. at 542.
100. Illinois Laws, 1871–1872, at 578.
101. "Argument for Plaintiff in Error," Bradwell v. State of Illinois, U.S. Supreme Court, December Term 1871, No. 67, at 2.
102. Bradwell v. State, 83 U.S. (16 Wall.) 130, 137 (1883).
103. Id. at 139.

edged that many individuals who were not citizens of the United States or of any state had been admitted to practice in state and federal courts. However, the right to control and regulate the granting of a license to practice law in a state court was not a power transferred to the national government.[104]

A concurrence by Justice Bradley insisted that the civil law, "as well as nature herself, has always recognized a wide difference in the respective spheres and destinies of man and woman." Echoing Blackstone's doctrine of coverture, he said that man "is, or should be, woman's protector and defender." The "natural and proper timidity and delicacy" of women made them "unfit" for many occupations. A "divine ordinance" commanded that a woman's primary mission is to the home. While many women are unmarried, a general rule imposed upon women the "paramount destiny and mission" to fulfill the offices of wife and mother. "This is the law of the Creator."[105]

Bradley recognized that contemporary society offered new avenues for the advancement of women and they "have my heartiest concurrence." But he was not prepared to see women in every office and position. It was in "the nature of things" that men and women are suited for different professions. In his opinion, "in view of the peculiar characteristics, destiny, and mission of woman," legislative bodies may decide which positions are to be discharged by men, including professions that "receive the benefit of those energies and responsibilities, and that decision and firmness which are presumed to predominate in the sterner sex."[106]

The attitudes of Bradley are reflected in an 1875 state court decision in Wisconsin. Lavinia Goodell requested permission to practice law before the Wisconsin Supreme Court. Unlike Myra Bradwell, she was not married. The Wisconsin Supreme Court denied her motion, explaining that the "law of nature" destined women to bear and nurture children, take care of the custody of homes, and love and honor their husbands.[107] Like the Bradwell case, Chief Justice Ryan acknowledged that many employments are "not unfit for female character." Yet he offered these reasons to exclude women from the profession of law:

The peculiar qualities of womanhood, its gentle graces, its quick sensibility, its tender susceptibility, its purity, its delicacy, its emotional impulses, its subordination of hard reason to sympathetic feeling, are surely not qualifications for forensic strife. Nature had tempered woman as little for the juridical conflicts of the court room, as for the physical conflicts of the

104. Id.
105. Id. at 141.
106. Id. at 142.
107. In re Goodell, 39 Wis. 232, 245 (1875).

battle field. Womanhood is moulded for gentler and better things. And it is not the saints of the world who chiefly give employment to our profession. It has essentially and habitually to do with all that is selfish and malicious, knavish and criminal, coarse and brutal, repulsive and obscene, in human life. It would be revolting to all female sense of the innocence and sanctity of their sex, shocking to man's reverence for womanhood and faith in woman, on which hinge all the better affections and humanities of life, that woman should be permitted to mix professionally in all the nastiness of the world which finds its way into courts of justice.[108]

Judge Ryan identified the kinds of "unclean issues" that found their way into a courtroom: sodomy, incest, rape, seduction, fornication, adultery, pregnancy, bastardy, legitimacy, prostitution, lascivious cohabitation, abortion, infanticide, obscene publications, libel and slander of sex, impotence, and divorce. All of those "vices and infirmities" of society pressed upon the legal profession and filled judicial reports "which must be read for accurate knowledge of the law. This is bad enough for men."[109] The kinds of discussions necessary in a courtroom "are unfit for female ears."[110]

Congress Enters

A rule adopted by the U.S. Supreme Court after the Civil War prohibited women from practicing there. Belva Lockwood, who had been admitted to the Washington, D.C., bar in 1873, drafted legislation and worked closely with members of Congress to overturn this rule. The bill provided that when any woman had been admitted to the bar of the highest court of a state, or of the supreme court of the District of Columbia, and was otherwise qualified as set forth in the bill (three years of practice and a person of good moral character, as with male attorneys), women may be admitted to practice before the U.S. Supreme Court. The bill became law within a year.

The bill reached the House floor on February 21, 1878, and quickly passed by a vote of 169 to 87. Chairman Benjamin Butler of the Judiciary Committee said he had no desire to debate the bill or to block debate. When asked if the committee's report was unanimous in supporting the bill, he said it was.[111] On

108. Id. at 245–46.
109. Id. at 246.
110. Id.
111. 7 Cong. Rec. 1235 (1878).

March 18, the Senate Judiciary Committee voted against the bill. It reasoned that "by the law as it has existed ever since the foundations of the Government the Supreme Court of the United States, as every other United States court, is authorized to make its own rules regulating the admission of persons to practice; so that there is no obstacle of law whatever to the admission of a woman to practice in those courts." Each federal court and the Supreme Court possessed the discretion to admit or bar women. The committee concluded that the bill "would make a distinction in favor of women, instead of removing a disability. There is no disability now whatever."[112]

The Senate Judiciary Committee handled this issue in the manner of a court. Precedents and customs, no matter how inapplicable to current conditions, should govern. There might not have been a formal disability in law, but there was certainly an informal disability in practice and a specific disability in judicial rules. The committee took a purist view of separation of powers. If the judiciary adopted these rules, it should be left to itself, without interference from the legislative branch. However, courts were advising that if the law needed to be changed, it should be done by legislative action, not by judicial rulings.

Senator Aaron Sargent offered an amendment to delete the text of the bill and replace it with: "That, no person shall be excluded from practicing as an attorney and counselor at law from any court of the United States on account of sex."[113] Instead of following the committee's reasoning about practices since the beginning of government, he spoke about contemporary values. The District of Columbia and many states had admitted women to the bar. The states included California, Illinois, Michigan, Minnesota, Missouri, North Carolina, Utah, and Wyoming. It seemed absurd to him to ask a woman to handle a case in state court and be forced to transfer it to a male attorney once it entered federal court. He added: "I think the Supreme Court should not have required further legislation, but they seem to have done so, and that makes the necessity for this legislation which I have now offered."[114] After the chairman of the Judiciary Committee promised to report the bill, Sargent agreed to have his amendment returned to the committee.[115]

A month later, the committee recommended the indefinite postponement of the bill on the ground that it was unnecessary. The committee then learned that the Chief Justice of the Supreme Court appeared to be waiting for Congress to pass legislation to clarify the law. At that point the bill was placed on

112. Id. at 1821.
113. Id. at 2704.
114. Id.
115. Id. at 2705.

the legislative calendar for consideration.[116] On May 29, the bill reached the floor for debate. Sargent's amendment produced a tie vote, 26 to 26. Twenty-four Senators were absent. Sargent announced he would try again.[117]

Senate debate continued on February 7, 1879. Once again the Senate Judiciary Committee reported the bill adversely, without written report. Sargent reviewed the progress made by women in various professions, including medicine and surgery. He reminded his colleagues that there was a time in England when it was improper and degrading for a woman to appear on stage. Female roles had to be filled by men. "No man," he argued, "has a right to put a limit to the exertions or the sphere of woman. That is a right which only can be possessed by that sex itself." Here he spoke in the manner of a lawmaker, looking to the present and the future, not solely to the past:

> I say again, men have not the right, in contradiction to the intentions, the wishes, the ambition, of women, to say that their sphere shall be circumscribed, that bounds shall be set which they cannot pass. The enjoyment of liberty, the pursuit of happiness in her own way, is as much the birthright of woman as of man. In this land man has ceased to dominate over his fellow—let him cease to dominate over his sister; for he has no higher right to do the latter than the former. It is mere oppression to say to the bread-seeking woman, you shall labor only in certain narrow ways for your living, we will hedge you out by law from profitable employments, and monopolize them for ourselves.[118]

Lawmakers disagreed on the level of deference they should extend to the Supreme Court. Should it be left alone to decide who should practice there? Senator George Hoar objected: "Now, with the greatest respect for that tribunal, I conceive that the law-making and not the law-expounding power in this Government ought to determine the question what class of citizens shall be clothed with the office of the advocate." Suppose the Court chose not to admit other disfavored groups to practice before it, such as persons who had fought with the South during the Civil War or black attorneys. Was there any doubt, he asked, that Congress would and could override those judicial policies?[119]

On this occasion the bill passed, 39 to 20. Seventeen Senators were absent. Of the 24 who were absent on the earlier tie vote of 26 to 26, 15 voted in favor

116. Id. at 3558–59.
117. Id. at 3889–90.
118. 8 Cong. Rec. 1084 (1879).
119. Id.

and 4 opposed. Five were absent.[120] The statute provided that any woman who shall have been a member of the bar of the highest court of any state or territory, or the Supreme Court of the District of Columbia, for the space of three years, and shall have maintained a good standing before such court and a person of good moral character, "shall, on motion, and the production of such record, be admitted to practice before the Supreme Court of the United States."[121]

As a result of this legislation, Belva Lockwood became the first woman admitted to practice before the U.S. Supreme Court. Later she appealed to the Court to practice in Virginia, which had denied her application. The Virginia statute provided that "any person duly authorized and practicing as counsel or attorney at law in any State or Territory of the United States, or in the District of Columbia, may practice as such in the courts of this State." Did the word "person" apply only to men or also to women? The meaning of the Privileges and Immunities Clause of the Fourteenth Amendment was again at issue. A unanimous U.S. Supreme Court left it to the state to determine the meaning of its statute.[122]

Little Help from the Judiciary

Within two years of *Bradwell,* the Supreme Court delivered another setback to women's rights. Virginia Minor brought a lawsuit, arguing that she was a "citizen" within the meaning of the Constitution and was therefore entitled to vote as one of the privileges and immunities protected by the Fourteenth Amendment. A unanimous Court agreed that women are citizens but denied that the Fourteenth Amendment added substantive rights to previous privileges and immunities. As interpreted by the Court, Section 2 of the Fourteenth Amendment limited voting to men. It pointed out that it took the Fifteenth Amendment to give blacks the right to vote. The Court concluded that women, like children, were "citizens" and "persons" in the constitutional sense, but that status did not automatically bring with it the right to vote.[123] A number of states allowed women to vote in federal and state elections, but the national right to vote did not come until the Nineteenth Amendment, ratified in 1920.

120. Id.
121. 20 Stat. 292 (1879). See Mary L. Clark, "The First Women Members of the Supreme Court Bar, 1879–1900," 36 San Diego L. Rev. 87 (1999); D. Kelly Weisberg, "Barred from the Bar: Women and Legal Education in the United States 1870–1890," 28 J. Legal Ed. 485 (1977); Alice L. O'Donnell, "Women and Other Strangers Before the Bar," Yearbook 1977, Supreme Court Historical Society, at 59–62, 114.
122. In re Lockwood, 154 U.S. 116 (1894).
123. Minor v. Happersett, 88 U.S. (21 Wall.) 162 (1875).

During this period there were a number of judicial rulings that might seem favorable to women, but they were premised not on the equality of women but on their inferiority. Those decisions covered what was called "protective legislation": statutes that singled out women for special treatment and relief. The Supreme Court in 1908 unanimously upheld Oregon's ten-hour day for women. Justice Brewer remarked: "Still again, history discloses the fact that woman has always been dependent upon man. He established his control at the outset by superior physical strength, and this control in various forms, with diminishing intensity, has continued to the present."[124] Although women had made some gains, as in the practice of law, Brewer concluded, "it is still true that in the struggle for subsistence she is not an equal competitor with her brother. Though limitations upon personal and contractual rights may be removed by legislation, there is that in her disposition and habits of life which will operate against a full assertion of those rights."[125]

After ratification of the Nineteenth Amendment, the Court in 1923 decided that protective legislation for women was no longer justified.[126] Yet the Court continued to uphold certain types of special legislation. The next year it upheld a New York law that prohibited women in large cities from working between 10 P.M. and 6 A.M.[127] The Court divided 5 to 4 in 1936 in striking down a New York minimum wage law for women and minors.[128] A year later, the Court, again split 5 to 4, accepted minimum wage legislation for women. States were entitled to consider "the fact that they are in the class receiving the least pay, that their bargaining power is relatively weak, and that they are the ready victims of those who would take advantage of their necessitous circumstances."[129]

Judicial attitudes about the rights of women had not advanced much farther by 1948. The Supreme Court upheld a Michigan law that prohibited female bartenders unless they were the wife or daughter of the male owner. A 6-to-3 Court decided that the law did not violate the Equal Protection Clause of the Fourteenth Amendment. Writing for the majority, Justice Frankfurter's opinion has a smug quality: "Beguiling as the subject is, it need not detain us for long. To ask whether or not the Equal Protection of the Laws Clause of the Fourteenth Amendment barred Michigan from making the classification the State has made between wives and daughters of owners of liquor places and wives and daughters of non-owners, is one of those rare instances where to state the ques-

124. Muller v. Oregon, 208 U.S. 412, 421 (1908).
125. Id. at 422.
126. Adkins v. Children's Hospital, 261 U.S. 525, 553 (1923).
127. Radice v. New York, 264 U.S. 292 (1924).
128. Morehead v. N.Y. ex rel. Tipaldo, 298 U.S. 587 (1936).
129. West Coast Hotel Co. v. Parrish, 300 U.S. 379, 398 (1937).

tion is in effect to answer it."[130] Three dissenters disagreed. To them, the state law arbitrarily discriminated between men and women.

In 1960, Frankfurter again wrote in the area of women's rights. On this occasion he rejected the "medieval view" that husband and wife are one person with a single will and therefore legally incapable of entering into a criminal conspiracy. To the extent that the Blackstonian concept of coverture rested on a legal fiction, the three dissenters believed the matter should be resolved by Congress, not the judiciary.[131] Medieval attitudes prevailed the next year when a unanimous Court agreed that women could be largely exempted from jury service because they are "still regarded as the center of home and family life."[132] Remnants of the law of coverture survived as late as 1966.[133]

Although Congress had passed legislation in 1879 authorizing women to practice before the U.S. Supreme Court, it was not until 1971 that the Court issued an opinion striking down sex discrimination. A unanimous Court declared invalid an Idaho law that preferred men over women in administering estates.[134] A study published that year condemned the judicial record: "Our conclusion, independently reached, but completely shared, is that by and large the performance of American judges in the area of sex discrimination can be succinctly described as ranging from poor to abominable."[135]

Continued Pressures for Change

Legal rights for women had progressed in Congress and state legislatures. Relying on the commerce power, Congress passed the Equal Pay Act in 1963 to prohibit employers in the private sector from discriminating on the basis of sex. Title VII of the Civil Rights Act of 1964 made it illegal for any employer to discriminate against anyone with respect to "compensation, terms, conditions, or privileges of employment" because of the person's sex. Congress passed Title IX of the Education Amendments of 1972 to withdraw federal financial assistance from any educational institution that practices sex discrimination.

Frustration with judicial attitudes about women's rights led members of the House of Representatives to support the Equal Rights Amendment (ERA). It

130. Goeseart v. Cleary, 335 U.S. 464, 465 (1948).
131. United States v. Dege, 364 U.S. 51 (1960).
132. Hoyt v. Florida, 368 U.S. 57, 62 (1961).
133. United States v. Yazell, 382 U.S. 341 (1966).
134. Reed v. Reed, 404 U.S. 71 (1971).
135. John D. Johnson Jr. and Charles L. Knapp, "Sex Discrimination by Law: A Study in Judicial Perspective," 46 N.Y.U. L. Rev. 675, 676 (1971).

passed overwhelmingly, 350 to 15. After the Senate granted its approval, this language was submitted to the states for ratification: "Equality of rights under the law shall not be denied or abridged by the United States or any State on account of sex." During debate in October 1971, Representative Martha Griffiths, a leading advocate of the ERA, issued this protest: "Mr. Chairman, what the equal rights amendment seeks to do, and all that it seeks to do, is to say to the Supreme Court of the United States, 'Wake up! This is the 20th century. Before it is over, judge women as individual human beings.'"[136] The ERA ran into many problems in the states, including the issues of abortion and women serving in the military. Although Congress extended the deadline for ratification, the amendment never attracted sufficient support for passage.[137]

Complete elimination of gender-based discrimination would make it impossible to provide legislative relief for pregnant women. A California law paid benefits to persons temporarily disabled from working and not covered by worker's compensation. However, payment was not allowed for certain disabilities attributable to pregnancy. The Supreme Court upheld that statute in 1974, but two years later it supported a disability plan by General Electric that gave benefits for nonoccupational sickness and accidents but not for benefits arising from pregnancy.[138] To the Court, the company's plan did not violate Title VII of the Civil Rights Act. The plan covered some risks but not others. The Court found no evidence that the company was motivated by sex discrimination. Three Justices dissented.

Congress held hearings to decide whether to revise Title VII. The Senate Committee on Human Resources concluded that the Court in the General Electric case had improperly interpreted the statute. The committee decided that the better argument had been made by the dissenting Justices.[139] The bill passed the Senate 75 to 11.[140] A report by the House Committee on Education and Labor agreed that the dissenting Justices "correctly interpreted" the statute.[141] The bill passed both Houses and became law in 1978. The statute amended Title VII to prohibit employment discrimination on the basis of pregnancy and to require fringe benefits and insurance plans to cover pregnant workers.[142]

This type of dialogue between Congress and the Court happens frequently. In the late 1980s, the Court began to backtrack from some of its rulings that

136. 117 Cong. Rec. 35323 (1971).
137. Jane S. Mansbridge, Why We Lost the ERA (1986).
138. General Electric Co. v. Gilbert, 429 U.S. 125 (1976).
139. S. Rept. No. 95-331, 95th Cong., 1st Sess. (1977)
140. 123 Cong. Rec. 29664 (1977).
141. H. Rept. No. 95-948, 95th Cong., 2d Sess. 2 (1978).
142. 92 Stat. 2076 (1978).

had upheld civil rights. That pattern became more pronounced during the spring of 1989, when the Court shifted the burden to employees to prove racial disparities at work.[143] Congress passed legislation to reverse or modify nine Court rulings dealing with employment discrimination. President George H. W. Bush vetoed the bill, and Congress was unable to override. Congress revised the bill slightly in 1991. Facing a probable override, Bush signed the Civil Rights Act of 1991.[144]

In 2007, the Court split 5 to 4 in deciding that Lilly Ledbetter had filed an untimely claim for pay discrimination with the Equal Employment Opportunity Commission (EEOC). From 1979 to 1998 she had worked at the Goodyear Tire and Rubber Company. In July 1998, she filed a formal charge of sex discrimination under Title VII and also a claim under the Equal Pay Act of 1963. A district court dismissed the latter claim but allowed the Title VII action to proceed to trial, where she prevailed and was awarded back pay and damages. She claimed that several supervisors gave her poor evaluations because of her sex. Goodyear maintained that the evaluations had been nondiscriminatory and that her claims were barred for any pay decision made before September 26, 1997, or 180 days before she filed her complaint with the EEOC. Ledbetter argued that evaluations during that 180-day period were defective because of discriminatory actions in previous years. The Eleventh Circuit held that she could not maintain her suit based on past discrimination because she failed to file timely charges during those periods. Writing for the Supreme Court, Justice Alito agreed with the Eleventh Circuit.[145]

Justice Ginsburg, in a dissent joined by three colleagues, noted the disparity between Ledbetter's monthly salary as area manager and those of her male counterparts for the end of 1997. The latter ranged from a high of $5,236 to a low of $4,286. Her monthly salary at the end of 1997 was $3,727. As to Ledbetter's failure to file discrimination charges before 1998, Ginsburg explained that comparative pay information is often hidden from employees. Also, initial pay discrepancies, even if modest, have the effect of accumulating over time. Referring to the Civil Rights Act of 1991, she wrote: "Once again, the ball is in Congress' court. As in 1991, the Legislature may act to correct this Court's parsimonious reading of Title VII."[146]

143. Wards Cove Packing Co. v. Atonio, 490 U.S. 642 (1989). Other decisions adverse to employees include Independent Fed. of Flight Attendants v. Zipes, 491 U.S. 754 (1989); Lorance v. AT&T Technologies, Inc., 490 U.S. 900 (1989); and Patterson v. McLean Credit Union, 491 U.S. 164 (1989).
144. Fisher and Harriger, American Constitutional Law, at 819–20.
145. Ledbetter v. Goodyear Tire & Rubber Co., 550 U.S. 618 (2007).
146. Id. at 661.

The House of Representatives passed legislation in 2007 to overturn the Court's decision, but the bill was filibustered in the Senate. Two years later, legislation was again considered and this time enacted. Representative George Miller said that the practical effect of the Court's decision would be that as long as employers could continue to hide discriminatory actions, "if they could get past 180 days, Ms. Ledbetter could be discriminated against and she would not be able to recover anything."[147] In support of legislative action, Senator Dick Durbin remarked: "We are saying to the Supreme Court, wake up to reality. You don't know what the person next to you is being paid. They don't publish it on a bulletin board."[148] The bill passed the Senate 61 to 36 and the House 250 to 177.[149] The statute, enacted on January 29, 2009, provides that an unlawful employment practice occurs when a discriminatory compensation decision is adopted. Nothing in the statute limits an employee's right to introduce evidence of an unlawful employment practice that occurs outside the time for filing a charge of discrimination.[150]

The capacity of Congress to protect individual and minority rights has a long and distinguished history, both in taking the initiative to safeguard those rights and to pass remedial legislation to correct misjudgments in the courts. This legislative capacity extends to many areas, including religious liberty, discussed in the next chapter. As with the rights of blacks and women, lawmakers have often defended religious values left unprotected by the courts. Nothing in the judicial record over the past two centuries offers any evidence that courts are especially gifted or reliable in protecting individual rights. That duty necessarily falls on all three branches, the fifty states, and the general public.

147. 155 Cong. Rec. H114 (daily ed., January 9, 2009).
148. Id. at S698 (daily ed., January 21, 2009).
149. Id. at S775 (daily ed., January 22, 2009) and H556 (daily ed., January 27, 2009).
150. 123 Stat. 5 (2009).

6

RELIGIOUS FREEDOM

Religious liberty has a unique quality. Although covered by constitutional text, statutes, presidential statements, and court rulings, religion is deeply personal and originates outside of government. It is rooted in values nurtured in the private sector: individual conscience, freedom of religious opinions, and the decision to conscientiously object to military service. Religion gains protection at times by congressional initiatives, presidential actions, and judicial decisions, but it would be a great error to treat religious freedom as something the government may define and regulate as though it is commerce or the taxing power. When Congress and the Supreme Court collided over the Religious Freedom Restoration Act of 1994, the Court insisted that once it announces a constitutional result, its word is final and may not be questioned or modified in any way by the elected branches or the general public. No branch of government has that authority or competence.

Struggles for Religious Liberty

A political (not merely judicial) process protects religious freedom. One study of church and state advised that it "advances the cause of realism in American constitutional law to say that the Constitution is what the judges say it is."[1] That attitude does not advance the cause of realism. It promotes illusion and misconception. Religious freedom is not best protected by courts or the belief in judicial supremacy. Perhaps a strained effort at rational analysis might lead in that direction, but history offers no support. It is helpful to recall what John Dickinson told his colleagues at the Philadelphia Convention: "Experience must be our only guide. Reason may mislead us."[2]

For those who want to know which branch of government best protects religious liberty, the answer is more likely to be Congress than the judiciary. The Supreme Court had barely begun to sketch out a jurisprudence of religious freedom before 1940.[3] In previous years, the task of protecting religious liberty had been left essentially to the regular political process, both national and state.

1. Frank J. Sorauf, The Wall of Separation: The Constitutional Politics of Church and State 3 (1976).
2. 2 Farrand 278.
3. Cantwell v. Connecticut, 310 U.S. 296 (1940).

Instead of federal courts functioning as the exclusive or even prominent guardian of individual rights, they generally performed a distinctly secondary role. Individuals and organizations disappointed by judicial rulings turned to Congress and the states for relief. Political scientist Leslie Goldstein correctly noted: "The Court has not been behaving as the counter-majoritarian force of its textbook description. It has instead been heeding quite carefully the policies endorsed by the majoritarian branches of government."[4]

Judicial decisions and doctrines about religious liberty did not guide the early settlers in America. They drew inspiration from their own hearts and minds. Independent and headstrong pioneers were willing to confront authority, suffer punishment, and face exile. An early and painful lesson came from the bitter religious wars of sixteenth-century Europe. As a response to religious abuse and oppression, Dutch revolutionaries drafted the Union of Utrecht of 1579, proclaiming that "each person must enjoy freedom of religion, and no one may be persecuted or questioned about his religion."[5] Authorities should have no control over religious opinions. What an individual believes is personal and private, not public.

That value became a bedrock principle in America, but only after centuries of bigotry, bloodshed, and personal suffering abroad and at home. Those who fled religious persecution in Europe in the early 1600s often carried their own brand of theocracy and intolerance to the New World. The Congregational Church in Massachusetts Bay levied taxes to support the clergy and the church, compelled everyone to attend church services, and subjected non-Congregationalists to trial and punishment for heresy, blasphemy, and idolatry.[6]

Roger Williams, landing at Boston in February 1631, battled against the doctrines and policies of the Puritans. He drafted articles of incorporation to extend political authority only to "civil things."[7] It was necessary to separate civil society and religious society. His book, *The Bloudy Tenent* (1644), reviewed the long history of religious prosecution against "so-called non-believers," yielding a "Nation of Hypocrites" and a record of forced worship that "stincks in Gods Nostrills."[8] In the 1600s, penalties inflicted on Americans who challenged religious authorities included imprisonment, fines, whipping, branding, ear cropping, tongue boring, and death by hanging.[9]

4. Leslie Friedman Goldstein, "The ERA and the U.S. Supreme Court," 1 Law & Policy Stud. 145, 154–155 (1987).
5. John Witte Jr., Religion and the American Constitutional Experiment 18 (2000).
6. R. Freeman Butts, The American Tradition in Religion and Education 19 (1950).
7. Gerald V. Bradley, Church–State Relationships in America 27 (1987).
8. Louis Fisher, Religious Liberty in America 34 (2002).
9. Id. at 35.

From its founding in 1682, Pennsylvania stood for "noncoercion of conscience."[10] William Penn urged not only liberty of conscience but opposition to taxes or tithes imposed on individuals to support a form of worship they did not profess.[11] Yet Penn at times would use government to require some religious activity and commitments in return for full civil and political rights.[12] Benjamin Franklin offered a bleak assessment of efforts to secure religious liberty: "If we look back into history for the character of present sects in Christianity, we shall find few that have not in their turn been persecutors, and complainers of persecution. The primitive Christians thought persecution extremely wrong in the Pagans, but practiced it on one another."[13]

Many lessons of religious liberty can be drawn from the experience of Virginia in the eighteenth century. Thomas Jefferson and James Madison worked jointly to enact the Virginia Statute for Establishing Religious Freedom in 1786. In distinguishing religious dogmas from moral principles, Jefferson wrote in 1816 that "all mankind, from the beginning of the world to this day, have been quarreling, fighting, burning and torturing one another, for abstractions unintelligible to themselves and to all others, and absolutely beyond the comprehension of the human mind."[14] For Jefferson, the free exercise of religion represented a fundamental human right over which the state could not intrude: "Our rulers can have authority over such natural rights, only as we have submitted to them. The rights of conscience we never submitted, we could not submit."[15] The reference to natural rights is telling. Conscience and religious opinions are fundamental to human freedom and should not be regulated by any part of government, judicial or nonjudicial.

Virginia's Declaration of Rights in 1776 proclaimed that religion "can be directed only by reason and conviction, not by force or violence; and therefore all men are equally entitled to the free exercise of religion, according to the dictates of conscience."[16] Several steps were taken to disestablish the Anglican Church in Virginia by repealing laws that required members of the church and dissenters to provide financial support. Virginia in December 1776 repealed its laws directed against heretics and nonattendance and exempted dissenters from

10. J. William Frost, A Perfect Freedom: Religious Liberty in Pennsylvania 2 (1990).
11. Id. at 15.
12. Fisher, Religious Liberty in America, at 36.
13. 5 Founders' Constitution 58.
14. 10 The Writings of Thomas Jefferson 67–68 (Ford ed.) (letter to Mathew Carey, November 11, 1816).
15. 3 The Writings of Thomas Jefferson 263 (Ford ed.).
16. 7 Thorpe 3814.

having to give financial support to the church.[17] Three years later, Virginia repealed laws requiring even members of the church to support their own ministry. Denied preferential treatment, the church urged a general tax to benefit all Christian religions and support teachers of Christianity. Taxpayers could designate a church to receive their share of the tax or direct funds to general educational efforts.[18]

Madison prepared a powerful attack on this legislation. He argued that religion must be left to the conviction and conscience of the individual, "wholly exempt" from government control. History taught him that ecclesiastical establishments did not maintain "the purity and efficacy of Religion." Instead, public financial support produced "pride and indolence in the Clergy; ignorance and servility in the laity; in both, superstition, bigotry and persecution."[19] Supported by other religious groups, Madison successfully defeated the general assessments bill. He then introduced Jefferson's Statute for Establishing Religious Freedom, which passed in January 1786. The statute provided: "Almighty God hath created the mind free; that all attempts to influence it by temporal punishments or burthens, or by civil incapacitations, tend only to beget habits of hypocrisy and meanness." No one could be "compelled to frequent or support any religious worship, place, or ministry whatsoever, nor shall be enforced, restrained, molested, or burthened in his body or goods, nor shall otherwise suffer on account of his religious opinions or belief."[20] A resolution passed by Congress in 1988 reflects a Madisonian sentiment: "Religion is most free when it is observed voluntarily at private initiative, uncontaminated by Government interference and unconstrained by majority preference."[21]

Early Constitutional Issues

Delegates at the Philadelphia Convention spent little time talking about religion. Charles Pinckney's draft constitution, specifying that Congress "shall pass no Law on the subject of Religion," was never acted upon.[22] Three days before the convention adjourned, Madison and Pinckney proposed to give Congress the power "to establish a University, in which no preferences or distinctions

17. H. J. Eckenrode, Separation of Church and State in Virginia 50–52 (1910).
18. Id. at 61–64.
19. 2 The Writings of James Madison 187 (Hunt ed.).
20. 12 The Statutes at Large: Being a Collection of All the Laws of Virginia 86 (1819–1823).
21. 102 Stat. 1772 (1988).
22. 3 Farrand 599; Leonard W. Levy, The Establishment Clause: Religion and the First Amendment 80 n.1 (rev. ed., 1994).

should be allowed on account of religion." With little debate, their motion lost on a vote of 4 to 6, with one state divided.[23]

The delegates agreed to place language in Article VI stating that members of Congress, members of state legislatures, and all executive officers (federal and state) "shall be bound by Oath or Affirmation, to support this Constitution." Oaths are associated with a belief in a deity. Affirmation carries no such implication.[24] Many Americans wanted to express their support for the Constitution without indicating a religious position. Article VI continues: "[B]ut no religious Test shall ever be required as a Qualification to any Office or public Trust under the United States." Religious tests provoked discussion at the Philadelphia Convention.[25] At the ratifying conventions, some delegates feared that eliminating a religious test might permit Catholics, pagans, deists, and Muslims to serve in public office.[26] James Iredell countered: under "the color of religious tests, the utmost cruelties have been exercised."[27]

The First Congress promoted religion by including this provision in the Northwest Territory Ordinance: "Religion, morality, and knowledge, being necessary to good government and the happiness of mankind, schools and the means of education shall forever be encouraged."[28] This general reference to religion would be replaced by assistance to a particular denomination. Legislation dealing with Native Americans often singled out Christianity as a driving motivation—if not said expressly in the statute, then very much implied in the legislative history.[29] Beginning in 1774, the Continental Congress authorized a chaplain to open legislative proceedings with prayers; that practice continued in 1789 with the First Congress and persists to the present time.[30] The First Congress debated giving exemptions from military service to conscientious objectors and recognizing their rights in the Second Amendment (discussed later in this chapter).

On June 8, 1789, Madison alerted his colleagues in the House of Representatives of his intention to propose a list of constitutional amendments. He recommended that the following language be inserted in Article I, section 9, between clauses 3 and 4: "The civil rights of none shall be abridged on account of religious belief or worship, nor shall any national religion be established, nor shall the full and equal rights of conscience be in any manner, or on any pretext,

23. 2 Farrand 616.
24. Fisher, Religious Liberty in America, at 44.
25. 2 Farrand 342, 468.
26. 2 Elliot 148; 4 Elliot 192.
27. 4 Elliot 192. See comment by Richard Spaight, 4 Elliot 208.
28. 1 Stat. 52, art. III (1789).
29. 1 Stat. 491, sec. 5 (1796); Fisher, Religious Liberty in America, at 147–51.
30. Fisher, Religious Liberty in America, at 49–51.

infringed." He also proposed adding this language to Article I, section 10, between clauses 1 and 2: "No State shall violate the equal rights of conscience, or the freedom of the press, or the trial by jury in criminal cases."[31] Under his proposal, the rights of conscience would bind both the national government and the states, but the prohibition on establishment controlled only the national government.

After much debate and changes by the House and the Senate, Congress settled on language that became the First Amendment: "Congress shall make no law respecting an establishment of religion, or prohibiting the free exercise thereof; or abridging the freedom of speech, or of the press; or the right of the people peaceably to assemble, and to petition the Government for a redress of grievances." The House language that prohibited states from infringing on the rights of conscience was deleted by the Senate and never submitted to the states for ratification. The Senate struck the word "conscience" from the First Amendment.[32]

Through what has become known as the Incorporation Doctrine, the Supreme Court has in a series of rulings incorporated most of the Bill of Rights into the Due Process Clause of the Fourteenth Amendment. The result: what was originally a limitation on Congress applies now to the states. The Court extended the Free Exercise Clause to the states in 1940 and the Establishment Clause in 1947.[33] State constitutions have their own provisions governing religious liberty. The meaning of the religion clauses in the First Amendment has been confused by the unfortunate metaphor of a supposed "wall of separation" existing between church and state. The phrase comes from a letter that President Jefferson wrote to the Danbury Baptist Association in 1802. He claimed that the intent of the framers in adopting the First Amendment was to build "a wall of separation between Church and State."[34] Jefferson was correct that in matters of religious opinions and conscience the government could not intrude in a zone of individual privacy. But contacts between church and state are permitted, as Jefferson's letter to the Baptist group clearly illustrates.

In upholding state assistance of transportation to parochial schools in 1947, Justice Hugo Black claimed that the First Amendment "has erected a wall between church and states. That wall must be kept high and impregnable. We could not approve the slightest breach. New Jersey has not breached it here."[35]

31. 1 Annals of Cong. 434–35 (1789).

32. For House and Senate debate on the First Amendment, see 1 Annals Cong. 729, 731, 755, 766 (1789); 1 S. Journal 70, 77 (1789).

33. Cantwell v. Connecticut, 310 U.S. 296, 303 (1940); Everson v. Board of Education, 330 U.S. 1, 15 (1947).

34. 16 The Writings of Thomas Jefferson 282 (Bergh ed., 1904).

35. Everson v. Board of Education, 330 U.S. 1, 18 (1947).

Black's rhetoric was false on multiple levels. First, no impregnable wall exists between church and state. Second, if a wall did exist, how could the judicial branch of government accept (much less decide) a religious issue? Third, a breach obviously occurred in the New Jersey case because the Court upheld the state's transportation assistance to religious schools.

A dissent by Justice Jackson highlighted the wide gap between Black's flowery language and his actual result. Jackson remarked that the case "which irresistibly comes to mind as the most fitting precedent" was that of Julia who, according to Byron's reports, "whispering 'I will ne'er consent,'—consented."[36] Justice Rutledge also had no patience for Black's judicial double-talk. In a dissent joined by Frankfurter, Jackson, and Burton, Rutledge wrote: "New Jersey's statute sustained is the first, if indeed it is not the second breach to be made by this Court's action. That a third, and a fourth, and still others will be attempted, we may be sure."[37] Rutledge's warning was on target. The breaches allowed by the Court in later years numbered in the dozens.

The wall imagery took another beating in 1948. A concurrence by Justice Jackson questioned the Court's reasoning in a case that analyzed an Illinois law that allowed religious teachers to give religious instruction in public school buildings. To the Court, using state funds to enable sectarian groups to give religious instruction to students in public schools violated the Constitution. Jackson predicted correctly that the Court would make "the legal 'wall of separation between church and state' as winding as the famous serpentine wall designed by Mr. Jefferson for the University he founded."[38] In this same case, Justice Reed offered apt advice: "A rule of law should not be drawn from a figure of speech."[39] A complete wall between church and state is neither possible nor desirable. Religious organizations have every right to petition and lobby government; government has every right to ensure various standards of safety, health, and curricula in religious schools. The objective has been to discover an accommodation that protects the interests and integrity of each side.

Congressional Challenges in the 1860s

The decision of Congress to assign chaplains to the military eventually required new legislative action to protect the interests of non-Christians. It had been the

36. Id. at 19.
37. Id. at 29.
38. McCollum v. Board of Education, 333 U.S. 203, 238 (1948).
39. Id. at 247.

practice to choose only Protestants to serve as military chaplains. Statutes specified that military chaplains were to be a regular ordained minister of a "Christian denomination."[40] When the Civil War started, the largely Jewish 65th Regiment of the Fifth Pennsylvania Cavalry had a Jewish layman serving as chaplain, but he left that post because of the statutory restriction.[41] A number of Christians and Jews signed petitions urging Congress to remove the sectarian statutory language.[42]

Jewish authorities finally decided to send Rabbi Arnold Fischel of New York to Washington, D.C., to speak to President Lincoln and congressional committees. Lincoln assured Fischel that he would "try to have a new law broad enough to cover what is desired by you in behalf of the Israelites." In a separate effort, Fischel explained to the Senate Committee on Military Affairs why a change in the statute would conform to the constitutional prohibition against a religious test. On this issue no one thought of taking the dispute to the courts for resolution. Within a year Congress deleted "Christian denomination" from the statute and inserted the words "some religious denomination." The regular political process worked. Acting by majority vote, Congress met the religious needs of a minority and safeguarded a constitutional principle.[43]

During this period Congress tackled another religious dispute. In 1860, Congress began debate on legislation to prohibit polygamy in the territories and to annul certain acts of the legislature of Utah that sanctioned multiple marriages. As with other constitutional issues relating to religion, Congress acted under its own independent interpretation without any assistance or guidance from the courts. A report by the House Judiciary Committee stated that "the whole civilized world regard the marriage of one man to one woman as being authorized by the law of God" and that marriage "is the foundation of civil society." The "law of God" here was clearly sectarian. The Jewish Old Testament recognized multiple marriages; the Christian New Testament did not. The House committee noted that every state treated polygamy as a crime, generally a felony.[44] The legislation passed the House, 149 to 60.[45]

40. 12 Stat. 270, sec. 9 (1861); 12 Stat. 288, sec. 7 (1861).

41. Bertrum Wallace Korn, American Jewry and the Civil War 58–60 (1951).

42. Id. at 65–68.

43. 12 Stat. 595, sec. 8 (1862). See Korn, American Jewry and the Civil War, at 70; Jonathan D. Sarna and David G. Dalin, Religion and State in the American Jewish Tradition 130 (1997); Albert Isaac Slomovitz, The Fighting Rabbis: Jewish Military Chaplains and American History 10–18 (2001 paper ed.).

44. H. Rept. No. 83, 36th Cong., 1st Sess. 1, 2 (1860). For debate see Cong. Globe, 36th Cong., 1st Sess. 1150–51, 1409–12, 1492–1501, 1512–23, 1540–46, 1557–60 (1860).

45. Cong. Globe, 36th Cong., 1st Sess. 1559 (1860).

The Senate, acting in 1862, passed the bill 37 to 2 and it became law.[46] Congress reasoned that it was not interfering with religious beliefs or "the dictates of conscience." It was prohibiting certain types of religious *practice*.[47] In 1879, the Supreme Court upheld the law by drawing the same distinction between belief and practice: "Laws are made for the government of actions, and while they cannot interfere with mere religious belief and opinions, they may with practices."[48]

Some members of Congress warned that Mormons would not obey any statute passed by Congress. They said there was no reason to expect a grand jury or petit jury of Mormons to indict or convict a fellow polygamist.[49] Their predictions proved correct. Prospects for compliance improved somewhat when Congress passed legislation in 1874 to give federal judges and federal officials greater authority over courts in Utah.[50] After the Mormon Church continued to refuse to comply with national policy, Congress passed legislation in 1882 to make polygamists ineligible to serve on juries, to vote, or to hold territorial or federal office.[51] The Supreme Court upheld that legislation.[52]

In 1887, Congress took it to the next level by confiscating Mormon Church property and repealing the act that incorporated the church. The statute exempted buildings occupied exclusively for the worship of God, parsonages related to those buildings, and burial grounds.[53] The Court upheld this law on several grounds, including the authority of Congress over the territories and the organic statute of the Territory of Utah that reserved to Congress the authority to disapprove and annul the acts of its legislature.[54] At that point the head of the Mormon Church, President Wilford Woodruff, issued an announcement against polygamy and advised all Mormons "to refrain from contracting any marriage forbidden by the law of the land." A general conference of Mormon representatives accepted his declaration on polygamy as "authoritative and binding."[55] Nevertheless, legal actions against polygamists continued throughout the twentieth and early twenty-first centuries.[56]

46. Cong. Globe, 37th Cong., 2d Sess. 2506–07 (1862).

47. 12 Stat. 501, sec. 2 (1862).

48. Reynolds v. United States, 98 U.S. 145, 166 (1879).

49. Cong. Globe, 36th Cong., 1st Sess. 1512 (Rep. John McClernand), 1520 (Rep. Eli Thayer).

50. 18 Stat. 253 (1874) (part 3 of vol. 18).

51. 22 Stat. 30 (1882).

52. Murphy v. Ramsey, 114 U.S. 15, 44 (1885).

53. 24 Stat. 635, 637 (sec. 13), 638 (sec. 17) (1887).

54. Mormon Church v. United States, 136 U.S. 1, 42, 44 (1890).

55. 2 Stokes 280; Orma Linford, "The Mormons and the Law: The Polygamy Cases" (Part II), 9 Utah L. Rev. 543, 582–83 (1965).

56. Fisher, Religious Liberty in America, at 26–27.

Conscientious Objectors

Some American citizens have offered a mix of religious and ethical reasons for refusing to serve in the military. This constitutional value arose not from the government but from personal beliefs and the community. The branch that initially recognized the right of conscientious objectors was the legislature, not the courts. Judges arrived late to this constitutional issue, generally upholding what had already been expressed in statutes and state constitutions. The colonies and early state governments made exceptions for individuals who presented religious objections to serving in the military. Legislation sometimes asked conscientious objectors to perform noncombatant services, such as extinguishing fires and caring for the wounded.[57]

On July 18, 1775, the Continental Congress debated plans to create a militia to prepare for the war of independence from England. It recognized the need to make an exception: "As there are some people, who, from religious principles, cannot bear arms in any case, this Congress intend no violence to their consciences, but earnestly recommend it to them, to contribute liberally in this time of universal calamity, to the relief of their distressed brethren in the several colonies, and to do all other services to their oppressed Country, which they can consistently with their religious principles."[58] Citizens whose conscience prohibited military action agreed to "bear our due share of the common civil taxes and burdens excepting the bearing of arms and weapons."[59]

After the break with England, several states added language to their constitutions to recognize the rights of conscientious objectors. The 1776 Constitution of Pennsylvania provided: "Nor can any man who is conscientiously scrupulous of bearing arms, be justly compelled thereto, if he will pay such equivalent."[60] The Vermont Constitution of 1777: no one "conscientiously scrupulous of bearing arms, [may] be justly compelled thereto."[61] The New Hampshire Constitution of 1784 followed the language in the Pennsylvania constitution.[62] The Maine Constitution of 1819 identified particular religious sects entitled to exemption: "Persons of the denomination of Quakers and Shakers . . . may be

57. Id. at 82–83.
58. 2 Journals of the Continental Congress 189 (1905).
59. Lillian Schliessel, ed., Conscience in America: A Documentary History of Conscientious Objection in America, 1757–1967, at 39–40 (1968).
60. Pa. Const. of 1776, VIII; 8 Swindler 278.
61. Vt. Const. of 1777, Ch. I, IX; 9 Swindler 490.
62. N.H. Const. of 1784, art. I, XIII; 6 Swindler 345.

exempted from military duty; but no other person . . . shall be so exempted, unless he shall pay an equivalent, to be fixed by law."[63]

This approach created problems. How would a legislative body distinguish between the denominations that qualify and those that fall short? Why should conscientious objection be limited to religious or sectarian beliefs instead of general ethical or philosophical principles? Those questions surfaced on June 8, 1789, when the House of Representatives debated the Second Amendment. Originally it included this language: "[B]ut no person religiously scrupulous of bearing arms shall be compelled to render military service in person."[64] Elbridge Gerry disliked the words "religiously scrupulous," insisting that the amendment be confined to persons belonging to a "religious sect scrupulous of bearing arms." James Jackson disagreed with those who predicted that "all the people of the United States would turn Quakers or Moravians." If someone expressed religious misgivings about military activity, it would be sufficient to pay an equivalent amount to earn an exemption.[65] Thomas Scott did not object to those he knew to be religiously scrupulous; he worried about those "who are of no religion."[66] The House version of the Second Amendment retained language exempting individuals who are religiously scrupulous, but the Senate deleted that exemption.[67]

During debate on the militia bill in 1790, members of Congress considered a religious exemption for the armed forces. They received a petition from the Quakers, "praying an exemption from militia duties and penalties on that account."[68] Lawmakers differed on the merits. Aedanus Burke disliked the idea of exemptions because it was inconsistent with religious liberty to recognize the rights of conscience but then require citizens to pay if they wanted to retain their religious beliefs.[69] James Jackson wondered how Congress could possibly identify which individuals were conscientiously scrupulous. Would it have to create some kind of tribunal to adjudicate those claims?[70] As the debate continued, Burke proposed exempting the people called Quakers "and all persons religiously scrupulous of bearing arms." Jackson feared that the effect of such a privilege "would be to make the whole community turn Quakers." He said if citizens wanted an exemption, they needed to pay.[71]

---

63. Me. Const. of 1819, art. VII, sec. 5; 4 Swindler 323.
64. 1 Annals of Cong. 434 (1789).
65. Id. at 750.
66. Id. at 767.
67. 1 Senate Journal 63–64, 71, 77 (1789).
68. 2 Annals of Cong. 1859 (1790).
69. Id. at 1865.
70. Id.
71. Id. at 1869–70.

Madison preferred not to look to particular religious denominations but to the more general principle of conscience. Responding to Jackson's concerns, he said he did not believe that Americans "would hypocritically renounce their principles, their conscience, and their God, for the sake of enjoying the exemption."[72] Madison proposed language giving an exemption for "all persons religiously scrupulous of bearing arms, who shall make a declaration of the same before a civil magistrate . . . but be liable to a penalty of _____ dollars."[73] The House decided to leave the matter to the states. Individuals who wanted to claim an exemption from military service had to depend on state laws and state constitutions. Courts had little role in this debate.

The issue returned to the national government after the outbreak of the Civil War. During debate in 1863 on a conscription bill, Senator Ira Harris proposed that all persons "who, being from scruples of conscience averse to bearing arms, are by the constitution of any State excused therefrom."[74] His language created a problem. Some states recognized the exemption for Shakers and Quakers in their statutes but not their constitutions. When several Senators raised that objection and others, Harris withdrew his amendment.[75] House members wanted to exclude individuals who seemed to be late converts just to avoid military service. A proposal to require that someone had been religiously scrupulous for a set period of time, such as one year or three years, was voted down, 18 to 95.[76] A Senate amendment required someone seeking an exemption to petition a federal judge. If granted an exemption, the individual would have to contribute toward "any public hospital or charitable service, a peace offering in accordance with his means." That proposal failed, 8 to 32.[77] The bill that gained enactment made no mention of conscientious objection.[78]

Quakers and other individuals could seek relief under another section of the statute. Any person drafted and notified to appear for military service may "furnish an acceptable substitute to take his place in the draft" or pay an amount to a person, authorized by the Secretary of War to receive payment, a sum not exceeding $300. Individuals who furnished a substitute or paid cash "shall be discharged from further liability under that draft."[79] Quakers had long opposed slavery but did not believe that war was the appropriate remedy. The Society of

72. Id. at 1871–72.
73. Id. at 1874.
74. Cong. Globe, 37th Cong., 3d Sess. 994 (1863).
75. Id.
76. Id. at 1261, 1292.
77. Id. at 1389–90.
78. 12 Stat. 731 (1863).
79. 12 Stat. 733, sec. 13 (1863).

Friends drafted language that Quakers could present to draft boards, relying on this provision of the law.[80]

Quakers met with members of Congress to develop a better national policy toward military service. In 1864, Congress passed legislation specifically mentioning conscientious objectors. An exemption applied to members of "religious denominations" who by oath or affirmation declare conscientious opposition to the bearing of arms and "are prohibited from doing so by the rules and articles of faith and practices of said religious denomination." They became noncombatants. The Secretary of War could assign them to duty in hospitals or to the care of freedmen, or they "shall pay the sum of three hundred dollars" to an individual designated by the Secretary to receive payment, "to be applied to the benefit of the sick and wounded soldiers."[81]

Those safeguards to religious minorities came from the regular political process, with no input from the judiciary. Quakers and other denominations understood that they could meet successfully with lawmakers and executive officials to craft a policy that served both national interests and their own. The result was an accommodation that could not have been found in the courts. President Lincoln, urged to compel Quakers, Mennonites, and other conscientious objectors to take up arms, refused: "No, I will not do that. These people do not believe in war. People who do not believe in war make poor soldiers. Besides, the attitude of these people has always been against slavery. If all our people held the same views about slavery as these people there would be no war.... We will leave them on their farms where they are at home and where they will make their contributions better than they would with a gun."[82]

Statutory policy changed over the years. During World War I, Congress eliminated the option of hiring substitutes or paying an amount to escape military service. Instead, there was an effort to distinguish between combatant and noncombatant duties.[83] Legal challenges in court claimed that exemptions for conscientious objectors violated the First Amendment by establishing or interfering with religion. Briefly dealing with that issue, a unanimous Court in 1918 found no constitutional problems with the policy that Congress had developed.[84]

Statutory language in 1917 granted exemptions to individuals "found to be a member of any well-recognized religious sect or organization" with a policy

80. Edward Needles Wright, Conscientious Objectors in the Civil War 15–16, 69–70 (1931).

81. 13 Stat. 9, sec. 17 (1864).

82. U.S. Selective Service System, Conscientious Objection 42–43 (Special Monograph No. 11, vol. I, 1950).

83. 39 Stat. 197, sec. 59 (1916); 40 Stat. 78, sec. 4 (1917).

84. Selective Draft Law Cases, 245 U.S. 366, 389–90 (1918).

against military service. Congress was prepared to retain that language in 1940 when it passed the Selective Training and Service Act. However, two Quakers met with Congress and the War Department and pointed out that the reference to a "religious sect" benefited them but was unfair. They wanted exemption to depend on individual conscience, not on membership. Other religious groups agreed with that critique. The 1940 statute contained a list of exemptions, including anyone who, "by reason of religious training and belief, is conscientiously opposed to participation in war in any form." Membership in a religious organization was not necessary.[85]

The statutory phrase "religious training and belief" raised another question. Did a conscientious objector need to believe in a Supreme Being? Would that language exclude objectors who depended on philosophical and political considerations? Not every religion is theistic. Could Congress constitutionally prefer theistic over nontheistic religions? The Supreme Court began to interpret the expression "a Supreme Being" in broad terms, meaning some force outside oneself, even if not a traditional deity. Drawing on a dissenting opinion from 1931, the Court decided that freedom of conscience "implies respect for an innate conviction of paramount duty," implying that it could embrace nontheistic beliefs.[86] Almost all of the effort to create exemptions for conscientious objectors came from private citizens and elected officials, not judges. Courts were not part of this dialogue until late in the game. Their contribution has not been central but rather working around the edges to parse statutory language.[87]

Compulsory Flag Salutes

In 1940, the Supreme Court upheld a compulsory flag salute that forced children to violate their religious beliefs. The opinion seemed final in the sense that it was issued with a commanding 8-to-1 majority. However, so defective was the Court's reasoning and so swift the public condemnation that within three years the Court decided to reverse itself to protect the religious interests of minorities. The outcome is explained not by judicial leadership or sensitivity to individual rights but by a broad public debate that forced some Justices to rethink their judicial doctrines and abandon them.

85. 54 Stat. 889, sec. 5(g) (1940). Fisher, Religious Liberty in America, at 96–99.
86. United States v. Seeger, 380 U.S. 163, 175–76 (1965), citing United States v. Macintosh, 282 U.S. 605, 634 (1931) (Hughes, C. J., dissenting).
87. Fisher, Religious Liberty in America, at 99–104.

The first flag-salute law appeared in Kansas in 1907. Other states began to pass legislation to compel schoolchildren to salute the flag. The Jehovah's Witnesses objected that the exercise violated their religious beliefs because they interpreted the Bible literally: "Thou shalt not make unto thee any graven image, or any likeness of any thing that is in heaven above, or that is in the earth beneath, or that is in the water under the earth. Thou shalt not bow down thyself to them, nor serve under them" (Exodus 20: 4–5). During the 1930s these laws survived judicial challenges in the lower courts, with the Supreme Court each time deciding not to get involved.[88]

In 1937, a federal district judge in Pennsylvania held this type of legislation to be unconstitutional. The case involved two children of Jehovah's Witnesses, Lillian Gobitas (13 years old) and her brother, William (12). The family name, incorrectly spelled "Gobitis" early in the litigation, remained misspelled at every level.[89] School authorities decided that the children's refusal to salute the flag constituted an act of insubordination that required expulsion from public schools. Pennsylvania had entered an area that the framers had held most private: individual conscience and religious opinions.

To the federal judge, religious beliefs could not be violated unless the state could demonstrate that the law was necessary for the public safety, health, morals, property, or personal rights.[90] He drew attention to the tradition of religious freedom in Pennsylvania. The state constitution provided that "all men have a natural and indefeasible right to worship Almighty God according to the dictates of their own consciences; . . . no human authority can, in any case whatever, control or interfere with the rights of conscience." He recalled that the state's founder, William Penn, had been expelled from Oxford University "for his refusal for conscience' sake to comply with regulations not essentially dissimilar [to the compulsory flag salute], and suffered, more than once, imprisonment in England because of his religious convictions."[91] The judge pointed to the religious intolerance that was "again rearing its ugly head in other parts of the world," as in Nazi Germany.[92]

---

88. Leoles v. Landers, 192 S.E. 218 (Ga. 1937), dismissed for want of substantial federal question, 302 U.S. 656 (1937); Hering v. State Board of Education, 189 A. 629 (N.J. 1937), dismissed for want of substantial federal question, 303 U.S. 624 (1938); Gabrielli v. Knickerbocker, 82 P.2d 391 (Cal. 1938), dismissed for want of jurisdiction, 306 U.S. 621 (1930); Johnson v. Deerfield, 25 F.Supp. 918 (D. Mass. 1939), aff'd, 306 U.S. 621 (1939).

89. Shawn Francis Peters, Judging Jehovah's Witnesses: Religious Persecution and the Dawn of the Rights Revolution 19 (2000).

90. Gobitis v. Minersville School Dist., 21 F.Supp. 581, 584 (E.D. Pa. 1937).

91. Id. at 585.

92. Id. at 586. See also Gobitis v. Minersville School Dist., 24 F.Supp. 271 (E.D. Pa. 1938).

His decision was upheld by the Third Circuit, which found defective a standard justification for the compulsory flag salute. It is "designed to better secure the state by inculcating in its youthful citizens a love of country that will incline their hearts and minds to its more willing defense."[93] The appellate court found it difficult to "find the essential relationship between infant patriotism and the martial spirit."[94] It preferred the values that George Washington expressed to the Quakers in October 1789: "I assure you very explicitly, that in my opinion the conscientious scruples of all men should be treated with great delicacy and tenderness; and it is my wish and desire, that the laws may always be as extensively accommodated to them, as a due regard to the protection and essential interests of the nation may justify and permit."[95]

After losing in district court and the Third Circuit, the school district appealed to the Supreme Court. The brief prepared for the Witnesses objected that the "form of salute is very much like that of the Nazi regime in Germany."[96] Instead of respecting the value of religious freedom and its heritage in America, some communities feared fifth column activities by Axis powers. During the spring of 1940, the German army moved relentlessly across Europe. On May 23, a mob in Del Rio, Texas, attacked three Witnesses they thought were Nazi agents. On June 2, the Gallup Poll reported that 65 percent of the public believed that Germany would attack the United States.[97] How would the Supreme Court respond to these pressures? Uphold individual rights? Safeguard "discrete and insular minorities," as Justice Stone had hoped in his famous footnote in 1938?[98]

The answer came on the last day of the Court's term, June 3, 1940. Writing for an 8-to-1 majority, Justice Frankfurter upheld the compulsory flag salute by subordinating individual rights to the national interest. He leaned heavily on two premises: (1) liberty requires unifying sentiments, and (2) national unity promotes national security. Using that formula, the value of conscience and the individual right to possess religious opinions would mean little. Frankfurter's family immigrated to the United States when he was 12 years old. The American flag represented something sacrosanct, a symbol of the assimilationist ideal he embraced.[99] He wrote for the Court: "The preciousness of the family rela-

93. Minersville School Dist. v. Gobitis, 108 F.2d 683, 692 (3d Cir. 1940).
94. Id.
95. Id. at 693.
96. Respondents' Brief, Minersville School Dist. v. Gobitis, at 3; 37 Landmark Briefs 375.
97. Francis H. Heller, "A Turning Point for Religious Liberty," 29 Va. L. Rev. 440, 447 (1943).
98. United States v. Carolene Products Co., 304 U.S. 144, 152–53 n.4 (1938).
99. Richard Danzig, "Justice Frankfurter's Opinion in the Flag Salute Cases: Blending Logic and Psychologic in Constitution Decisionmaking," 36 Stan. L. Rev. 675, 696–97 (1984).

tion, the authority and independence which give dignity to parenthood, indeed the enjoyment of all freedom, presuppose the kind of ordered society which is summarized by our flag. A society which is dedicated to the preservation of these ultimate values of civilization may in self-protection utilize the educational process for inculcating those almost unconscious feelings which bind men together in a comprehending loyalty, whatever may be their lesser differences and difficulties."[100]

The Jehovah's Witnesses hoped that the Supreme Court would protect the value of religious pluralism as it had been defended in the lower courts. Frankfurter disagreed, saying the proper course was for them to present their case "in the forum of public opinion and before legislative assemblies rather than to transfer such a contest to the judicial arena."[101] In this way he conceded that individual and minority rights would find protection not in the courts but rather through the regular political process. A powerful dissent from Justice Stone rejected Frankfurter's arguments, especially his doctrine of judicial self-restraint. To defer to legislative judgment and the democratic process, Stone said, "seems to me no less than the surrender of the constitutional protection of the liberty of small minorities to the popular will."[102]

Stone's dissent had little impact. According to his law clerk, Stone walked into the conference room deciding to defend the religious liberty of the Witnesses but did not articulate his misgivings about Frankfurter's position. Nor did he circulate his dissent sufficiently early to draw colleagues to his side.[103] Justices Black, Douglas, and Murphy, as relative newcomers to the Court, decided to defer to Frankfurter because of his reputation as a civil libertarian. By the time they saw Stone's dissent they felt it was too late to abandon Frankfurter.[104] Murphy's initial instinct was to write a dissent. He actually drafted one before deciding not to circulate it to the Justices.[105]

Frankfurter's opinion was assailed by law journals, the press, and religious organizations. The *New Republic,* which Frankfurter had helped found, warned that the country was "in great danger of adopting Hitler's philosophy in the effort to oppose Hitler's legions" and accused the Court of coming "dangerously close to

---

100. Minersville School District v. Gobitis, 310 U.S. 586, 600 (1940).

101. Id.

102. Id. at 606.

103. Alpheus Thomas Mason, Harlan Fiske Stone: Pillar of the Law 528, asterisked footnote (New York: Viking Press, 1956).

104. William O. Douglas, The Court Years, 1939–75, at 45 (1981).

105. J. Woodford Howard Jr., Mr. Justice Murphy: A Political Biography 251 (1968); Peters, Judging Jehovah's Witnesses, at 65–66.

being a victim of [war] hysteria."[106] Later it added sarcasm: "Already Mr. Justice Frankfurter has been heroically saving America from a couple of school children whose devotion to Jehovah would have been compromised by a salute to the flag."[107] Out of 39 law reviews that discussed *Gobitis,* 31 were critical. Newspapers condemned the Court for violating individual rights and buckling to popular hysteria.[108] Editorials in 171 newspapers ripped Frankfurter's opinion.[109]

After the release of *Gobitis,* a wave of violence against Witnesses swept the country. By one estimate, the persecution of Witnesses from 1941 to 1943 marked the greatest outbreak of religious intolerance in twentieth-century America.[110] Branded as disloyal, Witnesses were easy targets for arrests, forced marches, threats, beatings, vandalism, arson, and destruction of buildings and property.[111] Justices Black, Douglas, and Murphy increasingly regretted their willingness to join Frankfurter's opinion. A few months after the decision, Douglas advised Frankfurter that Black was having second thoughts about his vote. Sarcastically, Frankfurter asked whether Black had spent the summer reading the Constitution. "No," Douglas replied, "he has been reading the papers."[112]

Far from having the last word on this constitutional issue, pockets of resistance to the decision appeared throughout the country. Several state courts, refusing to follow Frankfurter's opinion, offered greater protection to schoolchildren who cited religious grounds for not saluting the flag.[113] In a 1942 ruling, Black, Douglas, and Murphy decided to publicly express their regret for joining Frankfurter. They now announced that *Gobitis* had been "wrongly decided."[114] Frankfurter's commanding majority of 8 to 1 shrank to a narrow 5-to-4 margin. Two Justices who had been part of the original eight-man majority retired and were replaced by Wiley Rutledge and Robert H. Jackson. Rutledge's opinions serving on the D.C. Circuit indicated that he would add his vote to those who opposed Frankfurter.[115] Jackson was likely to go in that direction also, pushing Frankfurter into a dissenting position with two colleagues.

106. "Frankfurter v. Stone," New Republic, vol. 102, at 843–44 (June 24, 1940).

107. Walton Hamilton and George Braden, "The Supreme Court Today," New Republic, vol. 103, at 180 (August 5, 1940).

108. David R. Manwaring, Render Unto Caesar: The Flag-Salute Controversy 158–60 (1962); Heller, "A Turning Point for Religious Liberty," 29 Va. L. Rev. at 452–53.

109. Alpheus Thomas Mason, Harlan Fiske Stone, at 532.

110. John T. Noonan Jr., The Believer and the Powers That Are 251 (1987).

111. Peters, Judging Jehovah's Witnesses, supra note 89, at 72–123.

112. H. N. Hirsch, The Enigma of Felix Frankfurter 152 (1981).

113. State v. Lefebvre, 20 A.2d 185 (N.H. 1941); In re Latrecchia, 26 A.2d 881 (N.J. 1942); State v. Smith, 127 P.2d 518 (Kans. 1942).

114. Jones v. Opelika, 316 U.S. 584, 624 (1942).

115. E.g., Busey v. District of Columbia, 129 F.2d 24, 38 (D.C. Cir. 1942).

Legislation passed by Congress in 1942 also weakened *Gobitis*. Instead of requiring flag salutes for the display and use of the American flag, the statute authorized this alternative: "[C]ivilians will always show full respect to the flag when the pledge is given by merely standing at attention, men removing the headdress."[116] The Justice Department cited this statute to demonstrate that the 1940 ruling supporting the compulsory flag salute had lost its authority. The Department emphasized that Witnesses had no objection to standing at attention during a flag-salute exercise.[117]

The issue returned to the Court in the fall of 1942, this time involving a case from West Virginia, with Jehovah's Witnesses again objecting to a compulsory flag salute. The district court did not feel bound by *Gobitis* because, of the seven current Justices who participated in that decision, "four have given public expression to the view that it is unsound."[118] The court held that the state could not force children to salute the flag when the action violated their religious beliefs and conscience. Justice Jackson, writing for a 6-to-3 majority, delivered a powerful and stirring defense of individual freedom and the Bill of Rights, but credit for the judicial reversal comes from those who refused to accept *Gobitis* as the last word on constitutional meaning and bluntly told the Court that it did not understand the Constitution, minority rights, or religious liberty. Part of Jackson's opinion, cited with admiration by those who champion religious liberty, is less impressive when his words are closely scrutinized. Consider this oft-quoted passage:

> The very purpose of a Bill of Rights was to withdraw certain subjects from the vicissitudes of political controversy, to place them beyond the reach of majorities and officials and to establish them as legal principles to be applied by the courts. One's right to life, liberty, and property, to free speech, a free press, freedom of worship and assembly, and other fundamental rights may not be submitted to vote; they depend on the outcome of no elections.[119]

The basic message: individual rights are protected in the courts, not by the elected branches. Jackson appeared to give no thought to the frequency with which the elected branches defended rights that could not be secured from

116. 56 Stat. 380, sec. 7 (1942).
117. Victor W. Rotnem and F. G. Folsom Jr., "Recent Restrictions upon Religious Liberty," 36 Am. Pol. Sci. Rev. 1053, 1064 (1942).
118. Barnette v. West Virginia State Board of Ed., 47 F.Supp. 151, 153 (D. W. Va. 1942).
119. West Virginia State Board of Education v. Barnette, 319 U.S. 624, 638 (1943).

courts. Among prominent examples: the rights of blacks in 1875 to have equal access to public accommodations, the rights of women in 1879 to practice law, and the rights of children not to be subjected to dangerous occupations at a young age. What offered those groups protection were elections and majority vote, not judicial rulings. Jackson's rhetoric ignores the complexity of political developments in America, including the creation of constitutional rights. Perhaps he was informed by the particular context of 1943: totalitarian governments abroad operating without any independent courts. Here is another passage from Jackson's opinion that is often admired:

> If there is any fixed star in our constitutional constellation, it is that no official, high or petty, can prescribe what shall be orthodox in politics, nationalism, religion, or other matters of opinion or force citizens to confess by word or act their faith therein. If there are any circumstances which permit an exception, they do not now occur to us.[120]

Jackson states that no official from the executive and legislative branches, high or petty, may announce what is orthodox in politics, nationalism, religion, and other matters of opinion. What of the Court? How often has the Court attempted to decide what is orthodox (that is, announcing the correct opinion or established doctrine)? Some examples: slavery (*Dred Scott*), women practicing law, federalism, economic regulation, mandatory sterilization (*Buck v. Bell* in 1927), child labor, the 1940 flag-salute case, abortion (*Roe v. Wade* in 1973), and more recently the 2010 campaign finance case of *Citizens United v. FEC*, supporting unlimited corporate spending on elections (to be discussed in subsequent chapters). When the Court claims it has the final word on the meaning of the Constitution, it is pretending it has authority to decide what is orthodox.

Religious Liberty in the Military

In 1986, the Supreme Court upheld an Air Force regulation that had prohibited an observant Jew in the military from wearing his skullcap (yarmulke) indoors while on duty. The Court split 5 to 4. Whether it had the "last word" depended on what Congress would do. Within one year, Congress passed legislation telling the military to rewrite the regulation to permit members of the military to wear religious apparel, provided it did not interfere with their mili-

---

120. Id. at 642.

tary duties. Constitutional liberties unavailable from the Court were protected by congressional statute.

Simcha Goldman, an Orthodox Jew and ordained rabbi, served for years as a captain in the U.S. Air Force. At the time of the litigation he worked in a mental health clinic as a psychologist. While in uniform and on duty, he wore a yarmulke at all times without incident. In April 1981, he appeared at a court-martial proceeding and testified on behalf of the defense and therefore against the Air Force. In what appeared to be a retaliatory move, on May 8 he was informed by the Air Force that wearing a yarmulke while on duty violated the military dress code.[121] His first response was to seek an administrative remedy by asking the Air Force to permit an exception in his case. The Air Force said no. At that point the dispute moved to the courts.

A district court ruled that the Air Force regulation violated Goldman's religious freedom under the First Amendment. The judge appeared to make light of the military's argument that allowing him to wear a yarmulke "will crush the spirit of uniformity, which in turn will weaken the will and fighting ability of the Air Force."[122] Another district court upheld the Air Force policy on yarmulkes, reasoning that departures from uniformity would adversely affect "the promotion of teamwork, counteract pride and motivation, and undermine discipline and morale, all to the detriment of the substantial compelling governmental interest of maintaining an efficient Air Force."[123] All three judges on a panel of the D.C. Circuit supported the Air Force position. As part of its argument, the Air Force said that if it accommodated Goldman's yarmulke, other members of the military would offer different religious claims: the use of turbans, robes, face and body paint, shorn hair, unshorn hair, badges, rings, amulets, bracelets, jodhpurs, and symbolic daggers.[124]

When the D.C. Circuit voted against a motion to hear the case en banc (full bench), three judges with quite familiar names dissented. Judge Kenneth Starr, who later served as Solicitor General in the Bush I administration and as independent counsel during the Whitewater investigation of President Clinton, objected that the panel's decision "does considerable violence to the bulwark of freedom guaranteed by the Free Exercise Clause."[125] Judges Ruth Bader Ginsburg and Antonin Scalia, who would later move to the Supreme Court, observed that

121. Goldman v. Weinberger, 475 U.S. 503, 511 (1986) (Stevens, J., concurrence, joined by White and Powell, J).
122. Goldman v. Secretary of Defense, 530 F.Supp. 12, 16 (D.D.C. 1981).
123. Bitterman v. Secretary of Defense, 553 F.Supp. 719, 725 (D.D.C. 1982).
124. Id. at 1539.
125. Goldman v. Secretary of Defense, 739 F.2d 657, 658 (D.C. Cir. 1984).

the Air Force policy suggested "callous indifference" to Goldman's religious faith and ran counter to the American tradition of accommodating spiritual needs.[126]

Action by the D.C. Circuit caught the attention of Congress. Congressman Stephen Solarz offered an amendment to the defense authorization bill in 1984, proposing that members of the armed forces may wear unobtrusive religious headgear, including a yarmulke, if religious observances or practices required the wearing of headgear. His amendment permitted the military to prohibit the headgear if it interfered with the performance of military duties.[127] Although Congressman William Dickinson warned that "we are flying in the face of a court decision just made," the Solarz amendment passed.[128] House and Senate conferees eliminated the amendment but required the Pentagon to report on changes in service regulations that would promote the free expression of religion to the greatest extent possible consistent with the requirements of military discipline.[129] The Pentagon study advised that courts would most likely defer to military judgments about the wearing of yarmulkes.[130]

Goldman's case now went to the Supreme Court. A brief submitted by Solicitor General Charles Fried supported the Defense Department by arguing that Goldman's position would force the military to choose between "virtual abandonment of its uniform regulations and constitutionally impermissible line drawing."[131] According to Fried, the entire purpose of uniform standards "would be defeated if individuals were allowed exemptions" and "make a mockery of the military's compelling interest in uniformity."[132] His argument was overdrawn. Military service regulations already allowed for "neat and conservative" religious apparel, including the wearing of crosses, the Star of David, and various rings, items of jewelry, and bracelets.[133]

Oral argument in 1986 was not too helpful. Some Justices seemed uncomfortable about second-guessing military regulations. Justice White asked Goldman's attorney if his client could satisfy his religious beliefs by wearing a toupee. The attorney conceded that a toupee would suffice, but his client wasn't bald. Moreover, it would "look somewhat strange" for someone with a full head of

126. Id. at 660.

127. 130 Cong. Rec. 14295 (1984).

128. Id. at 14298.

129. H. Rept. No. 98-1080, 98th Cong., 2d Sess. 293–94 (1984); 98 Stat. 2532–33, sec. 554 (1984).

130. Joint Service Study on Religious Matters 21, 25 (March 1985).

131. Brief for the Respondents, Goldman v. Weinberger, No. 84-1097, U.S. Supreme Court, October Term, 1985, at 19.

132. Id. at 49–50.

133. Id. at 3–4.

hair to wear a toupee. White countered: "It doesn't in the courtrooms in London where they are required to wear a wig."[134] Kathryn Oberly of the Justice Department advised the Justices to leave the dispute to the elected branches: "If Congress thinks that further accom[m]odation is either required or desirable it can legislate it."[135]

By the vote of 5 to 4, the Court held that the First Amendment did not prohibit the Air Force regulation. It accepted the Air Force judgment that the outfitting of military personnel in standardized uniforms "encourages the subordination of personal preferences and identities in favor of the overall group mission."[136] The Court placed substantial weight on the values of uniformity, hierarchy, unity, discipline, and obedience to ensure military effectiveness. In a concurrence, Justices Stevens, White, and Powell warned that if the military departed from a single standard by accommodating Goldman, it would be faced with other religious claims, including the wearing of a turban by a Sikh, a saffron robe by a Satchidananda Ashram-Integral Yogi, and dreadlocks by a Rastafarian.[137]

In a dissent, Brennan (joined by Marshall) offered contradictory arguments regarding the branch of government that has the primary duty to protect individual rights. On the one hand, he objected that the majority's decision represented an abdication of the Court's role "as principal expositor of the Constitution and protector of individual liberties in favor of credulous deference to unsupported assertions of military necessity."[138] At the same time, he acknowledged that other branches also have a duty to protect religious freedom: "Guardianship of this precious liberty is not the exclusive domain of federal courts. It is the responsibility as well of the States and of the other branches of the Federal Government."[139] He urged Congress to fix the Court's mistake: "The Court and the military have refused these servicemen their constitutional rights; we must hope that Congress will correct this wrong."[140]

Given its previous consideration of the Solarz amendment, Congress was primed to deliver a quick legislative answer to the Court. There was never any question that Congress possessed authority to trump the Court. The Constitution provides that Congress shall "make rules for the Government and Regulation of the land and naval Forces."[141] Within two weeks of the Court's decision,

---

134. Oral argument, Goldman v. Weinberger, U.S. Supreme Court, January 14, 1986, at 21–24.
135. Id. at 45.
136. Goldman v. Weinberger, 475 U.S. 503, 508 (1986).
137. Id. at 512–13.
138. Id. at 514.
139. Id. at 523.
140. Id. at 524.
141. U.S. Const., art. I, sec. 8, cl. 14.

legislation was introduced to permit members of the armed forces to wear items of apparel not part of the official uniform. Members of the military could wear any "neat, conservative, and unobtrusive" item of apparel to satisfy the tenets of a religious belief. The Secretary of the military service could prohibit the wearing of the item after determining that it "significantly interferes with the performance of the member's military duties."[142] The phrase "neat and conservative" was lifted from military service regulations. The bill passed the House in 1986 but was held up in the Senate. The next year, reflecting some switches by some Senators and the results of the 1986 elections, the bill passed the Senate 55 to 42. Lobbying against the provision was fierce in both chambers, including opposition from the American Legion, the Military Coalition, Secretary of Defense Caspar Weinberger, and the Joint Chiefs of Staff, but the bill became law.[143]

A Minority Within a Minority

This book offers many illustrations of how Congress, voting by majority, has protected the interests of a minority. At times it even defends the interest of a minority within a minority. As part of the "termination" policy in the 1950s, federal supervision over Klamath Indian property came to an end. Adult members of the tribe were asked to make a choice: hold their land interests in common under Oregon law, or convert the interests into cash. In 1958, approximately 77 percent of the tribal members voted to sell a portion of their property. Edison Chiloquin, a tribal member, disagreed with their decision. He wanted to retain his interests in the land. After the vote, 631,000 acres of Indian property were sold to a private corporation (91,000 acres), the Department of the Interior (15,000), and the Department of Agriculture (525,000).[144] The federal government used the land to create the Winema National Forest.

A second vote occurred in 1969, selling the remaining portion of the Klamath Indian property. Congress passed legislation in 1973 directing the Secretary of Agriculture to acquire 135,000 acres to be added to the Winema National Forest. Each Indian beneficiary received $270,000 from this land transfer. Chiloquin, who had helped create the Committee to Save the Remaining Klamath

142. 132 Cong. Rec. 6655 (1986) (Senator Alfonse D'Amato); id. at 7042, 7211 (Senator Frank Lautenberg).

143. 101 Stat. 1086–87, sec. 508 (1987). For examples of opposition by lobbyists and some lawmakers, see Fisher, Religious Liberty in America, at 120–21.

144. Background on the Edison Chiloquin bill comes from H. Rept. No. 1406, 96th Cong., 2d Sess. (1980); Garrett Epps, To an Unknown God: Religious Freedom on Trial 49–52 (2001); and Theodore Stern, The Klamath Tribe: A People and Their Reservation 249–52 (1965).

Indian Lands, refused the money and insisted that land be set aside to establish a village founded on traditional values and the preservation of Indian culture, ways, and spiritual beliefs. As a sign of his determination, he built a tipi in the forest, became a squatter, and kept a sacred council fire lit. He was now outside the law and had no possible protection in the courts.

Members of Congress supported a private bill on his behalf. As explained by Senator Mark Hatfield, Chiloquin became a squatter "because of his deep conviction that the Indian tribe had no right to divest itself of these ancestral lands." The bill would permit him to live "on this land in this native habitat and to continue the culture and the heritage of the proud Klamath Indian tribe." The purpose of the legislation was to avoid "confrontation and all other kinds of unpleasantries of trying to expel this man from the lands that are his ancestral home."[145] The bill specified that the property set aside for Chiloquin "shall not be inconsistent with its cultural, historical, and archeological character." The size of his property would approximately equal the money he declined ($270,000). If he or his heirs attempted to use the land for other than "traditional Indian purposes," it would revert to the United States to protect archeological, cultural, and traditional values associated with the property.[146]

Religious Use of Peyote

In 1984, Oregon denied unemployment benefits to an American Indian and a white man because they had ingested peyote during a religious ceremony. Their conduct violated an agreement to abstain from drugs while working as drug counselors for an agency. Peyote grows in small buttons at the top of a spineless cactus and has hallucinogenic properties. After the Supreme Court in 1990 sustained the denial of benefits, both Oregon and Congress passed legislation authorizing the use of peyote as part of a religious ceremony. Congress also enacted a law in 1993 to restore religious freedom to its doctrinal position before the 1990 decision. The Court struck down that legislation as unconstitutional because it was in conflict with the 1990 ruling. The Court insisted that its word on the meaning of the Constitution was final. These confrontations reveal both the strength and weakness of congressional efforts to protect religious liberty.

Alfred Smith, a Klamath Indian, served as a counselor for alcoholics since 1971. The agency he worked for required counselors to abstain from alcohol and mind-altering drugs and warned him that he could be fired for using pey-

145. 126 Cong. Rec. 30379 (1980).
146. 94 Stat. 3613 (1980).

ote, even as part of a religious ceremony. During a weekend service conducted by the Native American Church (NAC), he ingested peyote. He lost both his job and unemployment benefits.[147] The Supreme Court of Oregon held that the agency's action violated the Free Exercise Clause, relying on the standard announced by the U.S. Supreme Court in *Sherbert v. Verner* (1963): the state must show that a restraint on religious activity is the "least restrictive" means of achieving a "compelling" state interest.[148] Smith's case became joined with litigation involving Galen Black, a non-Indian who had been fired and denied unemployment benefits for ingesting peyote during a religious ceremony conducted by the NAC.

In 1988, the U.S. Supreme Court vacated the Oregon ruling and asked the Oregon Supreme Court this question: was the religious use of peyote legal in that state? If Smith and Black had been fired for engaging in criminal conduct, the U.S. Supreme Court suggested that *Sherbert* might not apply.[149] The Oregon Supreme Court looked at a range of judicial and nonjudicial sources, including congressional judgments and statutes, to conclude that federal drug laws contained an exemption for the religious use of peyote.[150] Dave Frohnmayer, Attorney General of Oregon, who had taken the case to the U.S. Supreme Court, now objected that the Oregon Supreme Court should not have relied on congressional interpretations of the Constitution: "The Oregon Supreme Court's holding is not a product of the court's independent assessment of what the first amendment requires. At most, it represents a choice to defer to congressional assumptions about the requirements of the federal constitution. . . . This process of canvassing congressional understanding to resolve an important first amendment question would be troubling under any circumstance."[151]

The U.S. Supreme Court agreed to take the case a second time. By that point, some conditions had changed to question whether the dispute was still a live controversy. As part of a federal consent decree, Smith's agency agreed that the religious use of peyote by NAC members would no longer be considered work-related misconduct. Under this change in policy, Smith and Black would not be denied unemployment benefits, and in fact both won back pay.[152] Although

147. Smith v. Employment Div., 721 P.2d 445–46 (Ore. 1986).
148. Id. at 446–49; Sherbert v. Verner, 374 U.S. 398 (1963).
149. Employment Div. v. Smith, 485 U.S. 660, 671 (1988).
150. Smith v. Employment Division, 763 P.2d 146, 149 (Ore. 1988); 21 C.F.R. §1307.31.
151. Petition for Writ of Certiorari to the Supreme Court of the State of Oregon, Employment Division v. Smith; 196 Landmark Briefs 425.
152. Brief in Opposition to Petition for Writ of Certiorari Employment Division v. Smith; 196 Landmark Briefs 2; Garrett Epps, "To an Unknown God: The Hidden History of Employment Division v. Smith," 30 Ariz. St. L. J. 953, 989 (1998).

Smith and Black had exhausted the unemployment benefits they received as a result of the first decision by the Oregon Supreme Court, under state law they could not be forced to repay the money even if the U.S. Supreme Court in a second decision reversed the state court.

The U.S. Supreme Court decided to resolve the dispute by eliminating the *Sherbert* standard and devising a new one. In a 6-to-3 decision, Justice Scalia ruled that state law may prohibit the possession and use of drugs even if it incidentally prohibits a religious practice, provided that the law is neutral and generally applicable to all individuals.[153] The state no longer needed to show a compelling interest or that its policy was the least restrictive means. The possibility of abandoning *Sherbert* was not before the Court. It had not been briefed or argued. For some reason Scalia decided to cite *Gobitis,* the 1940 flag-salute decision that had been bitterly attacked and survived only three years before being reversed.[154] He acknowledged that his new test would put religious minorities at the mercy of the political process, but such discriminatory treatment was an "unavoidable consequence of democratic government."[155] He could have added that discriminatory treatment can also be the consequence of judicial rulings, with remedies supplied by democratic institutions.

In addition to dissents from Justices Blackmun, Brennan, and Marshall, a concurrence by O'Connor sharply disagreed with Scalia. She objected that his ruling "dramatically departs from well-settled First Amendment jurisprudence, appears unnecessary to resolve the question presented, and is incompatible with our Nation's fundamental commitment to individual religious liberty."[156] She faulted Scalia for giving a "strained reading of the First Amendment" and presenting a "parade of horribles."[157] Why did she express those views in a concurrence rather than a dissent?

The fact that the Court accepted the Oregon case under these circumstances and announced a retreat from *Sherbert*—without any informed participation by the litigants—created an immediate protest. A broad coalition of religious groups asked that the case be reheard because Scalia's new standard would require a "massive reordering of the delicate relationship between individuals and religious organizations and the power of the state." Moreover, the new standard put pressure on states to enact legislation that might affect such religious

153. Employment Division v. Smith, 494 U.S. 872 (1990).
154. Id. at 879.
155. Id. at 890.
156. Id. at 891.
157. Id. at 892, 902. See Carolyn N. Long, Religious Freedom and Indian Rights: The Case of *Oregon v. Smith* (2000).

practices as the Jewish and Muslim ritual slaughter of animals, circumcision, and the use of communion wine by Christians.[158] The Court denied the motion for a rehearing.[159]

Congress Responds

There was now a broad gap between the Court's notion of religious liberty and the positions of religious organizations. Interest groups put pressure on Congress to reverse the Court. The result was the Religious Freedom Restoration Act (RFRA), drafted to reinstate the *Sherbert* standard. This was a tactical mistake. Congress could have devised legislative language to protect religious liberty to a greater degree than the Court. The legislative branch can always expand rights and liberties. It was a political miscalculation to take a standard that the Court had discarded and shove it down its throat. It was not difficult to predict how the Justices would respond.

While members of Congress and interest groups moved this bill along, the Oregon legislature enacted legislation to protect the sacramental use of peyote by the NAC. Al Smith, appearing in support of the bill, testified that the "drug we have to worry about is alcohol."[160] The Oregon statute provided that in any prosecution involving the manufacture, possession, or delivery of peyote, it would be an affirmative defense that the peyote is used in connection with the good-faith practice of a religious belief and is not dangerous to the health of the user or others nearby.[161]

During hearings by the House Judiciary Committee in 1992, Congressman Henry Hyde stated that Congress had no authority to enact RFRA: "Congress is constitutionally unable to restore a prior interpretation of the first amendment once the Supreme Court has rejected that interpretation. We are a legislature, not the Court."[162] In part he was correct. It was a mistake to try to restore the precise standard the Court had rejected. But throughout its history Congress has often disagreed with and countermanded the Court on constitutional issues. The

---

158. "High Court Urged to Reconsider," Washington Post, May 12, 1990, at C11. See "Hail Mary Pass," Legal Times, May 14, 1990, at 11.

159. Employment Division v. Smith, 496 U.S. 913 (1990).

160. "Panel Listens to Peyote Testimony," Salem, Oregon, Statesman Journal, April 6, 1991, at D1.

161. Oregon Laws, ch. 329, sec. 1 (June 24, 1991), reprinted in 1995 Oregon Revised Statutes 475.992, sec. 5 (vol. 9, p. 80).

162. "Religious Freedom Restoration Act of 1991," hearings before the House Committee on the Judiciary, 102d Cong., 2d Sess. 7 (1992).

Court may have authority to set a floor of constitutional rights below which Congress may not go. Nothing prevents Congress from establishing rights above the judicial floor. Hyde's position on the division between the branches was too rigid. He might equally have said: "The Court is a judicial body, not a legislature."

At the hearing, Nadine Strossen of the ACLU urged Congress to act: "The Supreme Court has cast us back into the good graces of this legislature, and it does depend on you, our elected representatives, to restore to all of us the religious freedom that should be protected by the Constitution but that the U.S. Supreme Court has refused to protect that way. Please restore our religious liberty through legislation."[163] Congress had every right and authority to do that, and indeed would legislate, as Oregon did in authorizing the religious use of peyote. But Congress should have developed independent legislative language rather than copy the *Sherbert* standard. Taking that route created a needless (and losing) confrontation with the Court.

In 1993, voting 35 to 0, the House Judiciary Committee reported a bill to create a "statutory right" to require the compelling governmental interest test whenever the free exercise of religion is burdened by a law of general applicability.[164] The committee picked up elements of *Sherbert* and Scalia's *Smith* decision. The bill did not require all states to permit the ceremonial use of peyote; it merely subjected any governmental restriction to the compelling interest standard.[165] The bill passed the House under suspension of the rules, which requires a two-thirds majority.[166] The Senate Judiciary Committee, voting 15 to 1, reported the bill for floor consideration.[167] As the bill headed for final passage, it had the support of 68 religious and civil liberties groups.[168] The bill cleared the Senate, 97 to 3.[169] Acting under a motion of unanimous consent, the House passed the Senate version.[170] The Religious Freedom Restoration Act provided that governments may substantially burden a person's religious exercise only if they demonstrate a compelling interest and use the least restrictive means of furthering that interest (*Sherbert*). The term "government" applied to any branch, department, agency, instrumentality, or official at the federal, state, and local levels.[171]

163. Id. at 64–65.
164. H. Rept. No. 103-88, 103d Cong., 1st Sess. 1–2 (1993).
165. Id. at 7.
166. 139 Cong. Rec. 9680–87 (1993).
167. S. Rept. No. 103-11, 103d Cong., 1st Sess. (1993).
168. "Disparate Groups Unite Behind Civil Rights Bill on Religious Freedom," Washington Post, October 16, 1993, at A7.
169. 139 Cong. Rec. 26416.
170. Id. at 27239–41.
171. 107 Stat. 1488 (1993).

In addition to this effort, Congress passed legislation in 1994 to permit the use of peyote by Native Americans during religious ceremonies.[172] In support of the bill, officials from the Drug Enforcement Agency (DEA) testified that the religious use of peyote by Indians had nothing to do with the vast and violent traffic in illegal narcotics that had swept the United States. The agency was unaware that peyote was diverted to any illicit market.[173] The trial record in lower courts showed that peyote is not a habit-forming substance.[174] There was evidence that Indians who took peyote as part of a religious ceremony were able to break their dependence on the drug that inflicted the greatest damage: alcohol.

In 1995, a district court found RFRA to be unconstitutional, arguing that in previous cases the Supreme Court had declared itself to be the ultimate interpreter of the Constitution. Therefore Congress could not enact legislation contrary to *Smith*.[175] That decision was overturned by the Fifth Circuit, which said that the duty of courts to say what the law is does not make that duty exclusive.[176] The executive and legislative branches "also have both the right and duty to interpret the Constitution."[177] It provided examples, such as in the area of voting rights, where Congress had protected constitutional rights to a greater degree than the Supreme Court.[178] Other lower courts also upheld the constitutionality of RFRA.[179]

Regardless of what happened next, the Supreme Court would inevitably acknowledge the crucial role of nonjudicial bodies in protecting religious liberty. If it upheld the statute it would recognize that religious groups, acting in concert with Congress, could define religious liberty more generously than the judiciary. If the Court invalidated RFRA, it would merely affirm a central proposition in *Smith* that the political process was superior to judgments by the courts: "It may fairly be said that leaving accommodation to the political process will place at a relative disadvantage those religious practices that are not widely engaged in; but that unavoidable consequence of democratic government must be preferred to a system in which each conscience is a law unto itself or in which judges weigh the social importance of all laws against the centrality of all religious beliefs."[180]

---

172. 108 Stat. 3125 (1994).
173. H. Rept. No. 103-675, 103d Cong., 2d Sess. 4 (1994).
174. State v. Whittingham, 504 P.2d 950, 953 (Ariz. 1972).
175. Flores v. City of Boerne, 877 F.Supp. 355, 357 (W.D. Tex. 1995).
176. Flores v. City of Boerne, Tex., 73 F.3d 1352, 1363 (5th Cir. 1996).
177. Id. at 1356.
178. Id. at 1363.
179. See the discussion in Fisher, Religious Liberty in America, at 194–95.
180. Employment Division v. Smith, 494 U.S. 872, 890 (1990).

A Lecture on Judicial Finality

In 1997, the Supreme Court held that Congress exceeded the scope of its enforcement power under Section 5 of the Fourteenth Amendment when it enacted RFRA.[181] To that extent it was a federalism case, with the Court deciding to protect the interests of the states against federal encroachment. Politically and institutionally, the Court announced a second theme: when it decides to dispose of a standard like *Sherbert* and create a new one, Congress should not attempt to revive the discarded rule. Congress had invited a black eye and got one.[182] But the reasoning and premises of the Court's decision are superficial, unpersuasive, and internally contradictory.

First, the Court announced that "under our Constitution, the Federal Government is one of enumerated powers."[183] Obviously that is false. There is no enumerated power of judicial review. Where did the Court locate the authority to hold a congressional statute void? It is an *implied*, not an enumerated, power. Second, in deciding that Congress exceeded its power under the Fourteenth Amendment, the Court said that Section 5 is limited to "enforcement" and "remedial" actions.[184] It further charged: "Legislation which alters the meaning of the Free Exercise Clause cannot be said to be enforcing the Clause. Congress does not enforce a constitutional right by changing what the right is." But RFRA did not "alter" the meaning of the Free Exercise Clause any more than is regularly done by judicial rulings that change standards, as the Court did when it decided to switch from *Sherbert* to *Smith*.

Third, the Court acknowledged, at it had to, that the "line between measures that remedy or prevent unconstitutional actions and measures that make a substantive change in the governing law is not easy to discern."[185] It is not only difficult for lawmakers and the public to discern, it is difficult for the Court to explain. Nothing in its decision added any clarity. Although "Congress must have wide latitude in determining where it lies, the distinction exists and must be observed."[186] How does Congress observe a line that is not only indistinct but apparently not capable of judicial explanation? Judicial vagueness continued when the Court advised that in future congressional action there "must be a congruence and proportionality between the injury to be prevented or reme-

181. Boerne v. Flores, 521 U.S. 507 (1997).
182. Neal Devins, "How Not to Challenge the Court," 39 Wm. & Mary L. Rev. 645 (1998).
183. 521 U.S. at 516.
184. Id. at 519.
185. Id.
186. Id. at 520.

died and the means adopted to that end."[187] Whatever that means, was the Court inviting Congress to redraft RFRA to make it more "congruent" and "proportional"? How would lawmakers go about that task? The Court added: "The appropriateness of remedial measures must be considered in light of the evil presented."[188] That guideline is too general and abstract for lawmakers to apply. If the Court's role is to "say what the law is," judicial speech must be intelligible and comprehensible.

In other passages, the Court suggested that constitutional defects in RFRA might be cured with additional congressional efforts: "RFRA is so out of proportion to a supposed remedial or preventive object that it cannot be understood as responsive to, or designed to prevent, unconstitutional behavior."[189] Also, the "sweeping coverage" of RFRA "ensures its intrusion at every level of government, displacing laws and prohibiting official actions of almost every description and regardless of subject matter."[190] *Smith* was similarly "sweeping" and "invasive." The Court's language was far too nebulous to provide helpful guidance.

Fourth, the Court stated: "The power to interpret the Constitution in a case or controversy remains in the Judiciary."[191] No one denies that. The Constitution expressly gives the Court the authority to decide what is a case or controversy, and of course it interprets the Constitution. Neither point makes the Court the exclusive or final interpreter of the Constitution. Citing language from *Marbury v. Madison,* the Court warned about the risk to constitutional government when Congress acts in the manner of RFRA: "If Congress could define its own powers by altering the Fourteenth Amendment's meaning, no longer would the Constitution be 'superior paramount law, unchangeable by ordinary means.' It would be 'on a level with ordinary legislative acts, and, like other acts, . . . alterable when the legislature shall please to alter it.'"[192]

History offers many examples of the Court using "ordinary means" to change and weaken constitutional government. In a related warning by the Court: "Shifting legislative majorities could change the Constitution and effectively circumvent the difficult and detailed amendment process contained in Article V."[193] The same result flows from Court decisions that reflect shifting judicial majorities. Legal scholar Michael McConnell offered this critique of the Court's

187. Id.
188. Id. at 530.
189. Id. at 532.
190. Id.
191. Id. at 524.
192. Id. at 529.
193. Id.

reasoning: "'Shifting legislative majorities' have no greater and no less capacity than shifting *judicial* majorities to 'circumvent' the amendment process of Article V."[194] As an illustration, two days before the Court invalidated RFRA it overruled its decision from 1985 that had limited federal assistance to parochial schools.[195]

The Court concluded with a clumsy assertion of judicial finality: "Our national experience teaches that the Constitution is preserved best when each part of the Government respects both the Constitution and the proper actions and determinations of the other branches. When the Court has interpreted the Constitution, it has acted within the province of the Judicial Branch, which embraces the duty to say what the law is."[196] Nothing in more than two centuries of constitutional practice and construction offers support for that mechanical and cramped formulation. Congress also has a duty to say what the law is.

Two questions remained. One concerned the application of RFRA not to the states but to the federal government. Several appellate courts held that the statute is a legitimate congressional action under Article I with respect to federal law.[197] The second development was legislation called "Son of RFRA," a bill that Congress passed in response to the Court's ruling. This time it acted not under the Fourteenth Amendment but under the commerce and spending powers. The bill, which became law in 2000, extends religious protections to land-use disputes and to the right of prisoners in state-run institutions to practice their faith.[198] There have been no effective legal challenges to this legislation.

On January 29, 1998, in response the Court's invalidation of RFRA, the House Judiciary Committee held a hearing on "Congress, the Court, and the Constitution." To my knowledge, this was the first time in the last four decades that Congress held general hearings on its duties to independently interpret the Constitution. I was among several individuals invited to testify on basic questions, such as: Is the legislative branch coequal with the judiciary in the task of interpreting the Constitution, or must it defer to the Court? Does *Marbury* mean that the Court is final and binding on other branches?[199] Hearings like this need to be held on a regular basis.

---

194. Michael W. McConnell, "Institutions and Interpretation: A Critique of City of Boerne v. Flores," 111 Harv. L. Rev. 153, 174 (1997) (emphasis in original).

195. Agostini v. Felton, 521 U.S. 203 (1997), reversing Aguilar v. Felton, 473 U.S. 402 (1985).

196. Boerne v. Flores, 521 U.S. at 535–36.

197. Kikumura v. Hurley, 242 F.3d 950 (10th Cir. 2001); In re Young, 141 F.3d 854 (8th Cir. 1998), cert. denied, sub nom. Christians, Trustee v. Crystal Evangelical Free Church, 525 U.S. 811 (1988).

198. 114 Stat. 803 (2000); see Fisher, Religious Liberty in America, at 200–01.

199. My testimony is available at http://www.loufisher.org/docs/ci/459.pdf.

The Court continues to provide vague direction on many constitutional issues, leaving final resolution to other parties. Certainly that is the case with religious liberty. Two current examples underscore this point. In 2009, a "unanimous" Court opinion on a Ten Commandments case managed to fracture into four separate concurring opinions, offering substantially different views on the Establishment Clause. A public park in Pleasant Grove City in Utah included a monument with the Ten Commandments. A religion called Summum (formed in 1975) insisted that its monument listing seven aphorisms of ethical principles be placed in the park. The Court held that the Ten Commandments monument was a form of "government speech" and not subject to scrutiny under the Free Speech Clause.[200]

Delivering the opinion for the Court, Justice Alito wrote: "The Free Speech Clause restricts government regulation of private speech; it does not regulate government speech." But he added: "This does not mean that there are no restraints on government speech." Whatever those restraints, for Alito they did not apply in this case. Stevens, joined by Ginsburg, concurred but found the "recently minted government speech doctrine" to be "of doubtful merit." Scalia, joined by Thomas, wrote a concurrence. Breyer and Souter wrote separate concurrences. The latter expressed "qualms" about the position that public monuments are "government speech categorically." The Court cannot possibly provide "judicial finality" when it writes in this manner.

Additional confusion came from a religious liberty case in 2010. In 1934, members of the Veterans of Foreign Wars (VFW) placed a six-foot cross on federal land in the Mojave National Preserve in California to honor American soldiers who died in World War I. In January 2002, Congress designated the cross a national memorial and authorized $10,000 to install a memorial plaque on it.[201] Six months later a district court held that plaintiffs objecting to the placement of a religious symbol on federal property had standing to sue and that the cross violated the Establishment Clause because it represented governmental endorsement of religion.[202] Congress responded in September 2003 with a land swap: transferring the property and the cross to a private party (the VFW) in exchange for privately owned land given to the preserve.[203]

After various appeals, the dispute reached the Supreme Court, which issued a 5-to-4 decision in 2010 reversing the lower court holdings that had enjoined the government from implementing the land-transfer statute. The case was

200. Pleasant Grove City v. Summum, 555 U.S. ___ (2009).
201. 115 Stat. 2278, sec. 8137 (2002).
202. Buono v. Norton, 212 F.Supp. 2d 1202 (C.D. Cal. 2002).
203. 117 Stat. 1100, sec. 8121 (2003).

remanded to the Ninth Circuit for further proceedings.[204] The Court's guidance in this case was confused because of multiple opinions. The decision was a plurality ruling (Kennedy wrote for the Court, joined by Roberts and Alito). Roberts added a short concurrence. Alito prepared a longer concurrence. Scalia and Thomas, representing the fourth and fifth votes for the majority, concurred only in the judgment, not the reasoning. A dissent by Stevens was joined by Ginsburg and Sotomayor. Breyer wrote a separate dissent. The lower courts now have to decide from this disjointed ruling if the congressional remedy is constitutional. If the Court wants to "say what the law is," it has a duty to speak with greater clarity.

Because of the public's broad involvement in basic constitutional questions of religious liberty, it is misguided on both political and legal grounds to look automatically (and optimistically) to the courts for the protection of minority rights. Vindication of religious values is just as likely to be found in legislative chambers as in courtrooms. Statutory rights gained from Congress and state legislatures, after interest groups and religious organizations intervene and add their support and understanding, can be as constitutionally sound as a judicial ruling. Courts have handed down a number of decisions supportive of religious minorities.[205] Other decisions have injured the cause of religious liberty. The larger lesson is that courts are only one participant in the complex national dialogue over religion and the Constitution.

204. Salazar v. Buono, 559 U.S. ___ (2010).
205. E.g., Largent v. Texas, 318 U.S. 418 (1943); Murdock v. Pennsylvania, 319 U.S. 105 (1943); Fowler v. Rhode Island, 345 U.S. 67 (1953); Wisconsin v. Yoder, 406 U.S. 205 (1972); Widmar v. Vincent, 454 U.S. 263 (1981); Lamb's Chapel v. Center Moriches School Dist., 508 U.S. 384 (1993); Rosenberger v. University of Virginia, 515 U.S. 819 (1995); Fisher, Religious Liberty in America, at 227–30.

7

INVESTIGATION AND OVERSIGHT

To protect constitutional government, Congress must closely oversee the executive branch. It can fulfill that duty by functioning as a coequal branch: holding hearings, writing reports, issuing subpoenas, invoking its contempt power, and relying on a mix of statutory and nonstatutory controls. Constitutional confrontations with the President emerged in the early years and have never stopped. In the late 1920s, the executive branch and Congress developed a "legislative veto" to permit broad delegations of congressional power to the President, subject to the check of a one-house or two-house veto. Legislative vetoes are not submitted to the President for his signature or veto. In *INS v. Chadha* (1983), the Supreme Court struck down the legislative veto as unconstitutional. Its ruling could not possibly be the final word. This method of congressional control survives, operating at the committee and subcommittee levels, because the two elected branches decided that an accommodation they fashioned long ago continues to satisfy their mutual needs.

Access to Documents

Not until 1927 did the Supreme Court recognize that Congress "cannot legislate wisely or effectively in the absence of information respecting the conditions which the legislation is intended to affect or change."[1] Lawmakers did not have to wait for more than a century to learn from the Court that they have an implied power to investigate and obtain information. Lawmakers understood that basic principle in the First Congress. Chapter 1 described the effort by Congress in 1790 to investigate a requested annuity for Baron von Steuben. Two other experiences from that period are well-known. One is properly understood: a House inquiry in 1792 into the military defeat of General St. Clair. The other is widely misunderstood: a House request in 1796 for documents related to the Jay Treaty.

On March 27, 1792, the House appointed a committee to investigate the military losses suffered by troops under Major General Arthur St. Clair to Indian tribes. Out of 1,400 U.S. soldiers, 657 were killed and another 271 wounded.[2]

---

1. McGrain v. Daugherty, 273 U.S. 135, 175 (1927).
2. George C. Chalou, "St. Clair's Defeat, 1792," in Congress Investigates, 1792–1974, at 7 (Arthur M. Schlesinger Jr. and Roger Bruns, ed., 1975).

The House authorized the committee "to call for such persons, papers, and records, as may be necessary to assist their inquiries."[3] Some lawmakers believed the matter should be left to the executive branch, but that proposal was rejected 21 to 35. The House supported its own independent inquiry, 44 to 10.[4] President Washington convened his Cabinet to decide how to respond to the House request for papers. According to notes taken by Secretary of State Thomas Jefferson, it was agreed

> first, that the House was an inquest, and therefore might institute inquiries. Second, that it might call for papers generally. Third, that the Executive ought to communicate such papers as the public good would permit, and ought to refuse those, the disclosure of which would injure the public: consequently were to exercise a discretion. Fourth, that neither the committee nor House had a right to call on the Head of Department, who and whose papers were under the President alone; but that the committee should instruct their chairman to move the House to address the President.[5]

After stating these principles, the Cabinet agreed that "there was not a paper which might not be properly produced."[6] President Washington directed Secretary of War Henry Knox to "lay before the House of Representatives such papers from your Department, as are requested by the enclosed Resolution."[7] He also asked Knox to make himself available to the House: "I should hope an opportunity would thereby be afforded you, of explaining your conduct, in a manner satisfactory to the public and yourself."[8] The House examined and evaluated papers furnished by the executive branch and listened to explanations from witnesses, including executive officials.[9]

Jefferson's notes raise several issues. First, they articulated the principle of executive privilege. The President could refuse papers "the disclosure of which would injure the public." The words here are important. Injury must be to *the public*, not to the President or the executive branch. The Cabinet did not suggest that the executive branch could withhold documents simply because they might prove embarrassing or had the potential for revealing improper or illegal

3. 3 Annals of Cong. 493 (March 27, 1792).
4. Id. at 493.
5. 1 The Writings of Thomas Jefferson 304 (Bergh ed., 1903).
6. Id. at 305.
7. 32 The Writings of George Washington 15 (Fitzpatrick ed., 1939).
8. Id. at 16.
9. 3 Annals of Cong. 1106–13 and Appendix, at 1052–59, 1310–17.

activities. Second, the Cabinet believed the House had no right to call upon the head of a department for papers that belonged to the President; those requests must be submitted to the President.

That abstract formality survived for a few years. In 1813, President Madison objected to a Senate resolution that authorized a committee to meet with him on the nomination of a minister to Sweden. He believed the Constitution permitted only two options: the Senate could request information directly from the President, or it could authorize a committee to meet with a department head. The appointment of a committee "to confer immediately with the Executive himself appears to lose sight of the coordinate relation between the Executive and the Senate which the Constitution has established, and which ought therefore to be maintained."[10] Informal contacts are now routinely practiced. Madison's successors regularly meet with congressional committees and individual lawmakers.

The Jay Treaty

The House request for papers concerning the Jay Treaty is generally misinterpreted. From many accounts, it appears that the House asked for documents and was rebuffed by President Washington for two principal reasons: (1) treaties require secrecy in foreign negotiations, and (2) the Senate is the exclusive legislative participant in treaty making. Both reasons are part of a cover story the administration found politically convenient, not constitutionally compelled. Washington's explanation does not bear up under scrutiny and marks possibly the only time that he made a public statement that was trite and disingenuous.

The treaty was highly controversial. Chief Justice John Jay negotiated the agreement with England. If the treaty were litigated, it might come before Jay in his judicial capacity.[11] Moreover, it was widely known that Jay decided to depart from his instructions and accepted substantial restrictions on American commerce.[12] Members of the House knew they had every right to protect their constitutional duties over commerce and the funding power. The treaty had cleared the Senate by the bare minimum two-thirds majority, 20 to 10, with lawmakers voting along party lines. Alexander Hamilton advised President Washington not to release the treaty instructions to the House, warning that the

10. 2 Richardson 516 (July 6, 1813).
11. Ralston Hayden, The Senate and Treaties, 1789–1817, at 69–70 (1920).
12. Abraham D. Sofaer, War, Foreign Affairs, and Constitutional Power: The Origins 85 (1976).

instructions were "in general a crude mass" and would do "no credit to the administration."[13]

Under these tense political conditions, the House requested Washington to release the treaty instructions, including correspondence and other related documents. The House extended some flexibility to Washington: "Excepting such of said papers as any negotiation may render improper to be disclosed."[14] That language applied to pending negotiations, not previous negotiations. Representative Edward Livingston identified the key constitutional power of the House on treaty matters: the House possessed "a discretionary power of carrying the Treaty into effect, or refusing it their sanction."[15] Basically, the President and the Senate could agree to any treaty they liked, but if the treaty depended on congressional authorization and appropriations, the House retained an independent judgment. It could vote as it liked. The House was excluded only from "self-executing" treaties—treaties that do not depend on any subsequent congressional action.

The House passed Livingston's resolution by a vote of 62 to 37.[16] Even before this face-off with President Washington, members of the House had already gained access to many of the treaty documents. One lawmaker explained that Livingston, as chairman of the House Committee on American Seamen, "together with the whole committee, had been allowed access to these papers, and had inspected them. The same privilege, he doubted not, would be given to any member of the House who would request it."[17] The legislation developed by the committee concerned the relief and protection of American seamen who had been forced into naval service by Great Britain.[18] One House member observed that with respect to papers on the Jay Treaty, "he did not think there were any secrets in them. He believed he had seen them all."[19] Another House member explained that his colleagues could have walked over to the office of the Secretary of the Senate to see the treaty papers, but why, he asked, "depend upon the courtesy of the Clerk for information which might as well be obtained in a more direct channel?"[20] Madison tried to weaken Livingston's resolution by permitting the President to withhold papers that, "in his judgment, it may not

13. Hayden, The Senate and Treaties, at 90.
14. Annals of Cong., 4th Cong., 1st Sess., at 400–01, 426.
15. Id. at 427–28.
16. Id. at 759.
17. Id. at 461 (remarks by Rep. Harper).
18. Id. at 802–20.
19. Id. at 642 (remarks of Rep. Williams).
20. Id. at 588 (remarks of Rep. Freeman).

be consistent with the interest of the United States, at this time, to disclose." Madison's amendment failed on a vote of 37 to 47.[21]

Washington offered several reasons for denying the House access to Jay Treaty documents. He referred to the need for caution and secrecy in foreign negotiations and the exclusive role of the Senate to participate as a member of the legislative branch in treaty matters.[22] Clearly he did not invoke executive privilege to block congressional access. He acknowledged that "all the papers affecting the negotiation with Great Britain were laid before the Senate, when the Treaty itself was communicated for their consideration and advice."[23]

His arguments for denying the House access to the documents were misleading. Members of the House did not need Washington to remind them that the Constitution excludes the House from treaty making. The text of the Constitution made that obvious. House members were not asking to be part of treaty making. The Jay Treaty had been negotiated and approved by the Senate. It was now time to consider legislation to authorize and fund its provisions. As part of that decision, the House was an equal partner with the Senate. The House had a right to gain access to documents needed for an informed judgment. Washington seemed to understand that point. A letter from Hamilton to Washington suggests that Washington initially agreed to give the House access to the treaty papers. Hamilton reasoned:

> The course you suggest has some obvious advantages & merits careful consideration. I am not however without fears that there are things in the *instructions* to Mr. Jay which good policy, considering the matter *externally* as well as *internally*, would render it inexpedient to communicate. This I shall ascertain to day [*sic*]. A middle course is under consideration— that of not communicating the papers to the house but of declaring that the Secretary of State is directed to permit them to be *read* by the *members individually*.[24]

Instead of Washington giving the papers to the House, the documents would be held by the Secretary of State, requiring House members to travel to his office to read the papers in the presence of an executive official. Few lawmakers would be happy with that arrangement. The editor of Hamilton's papers observed that

21. Id. at 438.
22. Id. at 759.
23. Id. at 761.
24. Letter from Hamilton to Washington, March 24, 1795, in 20 The Papers of Alexander Hamilton 81–82 (Syrett ed., 1974) (emphasis in original).

Washington "apparently suggested that he planned to comply with the request in Livingston's resolution."[25] Hamilton later urged Washington to deny the House access to the treaty papers, fearing that the documents "cannot fail to start [a] new and unpleasant Game—it will be fatal to the Negotiating Power of the Government if it is to be a matter of course for a call of either House of Congress to bring forth all the communication however confidential."[26] Hamilton would have blocked access not only to the House but the Senate as well. For reasons explained later, regarding the Algerine treaty of 1793, Hamilton's argument was poorly grounded.

Shortly after Washington advised the House that it would have no access to the Jay Treaty papers, Representative Thomas Blount introduced two resolutions, each adopted by the vote of 57 to 35, restating the principles of Livingston's resolution:

[W]hen a Treaty stipulates regulations on any of the subjects submitted to the Constitution to the power of Congress, it must depend, for its execution, as to such stipulations, on a law or laws to be passed by Congress. And it is the Constitutional right and duty of the House of Representatives, in all such cases, to deliberate on the expediency or inexpediency of carrying such Treaty into effect, and to determine and act thereon, as, in their judgment, may be most conducive to the public good.[27]

Washington needed $90,000 from Congress to implement the Jay Treaty.[28] The House could use this leverage to gain access to the treaty documents by refusing to support funding until it had the information it needed. After a lengthy debate, the appropriation passed the House by the narrow vote of 51 to 48.[29] An earlier test vote was even closer. The House divided 49 to 49, with the Speaker willing to break the tie to support funding.[30] The appropriation became law.[31] Had the House held firm on its institutional needs, Washington would have faced a difficult choice: share whatever documents were necessary to attract the extra votes, or have the treaty fail of implementation.

25. Id. at 66 (editor's introductory note to letter from Hamilton to Washington, March 7, 1796).
26. Id. at 68 (letter from Hamilton to Washington, March 7, 1796).
27. Annals of Cong., 4th Cong., 1st Sess. 771 (1796). For the votes, see id. at 782–83. See remarks by Madison on these resolutions, id. at 773, stating that it belonged to the House, not to the President, to decide what information it needed to vote in an informed manner.
28. Id. at 991.
29. Id. at 1291.
30. Id. at 1280.
31. 1 Stat. 459 (1796).

Washington's constitutional argument about the need to exclude the House in treaty matters was especially shallow, given his earlier experience with the Algerine treaty of 1793. He inherited the offensive practice from the Continental Congress of having to pay bribes ("tributes") to four countries in North Africa—Morocco, Algiers, Tunis, and Tripoli—to permit American merchant vessels to operate safely in those waters.[32] Those countries had imprisoned a number of American seamen, requiring appropriations from Congress for their release. In 1792, the issue was whether Washington should make a treaty with the Algerines by relying only on the Senate, or recognize that the House had to vote on the necessary funds. Washington thought about taking out a loan, but the loan would have to be repaid, again requiring action by both houses of Congress.

Secretary of State Thomas Jefferson did not think abstractly about treaty making being solely the prerogative of the President and the Senate. He understood that the House of Representatives was an essential partner in questions of funding. Jefferson posed a very practical question. Just as Senators "expect to be consulted beforehand" about a pending treaty, if Representatives need to fund a treaty, "why should not they expect to be consulted in like manner, when the case admits?"[33] Washington agreed to seek support from each house for the Algerine treaty.

Some Senators objected to opening the door to any House participation in treaty matters. If the House had to vote, "it would not be a secret."[34] For his part, Washington "had no confidence in the secrecy of the Senate" and decided against the option of borrowing money.[35] In a message to Congress on December 16, 1793, he forwarded to both the Senate and the House documents regarding a treaty with Morocco for paying ransom and for establishing peace with Algiers. He asked the lawmakers to protect the confidentiality of certain letters.[36] Whatever information he sent the Senate he shared with the House. In secret session, the House debated the treaty and supported the funding.[37] The treaty included an annual amount to be paid to the ruler of Algiers.[38]

32. Gerhard Casper, Separating Power: Essays on the Founding Period 45–50 (1997).
33. "The Anas," 1 Writings of Thomas Jefferson 294 (Bergh ed., 1903).
34. Id. at 306.
35. Id.
36. 4 Annals of Cong. 20–21 (1793).
37. Id. at 150–55; 8 Stat. 133 (1795); see Casper, Separating Power, at 51–65.
38. 8 Stat. 136 (art. XXII); see Fisher, the Politics of Executive Privilege, at 30–33.

Exploiting Legislative Leverage

When lawmakers are denied access to executive branch documents and executive officials refuse to testify before legislative committees, members of Congress have many powerful tools to compel an administration to cooperate.[39] Both sides can cite various constitutional principles to justify their actions, but the resolution is more likely to depend on how determined Congress is in obtaining what it needs. As pointed out by constitutional scholar Morton Rosenberg, legislative success depends on "how badly Congress wants to protect its institutional interests, and how skilled and determined the committees are in utilizing the powers, rules, and tools available to them."[40] The executive branch will want to stretch out the confrontation, hoping that the legislative branch will lose interest in the press of other business. Congress needs to play its cards effectively. When lawmakers fail to obtain executive branch information needed for congressional deliberation, the loss spreads outward. It weakens public control, democratic principles, and constitutional government.

A tangible example of legislative leverage is from 1986. President Reagan refused to give the Senate Judiciary Committee certain documents that his nominee for Chief Justice, William Rehnquist, had written while heading the Office of Legal Counsel (OLC) from 1969 to 1971. Each side presented reasonable arguments. The committee wanted the documents to enable it to determine Rehnquist's qualifications. The executive branch insisted that it was necessary to protect the confidentiality and candor of sharing legal advice with Presidents and their aides.[41] Although OLC memos are often made public, at times they are not. Rehnquist agreed to have his memos released to the committee, but the White House refused.[42]

Whatever the legal and constitutional merits of this confrontation, the political leverage favored Congress. If the administration decided to withhold the memos, the Senate Judiciary Committee could simply refuse to hold a hearing. Not only would there be no vote on Rehnquist, but there would also be no action on Antonin Scalia to be Associate Justice. The Senate had scheduled a

---

39. Louis Fisher, "Congressional Access to Information: Legislative Will and Leverage," 52 Duke L. J. 323 (2002).

40. Morton Rosenberg, When Congress Comes Calling: A Primer on the Principles, Practices, and Pragmatics of Legislative Inquiry 3 (2009).

41. Al Kamen and Ruth Marcus, "Reagan Uses Executive Privilege to Keep Rehnquist Memos Secret," Washington Post, August 1, 1986, at A1.

42. Id.

vote on both nominations on August 14.[43] In an op-ed article for the *Los Angeles Times,* Senator Ted Kennedy issued a blunt warning: "Rehnquist: No Documents, No Senate Confirmation."[44] The committee developed bipartisan support for its subpoena: eight Democrats and two Republicans.

The administration faced a choice. It could stick to its original constitutional position and sacrifice Rehnquist, or it could strike a deal. It chose the latter. President Reagan agreed to give the committee access to some of Rehnquist's OLC memos. Instead of the original request for all memos on such broad topics as "civil rights" and "civil liberties," the list narrowed to about 25 to 30 documents.[45] Six Senators and six staff members were allowed to read the memos.[46] The committee later requested and received additional Rehnquist documents from his service in the Justice Department.[47] The Senate confirmed Rehnquist and Scalia on September 17. Similar document fights occur with other judicial nominations.[48] If an accommodation cannot be worked out, judicial or other nominees may decide to withdraw their name, as Miguel Estrada did in 2003.[49]

An informal practice allows any Senator to place a hold on a bill or nomination, not necessarily because of opposition to the bill or nomination but because the Senator is tired of waiting for documents from the executive branch. In 1989, two committee chairmen, Donald Riegle and Alan Cranston, advised the White House that they would not schedule nomination hearings on the agencies within their jurisdiction until the administration turned over FBI reports on the nominees to the majority and minority staff directors. The agencies included the Department of Housing and Urban Development, the Council of Economic Advisers, the Securities and Exchange Commission, and the Department of Veterans Affairs. Faced with this threat, White House Counsel C. Boyden Gray agreed to release the FBI reports to the committee chairmen and ranking minority members.[50]

43. George Lardner Jr. and Al Kamen, "Senators to Push for Rehnquist Memos," Washington Post, August 5, 1986, at A4.
44. Edward M. Kennedy, "Rehnquist: No Documents, No Senate Confirmation," Los Angeles Times, August 5, 1986, Part II, at 5.
45. Al Kamen and Howard Kurtz, "Rehnquist Told in 1974 of Restriction in Deed," Washington Post, August 6, 1986, at A1.
46. Howard Kurtz and Al Kamen, "Rehnquist Not in Danger over Papers," Washington Post, August 7, 1986, at A1, A14.
47. "Senators Are Given More Rehnquist Data," Washington Post, August 8, 1986, at A3.
48. Fisher, The Politics of Executive Privilege, at 76–81.
49. Id. at 79–81.
50. Ann Devroy, "White House, Senators Feud on FBI Data," Washington Post, May 19, 1989, at A1. For other uses of Senate holds to gain access to executive branch information, see Fisher, The Politics of Executive Privilege, at 85–86.

As part of the congressional power of inquiry, both houses of Congress authorize their committees and subcommittees to issue subpoenas to require the production of documents and the attendance of witnesses from executive agencies and the private sector. A committee subpoena identifies the date, time, and place of a hearing a witness must attend, and the particular kind of documents sought. The Supreme Court recognizes that issuance of a committee subpoena pursuant to an authorized investigation is "an indispensable ingredient of lawmaking."[51] The committee need not have in mind a particular bill or legislative measure. The Court explained: "The very nature of the investigative function—like any research—is that it takes the searchers up some 'blind alleys' and into nonproductive enterprises. To be a valid legislative inquiry there need be no predictable end result."[52]

Of course there are limits to legislative investigations. Congressional inquiries may not interfere with the independence of decision makers in particular adjudicatory proceedings before a department or agency.[53] Even so, Congress may use its oversight powers to monitor the general adjudicatory process.[54] It is rare for an executive official to wholly sidestep a congressional subpoena. They will appear, even if it requires that they invoke the constitutional right against self-incrimination.[55] In 1981, Attorney General William French Smith suggested that administration compliance would be more likely when Congress issued a subpoena to seek information for legislative purposes and less likely when the subpoena is part of a "legislative oversight inquiry."[56] There is no merit to that distinction. Congress has as much constitutional authority to oversee the execution of laws as it does to pass them. As a practical matter, Congress could easily obliterate the distinction by introducing a bill to justify every oversight effort. Subpoenas are often effective in producing both documents and witnesses.[57]

If a witness refuses to testify or produce papers in response to a committee subpoena and the committee votes to report a resolution of contempt to the floor, either the House or Senate may vote to support the contempt citation. The legislative power of contempt is not expressly stated in the Constitution

51. Eastland v. United States Servicemen's Fund, 421 U.S. 491, 505 (1975).

52. Id. at 509.

53. Pillsbury Co. v. FTC, 354 F.2d 952, 963 (5th Cir. 1966).

54. ATX, Inc. v. U.S. Department of Transportation, 41 F.3d 1522 (D.C. Cir. 1994); State of California v. FERC, 966 F.2d 1541 (9th Cir. 1992); Power Authority of the State of New York v. FERC, 743 F.2d 93 (2d Cir. 1984); Peter Kiewit Sons' Co. v. U.S. Army Corps of Engineers, 714 F.2d 163 (D.C. Cir. 1983).

55. HUD Secretary Samuel Pierce took that option in 1989; Fisher, The Politics of Executive Privilege, at 93.

56. 5 Op. O.L.C. 27, 29–30 (1981).

57. Fisher, The Politics of Executive Privilege, at 95–109.

but exists as an implied power to further congressional objectives. In 1821, the Supreme Court stated that a legislative branch lacking that power would be "exposed to every indignity and interruption that rudeness, caprice, or even conspiracy, may mediate against it."[58] If either house votes for a contempt citation, the President of the Senate or the Speaker of the House shall certify the facts to the appropriate U.S. attorney, "whose duty it shall be to bring the matter before the grand jury for its action."[59] Individuals who refuse to testify or produce requested papers are subject to criminal contempt, leading to fines of not more than $100,000 and imprisonment up to one year.[60]

This statutory policy was challenged by the Reagan administration in 1982 after the House voted to hold in contempt EPA Administrator Anne Gorsuch for failing to turn over certain documents needed for congressional investigation. Fifty-five Republicans joined 204 Democrats to produce a top-heavy majority of 259 to 105, supporting contempt. The Speaker certified the facts and referred them to the U.S. attorney for presentation to a grand jury. Instead of moving toward prosecution, the Justice Department asked a district court to declare the House action an unconstitutional intrusion into the President's authority to withhold information from Congress.[61] The court dismissed the government's suit on the ground that judicial intervention in executive–legislative disputes "should be delayed until all possibilities for settlement have been exhausted."[62] The Justice Department did not appeal this ruling. The administration agreed to release "enforcement sensitive" documents to the House Public Works Committee, starting with briefings, then redacted copies, followed by unredacted documents, which could be examined by committee members and up to two committee staff persons.[63]

A subcommittee of the House Energy and Commerce Committee rejected this offer. It insisted that it receive the sensitive documents and read them in executive session, reserving for itself the right to release documents and use them in public session. As to staff access, the chairman and ranking minority member

58. Anderson v. Dunn, 6 Wheat. (19 U.S.) 204, 228 (1821).

59. 2 U.S.C. §194 (2006).

60. Id. at §192.

61. Dale Russakoff, "Prosecution of Gorsuch Ruled Out," Washington Post, December 12, 1982, at A1.

62. United States v. U.S. House of Representatives, 556 F.Supp. 150, 152 (D.D.C. 1983).

63. "Memorandum of Understanding Between the Committee on Public Works and Transportation and the Department of Justice Concerning Documents Subpoenaed from Environmental Protection Agency," February 18, 1983; H. Rept. No. 323, 98th Cong., 1st Sess. 18–20 (1983).

would decide that issue. The legislative position prevailed.[64] As part of this investigation, the House voted 413 to 0 to hold Rita M. Lavelle, an EPA official, in contempt for defying a committee subpoena to testify. She was sentenced to six months in prison, five years' probation, and a fine of $10,000 for lying to Congress about her management of the Superfund program.[65]

A second challenge to the contempt power developed during the administration of George W. Bush. In 2008, the House Judiciary Committee voted to hold two officials in contempt: White House Counsel Harriet Miers for refusing to testify, and White House Chief of Staff Joshua Bolten for withholding specified documents. After the House held each in contempt, the Justice Department once again decided not to comply with the statutory requirement to prosecute each individual. The House filed a suit in district court to require the administration to comply with the statute. The court held that Miers was required to appear to testify before the committee and that the administration had no valid excuse for Bolten refusing to produce nonprivileged documents.[66] However, the D.C. Circuit decided to leave the dispute to the incoming administration of President Barack Obama.[67] Apart from those two incidents, the legislative contempt power has been an effective instrument in forcing Cabinet officers and other high officials to testify and surrender documents to Congress.[68]

Congressional Autonomy

To protect its institutional powers, Congress may find it necessary to engage in a direct confrontation with the judiciary. In 1970, the House Committee on Internal Security prepared a report entitled "Limited Survey of Honoraria Given Guest Speakers for Engagements at Colleges and Universities." By including the names of leftist and antiwar speakers and the amounts they received, the committee hoped that university alumni would object to this use of college funds and threaten to withhold future contributions. The report placed the speakers

64. "EPA Document Agreement," CQ Weekly Report, March 26, 1983, at 635.
65. Fisher, The Politics of Executive Privilege, at 129.
66. "Reining in the Imperial Presidency: Lessons and Recommendations Relating to the Presidency of George W. Bush," House Committee on the Judiciary Majority Staff, Final Report to Chairman John Conyers Jr., March 2009, at 40–41.
67. For details on this dispute, see Mark J. Rozell, Executive Privilege: Presidential Power, Secrecy, and Accountability 169–79 (3d ed., 2010).
68. Fisher, The Politics of Executive Privilege, at 111–34.

under such organizations as the Black Panther Party, Communist Party of the United States of America, Socialist Workers Party, and Students for a Democratic Society (SDS). The ACLU managed to obtain a copy of the galleys of the committee report and asked a federal judge to issue an injunction prohibiting its publication.

District Judge Gerhard Gesell did precisely that, ordering that the report not be printed. The committee had ordered 6,000 copies.[69] To Gesell, the case "unquestionably presents an immediate issue of free speech and assembly."[70] The committee defended the report in part under the Speech or Debate Clause: "The Senators and Representatives . . . for any Speech or Debate in either House . . . shall not be questioned in any other Place."[71] Gesell agreed he could not interfere with lawmakers speaking about the report on the floor of Congress, but he decided he had authority to enjoin the Public Printer and the Superintendent of Documents from printing the report or even any "facsimile" of it. Gesell reasoned that "[n]othing in the Constitution or the cases suggests, however, that a committee report is a necessary adjunct to speech or debate in Congress."[72] As an alternative, Gesell suggested that Congress could print the report in the *Congressional Record* if it wanted to.[73]

Did the committee or Congress wait for relief from a higher court? No. Gesell issued his decision on October 28, 1970. Less than two months later, on December 14, the House brought the constitutional issue to the floor to debate legislative privileges. Members explained that it is not the rule or practice of the House to print the full text of committee reports in the *Congressional Record*.[74] To that extent, Gesell's order ran into problems not just with the Speech or Debate Clause but with Article I, Section 5, Clause 2, which authorizes each House to "determine the Rules of its Proceedings."[75] It was pursuant to that authority that the House promulgated Rule XI, creating the standing committees and requiring them to report to the House on the subject areas committed to it.[76] Moreover, House Rule XIII required the reference and printing of committee reports. Representative Richard Ichord, who led the debate, said that Judge Gesell's order restraining the printing of the House report "was acting clearly in excess of his powers and jurisdiction," constituted "a material obstruc-

69. Hentoff v. Ichord, 318 F.Supp. 1175, 1177 (D.D.C. 1970).
70. Id. at 1178.
71. U.S. Const., art. I, sec. 6, cl. 1.
72. Hentoff v. Ichord, 318 F.Supp. at 1180.
73. Id. at 1179, 1180, 1182, 1183.
74. 116 Cong. Rec. 41358 (1970) (statement by Rep. Ichord).
75. Id.
76. Id. at 41359.

tion of the constitutional duties of the House," and marked "a breach of the privileges" of the House.[77]

For those who preferred to let the case be appealed to the D.C. Circuit on the assumption that it would reverse the Gesell order, Ichord replied: "[T]he quality or content of the report was not an issue cognizable by the court. The court had no business entering into an examination of its contents."[78] If the House intended to assert its constitutional duty, "we are under an obligation to resist this encroachment immediately and in clear and unmistakable terms."[79] The House debated a resolution that directed everyone, including the courts, to get out of the way of the printing of the report: "All persons, whether or not acting under color of office, are hereby advised, ordered, and enjoined to refrain from doing any act, or causing any Act to be done, which restrains, delays, interferes with, obstructs, or prevents the performance of the work ordered to be done."[80]

Representative Don Edwards objected that the House resolution would interfere with the capacity of courts to interpret the Constitution: "This case then presents a question of law requiring an interpretation of the Constitution—a task which our system of government has placed on the courts."[81] The resolution ordering the printing of the committee report, he said, was a "lawless disregard of a court injunction."[82] Edwards was correct that courts interpret the Constitution, but so does Congress, especially when its institutional privileges are at stake. He attracted few colleagues to his effort to table the resolution, which passed on a vote of 302 to 54.[83] The House report was printed that very day.[84]

Testimony by White House Officials

Department and agency officials are accustomed to appearing before congressional committees to testify and produce documents. Over the years, administrations have claimed that this obligation does not apply to White House aides, who are said to be exempt from such requirements. White House Counsels have

77. Id.
78. Id. at 41362.
79. Id. at 41363.
80. Id. at 41368.
81. Id. at 41370.
82. Id.
83. Id. at 41373–74.
84. H. Rept. No. 91-1732, 91st Cong., 2d Sess. (1970).

advised lawmakers that "it is a longstanding principle, rooted in the Constitutional separation of powers and the authority vested in the President by Article II of the Constitution, that White House officials generally do not testify before Congress, except in extraordinary circumstances not present here."[85] The giveaway phrases here are "generally" and "except in extraordinary circumstances." The record is clear that White House aides do testify, and in large numbers.

On March 2, 1973, President Nixon refused to let White House Counsel John Dean testify at Senate hearings. Leaning primarily on separation of power grounds, he argued that the advice he received from Dean could not be interfered with by Congress: "[T]he manner in which the President personally exercises his assigned powers is not subject to questioning by another branch of Government. If the President is not subject to such questioning, it is equally appropriate that members of his staff not be so questioned, for their roles are in effect an extension of the Presidency."[86] Dean, he later explained, had "a double privilege, the lawyer–client relationship, as well as the Presidential privilege."[87]

As political pressures intensified, Nixon agreed to let Dean testify under certain conditions. White House aides could testify before the Senate Select Committee, chaired by Senator Sam Ervin, under four ground rules: initially they would appear "in executive session, if appropriate"; executive privilege "is expressly reserved and may be asserted during the course of the questioning as to any question"; the proceedings could be televised; and White House staff would appear "voluntarily" (that is, not in response to a committee subpoena) and testify under oath and "answer fully all proper questions."[88]

Under those conditions, not only did Dean appear, but so did many other White House aides: chief domestic adviser John Ehrlichman, White House aide H. R. Haldeman, consultant Patrick Buchanan, deputy assistant Alexander Butterfield, staff coordinator General Alexander M. Haig Jr., Nixon's personal attorney Herbert W. Kalmbach, special assistant Jeb Magruder, Nixon's personal secretary Rose Mary Woods, and others.[89] Butterfield told committee staff about the existence of listening and recording devices in the Oval Office.

Some of those tapes ended up with District Judge John Sirica, revealing unquestionable evidence of obstruction of justice, such as Nixon's remark at a

85. Letter from White House Counsel Jack Quinn to Rep. William H. Zeliff Jr., Chairman, Subcommittee on National Security, International Affairs, and Criminal Justice, May 8, 1996.

86. Public Papers of the Presidents, 1973, at 185.

87. Id. at 203.

88. Id. at 298–99.

89. Fisher, The Politics of Executive Privilege, at 200. See also Louis Fisher, "White House Aides Testifying Before Congress," 27 Pres. Stud. Q. 139 (1997).

March 22, 1973, meeting: "And, uh, for that reason, I am perfectly willing to— I don't give a shit what happens. I want you to stonewall it, let them plead the Fifth Amendment, cover-up or anything else, if it'll save the plan."[90] "Saving the plan" meant keeping Nixon in office. Release of the tapes, Nixon recognized, made impeachment "virtually a foregone conclusion."[91] He announced his resignation on August 8, 1974, effective the next day.

During this period, the Senate Judiciary Committee asked White House aide Peter Flanigan to testify about an antitrust action involving the International Telephone and Telegraph Corp. (ITT). The White House refused, citing constitutional principles and "long-established historical precedents."[92] When it became clear that the Senate would take no action on the nomination of Richard Kleindienst as Attorney General unless Flanigan testified, the White House aide appeared.[93] In 1975, the House Select Committee on Intelligence took testimony from several White House aides, former and current: Henry Kissinger, McGeorge Bundy, Arthur Schlesinger, and William G. Hyland. In that same year a Senate committee received testimony from a number of former White House aides, including Clark Clifford, Morton Halperin, and Ted Sorensen.[94]

In 1980, a special Senate subcommittee investigated whether Billy Carter, the President's brother, had committed criminal activities in his dealings with Libya. President Carter instructed all members of the White House staff to cooperate fully with the subcommittee. White House Counsel Lloyd Cutler and National Security Adviser Zbigniew Brzezinski appeared to testify.[95] The Iran-Contra crisis in 1986 put President Reagan at risk of impeachment. He announced that he had "already taken the unprecedented step of permitting two of my former national security advisers [Robert McFarland and John Poindexter] to testify before a committee of Congress."[96] Other former White House aides testified, including Bretton G. Sciaroni, Lieutenant Colonel Oliver North, and North's secretary, Fawn Hall. To demonstrate his willingness to support the congressional investigation, Reagan took the extraordinary step of waiving executive privilege in its entirety. Current and former White House aides could share

90. John J. Sirica, To Set the Record Straight 162 (1979).
91. Public Papers of the Presidents, 1974, at 622.
92. "Sen. Ervin Hints Filibuster on Kleindienst After Panel Rejects Calling of Nixon Aide," Wall Street Journal, April 13, 1972, at 4.
93. Fisher, The Politics of Executive Privilege, at 71–73.
94. Id. at 200–01.
95. "Inquiry into the Matter of Billy Carter and Libya" (vol. II), hearings before the Subcommittee to Investigate the Activities of Individuals Representing the Interests of Foreign Governments, Senate Committee on the Judiciary, 96th Cong., 2d Sess. (1980).
96. Public Papers of the Presidents, 1986, II, at 1595.

with the Iran-Contra Committee in public hearings their conversations and communications with Reagan.[97]

The power of the purse remains a hefty tool to compel White House aides to testify. In 1981, Martin Anderson, President Reagan's assistant for policy development, refused to appear before a House Appropriations subcommittee to defend his budget request of $2,959,000 for the Office of Policy Development. The subcommittee, noting that previous heads of the office had appeared, responded by deleting all of the funds.[98] White House Counsel Fred F. Fielding defended Anderson's decision, pointing out that Anderson was part of a deliberative process that required "frank and candid advice" in an atmosphere that preserved confidentiality.[99] That argument is unpersuasive. Cabinet heads are part of a deliberative process that requires candor and confidentiality, but they appear regularly before congressional committees. If a question at a hearing threatens the value of confidentiality, a Cabinet head may say so. Anderson could have done that. Eventually he met informally with the committee. Congress reduced his budget to $2,500,000.[100]

In the Clinton years, many White House aides testified on various matters. A hearing in 1994 concerned whether they had inappropriately learned about an investigation by the Resolution Trust Corporation (RTC) into the failed Madison Guaranty Savings and Loan.[101] Congressional hearings in 1995 and 1996 explored the firings in 1993 of seven employees of the White House Travel Office, the handling of documents after the death of White House aide Vincent Foster, and access by White House aides to confidential FBI files regarding individuals who had worked in the Reagan and Bush administrations. Current and former White House aides appeared to testify.[102] Clinton's use of the pardon power to grant clemency to Puerto Rican terrorists and a pardon to Marc Rich brought additional White House aides before congressional committees from 1999 to 2001.[103]

On March 25, 2004, White House Counsel Alberto Gonzales wrote to the 9/11 Commission, which Congress had created by statute. He explained why National Security Adviser Condoleezza Rice could not testify in public. Acknowl-

97. Lawrence B. Walsh, Firewall: The Iran-Contra Conspiracy and Cover-up (1997); William S. Cohen and George J. Mitchell, Men of Zeal: A Candid Inside Story of the Iran-Contra Hearings 45–50 (1988).

98. H. Rept. No. 97-171, 97th Cong., 1st Sess. 30 (1981).

99. Id. at 62.

100. Budget of U.S. Government: Appendix, Fiscal Year 1983, at I-C5.

101. Fisher, The Politics of Executive Privilege, at 204.

102. Id. at 203–08.

103. Id. at 211–20.

edging that some national security advisers had testified earlier before Congress, he noted that the appearances were either in closed sessions or involved a matter connected with potentially improper or illegal conduct. He could find no example of a "sitting National Security Advisor appearing publicly before a legislative body outside the context of potential improper or illegal conduct."[104] Gonzales referred to "the principles underlying the Constitutional separation of powers" to support his position. In order for President George W. Bush and his successors to receive candid advice from White House staff on counterterrorism and national security issues, "it is important that their advisers not be compelled to testify publicly before congressional bodies such as the Commission."

Speaking with reporters, White House spokesman Scott McClellan insisted that Rice could not appear in public before the commission because "it's a matter of principle. It's a matter of separation of powers." When Rice appeared on *60 Minutes* on March 28, she told Ed Bradley that "I'm not going to say anything in private that I wouldn't say in public. I'm legally bound to tell the truth, I'm morally bound to tell the truth." Her statement removed any principled objection to public testimony of any kind. A reporter called to ask for my views. I predicted the administration would reverse itself within a matter of days. On March 30, the administration decided to fold. Gonzales wrote to the commission to say that President Bush agreed to let Rice testify before the commission in public and under oath. The accommodation reflected not rigid principles of separation of powers but, as Gonzales put it, "a matter of comity."[105] It was also a matter of the administration exercising better judgment.

Agency Whistleblowers

Members of Congress should not rely solely on information from agency heads. Lawmakers need access to employees within the agency who are aware of inefficiencies, misconduct, and illegality that agency heads either do not know about or prefer to keep from congressional and public view. Several Presidents took steps to block agency information from Congress. In 1902, a "gag order" from President Theodore Roosevelt prohibited agency employees from seeking to influence legislation "individually or through associations" except through the heads of the departments. Failure to abide by the presidential order could result

104. Quotations for the Condoleezza Rice story come from Louis Fisher, "Talking About Secrets," Legal Times, April 19, 2004, at 66–67, available at http://www.loufisher.org/docs/ep/472.pdf.
105. Id.

in dismissal from government service.[106] Seven years later, President William Howard Taft issued another gag order, forbidding any bureau chief or subordinate in the executive branch to communicate with either house of Congress, any committee of Congress, or any member of Congress, with regard to legislation, appropriation, or congressional action of any kind, "except with the consent and knowledge of the head of the department; nor shall any such person respond to any request for information from either House of Congress, or any committee of either House of Congress, or any Member of Congress, except through, or as authorized by, the head of the department."[107]

Congress responded to the Roosevelt and Taft gag orders by adding language to an appropriations bill in 1912. During debate, lawmakers objected to hearing "only one side of a case" (the views of Cabinet officials and agency heads). Members of Congress refused to place the welfare of their constituents "in the hands and at the mercy of the whims of any single individual, whether he is a Cabinet officer or anyone else."[108] Lawmakers insisted on access to the rank and file, especially agency employees who had complaints about the conduct of their supervisors.[109] The purpose of the new legislative language was to ensure that government employees could exercise their constitutional rights to free speech, peaceable assembly, and to petition the government for redress of grievances.[110]

Lawmakers resented the gag orders because it prevented Congress "from learning the actual conditions that surrounded the employees of the service."[111] Relying solely on agency heads was unacceptable. If those officers "desire to withhold information and suppress the truth or to conceal their official acts it is within their power to do so."[112] One member of the House remarked: "The vast army of Government employees have signed no agreement upon entering the service of the Government to give up the boasted liberty of the American citizens."[113] That attitude is reflected during Senate debate on the amendment: "Mr. President, it will not do for Congress to permit the executive branch of this Government to deny to it the sources of information which ought to be free and open to it, and such an order as this, it seems to me, belongs in some other country than the United States."[114]

---

106. The 1902 order is reprinted at 48 Cong. Rec. 4513 (1912).
107. Id.
108. Id. at 4657 (statement of Rep. Reilly).
109. Id.
110. Id. at 5201 (statement of Rep. Prouty).
111. Id. at 5235 (statement of Rep. Buchanan).
112. Id. at 5634 (statement of Rep. Lloyd).
113. Id. at 5637 (statement of Rep. Wilson).
114. Id. at 10674 (statement of Senator Reed).

The language used to nullify the gag orders is known as the Lloyd-LaFollette Act, adopted as Section 6 of the Postal Service Appropriations Act of 1912.[115] It was carried forward and supplemented by the Civil Service Reform Act of 1978 and codified as permanent law.[116] The conference report explains the importance of agency employees disclosing information to Congress and the need for procedural safeguards to protect employees from reprisal or retaliation by supervisors.[117] The Whistleblower Protection Act of 1989 stated that disclosures by federal employees "serve the public interest by assisting in the elimination of fraud, waste, abuse and unnecessary Government expenditures." Protecting employees who disclose government "illegality, waste, and corruption is a major step toward a more effective civil service."[118] In signing the bill, President Bush praised the whistleblower as "a public servant of the highest order.... [T]hese dedicated men and women should not be fired or rebuked or suffer financially for their honesty and good judgment."[119]

In fact, whistleblowers are routinely fired, rebuked, and suffer financially for disclosing problems within their agencies. The agencies that are supposed to protect employees from retaliation (the Office of Special Counsel, the Merit Systems Protection Board, and the Federal Circuit) have rarely provided that protection. At House hearings in 1985, the presiding officer concluded: "There is no dispute—whistleblowers have no protection. We urge them to come forward, we hail them as the salvation of our budget trauma, and we promise them their place in heaven. But we let them be eaten alive."[120] The Whistleblower Protection Act (WPA) of 1989 and amendments to it in 1994 did little to protect agency employees who disclosed agency abuse. A House committee in 1994 noted: "The WPA has created new reprisal victims at a far greater pace than it is protecting them."[121]

Statutes encouraging whistleblowing did not cover the intelligence community, consisting of the CIA, NSA, and other intelligence agencies. This omission reflected what I considered to be a misconception about congressional access to executive branch information. It was widely agreed that legislative access to domestic agency information was necessary but access to national security was not. I wrote frequently against that distinction and testified before a House

115. 37 Stat. 555, sec. 6 (1912).
116. 5 U.S.C. §7211 (2006).
117. S. Rept. No. 95-1272, 95th Cong., 2d Sess. 132 (1978).
118. 103 Stat. 16, sec. 2(a) (1989).
119. Public Papers of the President, 1989, I, at 391.
120. Comments by Rep. Pat Schroeder, "Whistleblower Protection," hearings before the House Committee on Post Office and Civil Service, 99th Cong., 1st Sess. 237 (1985).
121. H. Rept. No. 103-769, 103d Cong., 2d Sess. 12 (1994).

committee in 1987 that both branches share in national security policy: "It is not true that under the Constitution national security or military policy or diplomacy is given only to the President as his prerogative." Congress, I said, "has explicit powers under the Constitution" to decide and implement national security policy.[122]

In 1998, the Senate Intelligence Committee asked me to evaluate an OLC memo that claimed for the President ultimate and unimpeded authority over the collection, retention, and dissemination of national security information. On that premise, OLC concluded that a pending bill granting limited whistle-blower rights to intelligence community employees was unconstitutional.[123] After completing a memo that rebutted OLC's analysis, I was asked to testify before the committee, which I did with Peter Raven-Hansen of the George Washington University law school. Our critiques of the OLC memo were similar.[124] The committee asked me to return a week later to testify again, this time sitting next to an attorney from OLC.[125] We shared our conflicting views with the committee. Two hours after the hearing I received a call from a committee staffer, saying that the committee agreed to report the "unconstitutional" bill for floor action. The committee vote was unanimous: 19 to 0.[126] The bill passed the Senate, 93 to 1.[127]

The House Intelligence Committee, taking a somewhat different approach with the bill, also rejected the administration's claim that the President exercised exclusive control over national security information. I testified before the House committee and helped draft the bill language.[128] In reporting the bill, the committee dismissed the existence of plenary presidential authority over national security information, describing national security as "a constitutional responsibility shared by the executive and legislative branches that proceeds according

122. Louis Fisher, testimony at "Computer Security Act of 1987," hearings before a subcommittee of the House Committee on Government Operations, 100th Cong., 1st Sess. 439 (1987). See also Louis Fisher, "Congressional Access to National Security Information," 45 Harv. J. on Legis. 219 (2008), available at http://www.loufisher.org/docs/ep/469.pdf.

123. Memo from Christopher H. Schroeder, Office of Legal Counsel, U.S. Department of Justice, to Michael J. O'Neil, General Counsel of the Central Intelligence Agency, November 26, 1996.

124. "Disclosure of Classified Information to Congress," hearings before the Senate Select Committee on Intelligence, 105th Cong., 2d Sess. 5–37 (1998).

125. Id. at 39–61 (Randolph D. Moss, Office of Legal Counsel).

126. S. Rept. No. 105-165, 105th Cong, 2d Sess. 2 (1998).

127. 144 Cong. Rec. 2871 (1998).

128. "Record of Proceedings on H.R. 3819, The Intelligence Community Whistleblower Protection Act," hearings before the House Permanent Select Committee on Intelligence, 106th Cong., 1st Sess. 32–53 (1998).

to the principles and practices of comity."[129] Congress enacted legislation with this language: "[N]ational security is a shared responsibility, requiring joint efforts and mutual respect by Congress and the President." The statute further provided that Congress, "as a co-equal branch of Government, is empowered by the Constitution to serve as a check on the executive branch; in that capacity, it has a 'need to know' of allegations of wrongdoing by the executive branch, including allegations of wrongdoing in the Intelligence Community."[130] The effectiveness of this statute depends on committee assertiveness, but it was important in law to establish and articulate those general principles.

From 2008 to 2010, Congress developed legislation to strengthen whistle-blower rights within the intelligence community. I testified before the House Committee on Oversight and Government Reform on May 14, 2009, and submitted several reports to the committee. One report rejected the Justice Department's claim that presidential plenary authority over national security information began in the administration of George Washington.[131] The second analyzed how lower courts had interpreted the Supreme Court's national security case of *Department of Navy v. Egan* (1988). It explained that dicta in the Court's decision implied some kind of plenary presidential power but the core holding was that Congress could intervene with statutory language to narrow the President's authority.[132] The House passed a strengthened whistleblower bill, but it was held up in the Senate until December 2010, when it failed to pass.[133]

Legislative Vetoes

Soon after arriving at the Library of Congress in September 1970, I began to work closely with the appropriations committees. They basically adopted me, opening their files and explaining how they monitored and controlled agency expendi-

129. H. Rept. No. 105-747, Part 1, 105th Cong., 2d Sess. 15 (1998).

130. 112 Stat. 2413, sec. 701(b) (1998). See H. Rept. No. 105-780, 105th Cong., 2d Sess. 19 (1998), and Thomas Newcomb, "In from the Cold: The Intelligence Community Whistleblower Protection Act," 53 Adm. L. Rev. 1235 (2001).

131. Louis Fisher, "Congressional Access to National Security Information: Precedents from the Washington Administration," Law Library of Congress, May 22, 2009, available at http://www.loufisher.org/docs/ep/467.pdf.

132. Louis Fisher, "Judicial Interpretations of *Egan*," Law Library of Congress, November 13, 2009, available at http://www.loufisher.org/docs/ep/466.pdf.

133. Richard Lardner, "Congress Set to Pass New Protections for Whistleblowers," Washington Post, December 2, 2010, at B3; "Whistleblower Provision," Washington Post, December 14, 2010, at B3; R. Jeffrey Smith, "Bill to Protect Whistleblowers Fails in Senate," Washington Post, December 23, 2010, at A3.

tures. Agencies begin the process by submitting detailed justifications for their projected budgets. Congress amends the justifications but does not appropriate with that level of detail. It includes money in large lump-sum accounts with the understanding that agencies will spend the money consistent with the amended justifications. Congressional control is partly statutory (money has to remain within the appropriation account unless Congress authorizes agencies to transfer funds from one account to another) and nonstatutory (agencies will observe a good-faith obligation to abide by the amended justifications).

As the fiscal year develops, an agency might decide that some of the amended justifications no longer make sense. It could ask the appropriations committees (usually its subcommittees) for permission to "reprogram" the money from a less needed area to one of more pressing priority. No legal violation occurs because the reprogrammed money remains within the appropriation account. This sophisticated system, built up over decades, satisfies two desires: agencies want lump sums to give them spending flexibility over the course of the fiscal year, and Congress is intent on controlling agencies that want to depart from amended justifications.

This type of agency–congressional accommodation yielded a "legislative veto" that met the needs of both branches. It was called a legislative veto because Congress did not follow the regular legislative process: passage of a bill by both houses, a conference committee to resolve differences between the two chambers, and submission of the bill to the President for his signature or veto. The reprogramming process required agencies to submit to designated committees proposed changes to amended justifications. At times agencies need merely notify the appropriations committees of the proposed changes. Other types of shifts require the agencies to seek and obtain the approval of the committees. Authorization committees are frequently included in this system of reviewing and approving reprogrammings.

The budget process is generally well covered with respect to two stages: how agencies and Presidents develop and present their budgets to Congress, and how Congress, through its authorization and appropriation processes, enacts the budget. Little attention is given to how agencies actually spend the appropriated money. In 1972, I began to write articles on presidential spending discretion, congressional control of budget execution, reprogramming of funds by the Defense Department, and the political context for legislative vetoes. Much of that material appeared in my book *Presidential Spending Power* (1975).

Legislative vetoes started to proliferate in the 1970s. Beginning at a modest level in the 1930s with the delegation of reorganization authority to the President, it quickly expanded to cover the Lend Lease Act of 1941, committee vetoes in the 1940s, federal salaries, the War Powers Resolution of 1973, the Impoundment Control Act of 1974, arms sales, presidential papers, deportation of aliens, and finally a broad assault by Congress on agency regulations.[134] By 1982, a case headed to the Supreme Court threatened to invalidate every type of legislative veto, from the inconsequential to the significant.

On February 21, 1982, for the *Washington Post,* I wrote an article called "Congress Can't Lose on Its Veto Power." It predicted that if the Court struck down the legislative veto, "the net result will more likely be less power for executive officials, a more convoluted legislative process, and continued congressional involvement in administrative decisions."[135] With or without the legislative veto, Congress would remain "knee deep in administrative decisions, and it is inconceivable that any court or any president can prevent this. Call it supervision, intervention, interference or plain meddling, Congress will find a way."[136] I had every reason to believe that the committee and subcommittee vetoes over reprogramming requests would continue. Members of Congress placed the article in the *Congressional Record* five times, promoting discussion during floor debate.[137]

There are many misconceptions about the legislative veto. It is widely believed that the procedure amounts to congressional encroachment upon the executive branch and is, for that reason, flatly unconstitutional. The story is far more complex. In 1854, Attorney General Caleb Cushing stated that a resolution passed by a house of Congress could not coerce a department head "unless in some particular in which a law, duly enacted, has subjected him to the direct action of each; and in such case it is to be intended, that, by approving the law, the President has consented to the exercise of such coerciveness on the part of either House."[138] In 1903 and 1905, Congress relied on simple resolutions (passed by one house) and concurrent resolutions (passed by both houses) to direct the Secretary of Commerce to make investigations and reports and to direct the Secretary of War to investigate matters relating to rivers and harbors.[139]

134. Louis Fisher, Constitutional Conflicts Between Congress and the President 89–90, 131, 137–48, 274–77 (5th ed., 2007).

135. Louis Fisher, "Congress Can't Lose on Its Veto Power: If the Supreme Court Blocks Its Use, the President Is Likely to Be the One Hurt," Washington Post, February 21, 1982, at D1, available at http://www.loufisher.org/docs/lv/legveto82.pdf.

136. Id. at D5.

137. Introduced by Rep. Trent Lott on February 22, 1982, 128 Cong. Rec. 1973–74; Rep. Elliott Levitas on February 23, 1982, 128 Cong. Rec. 2200–01; Senator Harrison Schmitt on March 23, 1982, 128 Cong. Rec. 5098–99; Rep. Levitas on December 1, 1982, 128 Cong. Rec. 28216–17; and Rep. Levitas on June 28, 1983, 129 Cong. Rec. 17882–83.

138. 6 Op. Att'y Gen. 680, 683 (1854).

139. 32 Stat. 829, sec. 8 (1903); 33 Stat. 1147, sec. 2 (1905). See 2 Hinds' Precedents §§1593–94.

The first major legislative veto involved the delegation of authority to the President to reorganize executive agencies, subject to the disapproval of a single house. The idea came not from Congress but from President Herbert Hoover. In order to have Congress grant him this authority for the purpose of achieving economies and efficiency, he was even willing to have his reorganization plans placed before a joint committee of Congress for review and approval.[140] It was not unusual to have executive proposals subject to disapproval without full legislative action by Congress, including bicameralism and presentment of a bill to the President. In *Currin v. Wallace* (1939), the Supreme Court upheld a delegation of authority to the Secretary of Agriculture to designate tobacco markets. No market could be designated unless two-thirds of the growers voting in a referendum favored it.[141] To a House committee, it seemed absurd "to believe that the effectiveness of action legislative in character may be conditioned upon a vote of farmers but may not be conditioned on a vote of the two legislative bodies of the Congress."[142]

Over the years, constitutional objections were frequently directed at legislative vetoes. In 1920, President Woodrow Wilson vetoed a bill that permitted Congress to remove the Comptroller General and the Assistant Comptroller General by concurrent resolution.[143] Congress revised the bill to change concurrent resolution to joint resolution (a legislative measure that goes to the President for his signature or veto). President Harding signed the bill into law.[144] Hoover's Attorney General, William Mitchell, regarded legislative vetoes as unconstitutional intrusions into the President's administrative duties.[145] President Wilson vetoed a bill in 1920 that allowed the Joint Committee on Printing, created by Congress, to determine regulations for the executive branch.[146] In 1933, Attorney General Mitchell objected to control of administrative matters by congressional committees.[147]

The use of committee vetoes has had a mixed history. They became a common feature during World War II because both branches concluded that the volume of wartime construction made it impracticable to do what had been the common practice: have Congress authorize each defense installation or public works project. By 1942, it was decided to submit all proposals for the acquisi-

---

140. Public Papers of the Presidents, 1929, at 432.
141. 49 Stat. 732, sec. 5 (1935); Currin v. Wallace, 306 U.S. 1 (1939).
142. H. Rept. No. 120, 76th Cong., 1st Sess. 6 (1939).
143. H. Doc. No. 805, 66th Cong., 2d Sess. (1920).
144. 42 Stat. 24, sec. 303 (1921).
145. 37 Op. Att'y Gen. 56 (1933).
146. H. Doc. No. 764, 66th Cong., 2d Sess. 2 (1920).
147. 37 Op. Att'y Gen. 56 (1933).

tion of land leases to the Naval Affairs Committees for their approval. This accommodation permitted Congress to pass general authorization statutes in lump sums, without specifying individual projects. Referred to as "coming into agreement" provisions, the procedure required the executive branch to seek the approval of the military committees when acquiring land and real estate transactions.[148]

At the time of the Eisenhower administration, Attorney General Herbert Brownell was prepared to condemn the committee veto as an unconstitutional infringement on executive duties.[149] It might have seemed an easy target for him, but he did not fully understand the options available to Congress. Lawmakers created another procedure that yielded precisely the same congressional control at the committee level. A bill was drafted to prohibit the appropriation of funds for certain real estate transactions unless the Public Works Committees first approved the contracts. Eisenhower signed the bill after Brownell explained that the procedure, based on the distinction between authorizations and appropriations, was fully within the constitutional power of Congress. The "veto" by the Public Works Committees was aimed not at the executive branch (which would have created a separation-of-powers dispute) but rather at the appropriations committees. The procedure was not executive–legislative. Instead, it was internal to one house of Congress. The form changed; the committee veto remained in force.

No "Last Word" from *Chadha*

These complexities were not understood by the Supreme Court when it held in *INS v. Chadha* (1983) that the legislative veto was unconstitutional. The case involved a one-house veto that allowed Congress to disapprove decisions by the Attorney General to suspend the deportation of an alien. On its face, the procedure may seem an obvious interference by Congress with executive duties, but the Justice Department had been happy with this arrangement. Previously the department needed to persuade Congress to enact a private bill to stop an individual's deportation. If one house agreed and the other did not, the effect was a one-house veto. Congress amended the law in 1940 to authorize the Attorney

148. Virginia A. McMurtry, "Legislative Vetoes Relating to Public Works and Buildings," in "Studies on the Legislative Veto," House Committee on Rules, 96th Cong., 2d Sess. 432–514 (1980).
149. 41 Op. Att'y Gen. 230 (1955), reprinted in 60 Dick. L. Rev. 1 (1955). See also 41 Op. Att'y Gen. 300 (1957).

General to suspend deportations subject to a two-house veto (disapproval by concurrent resolution).[150] Congress later authorized a one-house veto for certain categories of aliens.

The Court concluded that the one-house veto directed against Jagdish Rai Chadha, whose pending deportation had been stayed by the Attorney General, violated two constitutional principles: bicameralism (legislative action by both houses) and presentment (requiring legislative action to be submitted to the President for his signature or veto). Writing for the majority, Chief Justice Burger said that whenever congressional action has the "purpose and effect of altering the legal rights, duties, and relations of persons" outside the legislative branch, Congress must act through both Houses in a bill presented to the President."[151] Justice Powell concurred in the judgment but expressed a preference for a more narrowly drawn holding. Justice White's dissent also advised the Court to decide the case on narrower grounds and leave for full consideration the constitutionality of other congressional review statutes that raised quite different concerns. Justice Rehnquist dissented only on the issue of severability. The legislative history persuaded him that Congress had delegated the authority to suspend deportations only on the condition that it retain a one-house veto. If the legislative veto fell, so should the Attorney General's authority because the two were inseverable.

Burger's opinion reveals little understanding of how the political branches interact. He argued that the mere fact that a law or procedure was "efficient, convenient, and useful in facilitating functions of government, standing alone, will not save it if it is contrary to the Constitution. Convenience and efficiency are not the primary objectives—or the hallmarks—of democratic government." Elsewhere he said that although the legislative veto might be a "convenient shortcut" and an "appealing compromise," it was "crystal clear from the records of the Convention, contemporary writings and debates, that the Framers ranked other values higher than efficiency."[152]

His analysis is highly simplistic and misleading. The decade from the break with England in 1776 to the Philadelphia Convention marks a persistent search for a form of government that could perform more efficiently than the Continental Congress and the Articles of Confederation. Perhaps Chief Justice Burger had in mind the famous dissent by Justice Brandeis in 1926, when he claimed that the separation of powers doctrine was adopted not for efficiency but to pre-

150. 54 Stat. 672, sec. 20(c) (1940). See Harvey C. Mansfield, "The Legislative Veto and the Deportation of Aliens," 1 Pub. Adm. Rev. 281 (1940).

151. INS v. Chadha, 462 U.S. 919, 952 (1983).

152. Id. at 944, 958–59.

clude the exercise of arbitrary power.[153] At best this is a half-truth. The framers did not adopt separation of powers on highly theoretical grounds, divorced from practicality. They believed that the model, if properly understood and implemented, would lead to more effective and reliable government.[154]

Second, Burger described the purpose of the Presentation Clause as a means of giving the President the power of self-defense against an encroaching Congress. If Congress attempted through a bill or resolution to invade executive powers, a President's veto would check "oppressive, improvident, or ill-considered measures."[155] His language is misleading. It suggests that the exercise of a legislative veto undermines executive independence and invites ill-considered measures. But the legislative veto was generally used against measures that the President submitted to Congress. The President retained total control over the substance of his proposal. Legislative amendment was not allowed. Lawmakers could vote only yes or no. For example, if either house defeated a reorganization plan submitted by the President, the structure of government remained as it was before. The one-house veto merely maintained the status quo. The same reasoning applies to the use of legislative vetoes directed against agency regulations, arms sales, and other executive proposals. The President did not need his veto for "self-defense."

Third, Burger claimed that the framers wanted congressional power exercised "in accord with a single, finely wrought and exhaustively considered, procedure." The records of the Philadelphia Convention and debates in the state ratification debates provide, he said, "unmistakable expression of a determination that legislation by the national Congress be a step-by-step, deliberate and deliberative process."[156] This highly abstract model has little application to procedures that are commonly used by Congress. The House of Representatives can "suspend the rules" and bring a bill to the floor in a manner that prohibits amendments. All that is required is a two-thirds majority. The House Rules Committee can decide which amendments are and are not allowed. If the rule is adopted, it binds all lawmakers. Bills can be enacted without ever going to committee or having hearings conducted. The Senate Majority Leader can ask unanimous consent to proceed to a vote without amendments. If no one objects, that procedure is followed.

Fourth, each house of Congress always has authority to alter the legal rights and duties of individuals outside the legislative branch without complying with

153. Myers v. United States, 272 U.S. 52, 293 (1926).
154. Louis Fisher, President and Congress 1–27, 241–70 (1972); Louis Fisher, "Efficiency Side of Separated Powers," 5 J. Am. Studies 113 (1971).
155. INS v. Chadha, 462 U.S. at 947–48.
156. Id. at 951, 959.

bicameralism and presentment. Each house may command witnesses to appear before congressional committees and apply sanctions to those who refuse to cooperate. The Supreme Court recognizes the authority of either house to issue subpoenas and to hold uncooperative witnesses in contempt.[157] True, prosecution of those held in contempt of Congress requires action by the Justice Department, but no one can deny the coercive effect of committee subpoenas and congressional votes on contempt.

Fifth, note 18 of Burger's opinion states that no constitutional provision allows Congress "to repeal or amend laws by other than legislative means pursuant to Art. I." When Congress adopted a one-house veto against the suspension of Chadha's scheduled deportation, it was not repealing or amending the immigration law. *It was fulfilling it.* The law was effectively amended when the Supreme Court, without the participation of the other branches, decided to delete the legislative veto and allow the balance of the statute to remain in force. Moreover, the President remains at liberty to "make law" unilaterally through executive orders and proclamations. According to *Chadha,* legislative shortcuts are available to the President and to the Court but not to Congress.

Finally, the Court appeared unaware that Congress could comply with *Chadha* in full and still retain a one-house veto. The Court insisted that Congress comply with bicameralism and presentment. Congress could drop the one-house legislative veto for reorganization plans and replace it with a joint resolution of approval, which satisfies bicameralism because both houses must act and it satisfies presentment because joint resolutions (like bills) are submitted to the President. Congress took precisely that course after *Chadha.* It replaced the one-house veto for reorganization plans with a joint resolution of approval. Under this procedure, the President submits a reorganization plan and must gain the approval of both chambers within a fixed time period.[158] If one house withholds support or simply ignores the President's proposal, the practical result is a one-house veto. If it wanted to, Congress could apply the joint resolution of approval to other areas of delegated authority, including arms sales and national emergencies.

Chadha's deficiencies ensured that it had no chance of fully resolving or settling the dispute over the legislative veto. Neither Congress nor the executive branch accepted the static and impractical model that the Court devised. An

---

157. Subpoena power: Eastland v. United States Servicemen's Fund, 421 U.S. 491, 505 (1975); contempt power: Anderson v. Dunn, 6 Wheat. 204 (1821).

158. 98 Stat. 3192 (1984). This authority expired a few months later. The Reagan administration found the requirement for a joint resolution of approval so burdensome that it never requested a renewal of reorganization authority for the President.

article that appeared in the *New York Times* in 1989 reviewed my findings that more than 140 legislative vetoes had been signed into law after *Chadha*.[159] The number of legislative vetoes enacted after 1983 now exceeds a thousand. The procedure survives not because of congressional intransigence but because the elected branches understand the value of submitting such matters as reprogramming to designated committees for prior approval. Agencies in their budget manuals carefully spell out the types of reprogrammings that are covered by notification and those that require committee approval.[160]

In the years after *Chadha*, Presidents consistently object to the presence of committee-veto provisions that are placed in bills submitted to them. In their signing statements, they state that the committee vetoes are unconstitutional under *Chadha* and will not be enforced. Nevertheless, executive agencies regularly ignore these presidential statements and honor committee vetoes because it is in their interest to do so. Contrary to what the Court held in *Chadha*, legislative control over executive agencies is not exercised exclusively through public laws with full adherence to bicameralism and presentment. If they wanted to, Presidents not only could complain about the continuation of legislative vetoes but could direct agencies to rewrite their budget manuals and eliminate existing obligations to comply with committee controls. It would be foolish to take that step. As a result, there is a wide gulf between (1) the formality of *Chadha* and presidential signing statements, and (2) the practice of agency–committee agreements.

Whether Congress receives the information it needs to perform vital constitutional duties depends on the willingness, skills, and ability of lawmakers to defend institutional interests. Lawmakers need to understand they are part of a system of checks and balances, not an arm of the White House. Congress has the theoretical edge in executive–congressional disputes because of the powerful

159. Martin Tolchin, "The Legislative Veto, an Accommodation That Goes On and On," New York Times, March 31, 1989, at A11. See also Louis Fisher, "The Legislative Veto: Invalidated, It Survives," 56 Law & Contemp. Prob. 273 (August 1993), available at http://www.loufisher.org/docs/lv/legveto93.pdf.

160. E.g., Department of Defense, "Reprogramming of DOD Appropriated Funds," DOD Financial Management Regulation, vol. 3, ch. 6 (August 2000); U.S. Department of Transportation, Reprogramming Guidance, May 2005, at 1, para. 3; Treasury Department, Strategic Management Manual, March 29, 2001, ch. 6–30, at 1; Department of Veterans Affairs, Reprogramming, at 1. For a survey of these committee vetoes that appear in agency budget manuals, see Louis Fisher, "Committee Controls of Agency Decisions," CRS Report No. RL33151, November 16, 2005, available at http://www.loufisher.org/docs/lv/2626.pdf.

tools available to it. Lawmakers will generally win if they want to. During his service as head of the OLC, Antonin Scalia offered good advice during congressional hearings in 1975. When congressional and presidential interests collide, the answer is likely to lie in "the hurly-burly, the give-and-take of the political process between the legislative and the executive. . . . [W]hen it comes to an impasse the Congress has means at its disposal to have its will prevail."[161]

In December 2009, I met with a Senator, his chief of staff, and a professional aide who specialized in budgetary issues. Toward the end of the meeting I asked the Senator if he remembered Representative David Skaggs. He couldn't recall the name. I explained that Skaggs had been a member of the House for many years and had served on the Appropriations and Intelligence Committees. After leaving Congress he continued to give talks about the powers of Congress. On one occasion he spoke to congressional staffers about the importance of oversight. He asked three questions. "How many of you work for a member's office?" I watched many hands go up. "How many of you work on committees?" More hands. "How many of you are proud to work for Congress?" Arms stayed down. The Senator looked at me with irritation: "I can't fire you but I can fire these if they aren't proud to work for Congress." They put their hands up. So did I.

161. "Executive Privilege—Secrecy in Government," hearings before the Subcommittee on Intergovernmental Relations of the Senate Committee on Government Operations, 94th Cong., 1st Sess. 87 (1975).

8

BUDGETARY CLASHES

For more than a century, Congress received what was called a "Book of Estimates": an uncoordinated pile of agency budget requests from executive agencies. That process grew increasingly unacceptable, especially after a string of deficits appeared at the end of the nineteenth century. Both branches worked on remedial legislation. The result: the Budget and Accounting Act of 1921, which placed on the President a personal duty to have agency estimates carefully reviewed to produce a responsible national budget. Deficits in the 1960s prompted Congress to pass another landmark bill, the Budget Act of 1974. It controlled presidential impoundment of funds and created what many hoped to be more effective budget procedures. Continued conflicts over spending and deficits yielded the misguided Gramm-Rudman statute of 1985 and the Line Item Veto Act of 1996, both of which the Supreme Court struck down as unconstitutional. Extraordinary deficits during the Bush II/Obama administrations generated new budget proposals in 2010, including a fiscal commission. What has been lost in recent decades is presidential leadership in presenting a responsible national budget.

Power of the Purse

In Federalist No. 58, James Madison described the power of the purse as the "most complete and effectual weapon with which any constitution can arm the immediate representatives of the people, and for obtaining a redress of every grievance, and for carrying into effect every just and salutary measure."[1] In terms of enacted legislation, the Constitution places that weapon squarely in the hands of Congress: "No Money shall be drawn from the Treasury, but in Consequence of Appropriations made by Law."[2] Madison underscored that basic constitutional value in Federalist No. 48: "[T]he legislative department alone has access to the pockets of the people."[3]

To those who drafted the Constitution, the power of the purse represented an essential power for lawmakers and democratic government. The framers were

1. The Federalist 391.
2. U.S. Const., art. I, sec. 9.
3. The Federalist 345.

familiar with the actions of English kings. When blocked by Parliament, kings sought extraparliamentary sources of revenue for military expeditions and other objectives. Some funds came from foreign governments, others from private citizens. Efforts to circumvent Parliament led to a bloody civil war, with Charles I losing first his office and later his head.[4] Joseph Story, Justice of the Supreme Court from 1811 to 1845, explained the essential republican principle of vesting in the representative branch the power of the purse and the decision to go to war:

> [T]he power of declaring war is not only the highest sovereign prerogative; but ... it is in its own nature and effects so critical and calamitous, that it requires the utmost deliberation, and the successive review of all the councils of the nations. War, in its best estate, never fails to impose upon the people the most burthensome taxes, and personal sufferings. It is always injurious, and sometimes subversive of the great commercial, manufacturing, and agricultural interests. Nay, it always involves the prosperity, and not infrequently the existence, of a nation. It is sometime fatal to public liberty itself, by introducing a spirit of military glory, which is ready to follow, wherever a successful commander will lead.[5]

The U.S. Constitution was drafted and ratified to avoid the British history of civil war and bloodshed. The power of the purse is vested in Congress. Article I empowers Congress to lay and collect taxes, duties, imposts, and excises; to borrow money on the credit of the United States; and to coin money and regulate its value. Madison argued against placing the power of Commander in Chief in the same hands as the power to go to war: "Those who are to *conduct a war* cannot in the nature of things, be proper or safe judges, whether *a war ought* to be *commenced, continued,* or *concluded.* They are barred from the latter functions by a great principle in free government, analogous to that which separates the sword from the purse, or the power of executing from the power of enacting laws."[6] At the Philadelphia Convention, George Mason warned that the "purse & the sword ought never to get into the same hands <whether Legislative or Executive>."[7] Many of the framers who debated constitutional principles during this period insisted that the purse and sword be kept separate.

---

4. Paul Einzig, The Control of the Purse: Progress and Decline of Parliament's Financial control 57–62, 100–06 (1959).

5. 3 Joseph Story, Commentaries on the Constitution of the United States 60–61 (1833).

6. 6 The Writings of James Madison 148 (Hunt ed.) (emphasis in original).

7. I Farrand 139–40.

Jefferson praised the founders' decision to transfer the war power "from the executive to the Legislative body, from those who are to spend to those who are to pay."[8]

For the first 70 years, taxing and spending powers were centralized in two committees: the House Ways and Means Committee and the Senate Finance Committee. They handled appropriations, taxes, tariffs, and banking and currency. In the 1860s, Congress created new committees to redistribute some of this jurisdiction: a separate committee for appropriations and another committee for banking and currency.[9] In subsequent years, authorization committees began to gain authority over spending decisions.

A major budget dispute in the 1830s turned on the status of the Secretary of the Treasury. Congress accepted the Secretaries of War and State as executive officers, but treated the Secretary of the Treasury as partly its agent because of his responsibilities over the power of the purse. By statute, Congress placed in the Secretary of the Treasury—not in the President—the duty to place government funds either in the national bank or state banks. President Andrew Jackson directed Secretary of the Treasury William Duane to place those funds in state banks. When Duane refused, Jackson removed him and appointed a successor to carry out his policy. A Senate resolution censured Jackson for assuming "authority and power not conferred by the Constitution and laws, but in derogation of both." Outraged that the Senate would censure him on the basis of unspecified charges and without any opportunity to defend himself, Jackson accused the Senate of violating the Constitution by charging him with an impeachable act without first waiting for the House to act.[10] Three years later, the Senate expunged the censure resolution.[11]

Throughout the nineteenth century, annual estimates of expenditures originated in the various bureaus and agencies of the executive branch. Presidents exercised no formal or statutory duty to review the estimates and assemble a national budget, but on an informal level, some intervened to change agency estimates.[12] In the period after the Civil War, Congress came under severe criticism for the way it authorized and funded rivers and harbors projects. Lawmakers defended the projects as necessary for the expanding economy. Yet Presidents gained the reputation as "guardian of the purse" for resisting and veto-

8. 5 The Writings of Thomas Jefferson 123 (Ford ed.).

9. H. Rept. No. 93-147, 93d Cong., 1st Sess. 8–9 (1973).

10. 3 Richardson 1288–1312.

11. Register of Debates, 24th Cong., 2d Sess. 379–418, 427–506 (1837); S. Journal, 24th Cong., 2d Sess. 123–24 (1837).

12. Louis Fisher, Presidential Spending Power 14–21 (1975).

ing those bills and also private pension bills, many of which were considered fraudulent efforts to compensate deserters and satisfy other irresponsible claims.[13]

A Presidential Budget

Revenues from tariffs had been sufficient to cover national expenditures. Toward the end of the nineteenth century, however, federal deficits began to appear and proceeded to skyrocket with outlays for World War I. Congress recognized the need to place on the President a vital role to produce a responsible national budget. Lawmakers in 1919 objected that estimates of federal agencies represented "a patchwork and not a structure. As a result, a great deal of the time of the committees of Congress is taken up in exploding the visionary schemes of bureau chiefs for which no administration would be willing to stand responsible."[14] It was assumed that economy and efficiency could be secure by making a single officer responsible for receiving and evaluating agency requests: "In the National Government there can be no question but that the officer upon whom should be placed this responsibility is the President of the United States."[15]

Some budget reformers sought to strengthen not only presidential responsibility but to weaken Congress. They found the British parliamentary system appealing because it placed stringent controls on what the legislative branch could do in changing executive proposals. John J. Fitzgerald, chairman of the House Appropriations Committee, wanted to prohibit Congress from appropriating any money "unless it had been requested by the head of the department, unless by a two-thirds vote, or unless it was to pay a claim against the government or for its own expenses."[16] Budget experts recommended that Congress not increase any budget item without executive approval.[17] "Uncle Joe" Cannon, Speaker of the House from 1903 to 1911, warned in 1919 that such proposals would surrender an essential element of representative government: "I

13. Harper's Weekly, August 12, 1882, at 497; Harper's Weekly, July 3, 1886, at 421; 5 Richardson 5001–02, 5028, 5033–34; Thomas B. Reed, "Spending Public Money: Appropriations for the Nation," 424 North Am. Rev. 319, 321 (1892); Talcott Powell, Tattered Banners (1933); Louis Fisher, Congressional Abdication on War and Spending 22–24 (2000).

14. H. Rept. No. 362, 66th Cong., 1st Sess. 4 (1919).

15. Id. at 5.

16. John J. Fitzgerald, "Budget Systems," Municipal Research, No. 62 (June 1915), at 312, 322, 327, 340.

17. Charles Wallace Collins, "Constitutional Aspects of a National Budget System," 25 Yale L. J. 376 (1916).

think we had better stick pretty close to the Constitution with its division of powers well defined and the taxing power close to the people."[18]

Congress rejected efforts to strengthen the President over Congress. The Budget and Accounting Act of 1921 empowered the President to submit a budget and be responsible for the estimates in it. To that extent it was an "executive budget." Thereafter it became a "legislative budget," permitting Congress to change the estimates any way it wanted: with increases, reductions, or total elimination. Changes could be made in committee and on the floor and in either place by simple majority vote. Congress was in no way subordinate to the President's budget. A House report carefully explained basic constitutional principles:

> It will doubtless be claimed by some that this is an Executive budget and that the duty of making appropriations is a legislative rather than Executive prerogative. The plan outlined does provide for an Executive initiative of the budget, but the President's responsibility ends when he has prepared the budget and transmitted it to Congress. To that extent, and to that extent alone, does the plan provide for an Executive budget, but the proposed law does not change in the slightest degree the duty of Congress to make the minutest examination of the budget and to adopt the budget only to the extent that it is found to be economical. If the estimates contained in the President's budget are too large, it will be the duty of Congress to reduce them. If in the opinion of Congress the estimates of expenditures are not sufficient, it will be within the power of Congress to increase them. The bill does not in the slightest degree give the Executive any greater power than he now has over the consideration of appropriations by Congress.[19]

Both houses of Congress recognized the need to centralize appropriations authority in a single committee. In 1920, the House of Representatives consolidated jurisdiction over all funding measures in the Appropriations Committee; two years later the Senate adopted the same reform. Over the years, the budget process began to fragment once again. Authorization committees were permitted to engage in various methods of "backdoor spending."

If the President took the lead in initiating a budget with responsible estimates for total revenues and outlays, Congress could work within those aggregates and alter the priorities as it liked through the regular legislative process. This system

18. Joseph G. Cannon, "The National Budget," H. Doc. No. 264, 66th Cong., 1st Sess. 28–29 (1919).

19. H. Rept. No. 14, 67th Cong., 1st Sess. 6–7 (1921).

functioned reasonably well from 1921 to 1974. The Budget and Accounting Act of 1921 created a General Accounting Office to investigate all matters relating to revenues, appropriations, and expenditures. The statute created a Bureau of the Budget, to be located in the Treasury Department, to provide assistance to the President.[20] President Roosevelt in 1939 used his reorganization authority to transfer the Budget Bureau to the newly formed Executive Office of the President. In 1970, the Budget Bureau was renamed the Office of Management and Budget (OMB).

Although Congress in 1921 attempted to make the President responsible and accountable for submitting a national budget, it began to weaken its power of the purse. One step was to give executive agencies borrowing authority. Instead of having to come to Congress for an appropriation, Congress authorized some agencies to borrow money from the Treasury Department or the public. As agencies repaid the loans they could borrow additional money, creating an account that was revolving, permanent, and independent of congressional appropriations. In 1932, Congress created the Reconstruction Finance Corporation, permitting it to spend tens of billions in debt receipts. Very little of those funds passed through the appropriations committees.

A second form of backdoor spending consists of contract authority, allowing executive agencies to enter into obligations in advance of an appropriation. Once an obligation is made, the appropriations committees must provide funds to liquidate the obligations. A third type of backdoor takes the form of "mandatory entitlements," including veterans' pensions, railroad retirement, and other outlays over which Congress had no control, other than to rewrite the entitlement legislation. The appropriations committees merely calculate what is needed to pay for entitlements. By 1973, a joint congressional committee estimated that the appropriations committees had "effective control over less than fifty percent of the budget."[21]

Another decline in congressional control over the budget is the creation of government-sponsored enterprises (GSEs), especially Fannie Mae and Freddie Mac. Technically they were not part of the government, but it was well understood (or should have been understood) that if they fell on their face, as happened in 2008, Congress—and the taxpayers—would have to step in and bail them out. The cost has been at least $145 billion and is likely to increase. This "contingent liability" was easily understood, and yet Congress and the executive branch did nothing to protect taxpayers.[22]

20. 42 Stat. 20 (1921).
21. H. Rept. No. 147, 93d Cong., 1st Sess. 9 (1973).
22. "2 Zombies to Tolerate for a While," New York Times, August 17, 2010, at B1; William

The Impoundment Battle

From the 1930s through the 1960s, there were periodic disputes over Presidents who refused to spend appropriated funds, an administrative action called "impoundment." It had long been the practice of the executive branch to regard some appropriations as permissive rather than mandatory. In 1896, Attorney General Judson Harmon explained that an appropriation was not mandatory "to the extent that you are bound to expend the full amount if the work can be done for less."[23] Congress encouraged economies but fought back against administrations that canceled legislative policy or projects. The constitutional requirement remained. Presidents had a duty to see that the laws were faithfully executed. If they could carry out a statute with fewer funds, there was no issue.

Over the years, a series of impoundment disputes emerged. President Franklin D. Roosevelt withheld funds from some public works projects. President Harry Truman impounded funds for the Air Force and canceled a supercarrier. Impoundments occurred during the Eisenhower, Kennedy, and Johnson administrations.[24] In those conflicts, Congress raised objections, agencies made adjustments, and the regular political process prevented disputes from ripening into a constitutional crisis. That spirit of accommodation and compromise disappeared in the Nixon years, forcing Congress and the courts to curb presidential abuses.

In 1972, as part of President Nixon's reelection effort, the character of impoundment took a decisive and ominous turn. Nixon and his top officials ridiculed Congress for being profligate and irresponsible with the budget. A presidential message of July 26 warned that congressional policy would lead to "higher taxes and more income-eating inflation in the form of higher prices."[25] In calling for a spending ceiling of $250 billion for fiscal 1973, Nixon blamed the "hoary and traditional procedure of the Congress, which now permits action on the various spending programs as if they were unrelated and independent actions."[26] The result, he said, is that Congress "arrives at total Federal spending in an accidental, haphazard manner."[27]

Nixon's campaign hyperbole had little relationship to facts. The Joint Committee on Reduction of Federal Expenditures prepared "scorekeeping reports"

Poole, "Say Goodbye to Fannie and Freddie," New York Times, August 12, 2010, at A25; "Freddie Mac Seeks More Aid After a Big Loss," New York Times, August 10, 2010, at B7.

23. 21 Op. Att'y Gen. 414, 415 (1896).

24. Fisher, Presidential Spending Power, at 161–67.

25. Public Papers of the Presidents, 1972, at 741.

26. Id. at 742.

27. Id.

and circulated them on a regular basis. This document, printed in the *Congressional Record,* informed lawmakers from month to month how congressional actions compared to the President's budget. The results revealed a systematic and responsible pattern, not chaos. Congressional totals generally remained within the ballpark of the President's budget aggregates. From fiscal years 1969 through 1973, Congress reduced Nixon's appropriation requests by $30.9 billion. During that same period, Congress increased spending authority on legislative bills (backdoor spending and mandatory programs) by $30.5 billion. The result was thus a wash. Over a period of four years, Nixon's budgets added more than $100 billion to the deficit.[28]

On the day that Nixon gave his speech, White House domestic adviser John Ehrlichman attacked the "credit-card Congress" for adding billions to the budget. He compared lawmakers to a spendthrift brother-in-law "who has gotten hold of the family credit card and is running up big bills" with no thought of paying them.[29] Instead of rebuking the President for submitting irresponsible and unrealistic budgets, and making false statements about Congress and its legislative record, many lawmakers turned against their own institution and decided it was essential for Congress to apologize for its shortcomings and adopt new budget procedures.

Within two years of Nixon's campaign attacks, Congress enacted a new budget process that mistakenly tried to make the legislative branch look more like the executive branch. A congressional study committee in 1973 blamed Congress and its legislative process for failing to control spending and the level of the national debt. The Joint Study Committee on Budget Control linked budget deficits to procedural inadequacies within Congress: "The constant continuation of deficits plus their increasing size illustrates the need for Congress to obtain better control over the budget." The committee concluded that the decentralized nature of Congress was a significant factor: "[T]he failure to arrive at congressional budget decisions on an overall basis" contributed, it said, to the pattern of deficits. No committee was responsible for deciding "whether or not total outlays are appropriate in view of the current situation." Each spending bill "tends to be considered by Congress as a separate entity, and any assessment of relative priorities among spending programs for the most part is made solely within the context of the bill before Congress."[30] That critique was greatly overdrawn. The budget system at that time was not nearly so fragmented, incoherent,

---

28. Louis Fisher, "Congress, the Executive and the Budget," 411 The Annals 102, 105 (1974).

29. "Nixon Message Warns Congress Democrats Against Voting 'Excessive' Money Bills," Wall Street Journal, July 27, 1972, at 3.

30. H. Rept. No. 147, 93d Cong., 1st Sess. 1 (1973).

and irresponsible. What was missing was a responsible presidential budget promised by the 1921 statute.

After Congress began to debate Nixon's request for the $250 billion spending ceiling, Nixon announced his intention to stay within that ceiling by withholding funds from various domestic programs. In response, Speaker Carl Albert berated Nixon's threat as making "a monkey out of the legislative process."[31] Under the administration's theory, congressional action on authorization and appropriation bills could be nullified by unilateral executive actions to impound funds. The President could shield defense spending while at the same time selecting which domestic programs to curb or terminate. Nixon's impoundments were unprecedented in their scope, severity, and truculence.[32]

During December 1972 and January 1973, the administration announced major cancellations and cutbacks of domestic programs. Unless statutory language compelled the obligation and expenditure of funds, the administration insisted that federal programs could be legally terminated. Sharp reductions hit programs in agriculture, clean water, housing, and other areas. Dozens of cases were filed in federal court, with most of the decisions going decidedly against the administration.[33] Each house of Congress held hearings and drafted legislation to curb presidential power. Of the half-dozen or so articles published on impoundment by 1971, I had written two, one for the *George Washington Law Review* in 1969 and the other for *Administrative Science Quarterly* in 1970. My articles concluded that a constitutional issue emerged only when Congress found that a legislative program had been canceled or abbreviated because the President considered the statutory purpose unwise, wasteful, or inexpedient: "He then no longer operates on the basis of legislative authority. On the contrary, he matches his will against that of Congress."[34]

My publications led to several assignments with Senator Sam J. Ervin Jr., chairman of the Subcommittee on Separation of Powers of the Senate Judiciary Committee. At hearings I sat behind him to provide assistance. On May 23, 1971, I listened to thoughtful testimony from a tall, lanky Justice Department attorney who had long sideburns and favored loud ties. One of his sentences was of special interest to me: "It may be argued that the spending of money is inherently an executive function, but the execution of any law is, by definition, an

31. Richard L. Lyons, "Opposing Lines Drawn for Battle on Spending," Washington Post, March 7, 1973, at A4.

32. Fisher, Presidential Spending Power, at 168–74.

33. Id. at 177–97.

34. Louis Fisher, "Funds Impounded by the President: The Constitutional Issue," 38 G.W. L. Rev. 124, 125–26 (1969). See also Louis Fisher, "The Politics of Impounded Funds," 15 Admin. Sci. Q. 361 (1970).

executive function, and it seems an anomalous proposition that because the Executive branch is bound to execute the laws, it is free to decline to execute them."[35] I recognized the language as similar to a passage in a Supreme Court decision from 1838. In the Court's words, to contend that "the obligation imposed on the President to see the laws faithfully executed, implies a power to forbid their execution, is a novel construction of the constitution, and entirely inadmissible."[36] The Justice Department attorney testifying at the 1971 hearing was Bill Rehnquist, head of the Office of Legal Council (OLC) in the Justice Department, later to be Chief Justice.

In response to misleading claims by the Nixon administration, I wrote an article for the *Washington Star* on February 25, 1973, entitled "Impoundment Relies on Weak Arguments." It examined the legal and political arguments offered by the administration and found none of them persuasive or credible. Executive officials told Congress that Nixon was simply following what had been done by President Jefferson, who withheld $50,000 for gunboats in 1803. OMB Director Caspar Weinberger had advised a Senate committee: "[W]e are doing not only nothing different than any other President since Thomas Jefferson has done; we are doing it to no greater degree."[37] Jefferson's action had zero application to Nixon's impoundments. The military emergency that Congress had anticipated in 1803 disappeared because of the Louisiana Purchase. Neither Jefferson nor Congress saw a need to immediately spend the money. Jefferson took time to study the most recent models of gunboats and a year later spent the money. His action was temporary and had the support and understanding of Congress. He did not unilaterally terminate programs, impose a spending ceiling, or attempt to dictate budget priorities over those enacted by Congress.[38]

35. "Executive Impoundment of Appropriated Funds," hearings before the Subcommittee on Separation of Powers of the Senate Committee on the Judiciary, 92d Cong., 1st Sess. 253 (1971). The sentence, altered somewhat in the hearing transcript, comes from a Justice Department memo by William Rehnquist, reprinted at 116 Cong. Rec. 345 (1970).

36. Kendall v. United States, 12 Pet. (37 U.S.), 524, 613 (1838).

37. "Caspar W. Weinberger to Be Secretary of Health, Education, and Welfare" (Part 1), hearings before the Senate Committee on Labor and Public Welfare, 93d Cong., 1st Sess. 29 (1973). HUD Secretary George Romney also cited the Jefferson precedent to defend Nixon's impoundments; "Department of Housing and Urban Development; Space, Science, Veterans, and Certain Other Independent Agencies Appropriations, Fiscal Year 1973," hearings before the Senate Committee on Appropriations, 92d Cong., 2d Sess. 565 (1972).

38. Louis Fisher, "Impoundment Relies on Weak Arguments," Washington Sunday Star and Daily News, February 25, 1973, at C2, reprinted at 119 Cong. Rec. 5801–03, 7087–88 (1973). For more details on the Jefferson "precedent" that had no application to the Nixon impoundments, see the analysis by Joseph Cooper at 119 Cong. Rec. 7065 (1973). Also on the impoundment dispute, see James P. Pfiffner, The President, the Budget, and Congress: Impoundment and the 1974 Budget Act (1979).

Each house of Congress drafted legislation to control presidential impound-ments. The general idea was to divide impoundments into two categories: first, actions to terminate programs ("rescissions"), and second, proposals to delay spending ("deferrals"). Lawmakers agreed to prohibit Presidents from canceling a program unless Congress specifically gave its approval by statute. The Presi-dent would have to submit a rescission proposal to Congress and have it approved within a designated number of days. Congress could ignore the request if it wanted to. The burden would be on the President to secure congressional support during the specified period of congressional review. If Congress refused to approve the rescission, the funds would have to be released and spent. For deferrals, lawmakers agreed that Congress could disapprove deferrals by some-thing short of a public law, either a one-house or two-house veto. Neither meas-ure goes to the President for his signature or veto.

When Senator Ervin held a markup on the Senate bill, he sat in a room with other committee members and they submitted amendments to him, either typed or handwritten. He would recognize a Senator, receive the piece of paper, and hold it in front of his eyes to read. Without making any comment he handed the paper to me, seated to his right. My duty was to offer thoughts about the amendments, particularly whether they strengthened or weakened congressional control and what changes might be made to the amendments. Seated around the table were such prominent Senators as Henry Jackson, Ed Muskie, Abe Ribi-coff, Chuck Percy, and Jacob Javits.

Congress Tries to Make the Budget

Several times the Senate passed impoundment legislation but lawmakers decided to wait. Members of Congress worried that the bill was pro-spending because its purpose was to release impounded funds and have them spent. In 1974, an election year, lawmakers wanted impoundment control combined with legisla-tion that promised control over spending and deficits. The result: the Congres-sional Budget and Impoundment Control Act of 1974, consisting of ten titles. When the bill went to conference committee to iron out House and Senate dif-ferences, I was asked to write the section of the conference report dealing with impoundment.[39] I also prepared a floor dialogue between Senators Ervin and Humphrey to explain the purpose of the impoundment title.[40]

39. H. Rept. No. 1101, 93d Cong., 2d Sess. 76–78 (1974).
40. The Humphrey–Ervin dialogue appears at 120 Cong. Rec. 20481–82 (1974).

Toward the end of this process, Senator Ervin asked me whether the impoundment title protected congressional interests. I told him it did. We did not talk about the other nine titles of the bill that radically revamped congressional procedures. Congress created new budget committees in each house. Their principal duty was to prepare budget resolutions that set totals for aggregates: total spending, revenues, and the resulting deficit or surplus. The budget resolution subdivided spending into broad functional categories, including national defense, agriculture, transportation, and other sectors. The bill established a new Congressional Budget Office (CBO) to provide analytical support to lawmakers.[41]

I had worked on some of those titles but was never comfortable with the idea that centralizing Congress was a good reform. Supporters of the legislation believed that if the executive budget of 1921 strengthened presidential control, a legislative budget would strengthen Congress. The Budget and Accounting Act had indeed added to presidential power by centralizing the budget process within the executive branch. But why assume that centralizing the budget process within the legislative branch would yield comparable benefits? The two branches have unique institutional qualities and capabilities. The President heads the executive branch and gains strength from a central budget office. There is no head in Congress and no possibility of a central budget office comparable to the Office of Management and Budget (OMB). Executive agencies are subordinate to the central control of the President and OMB. No such control could ever be exercised by CBO.

Compared to the executive branch, Congress is by nature decentralized. It is split into two chambers with rival political parties vying for control. The executive branch has two elected officials, the President and Vice President. Congress has 535, each with an independent political base. The legislative branch is driven by committees and subcommittees that operate with a certain level of autonomy. The executive branch is largely hierarchical. Congress is essentially collegial in its operations. Even in the House of Representatives, run basically by majority vote and a strong Speaker, lawmakers are at liberty to vote against their own party in order to protect their local base back home.

Nevertheless, Nixon's campaign attack in 1972 on congressional procedures had taken its toll. Many lawmakers refused to defend their budget process and felt obliged to advocate something that looked better even if it might function worse. President Nixon signed the bill on July 12, 1974. In recognition of the work I did on the legislation, especially the impoundment title, I received from

41. 88 Stat. 297 (1974).

him a signing pen and personal letter, dated July 22, just a few weeks before he resigned from office. The letter did not state, but could have: "Thank you for curbing my power."

The 1974 statute assumed that members of Congress would behave more responsibly by having to vote explicitly on budget aggregates, facing up to totals rather than voting in "piecemeal" fashion on separate authorization, appropriation, and revenue bills. In 1974, it proved nearly impossible to defend fragmentation, splintering, and decentralization within the legislative branch. Reformers eagerly embraced and championed such abstractions as "coordination" and a "unified budget process," even if those words were impossible for anyone to understand, much less anticipate their consequences.

The 1974 statute weakened a central purpose of the Budget and Accounting Act of 1921: the personal and nondelegable duty of the President to prepare a responsible budget. As an elected official, the President had a statutory duty to get the budget off to a reasonable start. In contrast, the 1974 statute generated multiple budgets: one submitted by the President, the House budget resolution, the Senate budget resolution, and the final budget resolution agreed to by both chambers. The statute required two budget resolutions a year, a tentative one for the spring and a final one for the fall. Those resolutions were internal to Congress and not submitted to the President. Therefore they were not legally binding.

After a few years, Congress eliminated the spring resolution. The President's budget had provided a fixed and visible benchmark, making it easy for people to know if congressional action was above or below the President's estimates. That reference point disappeared. Instead of keeping within the President's aggregates, lawmakers could vote on generous ceilings in budget resolutions and tell their constituents they had "stayed within the budget," even if their actions exceeded the President's budget.

When Representative Tom Steed managed an appropriations bill for fiscal 1977, he stated: "Although we are over the President's budget, we are under the legislative budget . . . this particular bill will be well within the limit set by the Committee on the Budget."[42] In 1983, members of Congress wondered whether a pending bill was below budget or above budget. House Majority Leader Jim Wright offered this assurance: "This bill is not over the budget; the amounts proposed in this amendment are well within the budgeted figures. The amounts that we have agreed to and have discussed are not in excess of the congressional budget resolution. That, of course, is the budget." He admitted that the amounts

42. 122 Cong. Rec. 17843 (1976).

might exceed the President's budget, but "that, of course is not the budget. Congress makes the budget; the President does not."[43]

The 1974 statute undercut the President's budget and the appropriations committees. To protect the reputation of Congress as fiscal guardian, it had been the custom of lawmakers to keep appropriations under the President's requests. They now found it difficult to resist amendments for more spending if their draft bill fell below the amount allocated to them in a budget resolution. Lawmakers pressured the appropriations committees to spend "up to" the figure in the budget resolution. A chief clerk in an appropriations committee complained that spending limits in a budget resolution had been set at far too generous a level, forcing the committee to "spend up to the full budget allocation."[44] In 1979, the chairman of the House Budget Committee, Bob Giaimo, admitted that budget resolutions up to that time had given "a sizeable incremental funding increase, almost regardless of its effectiveness."[45]

President Reagan was more than willing to step aside and let Congress make the budget. He found the new arrangement politically advantageous. In 1985, he announced his acceptance of appropriations bills "even if above my budget, that were within the limits set by Congress's own budget resolution."[46] If Presidents ducked their statutory duty under the 1921 statute to prepare a responsible budget, Congress lacked the institutional capacity to convert an irresponsible presidential budget to a responsible one. Once a President submitted a budget with a deficit of several hundred billion, Congress could not provide a remedy. Lawmakers would have to drastically cut spending and radically increase taxes. Politically, they could not do that. Instead of the 1974 statute leading to more responsible budgeting, it invited the opposite. Eventually it produced the hapless Gramm-Rudman Act, discussed in the next section.

Most budget reformers in 1974 argued that centralization is better than decentralization, comprehensive action excels fragmentation, and large legislative vehicles (budget resolutions) are superior to small ones. After seeing the damage done by the 1974 budget process, former CBO Director Rudolph Penner offered refreshing observations during a House hearing in 1990. He concluded that Congress operating under a decentralized and informal system had been more coherent and responsible. Congress and the President had acted comparatively well under the older fragmented political process: "I have always been

43. 129 Cong. Rec. 25417 (1983).
44. Allen Schick, Congress and Money: Budgeting, Spending, and Taxing 313 (1980). See also Joel Havemann, Congress and the Budget 152–53 (1978).
45. 125 Cong. Rec. 9028 (1979)
46. Public Papers of the Presidents, 1985, II, at 1401.

struck by the fact in looking at the history of the [budget] process that it appeared chaotic in the late 19th century and early 20th century, but the results were very good in terms of budget discipline, yielding balanced budgets and surpluses most of the time, unless there was really a good reason to run a deficit." Although the 1974 Budget Act created a process "that looks very elegant on paper," it had led to "very dishonest and disorderly results." Penner concluded that those who criticized the 1974 statute as "too complex and too time consuming, are right on the mark."[47]

Reagan and Gramm-Rudman

The architects of the 1974 Budget Act believed that centralizing the congressional budget process would strengthen the legislative branch and weaken the President. The first year of the Reagan presidency proved them wrong. By attracting votes from conservative Democrats, President Reagan gained control of the budget resolution and used it as a blueprint to cut taxes, increase defense spending, and reduce some domestic programs. By seizing control of the budget resolution, he could largely control appropriations bills and the tax bill. He also gained control of the reconciliation process, created by the 1974 statute, to ensure that the separate spending and tax bills were consistent with the budget resolution.

Those steps were ideal vehicles to implement White House policy. The budget resolution in 1981 advanced presidential, not congressional, objectives. When Reagan's theory of supply-side economics failed to generate predicted revenues, the nation did not face the annual deficits of $25 billion experienced during the Nixon years. They now exploded to $200 billion a year. The Budget Act of 1974, with its supposedly superior capacity for dealing with budget aggregates, proved to be helpless.

Could the political and economic miscalculations of 1981 have happened without budget resolutions and the reconciliation process? Highly unlikely. Reagan would have faced almost insurmountable hurdles had he tried to enact his economic program in the decentralized legislative system that existed before 1974. His proposals would have undergone separate scrutiny by subcommittees and committees, chopped to bits and pieces. What emerged from that process would have differed greatly from what the White House wanted. Incremental

47. "Budget Process Reform," hearing before the House Committee on the Budget, 101st Cong., 2d Sess. 20–21 (1990).

decisions by a series of legislative players had placed an effective brake on presidential designs.[48]

The Budget Act of 1974 empowered Reagan by forcing Congress to vote on an overall budget plan. David Stockman, OMB Director from 1981 to 1985, explained why the centralized congressional process helped implement White House goals. The constitutional prerogatives of Congress "would have to be, in effect, suspended. Enacting the Reagan administration's economic program meant rubber stamp approval, nothing less. The world's so-called greatest deliberative body would have to be reduced to the status of a ministerial arm of the White House."[49] For Reagan's budget plan to succeed, Congress had to "forfeit its independence."[50] The effect of the Budget Act of 1974 was to replace the constitutional system of separation of powers with a British-style parliamentary government, with the executive branch very much in control.

Members of Congress, with far more expertise in budget matters than Stockman, regularly deferred to his leadership and analysis. He proved to be facile with numbers and always spoke with great confidence. But it is the job of lawmakers to challenge statements and insist on credible documentation, regardless of who testifies. Why did seasoned lawmakers defer to him? After leaving office, Stockman admitted: "[A] plan for radical and abrupt change required deep comprehension—and we had none of it."[51] He explained that the administration had "built an edifice of doctrine, but not a theory of governance."[52] Instead of depending on the new analytical capability of CBO and the budget committees, Congress routinely embraced the administration's flawed and false premises.

It took almost two centuries—from 1789 to 1981—to accumulate a national debt of $1 trillion. Much of that resulted from previous wars. By the end of Reagan's first term, the national debt had doubled to $2 trillion. By the time he left office four years later, it climbed to $3 trillion. This astonishing growth of budget deficits after 1981, combined with Reagan's refusal to offer constructive solutions, led to the irresponsible Gramm-Rudman-Hollings (GRH) deficit control act of 1985. This statute represents many things. It admitted that the congressional budget process created in 1974, supposedly with a heightened capacity to handle budget aggregates and deficits, could not be counted on. GRH was

48. Rudolph G. Penner, "An Appraisal of the Congressional Budget Process," in Crisis in the Budget Process 69 (1986); Allen Schick, "How the Budget Was Won and Lost," in Norman J. Ornstein, ed., President and Congress: Assessing Reagan's First Year 25 (1982).
49. David A. Stockman, The Triumph of Politics: How the Reagan Revolution Failed 59 (1986).
50. Id. at 200.
51. Id. at 91.
52. Id. at 245.

similarly useless. It allowed deficits to climb while both branches sought refuge in dishonest projections, budget manipulation, escapism, and new forms of accounting ingenuity. The regular political process was replaced by a supposedly automatic, mechanical solution. By 1990, when the ineffectiveness of this experiment was obvious to almost everyone, Congress jettisoned GRH.

Gramm-Rudman established a statutory schedule to eliminate deficits by fiscal 1991. Beginning with a deficit of $171.9 billion for fiscal 1986, the statute promised a cut in the deficit by $36 billion a year over five years, leading to a zero deficit. The President with his budget and Congress with its budget resolutions were obliged to honor those statutory mandates. If in any fiscal year the projected deficit exceeded the statutory allowance by more than $10 billion, another mechanical solution kicked in. A "sequestration" process required across-the-board cuts to protect the statutory target. Half of the reductions came from national defense. Specified social programs were exempt from automatic cuts.

The Senate did not hold hearings on GRH to examine its constitutionality. Draft legislation relied on congressional offices (CBO and GAO) to carry out what seemed to be clearly executive duties, especially with the sequestration process. One bill required the OMB and CBO Directors to estimate the levels of total revenues and budget outlays to determine whether the deficit for a particular year would exceed the statutory limit. The directors had to specify the degree to which expenditures needed to be cut to eliminate the excess deficit.[53] Upon receiving the joint OMB–CBO report, it was the duty of the President— without exercising any discretion—to issue an order to eliminate the excess deficit.

The House Committee on Government Operations held a hearing on Gramm-Rudman on October 17, 1985. I was one of four invited to testify. The others were Comptroller General Charles Bowsher, OMB Director Jim Miller, and CBO Director Rudolph Penner. They did not analyze the constitutional issue. That was left to me. I objected that GAO and CBO, because they were part of the legislative branch, should not be given "substantive enforcement responsibilities, as would be the case with Gramm-Rudman."[54] I looked partly to the Supreme Court's decision in *Buckley v. Valeo* (1976), which prohibited Congress from vesting substantive and enforcement responsibilities in legislative officers. GRH affected the balance of power between the executive and legislative branches. For that reason, constitutional analysis belonged to Congress, not the courts. I testified that the judicial branch in the past had made it clear "that you cannot expect other branches of government to protect your own pow-

53. "The Balanced Budget and Emergency Deficit Control Act of 1985," hearing before the House Committee on Government Operations, 99th Cong., 1st Sess. 26–27 (1985).

54. Id. at 200. See also 198–200, 207–12.

ers. You have to do that for yourselves."[55] Representative Mike Synar said to me at the hearing: "[Y]ou sit there as the only person whom I can find in this city or anywhere in this country who has done the type of constitutional scrutiny and analysis which is necessary to give any of us assurances that we are not going down a path that may be dangerous."[56]

The bill that emerged from conference committee authorized the Comptroller General to certify the results submitted by CBO and OMB. Senator Bob Packwood concluded that the addition of GAO, "which indeed is an executive agency . . . cures the allegation of unconstitutionality."[57] GAO is not an executive agency. It functions essentially as a research arm of Congress. Given the constitutional issues that had been raised, Congress should have resolved them. Instead, it chose to punt to the judiciary by authorizing any member of Congress to take the issue to court, following an expedited process that began with a three-judge court and from there directly to the Supreme Court.[58]

Several lawmakers strongly condemned this transfer of congressional power to CBO, OMB, GAO, and the courts.[59] Senator Robert Byrd objected that "this process represents the most significant abdication of the responsibility of Congress to determine the fiscal priorities of the Nation that I have seen in my 33 years on Capitol Hill."[60] Nonetheless, the conference report was accepted by the House, 271 to 154, and by the Senate, 61 to 31.[61] The three-judge court held that the delegation of executive powers to the Comptroller General was unconstitutional.[62] The Supreme Court affirmed.[63]

By focusing primarily on a particular fiscal year to project a deficit result, Gramm-Rudman encouraged budgetary games by both branches. One trick was to shift costs from a current year to the next, or even to a previous one. Revenue might be raised for the current year at the cost of losing much larger revenues for future years.[64] Other gimmicks were attractive: selling federal assets, accelerating the payment of loans, moving items off budget, and making improbable estimates of higher revenue.[65] Budget analyst Allen Schick captured the result

55. Id. at 200.
56. Id. at 221.
57. 131 Cong. Rec. 30274 (1985).
58. 99 Stat. 1098, sec. 274 (1985).
59. Fisher, Congressional Abdication on War and Spending, at 134.
60. 131 Cong. Rec. 35915 (1985).
61. Id. at 36102–03, 35916.
62. Synar v. United States, 626 F.Supp. 1374, 1391–93 (D.D.C. 1986) (three-judge court).
63. Bowsher v. Synar, 478 U.S. 714 (1986).
64. "Budget Reform Proposals," joint hearings before the Senate Committees on Governmental Affairs and the Budget, 101st Cong., 1st Sess. 3 (1989).
65. Allen Schick, The Capacity to Budget 204 (1990).

nicely: "GRH started out as a process for reducing the deficit and has become a means of hiding the deficit and running away from responsibility."[66]

The budget process of 1974 and Gramm-Rudman weakened the appropriations committees. Why make cuts in programs if they faced another reduction through sequestration?[67] If Congress failed to pass appropriations bills, the national government had to rely on stopgap continuing resolutions, creating further uncertainty in executive agencies. With the regular legislative process at a standstill, both branches decided to hold "budget summits" at the White House and other locations. The result: further damage to representative and democratic government. Senior lawmakers were excluded from those summits and had no way to participate in "the normal give and take of congressional deliberations."[68] Those who did attend were likely to be congressional party leaders who lacked the expertise and experience of committee members.

Gramm-Rudman proved easy to finesse. Both branches could offer imaginary budget projections of spending and revenue that seemed to satisfy the deficit targets. President Reagan started the process by presenting wildly optimistic numbers. Representative Martin Russo, a member of the House Budget Committee, noted that Congress "attacks the assumptions and proposals as phony, but uses them in the budget resolution anyway."[69] Congress adopted Reagan's suspect figures, although honest numbers (available from CBO and other sources) would have vastly increased the projected deficit and made Congress look like the "big spender." If the President submitted a disingenuous budget, Congress had political incentives to embrace it.

Gramm-Rudman never met any of its deficit targets. The deficit ceiling for fiscal 1986 was $171.9 billion. The actual deficit climbed to $221.1 billion. The next year's target was $144 billion. The actual deficit was close: $149.8 billion. The deficit for fiscal 1988 was supposed to be $108 billion. It closed at $155.2 billion. When it became obvious that the targets of GRH could not be met, Congress enacted a revision in 1986 known as GRH II. It pushed budget escapism into the future by two years, projecting a deficit of zero by fiscal 1993. The actual deficit for that year: $255 billion.[70]

66. Id. at 205.
67. 134 Cong. Rec. 587 (1988) (remarks by Rep. David Obey).
68. Raphael Thelwell, "Gramm–Rudman–Hollings Four Years Later: A Dangerous Illusion," 50 Pub. Admin. Rev. 190, 197 (1990).
69. "Budget Process Reform," hearings before the House Committee on the Budget, 101st Cong., 2d Sess. 1 (1990).
70. For analysis of the enactment and implementation of GRH, see Jasmine Farrier, Passing the Buck: Congress, the Budget, and Deficits 82–128 (2004).

Championing an Item Veto

In response to the stunning budget deficits of the 1980s, members of Congress debated different kinds of procedures to give the President greater power to rescind (cancel) appropriated funds. Politically and constitutionally, this move seemed bizarre. President Reagan's irresponsible budget in 1981 eventually tripled the national debt, but lawmakers now wanted to reward him with additional budget authority.

Some item-veto proposals, preposterous on their face, were introduced and debated. In 1984, Senator Mack Mattingly offered an amendment to give the President item-veto authority over appropriations bills. He proposed a congressional override not of the two-thirds required by the Constitution but by a simple majority.[71] Senator Lawton Chiles asked how Congress could consider rewriting the Constitution by statute. Senator Alan Dixon admitted that as a lawyer he had "some difficulty" about the amendment but advised: "[I]t is for the courts, not the Senate. Nobody knows, because the courts have never ruled. . . . It comes down, then, to the question of whether this is a good idea."[72] It was also a question of whether lawmakers take an oath to support and defend the Constitution. Several Senators objected to passing a patently unconstitutional bill and tossing it to the courts.

Chiles raised a point of order that the Mattingly bill "is legislation which changes the Constitution of the United States."[73] Mattingly moved to table the point of order. He lost on the remarkably close vote of 45 to 46. Chiles conceded that no court had ruled on the points raised by the Mattingly amendment, but only because the issue was "so clear that no court, from a justice of the peace on, has ever had to rule on it."[74] Dixon countered that the law was "unsettled" and the "only question is whether we have the courage to let the Supreme Court of the United States decide. This Senate is not the place where 100 separate Senators make that kind of judicial decision."[75] It takes no courage to punt a constitutional issue to the courts, particularly one that involves the prerogatives of Congress. Senator Paul Sarbanes asked how lawmakers would respond if someone proposed changing the terms of the President from four years to two, the Senate from six years to four, and the House from two years to three. Would it be appropriate to transfer those constitutional questions to the judiciary? Senator

71. 130 Cong. Rec. 10844 (1984).
72. Id. at 10852.
73. Id. at 10851, 10859–60.
74. Id. at 10861.
75. Id.

Dale Bumpers reminded his colleagues that each had taken an oath to support and defend the Constitution.[76] The Senate supported the Chiles point of order, 56 to 34.[77]

Another idea preoccupied Congress from 1987 to 1994: the claim that the President possesses an "inherent item veto." A theory advanced by Stephen Glazier in the *Wall Street Journal* stimulated many law review articles and congressional hearings. His conclusion: the Constitution included an item veto from 1789 to the present, although no one had noticed it for almost two centuries. Glazier argued that the President was justified in using an item veto because Congress had resorted to "omnibus" legislation (measures much larger than the standard appropriations bills) that undercut the President's original veto power. Acting in self-defense, the President could "unbunch" those bills by vetoing line items and riders.[78]

Glazier promoted several misconceptions. Omnibus bills are not a modern invention. In 1789, Congress passed an "omnibus" appropriations bill that consisted of four lump-sum amounts for the whole of government. The bill covered 13 lines in the U.S. statutes.[79] A similar omnibus appropriation bill appeared the next year.[80] President Washington never objected to receiving omnibus bills. Writing in 1793, he expressed this view of the veto power: "From the nature of the Constitution, I must approve all the parts of a Bill, or reject it in toto."[81] There was nothing new about appropriation riders. At the Philadelphia Convention, the delegates debated the procedure for passing tax bills in the House and allowing amendments in the Senate. George Mason expressed concern that Senators might follow "the practice of tacking foreign matters to money bills."[82]

Several members of Congress after 1987 thought it was a good idea to support the inherent item veto and see what courts would do. As explained throughout this book, "inherent" refers to powers possessed by the President that are not subject to legislative and judicial checks. Senator Bob Dole, running for President in 1988, said that although no President had used an inherent item veto, or

76. Id. at 10862.

77. Id. at 10870.

78. Stephen Glazier, "Reagan Already Has Line-Item Veto," Wall Street Journal, December 4, 1987, reprinted at 133 Cong. Rec. 34208 (1987).

79. 1 Stat. 95, ch. XXIII (1789).

80. Id. at 104 (1790).

81. 33 The Writings of George Washington 96 (Fitzpatrick, ed.) (letter to Edmund Randolph, September 23, 1793).

82. 2 Farrand 273. For additional details on the history of legislative riders, see Robert J. Spitzer, Saving the Constitution from Lawyers: How Legal Training and Law Reviews Distort Constitutional Meaning 75–77 (2008).

even claimed it, "it might be worth a try." If it meant provoking a constitutional test, he promised that if he received a bill as President "larded with fat, I will do it. Then we'll let the courts decide."[83] Other lawmakers, including Senator William Roth and Representative Chalmers Wylie, urged President Reagan to use the inherent item veto.[84]

In 1988, I participated in an all-day conference that explored the merits of the inherent item veto. Throughout the day I joined with other speakers in saying the idea had no substance in law or history. Charles Cooper, who had headed the OLC, found nothing in the constitutional text, structure, or history to support the idea. He had authored a lengthy OLC memo that found not the slightest support for an inherent item veto.[85] The audience stirred uneasily. Two conservative groups had financed the event and were disappointed to hear most speakers refer to the inherent item veto as a pipe dream. The last person to speak was Robert Bork. Surely he would come to the rescue. Bork, like the rest of us, found it ludicrous that a constitutional power could sit around for two centuries, without any notice, and suddenly come to light.[86]

Three years later, four Senators and 48 House members urged President George H. W. Bush to try an inherent item veto and see what would happen in court.[87] Within a year, he announced that constitutional advisers convinced him that no legal justification could be found for an inherent item veto: "[O]ur able Attorney General [William Barr], in whom I have full confidence, and my trusted White House Counsel [C. Boyden Gray], backed up by legal opinion from most of the legal scholars, feel that I do not have that line-item veto authority. And this opinion was shared by the Attorney General in the previous administration."[88]

The issue resurfaced during the Clinton administration. In 1994, the Senate Judiciary Committee held a hearing on a bill expressing the sense of the Senate that the President "currently has authority under the Constitution to veto individual items of appropriation and that the President should exercise that authority without waiting for the enactment of additional authorization."[89] The sponsor of the legislation, Senator Arlen Specter, concluded that the notion of an

83. Congressional Quarterly Weekly Report, May 14, 1988, at 1284.
84. Id.
85. 12 Op. O.L.C. 128 (1988).
86. Pork Barrels and Principles: The Politics of the Presidential Veto (National Legal Center for the Public Interest, 1988). The sponsors of the conference were the National Tax Limitation Foundation and Citizens for America.
87. "Resolution Urges President to Try Line-Item Veto as a Test of Power," Roll Call, May 20, 1991, at 3.
88. Public Papers of the Presidents, 1992, II, at 479.
89. "Line Item Veto: The President's Constitutional Authority," hearing before the Senate Committee on the Judiciary, 103d Cong., 2d Sess. 197 (1994).

inherent item veto was one "on which reasonable minds could differ, and, that being the case, why not submit it to the Supreme Court and have the dispute settled there?"[90]

There are two basic objections to his proposal. First, Congress should not transfer its authority to the President and await a judicial answer. Each branch is supposed to defend its own powers. Second, the claim of an inherent item veto is not one on which reasonable minds could differ. For reasonable minds to debate an issue, there must be reasons on each side. I sent the Senate Judiciary Committee a detailed analysis explaining why the arguments used by advocates of an inherent item veto were baseless.[91] Those who promoted the inherent item veto, including articles published in law reviews, regularly misstated and misinterpreted the material they reviewed.[92]

A GAO report in 1992 offered support for an item veto. Although the agency subsequently acknowledged that its analysis was faulty, the report continues to be cited as reasonable grounds for granting the President an item veto. GAO's study concluded that if President Reagan had possessed an item veto, he could have saved up to $70 billion over a six-year period.[93] Senator Byrd asked me to evaluate the report. It seemed awkward for me, working at the Congressional Research Service (CRS), to critique a report from another legislative agency. I suggested that he might want me to do the analysis but have it released as a study from the Senate Appropriations Committee. He said he wanted the report to come from me. CRS alerted GAO to my pending study, and Comptroller General Bowsher asked me to meet with the authors of the report. I did so and learned of additional problems with their analysis.

Examining the same data available to GAO, a more realistic and useful estimate of savings over the six-year period seemed to me not $70 billion but $2–3 billion at most and probably less. Also interesting: armed with an item veto, a President could use that power to push spending up. I said that Presidents "have their own programs and activities that they advocate, and the availability of an item veto could be an important weapon in coercing legislators to support White House spending priorities." A President could tell legislators that their projects will be item-vetoed unless they support the administration's spending goals. An amicable agreement would support each side, sending spending up.[94]

90. Id. at 190.

91. Id. at 200–05.

92. Spitzer, Saving the Constitution from Lawyers, supra note 82, at 80–89.

93. U.S. General Accounting Office, Line Item Veto: Estimating Potential Savings (GAO/AFMD-92-7), January 1992.

94. 138 Cong. Rec. 9981–82 (1992).

After my report went to GAO, Comptroller General Bowsher wrote to Senator Byrd and said that actual savings over the six years would have been much less than $70 billion. Such savings, Bowsher now said, could be "close to zero." He admitted that one could conceive of situations where the "net effect of item veto power would be to increase spending." Presidents intent on attracting legislative support for their spending programs could endorse projects desired by lawmakers. Bowsher expressed regret that the $70 billion figure created a "misleading impression."[95] Even though GAO disowned its report, it would be cited some years later during debate on the Line Item Veto Act of 1996.

Line Item Veto Act

From 1985 to 1995, lawmakers explored different ways of granting the President some form of expanded impoundment power. The purpose was to give the President a rescission power greater than what was allowed under the Impoundment Control Act (Title X of the Budget Act of 1974). Over that period I testified eleven times against different proposals for an item veto: separate enrollment, a constitutional amendment, the inherent item veto, expedited rescission, and enhanced rescission. Most of the proposals fell by the wayside. One became law.

In 1992, 1993, and 1994, the House passed legislation to make it easier for the President to rescind funds. Instead of allowing Congress to ignore a President's rescission proposals, as with Title X, "expedited rescission" required at least one house to vote on the President's recommendation. The Senate preferred a different version ("enhanced rescission") designed to greatly increase presidential power. Under this procedure, the President's decision to rescind funds became law unless Congress disapproved. If it did, and the President vetoed the disapproval resolution, Congress would need a two-thirds majority in each chamber to override the veto. With the Republican victories in the 1994 elections and the drafting of the "Contract with America" by House Republicans (advocating an item veto), Congress had the platform and the votes for enhanced rescission.

The House faced a practical problem. Speaker Newt Gingrich, interested in demonstrating his commitment to smaller government, cut House committee staff by a third. A Republican attorney on the House Committee on Government Reform and Oversight, aware of my consistent record in opposing an item

---

95. 142 Cong. Rec. 6513 (1996) (Bowsher's letter is dated July 23, 1992).

veto, nevertheless asked me to write the committee report. With the understanding that the report reflected the committee's position, not mine, I agreed to do so. The House counsel called the general counsel of the Senate Committee on Governmental Affairs, suggesting they might want me to write their report. I agreed to do that as well. Democrats on the Senate committee, discovering that a report was being written for an item veto, insisted that hearings be held. The committee chairman agreed.

The Democrats asked me to appear at the hearing. My public testimony explained why the bill was unconstitutional and would weaken not only legislative power but judicial independence. At the end of the hearing, after everyone had left the hearing room, the committee chairman asked the general counsel: "Did you tell me Lou is writing the committee report?" She said yes. He asked, based on what he had heard of my testimony: "Can he do that?" She said I could. I did. I was willing to help committees with their reports, knowing the product was theirs alone. If asked to testify, I would express my own views.

The Senate ended up reporting two versions of the item veto: enhanced rescission from the Committee on Governmental Affairs, and expedited rescission from the Committee on the Budget.[96] On the floor, those bills were pulled in favor of a third version: "separate enrollment." That procedure would convert the 13 appropriation bills into about 10,000 bills. After an appropriation bill passed both chambers, a clerk would break it into separate paragraphs, sections, and numbers, with each piece made into a bill and presented to the President. The Senate passed that version. Republicans delayed going to conference because they did not want to pass legislation to give President Clinton access to an item veto in the middle of an election year. By delaying, Republicans were criticized for being hypocritical. If they were so eager to give the President an item veto, why not go to conference and get a statute?

Senator Dole, now a declared candidate for President, wanted to demonstrate his leadership ability by moving the bill to enactment. One of the arguments in the conference report was GAO's original claim that an item veto could save $70 billion over a six-year period, a conclusion that GAO had disowned.[97] During floor debate on the conference report, Senator John McCain and Representative John Duncan both cited the $70 billion figure.[98] Information, accurate or

96. S. Rept. No. 9, 104th Cong., 1st Sess. (1995); S. Rept. No. 10, 104th Cong., 1st Sess. (1995); S. Rept. No. 13, 104th Cong., 1st Sess. (1995); S. Rept. No. 14, 104th Cong., 1st Sess. (1995).

97. H. Rept. No. 104-491, 104th Cong., 2d Sess. 15 (1996).

98. 142 Cong. Rec. 6502, 6883 (1996).

not, obviously remains in the intellectual stream forever. The Item Veto Act of 1996 adopted the model of enhanced rescission.[99]

Although enacted on April 9, the bill did not take effect until January 1, a delay intended to deny Clinton an item veto. To the surprise of many Republicans, he was reelected and made use of the item veto. Budget savings, however, were exceedingly modest. Over a five-year period, total savings came to less than $600 million.[100] In 1997, a district court held that the statute was unconstitutional because it violated the legislative procedures set forth in Article I.[101] On appeal, the Supreme Court ruled that the plaintiffs (members of Congress) lacked standing to bring the case.[102] The following year, a district court in a separate case found standing for private plaintiffs and held the statute unconstitutional for failing to follow the procedures of Article I. The Court affirmed.[103] It took another branch of government to provide the constitutional analysis that Congress should have performed by itself.

Balanced Budget Amendment

Throughout the 1980s and 1990s, members of Congress debated whether to add a balanced budget amendment to the U.S. Constitution. The net effect was to advertise that the new procedures of the Budget Act of 1974 were incapable of controlling deficits. Nor could anyone count on the automatic, mechanical remedy of Gramm-Rudman. Representative Gerald Solomon defended the balanced budget amendment in this manner: "Madame Speaker, Congress has repeatedly shown that it is not prepared to deal responsibly with the problems without some kind of a prod. The enactment of a balanced budget amendment will help to give Congress—and this is the point—it will help to give Congress that prod, that spine, that backbone and, for some who need it, the excuse to do what the American people have to do, and that is to live within our means."[104]

The American people can be credited with many virtues, but few live within

99. 110 Stat. 1200 (1996).

100. "The Line Item Veto," hearing before the House Committee on Rules, 105th Cong., 2d Sess. 13 (1998).

101. Byrd v. Raines, 956 F.Supp. 25 (D.D.C. 1997). The court concluded that presidential cancellations were equivalent to repeal and that repeal can be accomplished only through the regular legislative process: passage by both houses and presentment of a bill to the President.

102. Raines v. Byrd, 521 U.S. 811 (1997).

103. Clinton v. City of New York, 524 U.S. 417 (1998), affirming City of New York v. Clinton, 985 F.Supp. 168 (D.D.C. 1998).

104. 141 Cong. Rec. 2361 (1995).

their means. They do not use cash to buy homes and cars. They go into debt. Consumer indebtedness climbed to record heights in recent decades. It is interesting that Solomon would focus only on the spinelessness of Congress. Why leave out the President? Under the Budget and Accounting Act of 1921, the President has a personal duty to present a responsible budget. If the President fails at that task, there is no political reason to expect Congress to radically change the aggregates of a President's budget. Undermining that sense of personal responsibility was a major defect of the 1974 statute.

In 1984, President Reagan told the public that a balanced budget amendment "would force the Federal Government to do what so many States and municipalities and all average Americans are forced to do—to live within its means and stop mortgaging our children's future."[105] First, if Reagan wanted a balanced budget, he could have submitted one instead of tripling the national debt in his eight years in office. Second, it is obvious that states and municipalities do not balance their budgets. If they did, we would not hear of state and municipal bonds or concerns about bond ratings. States and municipalities do not live within their means. They borrow vast sums of money. If states spent only what they received in revenues, there would be no need for the limits on indebtedness placed in state constitutions.

In fact, state constitutions do not require balanced budgets. States have two budgets: an operating (or general) budget, which is supposed to be in balance, and a capital budget. The latter provides funds for roads, education, sewerage, housing, and urban renewal. Justice Shirley S. Abrahamson of the Wisconsin Supreme Court spoke about this budgetary double-talk: "The history of the Wisconsin constitutional provisions concerning municipal debt manifests both an abhorrence of public debt and a willingness to increase the debt limit, particularly for school purposes."[106] Requirements for a balanced budget (even in constitutions) always make room for indebtedness. It was dishonest for Reagan and other public officials to claim that a balanced budget at the federal level would end federal borrowing. It would not. Those points, and others, appeared in my testimony against a balanced budget amendment in 1992 before the House Budget Committee, and two years later before the Senate Appropriations Committee.[107]

---

105. Public Papers of the Presidents, 1984, II, at 1228.
106. Dieck v. Unified School Dist. of Antigo, 477 N.W.2d 613, 617–18 (Wis. 1991).
107. Louis Fisher, "Balanced Budget Amendment," reprinted in "The Balanced Budget Amendment" (vol. 1), hearings before the House Committee on the Budget, 102d Cong., 2d Sess. 185–205, 219–38 (1992); Louis Fisher, "Balanced Budget Amendment," reprinted in "Balanced Budget Amendment—S. J. Res. 41," hearings before the Senate Committee on Appropriations, 103d Cong., 2d Sess. 275–89, 304–14 (1994).

States have discovered many techniques for circumventing the balanced budget requirement. Limits on borrowing usually apply only to "full faith and credit debt" (debt secured by the general revenues of the government). It takes little imagination to create nonguaranteed bonds. A balanced budget requirement posed other costs to Congress. Governors use those requirements to justify greater power over spending (item-veto authority, impounding funds, shifting expenditures to the next fiscal year). Presidents would want the same powers, further subordinating Congress and weakening representative government.

A balanced budget amendment necessarily shifts politically sensitive decisions to the courts. Judges are asked to monitor spending, taxing, and indebtedness actions to ensure that they conform to the amendment. State judges are not shy about exercising those responsibilities.[108] There is no evidence that they have special skills or expertise to resolve fiscal disputes. Why should the power of the purse be exercised not by elected officials, with their duty to voters, but by federal judges? A move in that direction is a step away from democratic government.

The power and prestige of Congress would suffer greatly when citizens learned the obvious: a balanced budget amendment does not produce a balanced budget. After the national debt continued to climb through the use of bookkeeping contrivances and new borrowing agencies, the reputation of Congress would be damaged. Deficits in annual budgets pose a serious threat to the nation. Of greater damage is the loss of trust in elected officials.[109]

Biennial Budgeting

Another budget reform idea is biennial budgeting. Instead of Congress acting each year on authorization bills, appropriation bills, and budget resolutions, some reform groups advocate a two-year cycle. In the first year, Congress would receive a two-year budget from the President, pass a two-year budget resolution, and enact two-year appropriations. The second year would be set aside for multiyear authorizations and congressional oversight. Initially, this proposal might

108. Chiles v. Children A, B, C, D, E, and F, 589 So.2d 260 (Fla. 1991); Bruneau v. Edwards, 517 So.2d 818, 824 (La. Ct. App. 1987); Nations v. Downtown Development Authority, 345 S.E.2d 581 (Ga. 1986); Bd. of Ed., Etc. v. Chicago Teachers, Etc., 430 N.E.2d 1111, 1116 (Ill. 1981).
109. Louis Fisher, "The Effects of a Balanced Budget Amendment on Political Institutions," 9 J. L. & Pol. 89 (1992).

seem appealing. Why do every year what can be done every other year? Biennial budgeting promises to reduce legislative workload, repetitive votes, and redundancy. The prospect of performing vigorous oversight in the off year may seem attractive.

Examining biennial budgeting more closely reveals many problems. It is argued that agency officials would have more time to manage their affairs without having to prepare and defend a budget every year. But when Congress in the off year turns its attention to oversight, who would be asked to testify? Agency officials. They would have to prepare reports, testify, and respond to questions raised. It is unlikely that agencies would have more free time under biennial budgeting to devote to management. Congress and OMB can be expected to intervene on a regular basis to ask for updates.

Political appointees join an administration in the first year of the President's four-year term. They must put together a budget for the next year. Only after a year or two are they sufficiently expert and experienced to do this job reasonably well. Yet after a year or two these officials will be leaving government. Imagine how much more difficult it would be to come in the first year and credibly draft a two-year budget. If that task is done poorly it would require major budget amendments the second year. The result: biennial budgeting in name only.[110]

Second, the likely effect of biennial budgeting is to give the executive branch a longer leash with two years of money. Could Congress properly supervise how funds are obligated and spent? If budget projections are difficult to make now (and they are), biennial budgeting promises greater errors. In 1993, the National Performance Review (the Gore Report) admitted that agency officials inflate their estimates, "driving budget numbers higher and higher." Many budget directors "regularly ask for 90 percent more than they eventually receive."[111] Forced to estimate spending an additional year out, agencies will hedge their bets even more. Agency padding can be expected to be greater under biennial budgeting.

Third, the inspiration for biennial budgeting comes basically from the states. The Gore Report pointed out that "[t]wenty states adopt budgets for 2 years."[112] If 20 states followed biennial budgeting at that time, 30 did not. Some states are forced to use biennial budgeting because their legislatures meet only every other year. Congress has met annually ever since 1789. The trend at the state level is

110. Stan Collender, "Hopelessly Retro Budget Ideas Make a Comeback," Roll Call, September 28, 2010, at 31.

111. "From Red Tape to Results: Creating a Government That Works Better and Costs Less," Report of the National Performance Review, Vice President Al Gore, September 7, 1993 (Washington, D.C.: Government Printing Office), at 15–16.

112. Id. at 17.

not toward biennial budgeting. It is toward annual budgeting, a fact not mentioned in the Gore Report. In 1940, almost all of the states used biennial budgeting. That number had been cut in half by 1993.[113] Although 20 states formally use biennial budgeting, about a dozen of those states meet annually and can revise their budgets. States that rely on biennial budgeting are generally less populous, suggesting that this method of budgeting has little application to the federal government.[114]

Fourth, if agencies are not properly staffed to prepare reliable two-year budgets, Congress can anticipate two unattractive choices. The first is to fund programs at minimal levels over the two-year period, forcing agencies to return for supplemental funds the next year. The budget workload for Congress the second year (supposedly reserved for oversight) would be heavy. The second option is to fund programs at generous levels over a two-year period to minimize the need for supplemental appropriations and remedial legislation. The side effect would be ironic, making it harder to control agency spending and the deficit. Annual appropriations are difficult to pass now. Contentious debates over a two-year appropriation would add huge complications.

How much in-depth oversight can be expected the second year? Congressional committees typically focus on immediate crises and emergencies. Routine oversight over all agencies and programs takes a backseat. Most authorization committees have shifted from annual authorizations to multiyear cycles or no authorization bill at all. Whatever gain there might be in additional oversight by authorizing committees under biennial budgeting would be lost by the annual oversight currently done by the appropriations committees. Citing those reasons, I testified three times against biennial budgeting and wrote articles identifying the problems.[115]

Current Reform Proposals

After the Supreme Court in 1998 struck down the Line Item Veto Act, members of Congress explored alternatives that might survive judicial scrutiny. In

---

113. Congressional Budget Office, "Biennial Budgeting," Staff Working Paper, November 1987, at 22.

114. Ronald K. Snell, "Annual v. Biennial Budgeting: No Clear Winner," 68 Spectrum 23 (1995).

115. Louis Fisher, "Biennial Budgeting," reprinted in "Concurrent Resolution on the Budget for Fiscal Year 1988" (vol. III of III), hearings before the Senate Committee on the Budget, 105th Cong., 1st Sess. 97–103 (1997); Louis Fisher, "Biennial Budgeting," reprinted in "S. 261—Biennial Budgeting and Appropriations Act," hearing before the Senate Committee on Governmen-

2000, a subcommittee of the House Judiciary Committee held a hearing on a constitutional amendment to grant the President line-item authority. The problem with the legislation, my testimony explained, was using the Pennsylvania constitution as a model. Under the proposal considered by the subcommittee, the President "may disapprove any item of appropriation in any bill." I pointed out that "one of the odd things about a constitutional amendment is that it would allow a President to veto items, but Congress doesn't put items in bills and you know that. You don't put items in bills. You put items in [committee] reports."[116] State appropriations bills "are highly specific" and it "is not unusual to see sums for $2,000 or $2,500 in state appropriations bills," enabling the governor to veto those items. Congress does not provide that level of itemization. It appropriates in large lump-sum amounts.[117] After this hearing, the subcommittee did not even bother to report the constitutional amendment for full committee consideration.

In 2006, with deficits mounting from a combination of tax cuts promoted by President Bush and two unpaid wars in Iraq and Afghanistan, Congress held hearings on item-veto authority. The proposal was a form of "expedited rescission." The President would sign an appropriations bill and then immediately put together a list of items to be rescinded. Unlike the 1974 impoundment statute, Congress could not ignore his proposals. The expedited procedures in the 2006 proposal required committee action and floor action. Lawmakers could not amend the President's list of rescissions. If one house voted against it, there would be no need for the other house to act. Rescissions could take effect only if both houses passed an approval bill. The bill containing rescissions would be returned to the President for his signature.

This process does not have the procedural deficiencies of the Line Item Veto Act. To that extent, it has a greater likelihood of passing muster in the courts. In my judgment, it is not sufficient that a bill merely satisfies the standards announced in *Clinton v. City of New York* (1998). On June 8, 2006, I testified before the House Budget Committee that although it is "useful to examine judi-

---

tal Affairs, 105th Cong., 1st Sess. 25–28, 31–34, 36–40, 102–11 (1997); Louis Fisher, "Biennial Budgeting," reprinted in "Biennial Budgeting," hearing before the House Committee on Rules, 106th Cong., 2d Sess. 169–79, 180–82, 184 (2000). See also Louis Fisher, "Biennial Budgeting in the Federal Government," 17 Public Budgeting & Finance 87 (1997); Albert J. Kliman and Louis Fisher, "Budget Reform Proposals in the NPR Report," 15 Public Budgeting & Finance 27 (1995); Louis Fisher and Albert J. Kliman, "The Gore Report on Budgeting," The Public Manager, Winter 1993–1994, at 19.

116. "Item Veto Constitutional Authority," hearing before the Subcommittee on the Constitution of the House Committee on the Judiciary, 106th Cong., 2d Sess. 19 (2000).

117. Id. at 25.

cial precedents, each Member of Congress has an obligation to support and defend the Constitution and needs to exercise independent judgment in fulfilling that task. The branch responsible for protecting the rights, duties, and prestige of Congress is not the judiciary. It is Congress. The framers expected each branch to defend itself."[118] To me, the constitutional answer did not lie in case law: "It lies in the willingness of each Member to determine what Congress must do to preserve its place in a system of coordinate branches. The true expert here is the lawmaker, not the judge. No one outside the legislative branch has the requisite understanding of congressional needs or can be entrusted to safeguard legislative interests."[119]

My testimony identified four costs to Congress. First, the bill sent "a clear message to the public that Congress has been irresponsible with its legislative work," and therefore empowers the President to pick through an appropriations bill to eliminate items he believes should not have been included. The procedure "signals that Members are not up to the task and cannot properly conduct their constitutional duties."[120] There are no grounds to elevate the President as the more trusted guardian of the purse or more qualified to decide which projects are appropriate for a lawmaker's district or state. Also, at the aggregate level the President is far more likely to promote big-spending items, including the space program, Medicare, Medicaid, supercolliders, the Supersonic Transport, military commitments, and entitlement programs (such as prescription drugs for the elderly).

The second damage is to Congress as a political institution. Once the President submits a list of proposed items to be canceled, he would automatically receive public acclaim for fighting against waste, even if few in the general public could distinguish between "justified" and "unjustified" programs. I told the House Budget Committee that he would win "on image alone, not substance or analysis." Third, if Congress failed to approve his list, it would receive public condemnation. The President could credibly argue that Congress asked him to find waste, he had made his careful selections, and lawmakers now refused to delete unwanted and unneeded funds. My advice to the committee: "If Congress has an interest in building support and credibility with the public, this is a procedure to avoid."[121]

A fourth damage: the bill would give the President a new tool to coerce law-

118. Louis Fisher, statement before the House Committee on the Budget, "Line-Item Veto—Constitutional Issues," June 8, 2006, at 1.
119. Id. at 1–2.
120. Id. at 2.
121. Id. at 3.

makers and weaken their independence. He or his aides could call members and alert them to a particular project in their district or state that appears on a draft list of programs to be rescinded. During the phone call, the member would be told that the administration now concludes that the project is valuable and every effort will be made to see that it is removed from the list. At that point, I said in my testimony, the conversation "shifts course to inquire whether the lawmaker is willing to support a bill, treaty, or nomination desired by the President."[122] Exercising that political leverage diminishes the constitutional independence of Congress and invites a quid pro quo that would push spending up, not down. I made similar arguments in testifying against the item veto on May 2, 2006, before the Senate Budget Committee. Congress did not enact the legislation.

In 2009 and 2010, with deficits climbing to extraordinary heights because of tax cuts, the deep recession, the expense of two wars, entitlements, and the financial bailout, the proposal for an item veto reappeared. Hearings were held in the House and the Senate. Few lawmakers seemed concerned that the legislation would give undeserved praise to the President. In an article for *Roll Call* on January 19, 2010, I repeated the arguments made in my 2006 testimony against item-veto legislation and ended with this point: "It is fully within the president's power to recommend a budget that balances expenditures and revenues." If the President wants to display fiscal responsibility, "he needs to do it when he is submitting the budget."[123]

In 2009, members of Congress debated the idea of creating a "fiscal commission" to confront massive federal deficits. One might hope that the elected branches would identify problems and deal with them, instead of pushing the deficit issue to an outside commission. The idea of a fiscal commission began in Congress under the sponsorship of several Representatives and Senators. Bills introduced in 2009 proposed a commission to develop legislation to "reform tax policy and entitlement benefit programs and ensure a sound fiscal future for the United States"—code words for raising revenue, cutting entitlements, and bringing budget deficits under control.[124] To guarantee bipartisan support, the commission would need a supermajority (for example, 12 of 16 members) to issue its recommendations.

Hearings on these bills typically blamed Congress for the fiscal crisis: a national debt of $12 trillion and a deficit in the most recent fiscal year exceed-

122. Id.
123. Louis Fisher, "Congress, Don't Cede Budgetary Power to President," Roll Call, January 19, 2010, at 4, available at http://www.loufisher.org/docs/ci/454.pdf.
124. H.R. 1557, 111th Cong., 1st Sess. (2009); S. 1056, 111th Cong., 1st Sess. (2009). See also S. 2853, 111th Cong., 1st Sess. (2009).

ing $1.4 trillion. The prospect for the next decade: an additional $9 trillion of debt. At a November 10, 2009, hearing by the Senate Budget Committee, Senator George Voinovich stated: "Congress is simply not willing or not capable of enduring short term pain for long term gain." A fair point, but the same could be said of Presidents. During the hearing, Senator Lamar Alexander asked: "What about the President? The President has to be involved. . . . He is the agenda setter. . . . No one else can come close to that." On December 7, 2009, the cover of *Newsweek* captured the matter dramatically with this headline: "How Great Powers Fall: Steep Debt, Slow Growth, and High Spending Kills Empires—And America Could Be Next." In the background was the Capitol, upside down. Where was the White House? It should have been upside down also. A statement by Senator Joe Lieberman on December 17, 2009, noted that facing the deficit problem required "hard choices Congress has shown in the past it hasn't got the stomach for." Presidents have shown no stomach for action either.

President Obama voiced support for a fiscal commission established by statute.[125] The Senate amendment to create a bipartisan debt commission, which needed 60 votes to pass, fell short on a vote of 53 to 46. At that point Obama issued an executive order on February 18, 2010, establishing a fiscal commission to study ways of controlling the deficit. An 18-member commission (including current members of Congress) would present a plan no later than December 1, 2010, after the November elections. Issuing the report required the approval of "not less than 14 of the 18."

Obama had provided little leadership on the deficit issue. His first budget message of February 26, 2009, stated: "[W]e cannot lose sight of the long-run challenges that our country faces and that threaten our economic health—specifically, the trillions of dollars of debt that we inherited." Explaining that his initial budgets would produce deficits because of the deep recession and the need to stimulate economic recovery, he said, "we must begin the process of making the tough choices necessary to restore fiscal discipline, cut the deficit in half by the end of my first term in office, and put our Nation on sound fiscal footing." Cutting the deficit "in half" appears to support this result: adding $4.5 trillion (not $9 trillion) to the debt over the coming decade. Obama's budget message of February 1, 2010, told the nation that "we cannot continue to borrow against our children's future" and spoke of "getting our fiscal house in order." Admitting that "our fiscal situation remains unacceptable," he opted for a fiscal commission instead of exercising direct presidential leadership on a budget proposal.

---

125. Elaine S. Povich and Eric Pianin, "Support Grows for Tackling Nation's Debt," Washington Post, December 31, 2009, at A10.

Obama's executive order offered this objective: "The Commission is charged with identifying policies to improve the fiscal situation in the medium term and to achieve fiscal sustainability over the long run. Specifically, the Commission shall propose recommendations to balance the budget, excluding interest payments on the debt, by 2015." For fiscal years 2013 through 2015, net interest was projected at these levels: $435.9 billion, $509.9 billion, and $571.1 billion.[126] Adding a trillion dollars of debt every other year is not a credible or responsible long-term solution. On July 13, 2010, when Obama announced his new OMB Director, Jacob Lew, it was reported that Lew would be responsible for reducing the federal deficit "to 3 percent of the size of the economy by 2015."[127] Based on the gross domestic product (GDP) of $19.190 trillion projected for fiscal 2015,[128] the annual deficit at that time would be $575.7 billion. That cannot be called fiscal discipline or a strategy to control deficits.

In December 2010, the fiscal commission failed to attract the necessary 14 votes for a deficit control plan. Obama's third budget, submitted on February 14, 2011, once again called attention to the problem of long-term deficits. He said: "The reason is simple: in the long run, we will not be able to compete with countries like China if we keep borrowing more and more from countries like China." Quite true, but nothing in his budget proposal dealt substantively with long-term debts. He made no proposals to deal with the largest part of the budget—entitlements—preferring to leave that to Congress and the Republicans. Modest cuts were recommended for some domestic programs, including a five-year freeze on all discretionary spending outside of national security and a two-year freeze on federal civilian worker salaries. At the same time, Obama proposed tens of billions of dollars for high-speed rail and other spending initiatives. Other than a $78 billion cut over a five-year period that Defense Secretary Robert Gates had already proposed, national security spending was untouched and uncontrolled. In February 2011, OMB Director Lew spoke the language of budget restraint, repeatedly saying that the Obama proposal "is a budget that lives within our means."[129] However, the budgets projected over the next decade remained heavily in debt.

President Obama's budget in February 2011 projected deficits of $8 trillion over the next decade. The CBO put the figure closer to $10 trillion. Only after

126. Historical Tables: Budget of the U.S. Government, Fiscal Year 2011, at 76.

127. Anne E. Kornblut and Ed O'Keefe, "Obama Taps New Budget Chief," Washington Post, July 14, 2010, at A3.

128. Historical Tables: Budget of the U.S. Government, Fiscal Year 2011, at 211.

129. Dana Milbank, "Keep Passing the Buck on Budget Reform? Yes, We Can," Washington Post, February 15, 2011, at A2.

the House and Senate offered debt-control proposals did Obama propose a plan on April 13 to cut deficits over the next 12 years by $4 trillion.[130]

When Presidents conclude that it is essential to achieve a balanced budget and constrain spending, they should demonstrate leadership with their budget proposals rather than wait for other parts of government or the private sector to step forward. The growth of deficits in recent decades has been so extraordinary that few can miss its significance. Presidents and members of Congress are elected to respond to developments that threaten the country's fiscal health and political stability. Although the Budget Act of 1974 promised more effective control over national aggregates and priorities, when serious deficits materialized, the two elected branches looked elsewhere for remedies, ranging from Gramm-Rudman to the item veto to the recent fiscal commission. Precious time is wasted when public officials fail to confront issues that are so well marked.

---

130. Mark Landler and Michael D. Shear, "Taking on G.O.P., Obama Unveils Debt Relief Plan," New York Times, April 14, 2011, at A1.

9

NATIONAL SECURITY POLICY

The framers expected Congress to play a leading role in deciding foreign and defense policy. They assigned to Congress many of the prerogatives previously vested in the English kings. Legislative power, after declining markedly in the 1930s and during World War II, plummeted further in 1950 when President Harry Truman committed troops to Korea without ever coming to Congress for authority, either before or after. Few lawmakers challenged his initiative, and they were similarly passive when President Lyndon Johnson escalated the war in Vietnam. Aware of its declining strength, Congress passed the War Powers Resolution of 1973, but it represented not legislative reassertion but surrender and an abject failure to understand the Constitution. Subsequent crises over national security include the Iran-Contra affair of 1987, the Kosovo War in 1999, and the Iraq Resolution of 2002, covered in this chapter.

Breaking with the English Model

For members of Congress to protect their constitutional powers and their constituents, they need to understand how (and why) the framers broke free of political systems that centered war-making and foreign policy in the Executive. That key principle, nurtured by the framers, is central to democratic and constitutional government. It separates America from most government systems. When that value is forgotten or ignored, or never even understood, Congress loses the capacity to defend itself and the public interest. With a weak Congress, decisions about military commitments turn from popular government and elected lawmakers to an executive branch with two elected officials and a long pattern of costly, poorly conceived, and unconstitutional military engagements. The framers anticipated and warned against the hazards of executive wars.

The framers understood that the existing models of government in Europe, especially in Great Britain, placed all of external affairs in the Executive. After careful study and consideration, they transferred many of those powers to the legislative branch to secure the principle of self-government and popular sovereignty. They understood that in a republican form of government, the sovereign power rests with the citizens and the individuals they elect to public office. To preserve the republic, they drafted a Constitution to allow "only Congress to loose the military forces of the United States on other nations."[1] As political scientist David Gray Adler has noted, self-government depends on the principle of collective judgment, shared power in foreign affairs, and "the cardinal tenet of republican ideology that the conjoined wisdom of many is superior to that of one."[2]

Legislative control over external affairs took centuries to develop. The English Parliament gained the power of the purse in the 1660s to restrain the king, but the power to initiate war remained a monarchical prerogative. In his *Second Treatise on Civil Government* (1690), John Locke identified three functions of government: legislative, executive, and "federative."[3] The last embraced "the power of war and peace, leagues and alliances, and all the transactions with all persons and communities without the commonwealth."[4] To Locke, the federative power (what today we call foreign policy) was "always almost united" with the Executive. Any effort to separate the executive and federative powers, he counseled, would invite "disorder and ruin."[5]

A similar orientation appears in the writings of William Blackstone, the British eighteenth-century jurist. In book 1 of the *Commentaries on the Laws of England* (1765), a work of central interest to the framers, he defined the king's prerogative as "those rights and capacities which the king enjoys alone."[6] Some of those powers he called *direct*—that is, powers that are "rooted in and spring from the king's political person," including the right to send and receive ambassadors and the power of "making war or peace."[7] His language is similar to that of some contemporary advocates of presidential power who rely on the notion of "inherent" power, to be discussed later. In placing in the king the sole power to make war, Blackstone observed that individuals who entered society and accepted the laws of government necessarily surrendered any private right to make war: "It would indeed be extremely improper, that any number of subjects should have the power of binding the supreme magistrate, and putting him against his will in a state of war."[8]

1. Edwin B. Firmage, "War, Declaration of," in 4 Encyclopedia of the American Presidency 1573 (Leonard W. Levy and Louis Fisher, eds., 1994).

2. David Gray Adler, "Foreign Policy and the Separation of Powers: The Influence of the Judiciary," in Judging the Constitution: Critical Essays on Judicial Lawmaking 158 (Michael W. McCann and Gerald L. Houseman, eds., 1989).

3. John Locke, Second Treatise on Civil Government §§145–46 (1690).

4. Id. at §146.

5. Id. at §§147–48.

6. 1 William Blackstone, Commentaries on the Laws of England 232 (1765) (hereafter "Blackstone, Commentaries").

7. Id. at 232–33.

8. Id. at 249.

Part of Blackstone's argument excluding private citizens from engaging in war is reflected in the U.S. Constitution, but the powers he rooted in the Executive were transferred to Congress. When England and France squared off militarily in 1793, President Washington issued what has come to be known as the Neutrality Proclamation, advising Americans not to take sides. Of course they did, some preferring England and others supporting France. His administration began to prosecute those who violated the proclamation. Writing under the pseudonym "Pacificus," Alexander Hamilton defended Washington's initiative. James Madison chose the pen name "Helvidius" to rebuke Hamilton for borrowing a theory of government based on British royal prerogatives.

Ever since that time, there have been many who champion Hamilton's theory of presidential power; others think that Madison's understanding of the Constitution was better grounded. However, both engaged in mere theories of government. President Washington had to deal with reality when he learned that jurors rebelled at the thought of finding someone guilty for violating a presidential proclamation. Perhaps that policy was law in England, where a king's proclamation could be nailed to a tree to announce criminal law, but not in America. Jurors—and Americans—insisted that criminal law be created by Congress through the regular legislative process. Washington got the message. In response to his request for legislative authority, Congress passed the Neutrality Act of 1794, giving Washington the firm legal footing he needed to prosecute violators.[9]

The Neutrality Act imposed criminal penalties on citizens who attempt to make war on another country.[10] It did not in any way embrace Blackstone's definition of war as an exclusive executive power. Quite the contrary. The statute treated war as the power of the *national government,* not the President. As explained later in a section on early judicial rulings, the Neutrality Act referred to the *congressional* power to go to war. All three branches understood that basic principle. That understanding remained in place for more than a century and a half, until Truman's initiative in 1950 with Korea.

Blackstone promoted other exclusive foreign policy powers for the Executive. The king could make "a treaty with a foreign state, which shall irrevocably bind the nation."[11] He could issue letters of marque (authorizing private citizens to use their ships and other possessions to undertake military actions against another nation) and acts of reprisal (military responses short of war). To Blackstone, that power was "nearly related to, and plainly derived from, that other of

9. Louis Fisher, Presidential War Power 26–29 (2004 ed.).
10. 1 Stat. 381–84 (1794).
11. 1 Blackstone, Commentaries 244.

making war."[12] Also, the king was "the generalissimo, or the first in military command," and he had "the sole power of raising and regulating fleets and armies."[13] The American framers either transferred those executive powers exclusively to Congress or divided them between the President and the Senate (as with treaties and the appointment of ambassadors).

Blackstone insisted that when the king exercises these external powers he "is and ought to be absolute; that is, so far absolute, that there is no legal authority that can either delay or resist him."[14] The idea that the Executive has certain absolute war powers that cannot be limited by any legal authority, including the legislative branch, surfaced after World War II, particularly during the Truman and Bush II presidencies. It sometimes parades under the name "inherent powers." As explained later, it is rooted in the British prerogative model that the framers fully repudiated.

Creating a Republic

Unlike England, with its long history of monarchy over which Parliament gradually gained some powers, America as a national government started with a legislative branch and no other. After America declared its independence from England, all national powers (including executive) were vested in a Continental Congress. The ninth article of the first national constitution, the Articles of Confederation, provided: "The United States in Congress assembled, shall have the sole and exclusive right and power of determining on peace and war." The single exception to that principle lay with the sixth article, which allowed states to engage in war if invaded by enemies or when threatened by Indian tribes. The powers of the new national government were limited by the need to receive approval from nine of the thirteen states when it wanted to engage in war, enter into treaties, borrow money, appropriate money, and make other commitments.

The framers could not have been more explicit in rejecting the British monarchy and Blackstone's model of an Executive who possesses exclusive control over external affairs. At the Philadelphia Convention, Charles Pinckney said he was for "a vigorous Executive but was afraid the Executive powers of <the existing> Congress might extend to peace & war which would render the Executive a Monarchy, of the worst kind, towit an elective one." John Rutledge wanted the executive power placed in a single person, "tho' he was not for giving him the

12. Id. at 250.
13. Id. at 254.
14. Id. at 243.

power of war and peace." James Wilson supported a single executive but "did not consider the Prerogatives of the British Monarch as a proper guide in defining the Executive powers. Some of these prerogatives were of a Legislative nature. Among others that of war & peace &c."

Edmund Randolph worried about executive power, calling it "the fœtus of monarchy." The delegates at the convention, he said, had "no motive to be governed by the British Governmt. as our prototype." If the United States had no other choice it might adopt the British model, but "the fixt genius of the people of America required a different form of Government." Correct. Town hall meetings, broad public debate, and years of community service—all directed toward self-government—set Americans apart. Wilson agreed that the British model "was inapplicable to the situation of this Country; the extent of which was so great, and the manners so republican, that nothing but a great confederated Republic would do for it."[15]

Breaking free of monarchy had profound implications. Blackstone looked to the British king as the "pater familias of the nation." As historian Gordon Wood explains, to be a subject of the king "was to be a kind of child, to be personally subordinated to a paternal dominion." Subjects were necessarily "weak and inferior, without autonomy or independence."[16] The American colonists refused to be subjects, either to the king or to Parliament. Self-government requires individuals to take charge of their lives and their communities, to be adults, not children. Republican government in the United States cannot operate if citizens (and members of Congress) look to the President as pater familias, deferring to executive claims and initiatives. Nor is it compatible with republican government to accept what five Justices of the Supreme Court decide as the last word on constitutional meaning.

It is quite true that Hamilton looked to the British system with admiration and affection. In a lengthy speech at the Philadelphia Convention, he admitted that in his "private opinion he had no scruple in declaring . . . that the British Govt. was the best in the world."[17] Having disclosed his personal preference, he then agreed that the models of Locke and Blackstone had no application to America and its commitment to republican government. Hamilton's draft constitution broke free of Blackstone by requiring the Executive to seek the Senate's approval for treaties and ambassadors. In another rejection of Blackstone, the Senate would have "the sole power of declaring war."[18]

15. 1 Farrand 64–66.
16. Gordon S. Wood, The Radicalism of the American Revolution 11–12 (1993).
17. 1 Farrand at 288.
18. Id. at 292.

By the time the delegates had completed their labors, they had vested in Congress most of Locke's federative powers and Blackstone's royal prerogatives. The power of initiating war was not left to the solitary action of a single executive. It requires full deliberation and authorization by Congress. The President has no exclusive authority to appoint ambassadors and make treaties. For those actions, he needs the approval of the Senate. The power of issuing letters of marque and reprisal, placed by Blackstone in the king, is vested in Congress by Article I. Although the President was made Commander in Chief, the authority to raise and regulate fleets and armies (placed by Blackstone with the king) went to Congress. Under Article I, Clauses 12 and 13, Congress is empowered to raise and support armies and provide and maintain a navy. Clauses 14 through 16 authorize Congress to make regulations for the land and naval forces, call forth the militia, and provide for the organizing, arming, and disciplining of the militia, certainly a far cry from Blackstone's model of the king as generalissimo.

Clause 10 empowers Congress "to define and punish Piracies and Felonies committed on the high Seas, and Offenses against the Law of Nations." This, too, marked a fundamental rupture with Blackstone. For him, the power to accept, reject, and propose modifications to the law of nations on behalf of Great Britain was part of the royal prerogative. The law of nations consisted of "mutual compacts, treaties, leagues, and agreements" between various countries.[19] At the Philadelphia Convention, Madison explained why national legislation adopted by Congress was essential. The Constitution would "prevent those violations of the law of nations & of Treaties which if not prevented must involve us in calamities of foreign wars."[20]

An early statute passed by Congress, in 1790, provided punishments for certain crimes against the United States. One provision established fines and imprisonment for any person who attempted to prosecute or bring legal action against an ambassador or other public minister from another country. Persons who took those actions were deemed "violators of the laws of nations" who "infract the law of nations."[21] The political actor here was Congress, not the President (other than his signature). James Kent, in his *Commentaries* (1826), stated that an action against foreign ambassadors and public ministers "tends to provoke the resentment of the sovereign whom the ambassador represents, and to bring upon the calamities of war."[22] Because of this relationship to the war power, it was necessary for Congress to define national policy by statute.

19. 1 Blackstone, Commentaries, at 43.
20. 1 Farrand 316.
21. 1 Stat. 112, 117–18, sec. 25–28 (1790).
22. 1 James Kent, Commentaries on American Law 170 (1826).

The Constitution vests in Congress the power to regulate foreign commerce, an activity the framers understood to have a close relationship to the war power. Commercial conflicts between nations were often a cause of war. In *Gibbons v. Ogden* (1824), Chief Justice John Marshall said of the commerce power that "it may be, and often is, used as an instrument of war."[23] Guided by history and republican principles, the framers placed that power and responsibility with Congress.

Initiating War

At the Philadelphia Convention, the framers were determined to withhold from the President the power to take the country to war against another nation. Pierce Butler wanted to give the President that power, arguing that he "will have all the requisite qualities, and will not make war but when the Nation will support it."[24] In that sentiment he stood alone. Madison and Elbridge Gerry moved to change the draft language from "make war" to "declare war," leaving to the President "the power to repel sudden attacks," but not to initiate war. Roger Sherman added: "The Executive shd. be able to repel and not to commence war." Gerry expressed shock at Butler's position. He "never expected to hear in a republic a motion to empower the Executive alone to declare war."[25] George Mason "was agst giving the power of war to the Executive, because not <safely> to be trusted with it." He was "for clogging rather than facilitating war."[26] The motion to insert "declare" in place of "make" was agreed to.[27]

Some argue from this debate that although Congress may "declare" war, the President is at liberty to "make" war. That was never the understanding. Such an interpretation would defeat everything the framers said about Congress being the only political body authorized to take the country from a state of peace to a state of war. The President has authority to "repel sudden attacks": *defensive* actions. Anything of an offensive nature, including making war, is reserved solely to Congress. In cases discussed later, such as President Jefferson's action against the Barbary pirates in 1801, it was clearly understood that anything beyond defensive actions required congressional authorization. In the *Smith* case of 1806, federal judges spoke explicitly about Congress not merely declaring war

23. 22 U.S. (9 Wheat.) 1, 192 (1824).
24. 2 Farrand 318.
25. Id.
26. Id. at 319.
27. Id.

but *making* it.[28] Hamilton, a strong defender of presidential power in external affairs, acknowledged that it was up to Congress "to declare or make war."[29]

In articles, books, and legal memos, law professor and former Justice Department official John Yoo has claimed that the purpose of the Declare War Clause is not to vest in Congress the authority to initiate war. He reaches that position by relying on the British model that the framers expressly jettisoned. To Yoo, the war power provisions of the Constitution "are best understood as an adoption, rather than a rejection, of the traditional British approach to war powers."[30] That false conclusion appears in other writings over the years.[31] On its face and in its details, his argument wholly lacks substance. Only one framer came close to supporting executive wars: Pierce Butler, discussed above. Every other delegate at the convention and ratification debates spoke against that position.

Yoo argues that the framers included the Declare War Clause "to facilitate the federal government's representation of the nation in international affairs, and to make clear that the declaration of war was a power of the national government, not the state governments." There is no need to interpret the Declare War Clause to understand that going to war is a national decision. Authority over national wars is expressly stated in Articles I and II. Section 10 of Article I provides: "No States shall, without the Consent of Congress . . . engage in war, unless actually invaded, or in such imminent Danger as will not admit of delay." Other war-related authorities are withheld from the states by Section 10, including letters of marque and reprisal.

Yoo distorts the Declare War Clause by claiming that a declaration of war "performed a primarily juridical function under eighteenth-century international law."[32] In the "eighteenth-century mind, a *declaration* of war was not the same thing as a domestic *authorization* of war."[33] A declaration of war "represented the judgment of Congress, acting in a judicial capacity (as it does in impeachments), that a state of war existed between the United States and another nation." Through this analysis, a declaration of war "could take place either before or after hostilities had commenced."[34] To Yoo, a declaration of war "did

28. The *Smith* case is discussed in this chapter in the section "Judicial Rulings, 1800 to 1863."

29. 21 The Papers of Alexander Hamilton 461–62 (Syrett ed., 1974).

30. John C. Yoo, "The Continuation of Politics by Other Means: The Original Understanding of War Powers," 84 Cal. L. Rev. 167, 242 (1996).

31. E.g., John Yoo, The Powers of War and Peace: The Constitution and Foreign Affairs After 9/11, at 19, 27, 30–54, 89, 91–92 (2005). For my evaluation of Yoo's analysis, see Louis Fisher, "Lost Constitutional Moorings: Recovering the War Power," 81 Ind. L. Rev. 1199, 1233–47 (2006), available at http://www.loufisher.org/docs/wp/420.pdf.

32. Yoo, "The Continuation of Politics by Other Means," 84 Cal. L. Rev. at 242.

33. Id. (emphases in original).

34. Id.

not create or authorize; it recognized."[35] In short, a declaration of war by Congress merely recognized a war initiated by the President.

In a book published in 2005, Yoo repeats his argument that the Declare War Clause "served as a recognition of the legal status of hostile acts, rather than a necessary authorization for hostilities."[36] Whatever Yoo would like to draw from the "eighteenth-century mind," the American framers rejected that view, as did Congress, Presidents, and federal courts. The purpose of the Declare War Clause is to preserve republican government by keeping the power to initiate war in the legislative branch. That position is made clear in statements at the Philadelphia Convention and the state ratification debates.

Preventing Executive Wars

The framers placed in Congress the authority to initiate wars because they believed that Executives, in their search for fame and personal glory, have a natural appetite for war. Moreover, their military initiatives are destructive to the interests of the people.[37] In Federalist No. 4, John Jay expressed his opposition to executive wars. If anyone could have been sympathetic to executive power in foreign affairs it would have been Jay, whose duties during the Continental Congress gave him special insights into the need for executive discretion in carrying out foreign policy. But to Jay, initiating war was fundamentally different from general foreign policy duties:

[A]bsolute monarchs will often make war when their nations are to get nothing by it, but for purposes and objects merely personal, such as a thirst for military glory, revenge for personal affronts, ambition, or private compacts to aggrandize or support their particular families or partisans. These, and a variety of other motives, which affect only the mind of the sovereign, often lead him to engage in wars not sanctified by justice or the voice and interests of his people.[38]

In Federalist No. 69, Hamilton wrote that the President shared with the Senate the treaty power, compared to the British king, who "is the *sole possessor* of

35. Id. at 246.
36. Yoo, The Powers of War and Peace, supra note 31, at 147.
37. William Michael Treanor, "Fame, the Founding, and the Power to Declare War," 82 Corn. L. Rev. 695 (1997).
38. The Federalist 101.

the power of making treaties."[39] He explained how the British and American models differed in the field of military activities. The power of the king "extends to the *declaring* of war and to the *raising* and *regulating* of fleets and armies."[40] Unlike the king of England, the President "will have only the occasional command of such part of the militia of the nation as by legislative provision may be called into the actual service of the Union."[41]

At the Pennsylvania ratifying convention, James Wilson expressed a prevailing sentiment that the system of checks and balances "will not hurry us into war; it is calculated to guard against it. It will not be in the power of a single man, or a single body of men, to involve us in such distress; for the important power of declaring war is vested in the legislature at large."[42] To Wilson, declaring war was not (as John Yoo maintains) a mere juridical act to acknowledge presidential wars. In North Carolina, James Iredell noted that the king of Great Britain "is not only the commander-in-chief but has power, in time of war, to raise fleets and armies. He has also authority to declare war." By contrast, the President "has not the power of declaring war by his own authority, nor that of raising fleets and armies. These powers are vested in other hands."[43] In South Carolina, Charles Pinckney assured his colleagues that the President's power "did not permit him to declare war."[44]

Article II designates the President as Commander in Chief, but that title does not carry with it an independent authority to initiate war or act free of legislative control. Article II provides that the President "shall be Commander in Chief of the Army and Navy of the United States, and of the Militia of the several States, when called into the actual Service of the United States." Congress, not the President, does the calling. Article I grants Congress the power to provide "for calling forth the Militia to execute the laws of the Union, suppress Insurrections, and repel invasions." Presidential use of the militia depends on policy enacted by Congress.

When Congress passed legislation in 1792 to establish national policy for the militia, it provided that before the President could call up the militia, he would first have to be notified of a military threat "too powerful to be suppressed by the ordinary course of judicial proceedings." Only after an Associate Justice or a federal district judge verified the President of those conditions could he call forth the militia to suppress an insurrection. That judicial check was removed

39. Id. at 450 (emphasis in original).
40. Id. at 446 (emphases in original).
41. Id.
42. 2 Elliot 528.
43. 4 Elliot 107.
44. Id. at 287.

when Congress revised the legislation in 1795, but Congress can at any time determine by law how and when the President uses the militia.[45]

The Commander in Chief Clause is often interpreted as an exclusive, plenary power of the President, free of statutory checks. It is not. Instead, it offers several protections for republican, constitutional government. First, it preserves civilian supremacy over the military. The individual leading the armed forces is an elected civilian, not a general or admiral. Attorney General Edward Bates in 1861 concluded that the President is Commander in Chief not because he is "skilled in the art of war and qualified to marshal a host in the field of battle." He has that title for a different reason. Whatever military officer leads U.S. armies against an enemy, "he is subject to the orders of the *civil magistrate,* and he and his army are always 'subordinate to the civil power.'"[46] Congress is an essential part of that civil power.

The framers understood that the President may "repel sudden attacks," especially when Congress is out of session and unable to assemble quickly. But the power to take defensive actions does not permit the President to initiate wars and exercise the constitutional authority of Congress. President Washington took great care in instructing his military commanders that operations against Indians were to be limited to defensive actions. Any offensive action required congressional authority. He wrote in 1793: "The Constitution vests the power of declaring war with Congress; therefore no offensive expedition of importance can be undertaken until after they have deliberated upon the subject, and authorized such a measure."[47]

In 1801, President Jefferson directed that a squadron be sent to the Mediterranean to safeguard American interests against the Barbary pirates. Commanders were instructed to "protect our commerce & chastise their insolence—by sinking, burning or destroying their ships & Vessels wherever you shall find them."[48] On December 8, he informed Congress of his actions, asking lawmakers for further guidance. He said he was "[u]nauthorized by the Constitution, without the sanction of Congress, to go beyond the line of defense." It was up to Congress to authorize "measures of offense also."[49] In 1805, after conflicts

45. 1 Stat. 264, sec. 2 (1792); 1 Stat. 424 (1795). For further details on this period, see Louis Fisher, "Domestic Commander in Chief: Early Checks by Other Branches," 29 Cardozo L. Rev. 961 (2008), available at http://www.loufisher.org/docs/wp/418.pdf.

46. 10 Op. Att'y Gen. 74, 79 (1861) (emphasis in original).

47. 33 The Writings of George Washington 73 (Fitzpatrick ed., 1939). For details on military actions in the Indian Wars, see Fisher, Presidential War Power, at 17–20.

48. 1 Naval Documents Related to the United States Wars with the Barbary Powers 467 (1939).

49. 1 Richardson 315.

developed between the United States and Spain, Jefferson issued a public statement that articulates fundamental constitutional principles: "Congress alone is constitutionally invested with the power of changing our condition from peace to war."[50] In the *Smith* case of 1806, discussed later, a federal circuit court acknowledged that if a foreign nation invaded the United States, the President had an obligation to resist with force. But there was a "manifest distinction" between going to war with a nation at peace and responding to an actual invasion: "In the former case, it is the exclusive province of congress to change a state of peace into a state of war."[51]

The second value of the Commander in Chief Clause is accountability. Hamilton in Federalist No. 74 wrote that the direction of war "most peculiarly demands those qualities which distinguish the exercise of power by a single hand." The power of directing war and emphasizing the common strength "forms a usual and essential part in the definition of the executive authority."[52] Presidential leadership is essential but it cannot operate outside legislative control. The President is subject to the rule of law, including statutory and judicial restrictions.

At various times Congress has controlled military operations not only through statutory language but through committee oversight, such as the Joint Committee on the Conduct of the War during Lincoln's presidency. The committee was subject to criticism but it "brought speed and energy into the conduct of the war; . . . ferreted out abuses and put their fingers down heavily upon governmental inefficiency; . . . [and] labored, for a time at least, to preserve a balance and effect a cooperation between the legislative and executive departments."[53] The committee strengthened Lincoln's long-delayed decision to remove General George B. McClellan, prepared the groundwork for abolishing slavery, uncovered corruption and inefficiency, and served as a "splendid propaganda agency" in furthering the war effort.[54]

Another study credits the committee with helping to "bolster the resolve to continue the war" but faults it for lacking military expertise and "refus[ing] to defer to the experts."[55] Lincoln, as with most Presidents, had little military expertise and experience. But in their capacity as elected officials, Presidents and

50. Id. at 377.

51. United States v. Smith, 27 Fed. Cas. 1192, 1230 (C.C.N.Y. 1806) (No. 16, 342).

52. The Federalist 473.

53. William Whatley Pierson Jr., "The Committee on the Conduct of the Civil War," 23 Am. Hist. Rev. 550, 575–76 (1918).

54. Hans L. Trefousse, "The Joint Committee on the Conduct of the War," 10 Civil War Hist. 5, 7–9 (1964).

55. Bruce Tap, Over Lincoln's Shoulder: The Committee on the Conduct of the War 255, 259 (1998).

members of Congress possess a political legitimacy that cannot exist with non-elected experts, whether military or civilian. Republican government depends on popular sovereignty operating through elected officials. Most of them are members of Congress. Both Lincoln and Secretary of War Edwin M. Stanton shared a "distrust of professional military men," and Lincoln came to have great doubts "about the value of military expertise."[56] American wars, by deferring automatically to military leaders and reputed civilian experts, have placed a heavy price on the public.

The Truman Committee (the Senate Special Committee to Investigate the National Defense Program) helped shape mobilization efforts for World War II, especially by investigating waste and corruption in defense contracts. It functioned from the summer of 1941 to the spring of 1944.[57] The principal failure of Congress in recent decades has been to routinely defer to presidential and military decisions instead of exercising the independent judgment that is essential for democratic and constitutional government.[58]

Assertions of Inherent Powers

The framers understood that all three branches exercise not only powers expressly enumerated in the Constitution but also *implied*: powers that can be reasonably drawn from enumerated powers. Beginning at least with the Truman administration, claims have been made for "inherent" executive powers: powers that are beyond and independent of enumerated and implied powers. These presidential powers are said to inhere in the office and operate beyond legislative and judicial controls. *Black's Law Dictionary* defines "inherent powers" as "authority possessed without its being derived from another. . . . powers over and beyond those explicitly granted in the Constitution or reasonably to be implied from express grants."[59]

The framers recognized only two sources of constitutional power: enumerated and implied. Congress has the express power to legislate. To legislate in an informed manner, it has an implied power to investigate, issue subpoenas, and

56. David Herbert Donald, Lincoln 351, 357 (1995).

57. Theodore Wilson, "The Truman Committee, 1941," in Congress Investigates, 1792–1974, at 325–50 (Arthur S. Schlesinger Jr. and Roger Bruns, eds., 1975).

58. F. Ugboaja Ohaegbulam, A Culture of Deference: Congress, the President, and the Course of the U.S.-Led Invasion and Occupation of Iraq (2007); Stephen R. Weissman, A Culture of Deference: Congress's Failure of Leadership in Foreign Policy (1995); Barbara Hinckley, Less Than Meets the Eye: Foreign Policy Making and the Myth of the Assertive Congress (1994).

59. Black's Law Dictionary 703 (5th ed., 1979).

hold uncooperative witnesses in contempt. The President has the express duty to see that the laws are faithfully carried out. If a senior executive official (such as a department head) prevents a law from being carried out, the President has an implied power to remove that individual. The framers did not recognize powers that inhere in the executive. That concept is found in such writers as Blackstone and the prerogatives he recognized as the king's. He defined the king's prerogative as "those rights and capacities which the king enjoys alone." He spoke of powers that are "rooted in and spring from the king's political person," including the power "of making war or peace."[60]

Justice Department memos written during the administration of George W. Bush claimed the existence of presidential war powers that could not be limited by Congress. Assistant Attorney General Jay Bybee wrote on August 1, 2002: "Any effort by Congress to regulate the interrogation of battlefield combatants would violate the Constitution's sole vesting of the Commander-in-Chief authority in the President."[61] His memo claims that Congress "lacks authority under Article I to set the terms and conditions under which the President may exercise his authority as Commander in Chief to control the conduct of operations during a war."[62] Here Bybee seems to derive plenary presidential power from an express power: the Commander in Chief Clause. But Congress, especially in the area of war power, has its own express powers to counterbalance and check that clause. In other arguments, the Justice Department looked solely to inherent and unexpressed presidential power.

The concept of inherent power for the President (or any branch) is alien to the U.S. constitutional system, which depends on limited powers and checks and balances. The claim of presidential inherent powers did not surface until the early 1950s, when the Truman administration argued that the President possessed inherent, emergency powers to seize steel mills to prosecute the war in Korea. The Supreme Court rejected that theory.[63] President Nixon's assertion that, the Fourth Amendment notwithstanding, he had inherent authority to conduct warrantless domestic surveillance was similarly dismissed by the Court.[64]

60. 1 Blackstone, Commentaries 232–33.

61. Memorandum for Alberto R. Gonzales, Counsel to the President, from Jay S. Bybee, Assistant Attorney General, "Standards of Conduct for Interrogation Under 18 U.S.C. §§2340–2340A," at 39 (August 1, 2002) (hereafter "Bybee Memo"), available at http://www .justice.gov/olc/docs/memo-gonzales-aug2002.pdf, superseded by "Legal Standards Applicable Under 18 U.S.C. §§2340–2340A" (December 30, 2004), available at http://www.justice.gov/ olc/18usc23402340a2 .htm.

62. Bybee Memo, at 34–35.

63. Youngstown Co. v. Sawyer, 343 U.S. 579 (1952).

64. United States v. United States District Court, 407 U.S. 297 (1972).

During the George W. Bush administration, the Justice Department advised a federal appellate court: "Throughout this country's history, Presidents have exercised their inherent authority as Commander in Chief to establish military commissions, without any authorization from Congress."[65] Strangely, the department reached back to the 1780 trial of John André, a British spy. In three amicus briefs in this litigation (*Hamdan*), I pointed out that the President in 1780 did not exist and that the military trial of André proceeded entirely on the basis of legislative authority.[66] The Court in 2008 found zero merit to the argument for inherent authority, requiring President Bush to comply with statutory policy established by Congress and seek additional statutory authority if he needed it.[67]

No hint of inherent presidential war powers appears in the early decades of the republic. In 1793, Secretary of State Thomas Jefferson understood that the power over marque and reprisal, vested in Congress, is inseparable from the power to wage war. Reprisals are responses to what a nation considers to be an unjust military action. The making of a military reprisal against a nation, Jefferson said, "is a very serious thing. . . . when reprisal follows, it is considered as an act of war, and never yet failed to produce it in the case of a nation able to make war." If it became necessary to invoke this power, "Congress must be called on to take it; the right of reprisal being expressly lodged with them by the Constitution, and not with the Executive."[68]

Also in 1793, Madison called war "[t]he true nurse of executive aggrandizement. . . . In war, the honours and emoluments of office are to be multiplied; and it is the executive patronage under which they are to be enjoyed. It is in war, finally, that laurels are to be gathered; and it is the executive brow they are to encircle. The strongest passions and most dangerous weaknesses of the human breast; ambition, avarice, vanity, the honourable or venial love of fame, are all in conspiracy against the desire and duty of peace."[69] Five years later, at the time

65. "Brief for Appellants," at 59, Hamdan v. Rumsfeld, No. 04-5393 (D.C. Cir. December 8, 2004).

66. I wrote three amicus briefs in the *Hamdan* case: in D.C. Circuit, when the plaintiffs sought certiorari from the Supreme Court, and after the Court granted review.

67. Hamdan v. Rumsfeld, 548 U.S. 557, 593 (2006). The Court stated in a footnote: "Whether or not the President has independent power, absent congressional authorization, to convene military commissions, he may not disregard limitations that Congress has, in proper exercise of its own war powers, placed on his powers." Id. at 593, n.23. For further analysis of inherent powers, see Louis Fisher, The Law Library of Congress, "The 'Sole Organ' Doctrine" (August 2006), available at http://www.loufisher.org/docs/pip/441.pdf; Louis Fisher, "Invoking Inherent Powers: A Primer," 37 Pres. Stud. Q. 1 (2007), available at http://www.loufisher.org/docs/pip/440.pdf.

68. 3 The Writings of Thomas Jefferson 250 (Bergh ed., 1903).

69. 6 The Writings of James Madison 174 (Hunt ed., 1906).

of the Quasi-War against France, he told Jefferson that the Constitution "supposes, what the History of all Govts demonstrates, that the Ex. is the branch of power most interested in war, & most prone to it. It has accordingly with studied care, vested the question of war in the Legisl."[70]

During the Quasi-War, Hamilton discussed his broad theory of executive power. However, when Congress passed legislation on May 28, 1798, authorizing the President to seize armed French vessels,[71] he was asked what ship commanders could do prior to the enactment of that bill. He was "not ready to say that [the President] has any other power than merely to employ" ships with authority "to *repel* force by *force,* (but not to capture), and to repress hostilities within our waters including a marine league from our coasts." Any actions beyond those measures "must fall under the idea of *reprisals* & requires the sanction of that Department [Congress] which is to declare or make war."[72]

In the greatest crisis ever experienced by America, President Lincoln did not claim inherent power. At the start of the Civil War, he took extraordinary actions with Congress out of session, issuing proclamations calling forth the state militia, suspending the writ of habeas corpus, and placing a blockade on rebellious states. In his book on crisis government, published in 1948, Clinton Rossiter included a section called "The Lincoln Dictatorship." He claimed that Lincoln was "the sole possessor of the indefinite grant of executive power in Article II of the Constitution."[73] By drawing broadly from the "executive power" of Article II, Rossiter did not rely on express or implied powers but rather on what he regarded as a residue of inherent powers set aside for the executive. When Lincoln later explained to lawmakers what he had done during their absence, Rossiter claims that his message "is a significant assertion of the inherent crisis power of the President."[74]

Yet at no point did Lincoln invoke inherent powers to defend his actions. When Congress came back into session in July 1861, he described the emergency steps he had taken, adding this qualification: "whether strictly legal or not."[75] Through that language he made clear he did not act fully within the law, stating frankly he had exceeded his Article II powers. That point came through plainly when he told lawmakers that he believed his actions were not "beyond

70. Id. at 312.
71. 1 Stat. 561 (1798).
72. 21 The Papers of Alexander Hamilton 461–62 (Syrett ed., 1974) (emphases in original).
73. Clinton Rossiter, Constitutional Dictatorship: Crisis Government in the Modern Democracies 225 (1963 ed.).
74. Id. at 228.
75. 7 Richardson 3225.

the constitutional competency of Congress."[76] With those words he admitted he had exercised both Article I and Article II powers. Instead of claiming unchecked inherent powers, Lincoln understood that the only branch of government capable of making his acts legal was Congress. That is not the language of a dictator. Lawmakers debated his request for retroactive authority and granted it, with the explicit understanding that his acts had been illegal.[77] Congress passed legislation "approving, legalizing, and making valid all the acts, proclamations, and orders of the President, etc., as if they had been issued and done under the previous express authority and direction of the Congress of the United States."[78]

The Empty "Sole Organ" Doctrine

During the Iran-Contra hearings in 1987, several members of the Reagan administration defended giving assistance to Iran (in violation of the administration's public pledge of neutrality in the Iran–Iraq war) and providing funds to the Contras in Nicaragua (in violation of statutory policy). A frequently heard justification at the hearings relied on the *Curtiss-Wright* case of 1936, which supposedly granted the President "plenary and exclusive power as sole organ" of the national government in the field of international relations, "a power which does not require as a basis for its exercise an act of Congress."[79] Here is one more claim of inherent presidential power. As research director for the House Iran-Contra Committee and author of the sections in the final report dealing with institutional and constitutional issues, I explained why the language from *Curtiss-Wright* was not merely extraneous to the issue before the Court but falsely portrayed the sole-organ doctrine.[80] The reasons for the Court's misconceptions are explained below.

In defending the secret warrantless surveillance program that President Bush

76. Id.

77. Cong. Globe, 37th Cong., 1st Sess. 393 (1861) (statement of Senator Timothy Howe).

78. 12 Stat. 316 (1861). See Louis Fisher, "Abraham Lincoln: Preserving the Union and the Constitution," 3 Albany Gov't L. Rev. 503 (2010), available at http://www.loufisher/org/docs/wi/431.pdf.

79. "Iran-Contra Investigation," joint hearings before the Senate Select Committee on Secret Military Assistance to Iran and the Nicaraguan Opposition and the House Select Committee to Investigate Covert Arms Transactions with Iran, 100th Cong., 1st Sess., vol. 100-2, at 558; vol. 100-5, at 419–21, 426; vol. 100-7, part II, 38–39, 133–34.

80. Iran-Contra Affair, H. Rept. No. 100-433, S. Rept. No. 100-216, 100th Cong., 1st Sess. 472–74 (November 1987).

authorized after the terrorist attacks of September 11, 2001, the Justice Department relied in part on the sole-organ doctrine. The Department claimed that the activities of the National Security Agency "are supported by the President's well-recognized inherent constitutional authority as Commander in Chief and sole organ for the Nation in foreign affairs."[81] Well recognized within the Department, perhaps, but not by anyone who reads *Curtiss-Wright* with care. In a Department memo written on September 25, 2001, Deputy Assistant Attorney General John Yoo reached out to the sole-organ doctrine: "As future Chief Justice John Marshall famously declared [in 1800]: 'The President is the sole organ of the nation in its external relations, and its sole representative with foreign nations. . . . The [executive] department . . . is entrusted with the whole foreign intercourse of the nation.' 10 Annals of Cong. 613–14 (1800)." On that ground, Yoo argued, "it has not been difficult for the executive branch to assert the President's plenary authority in foreign affairs ever since."[82]

The sole-organ doctrine was popularized and misrepresented by Justice George Sutherland in *Curtiss-Wright*. The case had nothing to do with presidential power, whether plenary or inherent. It involved only *legislative power*: how much could Congress delegate *its* power to the President in the field of international affairs? In upholding the delegation, Sutherland added pages of dicta that were wholly irrelevant to the issue before the Court. He claimed that the principle that the federal government is limited to enumerated and implied powers "is categorically true only in respect to our internal affairs."[83] In arguing for independent and exclusive presidential powers in the field of foreign affairs, he relied on Marshall's speech in 1800.

What Sutherland (and Yoo) failed to do is to put Marshall's speech in proper context. When that is done, it is clear that Marshall never made a case for inherent, plenary, or independent powers for the President in foreign affairs.[84] Some members of the House of Representatives were prepared to censure or impeach President John Adams for turning over to Great Britain a British subject charged with murder. Marshall took the floor to explain why no grounds existed to

81. Memo from Attorney General Alberto R. Gonzales to the Majority Leader of the U.S. Senate, "Legal Authorities Supporting the Activities of the National Security Agency Described by the President," at 1, January 19, 2006 (hereafter "Gonzales Memo"), available at http://www .justice.gov/olc/2006/nsa-white-paper.pdf.

82. Memo opinion for Timothy Flanigan, Deputy Counsel to the President, from John C. Yoo, Deputy Assistant Attorney General, "The President's Constitutional Authority to Conduct Military Operations Against Terrorists and Nations Supporting Them," September 25, 2001 (hereafter "Yoo Memo"), reprinted in The Torture Papers 9 (Karen J. Greenberg and Joshua L. Dratel, eds., 2005).

83. United States v. Curtiss-Wright Corp., 299 U.S. 304, 315 (1936).

84. 10 Annals of Cong. 596, 613 (1800).

rebuke Adams. The Jay Treaty provided for extradition in cases involving the charge of murder. Adams was therefore not acting on the basis of any plenary or inherent power but rather on the express language in a treaty, with treaties under Article VI of the Constitution included as part of the "supreme Law of the Land."[85] Adams was thus acting on the basis of authority granted him by law.[86] Marshall's sole-organ speech had everything to do with express powers and the President's acting under authority granted by Congress, whether by treaty or by statute. It had nothing to do with inherent or plenary powers.

In his most recent book, *Crisis and Command* (2009), John Yoo repeats the passage in *Curtiss-Wright* where John Marshall describes the President as the "sole organ of the nation in its external relations."[87] Yoo does not give the reader any clue of what Marshall meant by those words. That understanding comes only by a careful reading of Marshall's entire speech.[88] In his later service as Secretary of State and Chief Justice of the Supreme Court, Marshall never advanced any notion of inherent, plenary, exclusive, or independent powers of the President in external affairs. As explained in the next section, Chief Justice Marshall looked solely to Congress in matters of war and understood that when a conflict arose between what Congress provided by statute and what a President announced by proclamation, in time of war, the statute represents the law of the nation.

Most scholarly studies of *Curtiss-Wright* have condemned Sutherland for his sloppy and dishonest misuse of Marshall's speech. Writing in 1944, C. Perry Patterson regarded Sutherland's position on the existence of inherent presidential powers to be "(1) contrary to American history, (2) violative of our political theory, (3) unconstitutional, and (4) unnecessary, undemocratic, and dangerous."[89] David M. Levitan, in 1946, repudiated Sutherland's theory, saying it marked "the furthest departure from the theory that [the] United States is a constitutionally limited democracy. It introduces the notion that national government possesses a secret reservoir of unaccountable power."[90] Law professor Michael Glennon

85. U.S. Const., art. VI, cl. 2 ("This Constitution, and the Laws of the United States which shall be made in Pursuance thereof; and all Treaties made, or which shall be made, under the Authority of the United States, shall be the supreme Law of the Land").

86. See Fisher, "The 'Sole Organ' Doctrine," supra note 67, at 7–9, and Louis Fisher, "Presidential Inherent Power: The 'Sole Organ' Doctrine," 37 Pres. Stud. Q. 139 (2007), available at http://www.loufisher.org/docs/pip/439.pdf.

87. John Yoo, Crisis and Command: The History of Executive Power from George Washington to George W. Bush 291 (2009).

88. Available at http://www.loufisher.org/docs/pip/444.pdf.

89. C. Perry Patterson, "In Re The United States v. The Curtiss-Wright Corporation," 22 Tex. L. Rev. 286, 297 (1944).

90. David M. Levitan, "The Foreign Relations Power: An Analysis of Mr. Justice Sutherland's Theory," 55 Yale L. J. 467, 493 (1946).

considered Sutherland's opinion "a muddled law review article wedged with considerable difficulty between the pages of the United States Reports."[91] Other scholarly evaluations of Sutherland's decision are similarly harsh.[92]

Some studies of *Curtiss-Wright* pay little or no attention to what Marshall meant by "sole organ," leaving the impression that he must have been talking about something of great and indefinite breadth. In one study, the historian Robert A. Divine provided excellent background on the litigation but concluded that Sutherland's ruling asserted "the supremacy of the President in conducting relations with other nations."[93] Divine did not explain that the case focused solely on congressional authority, not presidential authority, and that the expansive language by Sutherland was pure dicta. Divine states that the powers that flowed to the President after 1941 "rested securely on the far-reaching opinion of the Court that the President was the sole agent of the nation in the conduct of foreign affairs."[94] "Sole agent" is Divine's substitute for "sole organ," but Divine did not discuss Marshall or attempt to understand his intent.

A recent analysis of *Curtiss-Wright* by law professor H. Jefferson Powell provides instructive background on the conditions in South America that prompted Congress to pass arms embargo legislation and the prosecution of the Curtiss-Wright Export Corporation for violating the embargo. Powell quotes extensively from Sutherland's opinion, including "the very delicate, plenary and exclusive power of the President as the sole organ of the federal government in the field of international relations." He refers to Marshall describing the President as "the sole organ of the nation in its external relations, and its sole representative with foreign nations."[95] Powell discusses critics who characterize Sutherland's language as dicta and regard his references to Marshall and sole organ as "a cheat," but does not offer his own views on what Marshall meant by the term.[96]

The Court continues to cite the sole-organ doctrine with some regularity to uphold broad definitions of presidential power in foreign relations and to sup-

91. Michael J. Glennon, "Two Views of Presidential Foreign Affairs Power: *Little* v. *Barreme* or *Curtiss-Wright*?," 13 Yale J. Int'l L. 5, 13 (1988).

92. For a review of these scholarly studies, see Louis Fisher, "The 'Sole Organ' Doctrine," supra note 67, at 20–23.

93. Robert A. Divine, "The Case of the Smuggled Bombers," in Quarrels That Have Shaped the Constitution 219 (John A. Garraty, ed., 1966 ed.).

94. Id. at 221.

95. H. Jefferson Powell, "The Story of *Curtiss-Wright Export Corporation*," in Presidential Power Stories 222 (Christopher H. Schroeder and Curtis A. Bradley, eds., 2009).

96. Id. at 230. In a footnote, Powell summarizes one of his articles on *Curtiss-Wright*, "concluding that the critics are right about the meaning of the 'sole organ' passage in Marshall's speech but that Marshall nevertheless thought the president enjoys independent policymaking authority over foreign affairs." The footnote does not explain why the critics are right.

port extensive delegations of legislative power to the President.[97] Those citations have a routine, mechanical quality, as though whoever wrote them never read Marshall's speech. Although some Justices in concurrences have described the President's foreign relations powers as "exclusive," the Court itself has never denied to Congress its constitutional authority to enter the field and limit, reverse, or modify presidential decisions in the area of national security and foreign affairs.[98]

Judicial Rulings, 1800 to 1863

On judicial authority to decide questions of war, John Yoo has written that the framers anticipated that federal courts "were to have no role at all."[99] That was not the intent of the framers and bears no relationship to early judicial rulings. Beginning in 1800, the Supreme Court accepted and decided a large number of war power cases, with few examples of efforts to sidestep them.[100] Federal courts understood that the decision to initiate war lay solely with Congress, not with the President, and that if a conflict arose between statutory limitations in time of war and what the President had ordered during those hostilities, the legislative judgment necessarily prevailed as national policy.

The first U.S. war against another country under the Constitution, the Quasi-War of 1798, underscored the primary authority of Congress over war. Congress did not declare war against France. Instead, it passed a number of statutes that authorized military preparation with the clear understanding that it was going to war. During debate in the House, Representative Edward Livingston considered the country "now in a state of war; and let no man flatter himself that the vote which has been given is not a declaration of war."[101] Attorney General Charles Lee, after reviewing the laws that Congress had passed, advised President John Adams that "there exists not only an *actual* maritime war between France and the United States, but a maritime war *authorized* by both nations."[102] In Federalist No. 25, Hamilton had earlier acknowledged that the "ceremony of a formal denunciation [declaration] of war has of late fallen into disuse."[103]

97. Fisher, "The 'Sole Organ' Doctrine," supra note 67, at 23–27.
98. E.g., Webster v. Doe, 486 U.S. 592, 605–06 (1988) (O'Connor, J., concurring).
99. Yoo, supra note 30, at 170.
100. The major period of courts avoiding war power cases was during the Vietnam War. Louis Fisher, "National Security Law: The Judicial Role," in Freedom and the Rule of Law 203–26 (Anthony Peacock, ed., 2010); Louis Fisher, "Judicial Review of the War Power," 35 Pres. Stud. Q. 466 (2005), available at http://www.loufisher.org/docs/wp/422.pdf.
101. 9 Annals of Cong. 1519 (1798).
102. 1 Op. Att'y Gen. 84 (1798) (emphases in original).
103. The Federalist 211.

In 1800 and 1801, the Supreme Court decided its first two cases involving the Quasi-War. It held that Congress has a constitutional choice when it initiates wars. It can issue a formal declaration, consistent with language in the Constitution, or pass authorizing statutes, as it did with the Quasi-War. The latter type of military conflict would be "limited," "partial," and "imperfect."[104] Justice Samuel Chase recognized that Congress had authorized for the Quasi-War "hostilities on the high seas" but not "hostilities on land."[105] Congress was fully empowered by the Constitution to set statutory limits and President Adams was bound by them. By law, Congress controlled the scope of the war power carried out by the Commander in Chief. A year later, Chief Justice John Marshall announced the decision in a second case involving the Quasi-War. In clear language, he underscored the primary role of Congress over war: "The whole powers of war being, by the constitution of the United States, vested in congress, the acts of that body can alone be resorted to as our guides in this enquiry."[106]

In 1804 the Court decided a third Quasi-War case, *Little v. Barreme*. Congress had authorized President Adams to seize vessels sailing *to* French ports. He issued a proclamation directing American ships to capture vessels sailing *to or from* French ports. Could his powers as Commander in Chief supersede the direction that Congress by statute had provided? Writing for a unanimous Court, Chief Justice Marshall held that the order by Adams "cannot change the nature of the transaction, or legalize an act which, without those instructions, would have been a plain trespass."[107] The policy decided by Congress in a statute necessarily prevailed over conflicting presidential orders. Congress not only initiated wars but through statutory action could define their scope and purpose.

A circuit court decision in 1806 further demonstrates the broad understanding that Congress is preeminent in matters of war. The government prosecuted Colonel William S. Smith under the Neutrality Act for engaging in military actions against Spain. In defense, he claimed that his military enterprise "was begun, prepared, and set on foot with the knowledge and approbation of the executive department of our government" (the Jefferson administration).[108] How could a court check his story? Subpoena administration officials and have them testify under oath? The court decided that was not necessary. It ruled that a President or his assistants could not somehow authorize military adventures that violated congressional policy. The court described the Neutrality Act as

104. Bas v. Tingy, 4 U.S. (4 Dall.) 37, 40, 43 (1800).
105. Id. at 43.
106. Talbot v. Seeman, 1 Cr. (5 U.S.) 1, 28 (1801).
107. Little v. Barreme, 6 U.S. (2 Cr.) 170, 179 (1804).
108. United States v. Smith, 27 Fed. Cas. 1192, 1229 (C.C.N.Y. 1806) (No. 16,342).

"declaratory of the law of nations; and besides, every species of private and unauthorized hostilities is inconsistent with the principles of the social compact, and the very nature, scope, and end of civil government."[109] Neither the President nor executive officials had any authority to waive or ignore the Neutrality Act: "The president of the United States cannot control the statute, nor dispense with its execution, and still less can he authorize a person to do what the law forbids."[110] The court asked: "Does [the President] possess the power of making war? That power is exclusively vested in congress."[111]

The Supreme Court's decision in *The Prize Cases* (1863), upholding Lincoln's blockade on the South at the start of the Civil War, is often cited as recognizing an independent and inherent presidential power over war. On January 19, 2006, the Justice Department released a 42-page "white paper" providing legal arguments in support of a secret surveillance program conducted by the National Security Agency. The program violated congressional policy under the Foreign Intelligence Surveillance Act (FISA), which requires a FISA Court authorization for electronic surveillance in most instances and certainly the NSA operation. Among other authorities, the Department referred to *The Prize Cases* as support for independent presidential authority to use military force to resist an invasion even in the absence of congressional approval.[112] A Justice Department memo by Deputy Assistant Attorney General John Yoo on September 25, 2001, stated that Lincoln's blockade, as upheld in *The Prize Cases*, "was a question 'to be *decided by him*' and which the Court could not question, but must leave to 'the political department of the Government to which the power was entrusted'"—that is, the President.[113]

If Lincoln's decision "could not be questioned" by the Court, why was it litigated, why did his lawyers have to mount a defense, and why did the Court split 5 to 4 on the merits? The case might have been restricted to the question of whether the ships were subject to confiscation and whether those who seized them were entitled to a bounty, but the Court addressed the broad constitutional powers of Congress and the President. The ruling in *The Prize Cases* did not sanction independent presidential actions to initiate war. In upholding the blockade, Justice Robert Grier said that in the event of foreign invasion the President was not only authorized "but bound to resist force by force. He does not initiate the war, but is bound to accept the challenge without waiting for any

109. Id.
110. Id. at 1230.
111. Id.
112. Gonzales Memo, supra note 81, at 9. See also id. at 38.
113. Yoo Memo, supra note 82, at 5–6 (emphasis in original).

special legislative authority."[114] His observation merely restates the framers' understanding that the President may "repel sudden attacks."

The Prize Cases had nothing to do with a foreign invasion of the United States or a U.S. offensive action against another country. Lincoln's blockade was a measure taken in time of civil war. Justice Grier carefully limited the President's power to defensive action: "Congress alone has the power to declare a national or foreign war." The President "has no power to initiate or declare a war against either a foreign nation or a domestic State."[115] Richard Henry Dana Jr., who represented the government in this case, took exactly the same position during oral argument. He said the blockade had nothing to do with "the right *to initiate a war, as a voluntary act of sovereignty.* That is vested only in Congress."[116]

In preparing for the case, Dana reviewed statutes to determine whether any existing legislation by Congress at the time of the firing on Fort Sumter restricted what President Lincoln could do with blockades and capture of vessels.[117] He wanted to be sure that Lincoln had acted consistently with congressional policy. He concluded that "no act of Congress had, when the capture was made, or has since, conflicted with the acts of the President."[118] That point is crucial. Dana understood that the President is controlled by statutory policy. He did not claim that the President possessed some kind of inherent authority in time of war to justify ignoring or violating existing law enacted by Congress.

Presidential Deceit

The framers' fear of executive wars has been validated by Presidents who wanted to gain new territory, pursue partisan objectives, and satisfy other political goals. They were willing to take the country to war through dissembling, misrepresentation, and stealth. Strong words, but look at the record. In doing so, let us concede that presidential deceit succeeds only with the assistance of public support backed by congressional and judicial acquiescence.

On December 2, 1845, President James Polk reviewed for Congress diplomatic efforts under way to settle several disputes with Mexico, including the boundary "between Mexico and the State of Texas."[119] Efforts were under way to negotiate an agreement on the border. Despite uncertainty about the bound-

114. The Prize Cases, 67 U.S. (2 Black) 635, 668 (1863).
115. Id.
116. Id. at 660 (emphases in original).
117. 3 Landmark Briefs 517.
118. Id. at 515.
119. 5 Richardson 2241.

ary line, on May 11, 1846, Polk told Congress about military hostilities between U.S. and Mexican soldiers. He said that Mexican forces "have at last invaded our territory and shed the blood of our fellow-citizens on our own soil."[120]

The message to Congress and the general public could not have carried more emotion: *American blood shed on American soil*. But there was no evidence that the territory on which Mexican and American forces clashed belonged to the United States. Nevertheless, Congress promptly passed legislation that "a state of war exists" between the two countries.[121] After Polk's misrepresentations became clear, the House of Representatives on January 3, 1848, censured him for "unnecessarily and unconstitutionally" beginning the Mexican War.[122]

When the war was over, Polk, in a message to Congress on July 6, 1848, admitted that the border remained uncertain and that a treaty presented to Mexico contained a "boundary line with due precision upon authoritative maps . . . to establish upon the ground landmarks which shall show the limits of both Republics."[123] Several weeks later, on July 24, Polk said that after Texas had won its independence, it had "asserted and exercised" title to certain territory along the border with Mexico but never legally occupied it.[124] An assertion is not legal title. He added: when war began, Mexico was "in possession of the disputed territory."[125] Somewhere in Polk's mind, disputed territory became American soil.

On February 15, 1898, the American battleship *Maine* exploded while sitting in the Havana harbor, killing two officers and 250 enlisted men. Fourteen of the injured later died, bringing the death toll to 266. A naval board of inquiry concluded that the blast resulted from a mine placed outside the ship. As to the possibility of the explosion coming from a magazine within the ship containing ammunition, the board said "there had never been a case of spontaneous combustion of coal on board the MAINE."[126] The board did not identify who might have placed the mine, but its report led many to accuse Spain of sabotage, helping to whet the public's appetite for military action. A declaration of war soon came from Congress.[127]

120. Id. at 2288.

121. 9 Stat. 9 (1846).

122. Cong. Globe, 30th Cong., 1st Sess. 95 (1848).

123. 5 Richardson 2438.

124. Id. at 2446.

125. Id. For additional details on Polk and the Mexican War, see Louis Fisher, The Law Library of Congress, "The Mexican War and Lincoln's 'Spot Resolutions,'" August 18, 2009, available at http://www.loufisher.org/docs/wi/433.pdf.

126. Official Report of the Naval Board of Inquiry into the Loss of the Battleship MAINE (Sampson Board), available at http://www.spanamwar.com/mainerpt.htm.

127. 30 Stat. 364 (1898).

There may not have been a case of spontaneous combustion on the *Maine,* but the board should have acknowledged that other U.S. ships had experienced spontaneous combustion of coal in bunkers. The board failed to call upon many technically qualified experts. George W. Melville, the Navy's chief engineer, doubted that a mine caused the explosion but was not asked for his views. He suspected that the cause of the disaster was a magazine explosion.[128] Philip R. Alger, the Navy's leading ordnance expert, told the *Washington Evening Star* a few days after the blast that the damage appeared to come from a magazine explosion.[129]

Many ships, including the *Maine,* had coal bunkers located next to magazines filled with ammunition, gun shells, and gunpowder. Only a bulkhead separated the two compartments. Fresh surfaces of newly broken coal oxidize as part of a chemical reaction that releases heat. If not dissipated, the heat accelerates the reaction and puts at risk the nearby magazines. Several weeks before the *Maine* exploded, an investigative board on January 27, 1898, warned the Secretary of the Navy about spontaneous coal fires that could detonate magazines.[130] Fires from coal bunkers happened frequently. From 1894 to 1908, more than 20 coal bunker fires were reported on U.S. naval ships.[131]

In 1974, Admiral Hyman G. Rickover asked naval historians and specialists to take another look at the sinking of the *Maine.* They determined that the explosion was, "without a doubt," internal.[132] Their study decided that the board of inquiry in 1898 was loath to place blame on either the design or construction of the ship, even though bunker fires were well-known, or on the competence of the commanding officer and his crew. There was a "natural tendency to look for reasons for the loss that did not reflect upon the Navy."[133]

A book by historian Lewis Gould in 1982 concluded that inadequate ventilation within the *Maine* led to a fire in the coal bunkers that set off nearby gunpowder.[134] Historian John L. Offner wrote his doctoral dissertation on the Spanish-American War. His book, published in 1992, noted that from 1895 to 1898 a total of 13 other American ships had fires associated with spontaneous combustion in coal bunkers.[135] In 1998, the National Geographic Society com-

128. H. G. Rickover, How the Battleship *Maine* Was Destroyed ix, xvii, 46 (2d rev. ed., 1995).
129. Id. at 46.
130. Thomas B. Allen, "Remember the *Maine?*," National Geographic, February 1998, at 108.
131. Rickover, How the Battleship *Maine* Was Destroyed, at 125.
132. Id.
133. Id. at 95.
134. Lewis L. Gould, The Spanish-American War and President McKinley 35 (1982).
135. John L. Offner, An Unwanted War: The Diplomacy of the United States and Spain over Cuba, 1895–1898, at 123 (1992).

missioned a study by Advanced Marine Enterprises (AME) to prepare a computer model to explore the cause of the *Maine*'s destruction. Although the assumptions that went into the computer model indicated that a coal fire "could have been the first step" in the sinking of the ship, AME concluded that a mine was the more likely cause, conceding that its findings were "not definitive."[136] These divergent and conflicting explanations were not available to members of Congress and the general public in 1898.[137]

On August 3, 1964, President Lyndon Johnson reported that on the previous day the North Vietnamese had attacked the U.S. destroyer *Maddox* in the Gulf of Tonkin.[138] The following day, in a radio and television address, he described a second attack, this one against two American destroyers.[139] He asked Congress to pass "a resolution making it clear that our Government is united in its determination to take all necessary measures in support of freedom and in defense of peace in Southeast Asia."[140] With little debate and no effort by Congress to independently determine the accuracy of Johnson's statements, the Tonkin Gulf Resolution passed the Senate on August 6 by a vote of 88 to 2, and the House a day later, 416 to 0. Johnson signed the resolution into law on August 10.[141]

From the start, there were doubts that the second attack had ever occurred. The commander of the *Maddox* sent this cable on August 4: "Review of action makes many recorded contacts and torpedoes doubtful. Freak weather effects and over-eager sonarman may have accounted for many reports. No actual visual sightings by *Maddox*. Suggest complete evaluation before any further action."[142] Other studies over the years, including a statement by former Secretary of Defense Robert McNamara in 1995, concluded there was no second attack.[143]

---

136. Thomas B. Allen, "A Special Report: What Really Sank the *Maine?*," Naval History, March–April 1998, at 5, 12–13, available at http://proquest.umi.com/pqdweb?index=2&did =83179245&SrchMode=3&sid=l&Fmt=3&Vlnst=PROD&VType=PQD&RQT=309&VNa me=PQD&TS=1249051089&clientld=45714.

137. For the various analyses of the sinking of the *Maine*, see Louis Fisher, The Law Library of Congress, "Destruction of the *Maine*," August 4, 2009, available at http://www.loufisher.org/docs/wi/434.pdf.

138. Public Papers of the Presidents, 1963–64, II, at 926–27.

139. Id. at 927–28.

140. Id. at 927.

141. 78 Stat. 384 (1964).

142. "The Gulf of Tonkin, the 1964 Incidents," hearing before the Senate Foreign Relations Committee, 90th Cong., 2d Sess. 54 (1968).

143. Keith B. Richburg, "Mission to Hanoi," Washington Post, November 11, 1995, at A21, A25. See also Joseph C. Goulden, Truth Is the First Casualty: The Gulf of Tonkin Affairs—Illusion and Reality (1969), and Edwin E. Moïse, Tonkin Gulf and the Escalation of the Vietnam War (1996).

It was particularly on the basis of the claimed second attack that Congress passed the Gulf of Tonkin Resolution. A "whereas" clause in the resolution states that North Vietnamese naval units had "deliberately and repeatedly" attacked U.S. naval vessels.[144] In 2005, the National Security Agency released a study that concluded what had long been suspected: *there was no second attack.* The NSA explained that what had been reported as a second attack consisted of late signals coming from the first.[145] This would be one of many times that the United States, with presidential encouragement, went to war on the basis of false information.

In November 1986, members of Congress learned that some officials of the Reagan administration had secretly violated the Boland Amendment, which prohibited assistance to the Contra resistance in Nicaragua. The amendment had been rewritten and tightened several times to block assistance of any kind, direct or indirect. Nevertheless, administration officials decided to continue the assistance. Denied funds from Congress, they sought financial assistance from private individuals and foreign governments. Those actions marked a fundamental violation of the Constitution and put President Reagan at risk of impeachment, had it been demonstrated that he personally knew about and authorized efforts to violate statutory policy and funding restrictions. Several individuals went to prison for their involvement. In December 1992, President George H. W. Bush issued pardons to six administration officials who faced prosecution and possible conviction. Although Congress investigated the Iran-Contra affair, the scope of illegality within the administration could never be adequately determined because key documents had been destroyed and concerted efforts were made to obstruct the work of the independent counsel, Lawrence Walsh.[146]

In October 2002, Congress passed the Iraq Resolution to empower President Bush to use military force against Iraq. The administration told lawmakers and the public that Iraq possessed weapons of mass destruction and had the capacity to inflict even greater damage on the United States than the 9/11 terrorist attacks. All of the executive claims about aluminum tubes, uranium ore from a country in Africa, the presence of al Qaeda in Iraq, the existence of chemical and biological weapons, mobile labs carrying biological agents, and drones capable

144. 78 Stat. 384 (1964).

145. Robert J. Hanyok, "Skunks, Bogies, Silent Hounds, and the Flying Fish: The Gulf of Tonkin Mystery, 2–4 August 1964," Cryptologic Quarterly, declassified by the National Security Agency on November 3, 2005, available at http://www.nsa.gov/public_info/_files/gulf_of _tonkin/articles/rel1_skunks_bogies.pdf.

146. Lawrence B. Walsh, Firewall: The Iran-Contra Conspiracy and Cover-up (1997).

of delivering WMDs were subject to skepticism and regularly discredited in the press.

Congressional committees with the capacity, but perhaps not the will, could have scrutinized those claims. Instead of passing the Iraq Resolution, lawmakers should have told the administration that the claims were too speculative and unsubstantiated to justify war. It was therefore necessary to send inspectors into Iraq to determine the facts. Congress did not take that easily available option. Within a short time, it became clear that all of the administration claims about Iraqi capability of possessing and using WMDs were entirely vacuous.[147]

Legislation was introduced in the House of Representatives in 2009 to apply criminal penalties to Presidents and executive officials who knowingly and willfully mislead Congress or the American people for the purpose of gaining support for the use of U.S. armed forces. Critics of the bill (H.R. 743) argued that it would chill speech protected by the First Amendment, but no public official has a constitutional right to dispense misleading information, especially about the need for war. In their defense, officials can say they thought at the time the information was correct and reliable. If criminal penalties make them hesitant to mislead Congress and the public, all well and good. I testified in favor of the bill at hearings before a subcommittee of the House Judiciary Committee on July 27, 2009.[148]

It is appropriate to condemn Presidents who present a false picture and prey upon fear. It is equally just to condemn Congress for not performing its role as a coequal branch and exercising independent judgment. The Iraq Resolution deferred to President Bush on the need for force, leaving to his determination whether the United States would rely "on further diplomatic or other peaceful means" to resolve the threat.[149] In that sense, the decision to go from a state of peace to a state of war, a fundamental step reserved to Congress under the Constitution, was left with President Bush. In my judgment: an unconstitutional war. For reasons explained in the next section, there were two other unconstitutional wars: Korea and Kosovo.

---

147. Analysis of all six administration claims about Iraqi WMDs appears in Louis Fisher, "Justifying War Against Iraq," in Rivals for Power 289–313 (James A. Thurber, ed., 2006).

148. My testimony is available at http://www.loufisher.org/docs/wi/435.pdf. See also Louis Fisher, "When Wars Begin: Misleading Statements by Presidents," 40 Pres. Stud. Q. 171 (2010), available at http://www/loufisher.org/docs/wi/432.pdf.

149. 116 Stat. 1501, sec. 3(b) (2002). For a critique of the manner in which the Bush administration and Congress (both Democrats and Republicans) passed the Iraq Resolution, see Louis Fisher, "Deciding on War Against Iraq: Institutional Failures," 118 Pol. Sci. Q. 389 (2003), available at http://www.loufisher.org/docs/wp/423.pdf.

Bypassing Congress Entirely

The record of the Bush administration and Congress with the Iraq Resolution in 2002 marked a serious failure by both branches. The deference and passivity of lawmakers in the wars against Mexico in 1846, Spain in 1898, and North Vietnam in 1964 represent other errors of judgment. Deficient as those legislative actions were, they resulted in some debate and passage of a statute. After World War II, there has developed the practice of Presidents going to war without ever coming to Congress. Lawmakers tolerate this with little protest and little understanding of their constitutional duties. Nor has there been much in the way of public debate or scholarly concern. The two major examples of Presidents bypassing Congress (and public control) are Korea in 1950 and Kosovo in 1999.

In June 1950, President Truman ordered U.S. troops to Korea without first requesting or receiving congressional authority. Secretary of State Dean Acheson advised Truman not to ask Congress for a joint resolution supporting the decision to use American troops against North Korea.[150] Nor did Truman return to Congress after he had taken his initiatives and request authority at that time, as Lincoln had done during the Civil War. Instead, Truman cited what he considered to be treaty commitments reflected in resolutions passed by the U.N. Security Council as sufficient authority to use military force against North Korea.[151]

U.N. resolutions are not a legal substitute for congressional authority. They cannot be. If they were, the President and the Senate through the treaty process could strip from the House of Representatives its constitutional role in deciding questions of war, and in fact strip the same authority from future House and Senate control. That process would radically amend the Constitution and undermine the commitment to a republic, self-government, public participation, Congress as a coequal branch, and the system of checks and balances.

The history of the U.N. Charter makes it very clear that all parties in the legislative and executive branches understood that the decision to use military force through the U.N. required prior approval from both houses of Congress. If the U.N. found it necessary to use military force against aggressors under Chapter VII, U.N. members would make available to the Security Council, "in accordance with a special agreement or agreements," armed forces and other assistance for the purpose of maintaining international peace and security. The agreements were to be concluded between the Security Council and member states, and "shall be subject to ratification by the signatory states in accordance with their respective

---

150. Glenn D. Paige, *The Korean Decision, June 24–30, 1950*, at 187 (1968).
151. *Public Papers of the Presidents, 1950*, at 491–92.

constitutional processes." At the time the Senate debated the Charter, Truman wired a cable from Potsdam to Senator Kenneth McKeller on July 27, 1945, making this pledge: "When any such agreement or agreements are negotiated it will be my purpose to ask the Congress for appropriate legislation to approve them."[152] His request would go to *Congress*—both houses—not just the Senate. With that firm understanding, the Senate approved the Charter by a vote of 89 to 2.[153]

Under the Charter, each member state of the U.N. had to decide how to fulfill its "constitutional processes." Initially, Secretary of State John Foster Dulles thought that special agreements would need the approval only of the Senate and not the full Congress.[154] Several Senators, citing language from Article I that vests war powers in Congress, not the Senate, disagreed with Dulles.[155] Dulles backtracked a bit. The central point he wanted to make, he said, was that the use of force "cannot be made by exclusive Presidential authority through an executive agreement." Whether Congress should act by treaty (Senate) or by joint resolution (both houses) he was less sure about.[156] It was in response to this debate that Truman sent his wire from Potsdam, stating he would seek approval of the full Congress.

Congress did not depend on the Potsdam cable. To determine by law how the United States would fulfill its commitment to provide military assistance to the Security Council, Congress passed the U.N. Participation Act of 1945. In the clearest possible language, Section 6 states that the agreements "shall be subject to the approval of the Congress by appropriate Act or joint resolution."[157] What Truman had pledged with his Potsdam message was now law. The restrictions on the President's power under Section 6 were modified somewhat by amendments adopted in 1949, allowing the President on his own initiative to provide military forces to the U.N. for "cooperative action." However, presidential discretion to deploy those forces was subject to stringent conditions: they can serve only as observers and guards, can perform only in a noncombatant capacity, and cannot exceed 1,000 in number.[158] In providing these forces to

152. 91 Cong. Rec. 8185 (1945).

153. Id. at 8190.

154. "The Charter of the United Nations," hearings before the Senate Committee on Foreign Relations, 79th Cong., 1st Sess. 298 (1945).

155. 91 Cong. Rec. 8021 (1945) (Senator Lucas); id. at 8021–24 (Senators McClellan, Hatch, Fulbright, Maybank, Overton, Hill, Ellender, and George).

156. Id. at 8027–28.

157. 59 Stat. 621, sec. 6 (1945). Section 6 offers the President some flexibility in other situations, but they do not negate the requirement for express approval from Congress for special agreements authorizing military action under an Article 43 act of aggression.

158. 63 Stat. 735–36, sec. 5 (1949).

the U.N., the President shall ensure that the troops not involve "the employment of armed forces contemplated by Chapter VII of the United Nations Charter."[159]

After this extensive debate and statutory action, supposedly adopting safeguards to protect congressional authority and the Constitution, Truman in 1950 went to war against Korea without seeking congressional authority, either before or after his commitment of troops. He violated his Potsdam pledge, the U.N. Charter, the U.N. Participation Act, and the Constitution, yet few members of Congress raised any objections. Truman told the nation that the U.N. Security Council had acted to order a withdrawal of North Korean forces to positions north of the 38th parallel, and that "in accordance with the resolution of the Security Council, the United States will vigorously support the effort of the Council to terminate this serious breach of the peace."[160] More injurious was Truman's breach of the Constitution.[161]

On June 29, 1950, Secretary of State Acheson claimed that all U.S. actions taken in Korea "have been under the aegis of the United Nations."[162] "Aegis" is a fudge word, meaning "shield" or "protection." He used the word to suggest that the United States was acting under the legal banner of the U.N., which was patently false. He argued that Truman had done his "utmost to uphold the sanctity of the Charter of the United Nations and the rule of law."[163] In fact, Truman committed forces before the council called for military action and acted against the rule of law. In his memoirs, Acheson admitted that "some American action, said to be in support of the resolution of June 27, was in fact ordered, and possibly taken, prior to the resolution."[164]

Even if a case could be made that the emergency facing Truman in June 1950 required him to act immediately without receiving congressional authority, nothing prevented him from returning promptly to Congress (as Lincoln did) to ask for a supporting statute to be applied retroactively.[165] Congress's reaction to Truman's usurpation of the war power was largely passive.[166] Academics might have

159. Id.

160. Public Papers of the Presidents, 1950, at 491.

161. Louis Fisher, "The Korean War: On What Legal Basis Did Truman Act?," 89 Am. J. Int'l L. 21 (1995), available at http://www.loufisher.org/docs/wp/425.pdf.

162. 23 Dep't of State Bull. 43 (1950).

163. Id. at 46.

164. Dean Acheson, Present at the Creation 408 (1969). See also Edwin C. Hoyt, "The United States Reaction to the Korean Attack: A Study of the Principles of the United Nations Charter as a Factor in American Policy-Making," 55 Am. J. Int'l L. 45, 53 (1961).

165. John Norton Moore, "The National Executive and the Use of the Armed Forces Abroad," 21 Naval War College Rev. 28, 32 (1969).

166. Fisher, Presidential War Power, at 100–02.

been a check, but instead of upholding constitutional principles they rushed to Truman's support with superficial and misinformed arguments. The names of these presidential apologists include Henry Steele Commager and Arthur M. Schlesinger Jr. Over a decade later, when the Vietnam War turned sour, both men publicly expressed regret for their positions in 1950. It is always helpful to admit one's errors, but the time for professional integrity was in 1950, not in the mid-1960s.[167]

On April 10, 2008, the House Foreign Affairs Committee held hearings on war power legislation "for the 21st Century." I testified that the bill under consideration (H.J. Res. 53) helped remedy serious deficiencies in the War Powers Resolution of 1973. I disagreed with language permitting military action on the basis of resolutions passed by the U.N. Security Council.[168] The bill was later amended to correct that provision, but neither house has demonstrated sufficient awareness of this issue to prohibit Presidents from using council resolutions as a substitute for legislative authority. The framers expected each branch to protect its constitutional powers. In the crucial area of war, Congress repeatedly fails to do that.

There is a third unconstitutional war: Kosovo in 1999. President Bill Clinton was unable to follow the Truman model of getting authority from the U.N. Security Council because it refused to endorse military action in Yugoslavia. In 1998, Clinton decided to turn to NATO countries to authorize military action. Like the U.N. Charter, NATO is a treaty. Like the U.N. Charter, the President and the Senate through the treaty process cannot transfer the constitutional powers of the House and the Senate to NATO countries.[169] Moreover, Section 8(a) of the War Powers Resolution of 1973 expressly states that authority to introduce U.S. forces into hostilities shall not be inferred "from any treaty heretofore or hereafter ratified unless such treaty is implemented by legislation specifically authorizing" the introduction of American troops.[170]

Clinton's foreign policy advisers consulted with members of Congress but not to obtain their approval.[171] Remarkably, Clinton was willing to seek the approval of each NATO country (Belgium, Denmark, Luxembourg, etc.). He

167. Id. at 102–04.

168. Louis Fisher, statement before the House Foreign Affairs Committee, "War Powers for the 21st Century: The Constitutional Perspective," April 10, 2008, available at http://www.loufisher/org/docs/wpr/428.pdf.

169. Louis Fisher, "Sidestepping Congress: Presidents Acting Under the U.N. and NATO," 47 Case W. Res. L. Rev. 1237 (1997), available at http://www.loufisher.org/docs/424.pdf.

170. 87 Stat. 558, sec. 8(a) (1973).

171. Helen Dewar and John M. Goshko, "Hill Signals Support for Airstrikes," Washington Post, October 2, 1998, at A35.

268 CHAPTER NINE

saw no reason to seek approval from the elected members of Congress, supported by their Article I constitutional authority. Legislatures in some NATO countries, including Italy and Germany, were forced to take votes to authorize military action in Yugoslavia.[172] The House and the Senate debated legislation on concurrent resolutions (H. Con. Res. 42 and S. Con. Res. 21) that could have no legal force. To be legally binding, a measure must either be a bill or a joint resolution presented to the President for his signature or veto. The House and the Senate debated and voted on these concurrent resolutions, but none gained a majority.[173] The war against Yugoslavia began on March 24, 1999, without any statutory or constitutional support.

War Powers Resolution

Congress, aware that its constitutional powers had declined sharply because of the wars in Korea and Vietnam (even though the latter had been authorized by the Tonkin Gulf Resolution), held hearings throughout the 1960s to determine what steps might be taken to curb presidential war power. Lawmakers had to rethink their institutional values. Senator J. William Fulbright had written in 1961 that "for the existing requirements of American foreign policy we have hobbled the President by too niggardly a grant of power."[174] Admitting it might be "distasteful and dangerous to vest the executive with powers unchecked and unbalanced," he asked whether "we have any choice but to do so."[175] That attitude was visible in August 1964 when Fulbright basically carried water for the Johnson administration in securing enactment of the Tonkin Gulf Resolution. Although he chaired the powerful Foreign Relations Committee, he seemed willing to function as a White House aide.

A year later, Fulbright broke with the administration's national security policy, especially over Johnson's military intervention in the Dominican Republic. He accused Johnson of relying on an exaggerated fear of communism.[176] By 1967, Fulbright could see "great merit in the checks and balances of our 18th century Constitution."[177] How many decades does it take a lawmaker to learn

172. Fisher, Presidential War Power, at 199.
173. Id.
174. J. William Fulbright, "American Foreign Policy in the 20th Century Under an 18th-Century Constitution," 47 Corn. L. Q. 1, 2 (1961).
175. Id. at 7.
176. 111 Cong. Rec. 23858–59 (1965).
177. "U.S. Commitments to Foreign Powers," hearings before the Senate Foreign Relations Committee, 90th Cong., 1st Sess. 3 (1967).

that? The Senate passed the National Commitments Resolution of 1969, challenging the right of the President to make commitments without seeking and obtaining congressional authority. In reporting the resolution, the Foreign Relations Committee noted the expansion of presidential war power and said that if blame is to be apportioned, "a fair share belongs to the Congress" because of its record of acquiescence and passivity.[178] It concluded that acquiescence was "probably the most important single fact accounting for the speed and virtual completeness of the transfer" of the war power from the legislative branch to the President.[179]

Mea culpas can be of value if they are well grounded and change attitudes and behaviors, but the Fulbright report rested on faulty analysis. It said that Congress "may have permitted itself to be overawed by the cult of executive expertise."[180] On what basis could a member of Congress (or the public), aware of the extensive pattern of misguided and faulty executive branch actions in national security affairs, including the claim of a "second attack" on the Tonkin Gulf, be "awed" by this record? The committee report speculated that the Senate's rejection of the Covenant of the League of Nations in 1919 and 1920 might have created in Congress "a kind of penance for its prewar isolationism, and the penance has sometimes taken the form of overly hasty acquiescence in proposals for the acceptance of one form or another of international responsibility."[181]

There was no need for legislative penance about the League of Nations. That is a canard. President Woodrow Wilson vigorously opposed Senator Henry Cabot Lodge's reservations to the covenant, claiming that they "cut out the heart" of the document and represented "nullification" of the treaty.[182] His language was irresponsible hyperbole, masking Wilson's decision to engage in a personal vendetta with Lodge even at the cost of losing the treaty. Wilson's principal advisers, including Secretary of State Robert Lansing, Bernard Baruch, Herbert Hoover, and Colonel Edward Mandell House, all urged Wilson to accept the reservations.[183]

In private correspondence, Wilson admitted that he had no principled objection to the Lodge amendments. Writing to Senator Gilbert Monell Hitchcock on March 8, 1920, he explained why he thought there was no need for Senate stipulations dealing with Article 10 of the covenant, under which the League of

178. S. Rept. No. 129, 91st Cong., 1st Sess. 8 (1969).
179. Id. at 15.
180. Id. at 16.
181. Id.
182. 63 The Papers of Woodrow Wilson 451 (Arthur S. Link, ed., 1990); 64 The Papers of Woodrow Wilson 47, 51 (Link ed., 1991).
183. Townsend Hoopes and Douglas Brinkley, FDR and the Creation of the U.N. 6 (1997).

Nations would take military action. Whatever obligations the U.S. government undertook "would of course have to be fulfilled by its usual and established constitutional methods of action," and there "can be no objection to explaining again what our constitutional method is and that our Congress alone can declare war or determine the causes or occasions for war, and that it alone can authorize the use of the armed forces of the United States on land or on the sea."[184] Those basic constitutional principles were embodied in the Lodge reservations.

Fulbright's committee report made a powerful point when it discussed the Tonkin Gulf Resolution. The statutory language appeared to put no limits on the scope of presidential military action, even if few members of Congress expected a full-scale war. Many thought they were helping to prevent a wider conflict by taking a firm stand against aggression. Whatever their political calculations, transferring such open-ended authority to Johnson was careless and irresponsible:

> In adopting a resolution with such sweeping language, however, Congress committed the error of making a *personal* judgment as to how President Johnson would implement the resolution when it had a responsibility to make an *institutional* judgment, first, as to what *any* President would do with so great an acknowledgment of power, and, second, as to whether, under the Constitution, Congress had a right to grant or concede the authority in question.[185]

The National Commitments Resolution, passed by a vote of 70 to 16, defined a national commitment as the use of U.S. armed forces on foreign territory, or a promise to assist a foreign country by using U.S. armed forces or financial resources, "either immediately or upon the happening of certain events." The resolution expressed "the sense of the Senate that a national commitment by the United States results only from affirmative action taken by the executive and legislative branches of the United States government by means of a treaty, statute, or concurrent resolution of both Houses of Congress specifically providing for such commitment."[186] Reference to a statute is constitutionally solid. Singling out a treaty or a concurrent resolution is not. The President and the Senate may not make national commitments, particularly with regard to the war power, by treaty. Moreover, a concurrent resolution has no legal effect because it is not presented to the President. The National Commitments Resolution, passed in the form of a Senate res-

184. 65 The Papers of Woodrow Wilson 68 (Link ed., 1991).
185. S. Rept. No. 129, 91st Cong., 1st Sess. 23 (emphases in original).
186. 115 Cong. Rec. 17245 (1969).

olution, has no legal effect but it does express constitutional principles by that body. Democrats supported it 43 to 3; Republicans voted in favor 17 to 13.

After years of intense debate, Congress passed the War Powers Resolution in 1973 in an effort to limit presidential power. The measure started off well in the Senate in terms of constitutional principles. By the time it passed both houses and was submitted to President Nixon, it had evolved into a hodgepodge of conflicting and contradictory values, wholly at odds with the Constitution and even language in the statute. Section 2(a) provides: "It is the purpose of this joint resolution to fulfill the intent of the framers of the Constitution of the United States and insure that the collective judgment of both the Congress and the President will apply to the introduction of United States Armed Forces into hostilities, or into situations where imminent involvement in hostilities is clearly indicated by the circumstances, and to the continued use of such forces in hostilities or in such situations."[187] Keep that statutory purpose in mind. Now compare it to the grant of authority to the President to use military force for any reason, anywhere in the world, for up to 90 days, without advance congressional approval. Nothing could more violate the framers' intent. By granting the President this unilateral authority, clearly the statute did nothing to ensure the "collective judgment" of both branches.

Senator Thomas Eagleton, a principal sponsor of the Senate bill, expressed dismay at House and conference committee action. He concluded that the bill that passed the two chambers was incompatible in constitutional principle, remarking that the House and the Senate "marched down separate and distinct roads, almost irreconcilable roads."[188] The bill that emerged from conference, he said, marked a "total, complete distortion of the war powers concept."[189] It represented a surrender of congressional power and a violation of the Constitution. Recalling the expansion of presidential power during the Vietnam War, he asked his colleagues: "[H]ow can we give unbridled, unlimited total authority to the President to commit us to war?"[190] He said the bill, after being carefully conceived in the Senate, "has been horribly bastardized to the point of being a menace."[191] The menace remains.[192] Recent efforts to replace the War Powers

187. 87 Stat. 555, sec. 2(a) (1973).
188. 119 Cong. Rec. 33555 (1973).
189. Id. at 36177.
190. Id.
191. Id. at 36178. See Louis Fisher, "Thomas F. Eagleton: A Model of Integrity," 52 St. Louis U. L. J. 97 (2008), available at http://www.loufisher.org/docs/wpr/429.pdf, and Susan R. Burgess, Contest for Constitutional Authority: The Abortion and War Powers Debates (1992).
192. Louis Fisher and David Gray Adler, "The War Powers Resolution: Time to Say Goodbye," 113 Pol. Sci. Q. 1 (1998), available at http://www.loufisher.org/docs/wpr/430.pdf.

Resolution with different procedures, such as the Baker–Christopher report of 2008, would simply shift greater powers to the President.[193]

Much of the decline in congressional power over national security flows from lawmakers who defer to "expertise" in the executive branch and the President. Whether Democrat or Republican, members of Congress have been unwilling to confront and critique presidential initiatives. Representative Jim Wright recalls how he and Speaker Tip O'Neill helped President Reagan on matters of foreign affairs: "He was our President. We owed him that."[194] No, no. Lawmakers owe the President (and, more importantly, the American people) their independent and informed judgments, including warnings not to move in a direction that is both unconstitutional and damaging to the country. Part of what keeps the nation secure is a vigorous use of checks and balances—privately if possible, publicly if necessary. Unless lawmakers exercise their independent judgment, they cannot protect their institution or their constituents, nor can they honor their constitutional oath of office.

The State Secrets Privilege

Because of a misguided Supreme Court decision in 1953, *United States v. Reynolds,* the executive branch has been able to exercise unchecked power in the field of national security even if it violates statutes, treaties, individual rights, and the Constitution. The case arose when three civilian engineers, who had provided assistance to the military, died while aboard a B-29 that exploded over Waycross, Georgia. Under the Federal Tort Claims Act of 1946, their widows sued the government for possible negligence. They asked to see, among other documents, the official accident report, which according to the government contained confidential information. The trial judge offered the Justice Department a choice: give me the report, which I will read in my chambers, or you lose. The government refused to release the report and lost the case.[195]

Writing for the Third Circuit, Judge Albert Maris affirmed the district court's decision. He concluded that a legitimate claim of confidentiality would be protected because the accident report would be read only in the privacy of the trial

---

193. Louis Fisher, "The Baker-Christopher War Powers Commission," 39 Pres. Stud. Q. 128 (2009), available at http://www.loufisher.org/docs/wpr/426.pdf; Louis Fisher, "When the Shooting Starts," Legal Times, July 28, 2008, at 44, available at http://www.loufisher.org/docs/wpr/427.pdf.

194. Jim Wright, Balance of Power: Presidents and Congress from the Era of McCarthy to the Age of Gingrich 382 (1996).

195. Brauner v. United States, 10 F.R.D. 468 (D. Pa. 1950).

judge's chambers. He refused to allow an agency official in a lawsuit, to which the government is a party, to decide what would and would not be shared with a court. Such a result would be "to abdicate the judicial function and permit the executive branch of the Government to infringe the independent province of the judiciary as laid down by the Constitution."[196] There was no danger, Maris said, in allowing judges in camera to review sensitive and classified materials: "The judges of the United States are public officers whose responsibility under the Constitution is just as great as that of the heads of the executive departments."[197] He might have added: judges do not have the vested interest of parties to a case.

The principles expressed by Judge Maris seem unassailable. Otherwise, the executive branch could violate the law, be challenged in court, and walk away unscathed after refusing to share certain documents with federal judges. Yet the Supreme Court invited precisely that result when it reversed the Third Circuit. Without looking at the accident report, it accepted the government's assertion that it contained highly sensitive information. Divided 6 to 3, the Court ruled that a court "must determine whether the circumstances are appropriate for the claim of privilege, and yet do so without forcing a disclosure of the very thing the privilege is designed to protect."[198] The word "disclosure" was a red herring. No one asked that the report be disclosed to the public, or even to the three widows and their attorneys. Disclosure was to the trial judge. If a court cannot read a relevant document, it cannot make an informed decision. It would be at the mercy of executive branch assertions, even if invalid or dishonest.

The Court's decision is extraordinarily incoherent. After advising courts that in confronting a claim of privilege it cannot force the disclosure of a privileged document, it wrote: "Judicial control over the evidence in a case cannot be abdicated to the caprice of executive officers."[199] Of course that is what the Court did. After deciding not to look at the accident report (or require the trial judge to do so), it was forced to speculate on its contents: "Certainly there was a reasonable danger that the accident investigation report would contain references to the secret electronic equipment which was the primary concern of the mission."[200] Suppose it did. The trial judge could redact such references and release the balance of the report to the three widows.

196. Reynolds v. United States, 192 F.2d 987, 997 (3d Cir. 1951).

197. Id. For background on the district court and Third Circuit decisions, see Louis Fisher, In the Name of National Security: Unchecked Presidential Power and the *Reynolds* Case 29–91 (2006).

198. United States v. Reynolds, 345 U.S. 1, 8 (1953).

199. Id. at 9–10.

200. Id. at 10.

As shallow as the Court's decision is, its careless and thoughtless nature is nearly matched by an exceedingly brief and cryptic dissent from Justices Black, Frankfurter, and Jackson. In two lines they dissented "substantially for the reasons set forth in the opinion of Judge Maris below."[201] Was it too much of a burden to write an actual dissent, offering reasons and arguments, including those of Judge Maris they agreed with? Would repetition of publicly available language from the Third Circuit place the nation at too great a risk?

The Court's decision to operate out of pure ignorance came back to haunt it (or should have). It had speculated that the accident report might have said something about the confidential mission of the B-29 and the confidential equipment it carried. In 1996, the Air Force declassified a number of accident reports, including one on the Waycross, Georgia, tragedy. Judith Loether, daughter of one of the civilian engineers who died on the plane, discovered the report in 2000 by browsing the Internet. She read the report, expecting to find references to the confidential mission and confidential equipment. The report said nothing about either.[202]

The executive branch had misled the judiciary. More accurately, the Supreme Court allowed itself to be misled by choosing to remain in the dark. Had the Justices read the report, they would have noticed two things. First was the absence of any confidential information. Second was the presence of information showing clear government negligence, such as the failure to install heat shields to minimize the risk of the engines overheating. The plane should have never been in the air.[203]

The three families decided to return to federal court in 2002, not as a tort claims action but on what is called a *coram nobis:* a motion to a court to review and correct its judgment because it was based on an error of fact. One might think the judiciary would resent being misled by a party, particularly when it is the government that is in court more than any other litigant. Yet the federal judges involved in this *coram nobis* did not seem to mind that the judiciary in *Reynolds* had been snookered by the government. A district court and the Third Circuit lethargically handled the case from 2003 to 2005, deciding each time against the families. On May 1, 2006, the Supreme Court decided not to take the case from the lower courts and perhaps review and rethink its own botched decision in *Reynolds.*[204]

201. Id. at 12.
202. Fisher, In the Name of National Security, at 166–68. For an excellent account of this case and its impact on the three families, see Barry Siegel, Claim of Privilege: A Mysterious Plane Crash, a Landmark Supreme Court Case, and the Rise of State Secrets (2008).
203. Fisher, In the Name of National Security, at 178–79.
204. For a review of this litigation from 2003 to 2006, see Fisher, In the Name of National Security, at 169–211.

From 2006 to 2010, I worked with both judiciary committees on legislation to make the courts exercise their independence in state secrets cases. Judges would look at documents in camera instead of taking at face value the government's assertions in various declaration and affidavits. I presented testimony before both committees in support of the legislation.[205] The committees marked up their bills and reported them, but did not bring them to the floor for debate and passage. Other than a change in Justice Department procedures in reviewing agency claims about state secrets, the policy of the Obama administration in court on the state secrets privilege is identical to that of the George W. Bush administration.

Congress made matters worse in 2008 by granting immunity to the telecoms that gave assistance to the illegal surveillance program initiated by the Bush administration after 9/11. Dozens of cases were filed against the administration and the telecoms, but the state secrets privilege was invoked each time to block the litigation. The immunity statute sent an unfortunate legislative message: disrespect for the rule of law and disrespect for Congress. Lawmakers dishonored their own institution because Congress in 1978 had enacted national policy with FISA. After learning that the law had been secretly violated, it gave immunity to private companies that helped the administration defy the law.[206]

The urgent need for legislation is underscored by the general ineptness and torpid quality of federal court decisions on state secrets cases, including the illegal NSA surveillance program and "extraordinary rendition" (sending individuals to other countries for interrogation and torture). Federal judges have been largely supine when faced with assertions of state secrets by the government.[207] A typically listless, apathetic ruling was issued by the Ninth Circuit on September 8, 2010, in the rendition case of *Mohamed v. Jeppesen Dataplan*. At one point the court cites a lower court in this manner: "[W]e must make an independent determination whether the information is privileged."[208] From the same case it understands that federal courts "take very seriously our obligation to review the [government's claims] with a very careful, indeed a skeptical, eye."[209] It then

205. E.g., "Examining the State Secrets Privilege: Protecting National Security While Preserving Accountability," Senate Committee on the Judiciary, February 13, 2008, available at http://www.loufisher.org/docs/ssp/450.pdf. For my other articles and testimony on the state secrets privilege, see http://loufisher.org/dev/ssp.html.

206. P.L. 110–261, 122 Stat. 2436, 2467–71 (2008).

207. Many of these cases are discussed in Louis Fisher, The Constitution and 9/11: Recurring Threats to America's Freedoms 248–360 (2008).

208. Mohamed v. Jeppesen Dataplan, Inc., 614 F.3d 1070, 1080 (9th Cir. 2010), citing Al-Haramain, 507 F.3d at 1202.

209. 614 F.3d at 1082.

swings around 180 degrees by citing the same case in which the lower court said: "[W]e acknowledge the need to defer to the Executive on matters of foreign policy and national security and surely cannot legitimately find ourselves second guessing the Executive in this arena."[210] I tried to locate a legal term that describes this method of reasoning. I finally settled for *gibberish*. Perhaps that word may seem too rude and disrespectful when referring to a decision by a federal court, but it fits. The dictionary defines gibberish as "unintelligible or meaningless language."

Presidents play a powerful card when they accuse opponents of lacking in patriotism, especially in times of emergencies and external threats. If lawmakers and the public swallow their misgivings about presidential announcements, the Constitution is put at risk along with the nation. We have been down that path many times: the Alien and Sedition Acts, the Red Scare after World War I, anticommunism after World War II, and executive branch abuses after 9/11. Patriotism does not mean mechanical deference to the President (or the Court). Democracy depends on the power of reason, open debate, and the courage to speak out, especially when the reigning guidelines are "no politics beyond the water's edge" and "my country, right or wrong." A healthier and more constructive response came from Senator Carl Schurz in 1872. He had been born in Germany, so some Senators branded his opposition to a pending amendment as unpatriotic. He explained why he objected to the amendment and then closed with: "My country, right or wrong; if right, to be kept right and if wrong, to be set right."[211]

210. Id. at 1081–82.
211. Cong. Globe, 42d Cong., 2d Sess. 1287 (February 29, 1872).

10

ANALYTICAL SUPPORT

To fulfill its legislative and constitutional duties, Congress turns to experts from executive agencies, universities, private organizations, lobbyists, and its own professional staff in member offices and committees. Each chamber has an office of general counsel to provide analytical support for constitutional issues. Beginning in 1914, Congress created agencies to help craft legislative bills, prepare for hearings, and monitor and check the executive branch. These agencies include the Congressional Research Service (CRS), Government Accountability Office (GAO), Congressional Budget Office (CBO), and the short-lived Office of Technology Assessment (OTA). They prepare objective and nonpartisan reports. Some attempt to embrace a model called "neutral competence" without understanding that it is incompatible with providing professional, authoritative, and analytical support. As explained in this chapter, this model—adopted at times by OTA and more recently by CRS—weakens the institutional powers of Congress.

Member and Committee Staff

House member staffs are fairly small for the broad range of work required to cover a member's district. The D.C. office typically has about eight to ten staffers, including the chief of staff, scheduler, communications director (or press secretary), legislative counsel, legislative correspondent, and staff assistants. The office needs to track current legislative issues, follow committee hearings of interest to the member, receive visitors to the office, and handle the flood of questions coming in from constituents by phone, letters, and e-mails. For a staff this small, there can be little specialization in substantive areas. Salaries for junior staff (as low as $30,000) create serious turnover because of the expense of living in the District of Columbia area. If Congress wants to retain talented staffers and the experience they acquire quickly on the job, those salaries need to be lifted. Salaries for more senior positions are adequate to hold staffers who enjoy working on Capitol Hill. Many are dedicated and remain for decades, sometimes switching to another office when a member retires or is defeated.

In addition to their D.C. offices, House members have several offices in their districts, each office having about eight staffers. District offices focus principally on issues brought to them by constituents, either public policy or individual needs. Senators, with their larger territory and population, require more staff.

Their D.C. office can range from 25 to 50 employees, depending on the population within the state, and another 10 to 40 who work in field offices. Counting personal, committee, and other support assistance, House and Senate staff totaled 15,907 in 2010: 9,808 in the House, 6,099 in the Senate.[1]

Most policy staff expertise exists within committees and subcommittees and leadership staff. Committee staff grew rapidly after 1974 in response to efforts by the Nixon administration to weaken Congress.[2] Some staff are assigned directly to individual Senators and Representatives who sit on those committees. Other professional staffers serve the offices of party leaders (such as House Speaker, House Minority Leader, Senate Majority Leader, Senate Minority Leader), congressional caucuses, and task forces. Both chambers have an Office of Legislative Counsel (46 employees in the Senate and 61 in the House, as of 2010) who help with bill drafting. In the 1970s, Congress created a special legal counsel in both bodies: the Senate Legal Counsel and the House General Counsel. These offices are small but highly expert—about six employees in the Senate and ten in the House. Their work is described in the next section.

When I began working for Congress in September 1970, I met and assisted professional staff who had been on the Hill for several decades and had learned to both honor and protect congressional powers. A half dozen subcommittee staffers could match wits with large executive agencies and through experience, perseverance, and dedication closely monitor agency actions. They built a career in Congress and were proud to do so. A study of congressional staffing in 1977 observed: "[A] career of being a Hill aide has developed."[3] As the decades passed by, I found fewer individuals with that commitment and interest. Many talented staffers now stay for a few years and move from Congress to higher salaried, private sector positions. That same opportunity existed in the 1970s, but for many, the Hill was a special place to apply one's energies. That seems less so today.

Studies often exaggerate the extent to which staff "run" Congress. No doubt lawmakers depend heavily on their staff, as they should, but personal and committee staff add value only when they are technically and politically competent and exercise good professional judgment. It has been said that members of Con-

1. R. Eric Petersen, Parker H. Reynolds, and Amber Hope Wilhelm, "House of Representatives and Senate Staff Levels in Member, Committee, Leadership, and Other Offices, 1977–2010," CRS Report R41366, August 10, 2010.

2. Kenneth Kofmehl, Professional Staffs of Congress xxiv–xxvii (1977 ed.); Michael J. Malbin, Unelected Representatives: Congressional Staff and the Future of Representative Government 4–8, 253 (1979).

3. Harrison W. Fox Jr. and Susan Webb Hammond, Congressional Staffs: The Invisible Force in American Lawmaking 62 (1977).

gress "do not have time to read; staff have time to read but not to think."[4] No one should underestimate the complexity of issues that enter a congressional office, but the members and staff I dealt with, from both parties, had time to think because they took time to think.

To do their work well, staffers need to be very clear about what a lawmaker wants. During my service at CRS, a House staffer called me about a budget issue that interested his member. Unable to determine what the issue was, even though we talked about it at some length, I sent the staffer some short pieces to see if that would clarify the request. It didn't. Finally, the office asked me to speak with the member. After about an hour in his office, with two staffers joining us but remaining silent, I shook the member's hand and promised to get him what he needed. As I left the office and started walking down the hall, the two staffers followed and asked: "Do you know what he wants?" I said I did, and they replied: "Thank God." His original request had been too general and they were unable, or unwilling, to translate it into something understandable. Staffers need to do that.

Members want direct (respectful) answers from their staff; they want to know what a staffer thinks. One office asked me to meet with a Senator in the Capitol just off the Senate floor. He came with three staff aides, who did not participate in the discussion. The topic was a complicated one that I reviewed before the meeting. At the end of our discussion, the Senator looked at me and asked: "How should I vote?" I said he should vote against. He stared at me for a while and then, with a smile, said: "You're right." He could just as easily have said: "I disagree." I had no control over his response. All I could do was offer my best professional judgment.

On another occasion, I was with a Senator who enjoyed calling experts in and asking them questions. He did that with me often. He was excellent at building a context and an understanding of the issues that interested him. He very kindly and generously described the credentials of a law professor seated before him. He then asked about a particular war power dispute: "What do you think the framers would have said about that?" The individual responded: "It would be very problematic." The vagueness of the reply produced disappointment on the Senator's face. He had asked a straight question and wanted a straight answer.

House and Senate Legal Counsel

In the 1960s, Congress debated the need for an in-house counsel to represent the institutional interests of Congress in court. On some occasions, the Justice

4. Bruce Bimber, The Politics of Expertise in Congress: The Rise and Fall of the Office of Technology Assessment 35 (1996).

Department had withdrawn its defense of congressional interests being litigated, forcing Congress to locate individuals to prepare briefs and participate in oral argument. As part of the Ethics in Government Act of 1978, Congress created the Senate Legal Counsel. The statute authorized the President Pro Tempore to appoint a Legal Counsel from individuals recommended by the Senate majority and minority leaders. The first Senate Legal Counsel, Michael Davidson, served from 1979 to 1995 and was followed by Thomas Griffith. The position then went to Patricia Bryan, assisted by Deputy Senate Counsel Morgan Frankel, who had joined the office in 1981. Bryan and Frankel later switched positions, with Frankel as Counsel and Bryan as Deputy Counsel.

The Senate has been well served by the remarkable continuity within the Senate Legal Counsel's office. The office advises lawmakers and committees when subpoenas are directed to the Senate, and provides advice to committees about their investigations and any legal or constitutional issues that might arise. The counsel may represent a committee in a civil action to enforce a committee subpoena. In 1980, the office was active in the investigation of President Carter's brother, Billy, and his connections to Libya. Later it assisted in the impeachment actions against federal judges and President Bill Clinton. The office became involved in the Billy Carter investigation partly because Ted Kennedy, the chairman of the Senate Judiciary Committee, which had jurisdiction over the matter, recused himself because he had challenged Carter for the Democratic nomination. That led to the recusal of his staff, including the committee's chief counsel, Stephen Breyer. A Senate agreement on July 24, 1980, directed the Senate Legal Counsel and Deputy Legal Counsel to work with the committee. A special counsel, retired federal appellate judge Philip Tone, was appointed and worked out of the Senate Legal Counsel office.[5]

In the 1980s, the Senate Legal Counsel was closely involved in constitutional questions surrounding the legislative veto, the Competition in Contracting Act, Gramm-Rudman, the independent counsel, and the pocket veto. The office prepared briefs and participated in oral argument, including several times in the Supreme Court. More recent cases include the item veto, a constitutional challenge to the practice of excluding the District of Columbia from the apportionment of congressional districts, and whether cost of living adjustments (COLAs) in a federal statute violate language in the Twenty-seventh Amendment. In the latter case, a federal court held that the member of Congress bringing the lawsuit lacked standing.[6]

5. Information received from Michael Davidson, former Senate Legal Counsel, October 9, 2010.
6. Schaffer v. Clinton, 240 F.3d 878 (10th Cir. 2001). See Louis Fisher, "Constitutional Analy-

The House of Representatives also recognized the need to have in-house counsel to defend its powers in court. Unlike the Senate, it did not rely on a statute to create the office. Instead, Speaker Tip O'Neill in 1979 selected Stanley Brand to be the first House General Counsel. In a case that helped shape the Speech or Debate Clause, Brand represented Speaker O'Neill as amicus curiae in arguments before the Supreme Court.[7] Brand was active in a confrontation with the Environmental Protection Agency, leading to a vote by the House to hold EPA Administrator Anne Gorsuch Burford in contempt for refusing to release documents.

Assisting Brand was the House Deputy General Counsel, Steven Ross, who became House General Counsel in 1983. Charles Tiefer, after serving as Senate assistant legal counsel from 1979 to 1984, moved to the House and filled the positions of Deputy General Counsel and Solicitor from 1984 to 1995. Brand, Ross, and Tiefer regularly appeared in court to defend the interests of the House. In the legislative veto case of *INS v. Chadha*, the House hired Eugene Gressman to argue the case before the Supreme Court, and Brand joined him on the briefs. Ross handled oral argument for the House in the Gramm-Rudman case and submitted a brief in a pocket veto case, *Burke v. Barnes*. Arguing the latter case was Morgan Frankel of the Senate Legal Counsel's office. Brand, Ross, and Tiefer frequently testified before congressional committees.

When the Republicans took over the House in 1995, Speaker Newt Gingrich made his appointments to the House General Counsel office. Initially, he turned to Cheryl Lau. After a short stint, she was replaced by Geraldine Gennet, who remained in that position until 2007. She was followed by Irvin Nathan. During Gennet's tenure, the office handled a number of constitutional disputes: the challenge to COLAs for members of Congress, a House rule that required a three-fifths majority for legislation increasing federal income taxes, qualified immunity for congressional staff, and use of the Speech or Debate Clause to protect against the compulsory disclosure of congressional investigative reports.[8]

A major issue involved the decision of the Justice Department on May 20, 2006, to obtain a search warrant and enter the Capitol Hill office of Represen-

sis by Congressional Staff Agencies," in Congress and the Constitution 75–77 (Neal Devins and Keith E. Whittington, eds., 2005); Charles Tiefer, "The Senate and House Counsel: Dilemmas of Representing in Court the Institutional Congressional Client," 61 Law & Contemp. Prob. 47 (1998); and Rebecca Mae Salokar, "Legal Counsel for Congress: Protecting Institutional Interests," 20 Cong. & the Presidency 131 (1993).

7. United States v. Helstoski, 442 U.S. 477 (1979). Brand also argued before the Court in Helstoski v. Meanor, 442 U.S. 500 (1979).

8. Fisher, "Constitutional Analysis by Congressional Staff Agencies," supra note 6, at 79.

tative William J. Jefferson. The search continued for 18 hours, from Saturday evening until Sunday morning. Once inside the office, the FBI refused to permit Gennet to enter while the search was proceeding. An appellate court held that the Justice Department could not review the seized files until Jefferson had an opportunity to determine which ones pertained to legislative work and were thus protected by the Speech or Debate Clause.[9] In 2008, the Supreme Court denied certiorari. Jefferson was later tried and convicted on other evidence and sentenced to 13 years in prison.

After becoming House Legal Counsel in November 2007, Irvin Nathan was quickly involved in the decision of the House to hold two White House officials in contempt: former White House Counsel Harriet Miers for refusing to testify, and White House Chief of Staff Joshua Bolten for refusing to submit requested materials. They were the first individuals held in contempt of Congress in over 25 years. When the administration refused to prosecute the contempt, the House took the matter to court. On July 31, 2008, District Judge John Bates held that Miers was not immune from congressional testimony and was required to appear and testify before the House Judiciary Committee. He also ruled that the administration had no valid excuse for refusing to produce nonprivileged documents.[10] These actions led to testimony by Miers and Karl Rove and the production of White House documents.

Other activities during Nathan's tenure involved defending in court the constitutionality of the 2007 amendments to the Lobbying Disclosure Act, promoting prosecutions by the Justice Department for false statements and perjury before Congress, seeking to advance in court the sovereign immunity of Congress, seeking and obtaining access by the House to grand jury information for use in House impeachment of two federal judges, filing amicus briefs in federal courts dealing with alleged violations of the Speech or Debate Clause, and attempting to negotiate with the Justice Department protocols for searches of the offices of members of Congress.

Government Accountability Office

Congress created GAO in 1921 to strengthen legislative control over executive agencies. Some details of that statute appear in Chapter 8. The enabling statute

9. United States v. Rayburn House, Room 2113, Washington, D.C., 497 F.3d 654 (D.C. Cir. 2007).
10. "Reining in the Imperial Presidency: Lessons and Recommendations Relating to the Presidency of George W. Bush," House Committee on the Judiciary, Majority Staff, March 2009, at 40–41.

directed the Comptroller General, as head of GAO, to investigate "all matters relating to the receipt, disbursement, and application of public funds" and gave GAO investigators "the right to examine any books, documents, papers, or records" held by executive agencies.[11] Those statutory authorities put GAO in a position to review and make recommendations on matters ranging from statutory interpretation to constitutional analysis.

GAO is the largest of the legislative support agencies. After cresting to a size of 5,300 by the early 1990s, it was severely cut by the Republican Congress in 1995 and lost more than a third of its staff and budget. To Republicans, GAO staff had gotten too close to Democrats, especially in the House, but that perception reflected the fact that the House had been controlled by Democrats for four decades. 1995 was also a time when Republicans, having taken over the House, wanted to demonstrate their commitment to cutting the size of the federal government. Even though cuts for the federal government were modest, for GAO they were substantial. It recovered some of its losses and has a current size of about 3,000. In 2004, Congress changed the name of GAO from General Accounting Office to Government Accountability Office, a modification that constantly baffles newspapers and reporters who are just as likely to call it General Accountability Office or Government Accounting Office. Much safer: GAO.

Over its history, GAO frequently clashed with the Justice Department over legal interpretations.[12] One of the collisions involved the Philadelphia Plan, an initiative of the Nixon administration that required contractors to set specific goals for hiring minorities as a condition for working on federally assisted projects. The Comptroller General concluded that the plan conflicted with Title VII of the Civil Rights Act of 1964, which prohibits employment discrimination on the basis of race, color, religion, sex, or national origin. The Secretary of Labor disagreed, stating that the interpretation of the statute was vested in the Justice Department and it had approved the policy. Federal courts upheld the legality of the Philadelphia Plan.[13]

GAO has access to agency documents, including records in the intelligence community. Over the years, its capacity to audit and evaluate those agencies was rebuffed. The Central Intelligence Agency interpreted its statutory authority to

11. 42 Stat. 25, sec. 312(a), and 26, sec. 313 (1921); 31 U.S.C. §712 (2006).
12. Joseph Pois, Watchdog on the Potomac: A Study of the Comptroller General of the United States 250–77 (1976).
13. Contractors Ass'n of Eastern Pa. v. Secretary of Labor, 442 F.2d 159 (3d Cir. 1971), cert. denied, 404 U.S. 854 (1971). See Robert P. Schuwerk, "The Philadelphia Plan: A Study in the Dynamics of Executive Power," 39 U. Chi. L. Rev. 723 (1972), and Louis Fisher, Constitutional Conflicts Between Congress and the President 106–107 (5th ed., 2007).

prevent GAO audits and investigations. Legislation has been introduced and hearings held to provide GAO with authority to evaluate programs and activities within the intelligence community.[14] Legislation passed in September 2010 does not give GAO full access to the intelligence community; it might move somewhat in that direction. The bill requires the Director of National Intelligence and the GAO to prepare a directive describing GAO access to records in the intelligence agencies.[15]

Constitutional issues emerge in various evaluations conducted by GAO. Much of the legal analysis is performed in the Office of General Counsel, consisting of about 150 lawyers. A major constitutional issue arose in 1985 when Congress granted the Comptroller General deficit-reduction authority under the Gramm-Rudman Act. As explained in Chapter 8, the Supreme Court held that the provision was unconstitutional because it attempted to give executive powers to a legislative officer.

GAO is responsible for overseeing the Federal Vacancies Act of 1998. By statute, agency employees are not permitted to fill positions requiring Senate confirmation for more than a fixed period of days. The reason: to protect the Senate's authority to advise and consent. The initial statutory limit of 30 days was regularly ignored, as was the more generous limit of 120 days. In 1998, Congress increased the limit to 210 days, although under some circumstances an employee may stay in a vacant position for longer periods. GAO has long monitored compliance with the statute.[16] Closely related to the Vacancies Act is the President's use of the recess appointment power, which can be abused and requires GAO to closely review this area.

In the mid-1980s, GAO conducted studies to determine whether there had been any illegality in giving federal funds to the Nicaraguan Democratic Resistance (called the Contras). It disclosed false receipts and use of funds to purchase ammunition and grenades, in violation of statutory policy. When the Iran-Contra affair became public in November 1986, GAO continued to investigate federal expenditures and assisted with the congressional inquiry into Iran-Contra. In August 1989, it reported on the refusal of the Justice Department to allow GAO employees to review compliance by the executive branch with congressional requests for documents related to Iran-Contra.[17]

14. Frederick M. Kaiser, "GAO: Government Accountability Office and General Accounting Office," CRS Report RL30349, September 10, 2008, at 9–11.

15. Eugene Mulero and Tim Starks, "Long-Delayed Authorization Bill Clears," CQ Weekly Report, October 4, 2010, at 2295.

16. E.g., General Accounting Office, "Presidential Appointments: Agencies' Compliance with Provisions of the Federal Vacancies Reform Act of 1998," May 2001, GAO-01-701.

17. Based on these GAO studies: No. 131994, study on disbursements of economic support

GAO helps Congress protect its power of the purse by analyzing agency expenditures to ensure that funds are spent in accordance with law, including proper implementation of the Impoundment Control Act of 1974. GAO experts often testify on such budget proposals as item veto authority for the President and adopting a biennial budget, which would require Congress to pass a two-year appropriations bill one year and concentrate on oversight the next (discussed in Chapter 8). In testimony presented in 1992, Assistant Comptroller General Harry Havens cautioned that a change in the rescission process to permit some kind of item veto "cannot be expected to be a major tool in reducing the deficit." The proposal would have applied only to discretionary spending, representing about 37 percent of the year's budget. He warned that an item veto would trigger "a major shift of power from Congress to the President in an area that was reserved to Congress by the Constitution and which has historically been one of clear legislative primacy."[18]

During the presidency of George W. Bush, GAO was asked by some members of Congress to obtain documents from the energy task force chaired by Vice President Dick Cheney. Representatives John Dingell and Henry Waxman wanted to know who served on the task force and whether it had met in private with "exclusive groups of non-governmental participants—including political contributors—to discuss specific policies, rules, regulations, and legislation."[19] Dingell and Waxman requested from GAO a list of each task force member and staff, including name, title, office, or employer he or she represented. The lawmakers were concerned that closed-door meetings by the task force "may violate the letter and spirit of the Federal Advisory Committee Act (FACA)."[20]

Cheney's counsel, David Addington, replied that FACA did not cover the task force because it "does not apply to a group 'composed wholly of full-time, or permanent part-time, officers or employers of the Federal Government.'" However, in the spirit of "comity between the legislative and executive branches," he agreed to provide information on the composition of the task force. He pointed out that task force members "have met with many individuals who are

funds to Honduras, December 2, 1986; No. 131728, study on controlling funds to the Nicaraguan Democratic Resistance, December 5, 1986; No. 542492, study on military activities in Central America, June 17, 1988; No. 139293, study of GAO authority to review executive branch compliance with congressional requests related to the Iran-Contra affair, August 9, 1989.

18. "Legislative Line-Item Veto Proposals," hearings before the House Committee on Rules, 102d Cong., 2d Sess. 274 (1992).

19. Letter of April 19, 2001, from Reps. Dingell and Waxman to Comptroller General David Walker, at 1.

20. Letter of April 19, 2001, from Reps. Dingell and Waxman to Andrew Lundquist, executive director of the task force, at 1.

not Federal employees to gather information relevant to the Group's work, but such meetings do not involve deliberations or any effort to achieve consensus on advice or recommendations."[21]

In releasing this information, Addington objected that a more extensive GAO investigation would interfere with the "exercise of the authorities committed to the Executive in the Constitution," including the President's authority to require the opinion, in writing, of the principal officer in each of the executive departments; the duty to take care that the laws be faithfully executed; and recommending to Congress "to their Consideration such Measures as he shall judge necessary and expedient." After citing this constitutional language, he objected that GAO intended "to intrude into the heart of Executive deliberations," including discussions among the President, the Vice President, members of the Cabinet, and presidential aides.[22]

Initially, the congressional request was quite broad, reaching to minutes, notes, logs, diaries, e-mails, voice mails, and computer tapes. GAO agreed to scale back the scope of its inquiry. Because GAO is a nonpartisan agency funded by Congress, it is usually extremely careful to avoid public statements that appear to be political or partisan. When the Cheney task force refused to release additional information, Comptroller General David Walker stated: "If all you have to do is create a task force, put the vice president in charge, detail people from different agencies paid by taxpayers, outreach to whomever you want and then you can circumvent Congressional oversight, that's a loophole big enough to drive a truck through."[23] Some Republicans concluded that GAO was conducting an overzealous and partisan inquiry. To House Majority Leader Dick Armey, GAO was "being pressured here on a partisan political basis, and they are wrong."[24] Senator Ted Stevens, ranking member of the Appropriations Committee, said he was "appalled" at GAO's pursuit of White House documents and warned that any effort by GAO to litigate the matter could damage the agency.[25]

GAO decided to take the dispute to district court. By that time, other lawsuits had required the administration to turn over thousands of pages of documents related to the Cheney task force. Reporters, by talking to private groups involved in task force meetings, learned about many of the companies and their

21. Letter of May 4, 2001, from David S. Addington, counsel to the Vice President, to Reps. Tauzin, Dingell, Burton, and Waxman, at 1.

22. Letter of May 16, 2001, from Addington to GAO General Counsel Anthony Gamboa, at 1.

23. Stephen Labaton and Richard A. Oppel Jr., "Bush Says Privacy Is Needed on Data from Enron Talks," New York Times, January 29, 2002, at A1.

24. Dave Boyer, "GOP Terms GAO's Request a Partisan Hunt," Washington Times, January 30, 2002, at A4.

25. Id.

contributions to political campaigns.[26] On December 9, 2002, District Judge John D. Bates dismissed the GAO complaint by holding that Comptroller General Walker lacked standing to bring the suit. Walker, said the court, had suffered no personal injury and any institutional injury would exist only "in his capacity as an agent of Congress—an entity that itself has issued no subpoena to obtain the information and given no expression of support for the pursuit of this action."[27]

There had been considerable debate within GAO about the wisdom of taking the matter to court. Similar resistance developed to an effort to appeal the decision by Judge Bates. In the end, GAO decided not to appeal but announced that, in the future, it would seek support from at least one full committee with jurisdiction over a records dispute before resorting to litigation.[28]

Congressional Research Service

CRS dates to 1914, when Congress passed legislation to fund a Legislative Reference Service (LRS) within the Library of Congress, "to employ competent persons to prepare such indexes, digests, and compilations of law as may be required for Congress and other official use."[29] Although LRS began largely as an organization to acquire facts and search for available documents, by 1946 it had grown to a staff of 131.[30] The Legislative Reorganization Act (LRA) of 1946 looked more ambitiously to "analysis, appraisal, and evaluation" of legislative proposals, prepared "without partisan bias."[31]

The 1946 statute authorized the Librarian of Congress to appoint a corps of "senior specialists" to cover such broad fields as American government and public administration, American public law, full employment, housing, international affairs, money and banking, taxation, and fiscal policy. The grade for senior specialist was set at not less than the highest grade in the executive branch "to which

26. Louis Fisher, The Politics of Executive Privilege 195 (2004).

27. Walker v. Cheney, 230 F.Supp.2d 51, 74 (D.D.C. 2002).

28. For further details on the Cheney task force dispute, see Fisher, The Politics of Executive Privilege, at 183–98; Peter Brand and Alexander Bolton, "GOP Threats Halted GAO Cheney Suit," The Hill, February 19, 2003, available at http://www.commondreams.org/headlines03/0219-12.htm; and Jordy Yager, "Federal Agencies Stiff-arm GAO on Info," The Hill, November 3, 2010, available at http://thehill.com/homenews/senate/68271-agencies-stff-arm-gao-on-info.

29. 38 Stat. 454, 463 (1914). For a careful study of CRS and its growth from the LRA, see Harold Relyea, "Across the Hill: The Congressional Research Service and Providing Research for Congress—A Retrospective on Origins," 27 Gov't Info. Q. 414, 416 (2010).

30. Id. at 417.

31. 60 Stat. 812, 836, sec. 203(a) (1946).

research analysts and consultants without supervisory responsibility are currently assigned."[32]

Much of the motivation behind the LRA of 1946 was to restore Congress to a coequal power with the executive branch. It was well understood that during the 1930s and World War II, the status, reputation, and capacity of Congress had plummeted.[33] At a congressional hearing in 1945, lawmakers listened to two Library of Congress officials describe the anticipated duties of senior specialists. In requesting funds for these experts, LRS Director Ernest Griffith said it was not the intention to have these individuals "giv[e] advice." Rather, they would prepare a study "without bias and without recommendations . . . [to] indicate a number of alternative recommendations if so requested."[34] Dr. Luther Evans, Chief Assistant Librarian, disagreed. The Library had already reached an agreement that LRS experts "would give scholarly research and counsel, and we say in another place that they would give expert opinions." He compared it to "the diagnosis of a physician who sometimes has to give an opinion on a medical case, but he gives it as an expert and not as a layman."[35] Griffith agreed that experts would say: "In my opinion, it would be thus and so, for the following reasons."[36]

The Legislative Reorganization Act of 1970 marked a second attempt to strengthen the research capacity of Congress. Lawmakers needed to better compete with resources available in the executive branch. In the decades following World War II, Congress had displayed increasing evidence that it was becoming a second-rate, second-class political institution, far too subordinate to presidential power. Years of congressional hearings and reports produced the LRA of 1970. This statute was far more explicit, directing the Library of Congress to prepare itself not merely for reference work but for high-level, analytical studies to help Congress with its substantive duties. The statute changed the name of LRS to Congressional Research Service (CRS), anticipating that it would triple in size and greatly deepen its analytical mission.

The statute authorized a number of senior specialists within CRS, to be compensated at "the highest grade in the executive branch of the Government to which research analysts and consultants without supervisory responsibility, are assigned."[37] That grade was GS-17. Congress specified broad fields for these senior specialists, including American government and public administration,

32. Id., sec. 203(b).
33. Relyea, supra note 29, at 417.
34. "Organization of Congress" (part 3), hearings before the Joint Committee on the Organization of Congress, 79th Cong., 1st Sess. 440 (1945).
35. Id. at 445.
36. Id. at 446.
37. 84 Stat. 1182 (1970).

American public law, international affairs, national defense, and taxation and fiscal policy. The clear intent was to create a congressional staff agency with the capacity and willingness to deliver to the legislative branch nonpartisan, professional, and expert analysis, especially for those appointed to the top level of senior specialist.

A Senate report specified that "sound congressional decisionmaking is rooted in the availability of accurate information and expert analysis."[38] Not just information but *analysis*. Experts had to review available information and subject it to the kinds of professional scrutiny that would yield a reasonable and thoughtful result. Analysts at the level of senior specialists were required to do more than present two sides of a question. If one side was stronger, they had a duty to say so. The same obligation applied to research specialists at the level of GS-16. Congress expected the work of CRS to involve "more creative effort than the mere acquisition, storage and retrieval of data and information produced elsewhere."[39] Obtaining and compensating "high caliber specialists and senior specialists" would provide research services to Congress "of the highest possible quality."[40]

I joined CRS in September 1970, after receiving my doctorate in political science at the New School for Social Research and teaching for three years at Queens College. With strong interests in all three branches of government and their interactions, I decided to relocate to Washington, D.C. My move from New York City coincided with the expanded CRS mission. It was a wonderful opportunity to do research and constantly test and apply it. Having done undergraduate and graduate work in chemistry and physical chemistry, I would be in the laboratory again, this time in the social sciences.

My outside writing and congressional testimony contributed to promotions within CRS. I entered as a GS-12 and by 1988 moved to GS-17 as Senior Specialist in Separation of Powers. At no time did my expression of expert opinions within CRS, or in my outside publications and speeches, ever prompt a member of Congress or legislative staffer to decline my assistance. Lawmakers and Hill staff are accustomed to hearing a variety of viewpoints. They expect, and want, reasoned and informed analysis, even when results challenge and conflict with their own positions. My research and writing on controversial matters created a close, constructive, and professional working relationship with lawmakers and their staff. As previous chapters make clear, I was blessed for more than three decades to work closely with lawmakers and their staff. I appeared regu-

38. S. Rept. No. 91-202, 91st Cong., 1st Sess. 18 (1969).

39. Id. at 19.

40. Id. at 42. Similar objectives are found elsewhere in the legislative history; H. Rept. No. 91-1215, 91st Cong., 2d Sess. 100 (1970).

larly on C-SPAN and NPR to express expert views on pending issues of controversial public policy. No one in CRS management raised any objections. Conditions changed markedly in 2004.

In 1988, there were 18 senior specialists. To be selected, they had to compete with other "nationally recognized experts." One cannot develop that reputation by being neutral and descriptive. CRS selected its last senior specialist through a competitive process in 1989. Since that time, CRS management has allowed the number of research senior specialists to drift down, by attrition and retirement. By 2011 there were four research senior specialists who competed for that position and were able to demonstrate a reputation as nationally recognized experts. All four are nearing retirement.

Similarly, CRS management allowed the number of research specialists (GS-16s) to drop from about 38 in the late 1980s to three by the end of 2011. That number will move to zero with pending retirements. Thus, over a period of two decades, CRS management eliminated the two top levels of experts within the agency that Congress had established by law to assist it with substantive duties and constitutional analysis.

The language above refers to "research" senior specialists and "research" specialists because those individuals were appointed on the basis of their analytical skills. From 1989 forward, CRS management began giving the titles "specialist" and "senior specialist" to officials who did not compete for those positions, were not nationally recognized experts, and lacked the education, experience, and academic skills to function in the substantive areas statutorily designated by Congress. By law, Congress announced: "We need substantive specialists with nationally recognized credentials to help us with our legislative and constitutional duties." By administrative action, CRS management decided: "No, you don't."

The next section explains a major shift in CRS policy. The primary purpose is to highlight a change that ran counter to what Congress authorized in the LRA of 1970. As a result, the institutional powers of Congress were weakened and damage was done to the constitutional system of checks and balances. I found myself in the middle of that change, leading to my transfer from CRS to the Law Library in 2006, but the larger message is that CRS analysts and specialists continue to pay a price for publicly expressing expert views. Details are provided to establish that point.

CRS Policy of Neutrality

In January 2004, CRS management directed its analysts to follow a new policy of "neutrality," both inside the institution and with outside speaking and writing. Nothing in the LRA of 1970 or its legislative history implied, invited, or required that policy. Congress understood then and understands now that it is necessary and appropriate for experts to speak and write publicly about their discipline. Lawmakers sought competent and professional opinions from CRS specialists and senior specialists. During my first 33 years at CRS, no one in management told me to avoid the expression of expert opinions. Quite the contrary. CRS Director Daniel Mulhollan often told me I was an ideal senior specialist because of my analytical reports to Congress, frequent testimony before congressional committees, and outside publications and talks.

In December 2003, I was asked to meet with Mulhollan and several of his aides to discuss an article I had written about the Iraq war. Entitled "Deciding on War in Iraq: Institutional Failures," it was published in the peer-reviewed academic journal *Political Science Quarterly,* located in New York City.[41] The journal, dating to the founding of the Academy of Political Science in 1880, promotes "objective, scholarly analysis of political, social, and economic issues." The journal has been published continuously since 1886.

By itself, my article was unlikely to attract much attention. However, David Broder of the *Washington Post* wrote an op-ed on December 7, 2003, devoted entirely to my article. The op-ed carried an eye-catching title: "Congress's Cop-out on War," virtually ensuring that senior lawmakers who voted on the Iraq Resolution would take notice and feel an obligation to respond.[42] Representative Henry Hyde, chairman of the House International Relations Committee that reported the Iraq Resolution, wrote a letter to the *Washington Post,* defending the resolution.[43] After the letter appeared, I spoke with his office several times. The staffer who prepared the letter told me that Hyde encouraged "competitive analysis" and "diversity of opinion." I had expressed my view. He had expressed his. To the congressional office, the matter was closed.

For CRS, the matter remained quite open. I had two lengthy meetings with CRS management. At the first, one of Mulhollan's legal advisers told me I had violated the CRS policy of "neutrality." Surprised, I replied that in my 33 years with the agency, I had never heard or seen the word. I understand that for many people the term may seem attractive, perhaps implying an absence of bias and being open and fair-minded. But neutrality for a research agency has serious limitations. Thomas Haskell, in his book *Objectivity Is Not Neutrality,* saw "nothing to admire in neutrality":

41. Louis Fisher, "Deciding on War in Iraq: Institutional Failures," 118 Pol. Sci. Q. 389 (2003), available at http://www.loufisher.org/docs/wp/423.pdf.

42. David S. Broder, "Congress's Cop-out on War," Washington Post, December 7, 2003, at B7.

43. Rep. Henry J. Hyde, letter to the Washington Post, December 23, 2003, at A20.

My conception of objectivity . . . is compatible with strong political commitment. It pays no premium for standing in the middle of the road, and it recognizes that scholars are as passionate and as likely to be driven by interest as those they write about. It does not value even detachment as an end in itself, but only as an indispensable prelude or preparation for the achievement of higher levels of understanding. . . . Detachment functions in this manner not by draining us of passion, but by helping to channel our intellectual passions in such a way as to ensure collision with rival perspectives.[44]

As the meeting with CRS management continued, I reminded Mulhollan and those in the room that CRS reviewers had consistently approved my congressional testimony, which regularly took positions for and against House and Senate bills, including their constitutionality or lack thereof. Nothing in my nearly 40 appearances before committees at that time could be called neutral. The same applied to my CRS reports and memos. I took positions based on nonpartisan, objective, professional analysis. I told Mulhollan it was my practice to give him copies of my books and articles, including a recent book called *Congressional Abdication on War and Spending* (2000), which was not neutral even in its title.

I prepared a memo for Mulhollan to review existing standards of CRS research. My set of values had always been clear and public: "Throughout my career at CRS I have been strongly committed to keeping political institutions strong, defending legislative prerogatives, and in maintaining a vigor and health to checks and balances. I do that because the concentration of political power in a single branch poses a threat to democratic values, representative government, legislative deliberation, and individual liberties." Those values directed my congressional testimony, reports, and memos, all of them reviewed and approved by CRS. Over the years, the agency had "supported my interest in and commitment to political institutions, separation of powers, and checks and balances."[45] As made clear from comments at previous CRS meetings and remarks by Mulhollan, "solid research allows us to get off dead center and reach a conclusion on the basis of the evidence assembled."[46]

In a memo of January 23, 2004, Mulhollan "admonished" me for the article in *Political Science Quarterly*. He stated that "damage has been done" because I had

44. Thomas L. Haskell, Objectivity Is Not Neutrality: Explanatory Schemes in History 150 (1998).

45. Memo from Louis Fisher, Senior Specialist in Separation of Powers, to Daniel P. Mulhollan, CRS Director, December 22, 2003, at 1.

46. Id. at 2.

criticized both branches on a war powers question, "the very subject for which you have responsibility as a CRS analyst." The result, he concluded, was "damage to CRS in fulfilling its responsibility to provide unbiased analysis to its congressional clients."[47] Mulhollan also objected that my article failed to include a disclaimer, as required by Library regulations. Quite true, but neither the Library nor CRS had ever enforced that regulation. Employees published articles with or without a disclaimer, with no one admonished for failing to include one. As I explained to Mulhollan, his reference to disclaimers was a "makeweight." Had my article on the Iraq Resolution been purely descriptive without expressing a personal view, or "insipid or bland," it would have passed without notice. The presence or absence of a disclaimer would have been immaterial.[48] Bland, pointless manuscripts, of course, are not published in a professional journal like *Political Science Quarterly*.

According to Mulhollan, CRS has a responsibility to provide "unbiased analysis" to Congress. That is not the agency's statutory mission. He reflects the views of Ernest Griffith at the 1945 hearing, a misconception that Luther Evans quickly corrected and from which Griffith hastily retreated. The duty of CRS is to provide professional analysis. If a draft bill violates express language in the Constitution or conflicts with court rulings, a CRS analyst is expected to say so. If a contemplated procedure violates House and Senate rules, a CRS analyst has a duty to point that out. Expert and informed judgments are required every day. As to my article in *Political Science Quarterly* being "critical of both branches" on a subject that I had "responsibility [for] as a CRS analyst," that had been true for 33 years on a range of issues, without incident.

Two days before I received the letter of admonishment, Mulhollan shared some personal thoughts at a CRS annual meeting. Ironically, his views mirrored those that had directed my research and writing for over three decades. He told agency analysts that CRS "faces many challenges in meeting its statutory mission," but "more and more daunting is helping Congress to sustain its constitutional prerogatives during a time of war where traditionally the executive branch has prevailed. It is incumbent upon each of us to undertake our individual roles in CRS in assisting the Congress directly or indirectly together to help sustain representative democracy as so exquisitely portrayed by the United States Congress."[49] A clear bias? No doubt, but an appropriate one for a legislative research agency. Another Mulhollan statement violated his new standard of neutrality:

47. Memo from Mulhollan to Fisher, January 23, 2004, at 2.
48. Memo from Fisher to Mulhollan, February 23, 2004, at 2.
49. "Director's Statement for the 2004 CRS Annual Meeting Presented on January 21, 2004," at 2.

"I have expressed to you in other venues my concern over the trend of Supreme Court decisions over the past decade to restrict congressional power in favor of the power of the states."[50]

On January 23, 2004, Mulhollan released a "Director's Statement" entitled "Outside Activities: Preserving Objectivity and Non-Partisanship." Actually, it was a policy statement on what CRS analysts could say both outside *and* inside the institution. He advised: "We must all see to it that our ability to serve the Congress . . . is not compromised by even the appearance that we have our own agenda as an agency." CRS could not "relax our guard against avoidable charges of bias."[51] Yet Mulhollan had expressed positions on the war power, objected to trends in Supreme Court rulings, and stated that CRS has a duty to protect the constitutional prerogatives of Congress and the nature of representative democracy. Those values, in fact, are embodied in the LRA of 1970, defining the analytical mission of CRS. In contrast, Mulhollan's Director's Statement told all CRS employees to "err on the side of caution" in their outside writings and remarks."[52] Everyone should "think carefully before taking a public position on matters for which you are responsible in your work. When addressing the issues for which you speak for CRS, please do so in full observance of the neutrality required of your work here."[53]

In a memo to Mulhollan, I expressed my concern that if "we err on the side of caution at every turn, we risk legitimate and much more serious criticism that our products lack analytical rigor, integrity, interest, and value. Most of the criticism of our work that I am familiar with, from CRS staff and Congress, is that our reports are too diffuse and rambling, without theme, direction, or conclusion." If lawmakers received from CRS only descriptive reports and background material, without thoughtful analysis, "Congress may decide it has to go elsewhere."[54] I noted that when the Congressional Budget Office (CBO) releases a budget projection or study, "it knows that not all readers on Capitol Hill will be happy with the result." It issues its best professional judgment and responds as necessary to criticism. "That is all it can do and all we can do. Congressional research arms cannot function if they fear criticism."[55]

A CRS attorney who specializes in ethics and federal personnel policy prepared a legal analysis of the Director's Statement, concluding that the new pol-

---

50. Id. at 4.
51. Daniel P. Mulhollan, Director's Statement, "Outside Activities: Preserving Objectivity and Non-Partisanship," January 23, 2004, at 1.
52. Id.
53. Id. at 2.
54. Fisher to Mulhollan, January 31, 2004, at 2–3.
55. Id. at 4.

icy of neutrality had no support in the Constitution, federal statutes, or Library of Congress regulations. The attorney expressed concern that the statement "is having the unfortunate, but perhaps the intended effect of chilling and intimidating staff who want or had planned to engage in professionally-related writing or lecturing activities outside of their CRS employment." This result "is detrimental not only to the individual employee, but to the professionalism, reputation and mission of the agency as a whole." The Director's Statement was "inconsistent and self-defeating for the agency to require, as a factor for promotion, recognition as an expert in one's field by the professional community outside of Congress, and then to discourage and intimidate employees from engaging in precisely those kinds of outside writing and scholarship activities which may garner such recognition."[56]

I brought the dispute to the attention of the Library's Office of the General Counsel, which advised that I had a constitutional, statutory, and Library right to express my professional views on the outside, including views that overlapped my assigned research areas in CRS. Attorneys in the office had read my article in *Political Science Quarterly* and concluded that it did not violate Library policy. They told me that any effort by CRS to punish me for writing in that manner would not be successful under Library policy.

Media Reactions to CRS

For close to two years, the dispute over my article in *Political Science Quarterly* remained within the Library. Various efforts were undertaken to negotiate an agreement that would be consistent with CRS's analytical mission. In December 2005, I completed a lengthy CRS report on national security whistleblowers. Chris Strohm, a reporter for *Government Executive,* asked for my views. I said that conditions for agency whistleblowers had worsened after the September 11, 2001, terrorist attacks; Congress and the courts had been overly deferential to the executive branch; and it must be frightening for agency employees to work under abusive managers who are rarely held accountable for their conduct. Strohm's article included statistics to demonstrate that whistleblowers had little chance in court.[57]

56. The rebuttal by the CRS attorney appeared in the union publication CREAgram, May 12, 2004.

57. Chris Strohm, "Report Finds Government Whistleblowers Lack Adequate Protections," Government Executive, January 10, 2006, available at http://www.govexec.com/dailyfed/0106/011006c1.htm.

Three days after this article appeared, I received a second memo of admonishment, this one from Robert Dilger, chief of the CRS division on Government and Finance. He said my remarks in *Government Executive* "appear to compromise your ability to be perceived as meeting CRS standards of impartiality and objectivity." Further: "Care must be taken to avoid compromising the Service's mission by providing the impression that we as an agency, or the analyst as an individual, have taken a position on an issue before the Congress, or that we are not impartial and objective when researching those issues."

When I received this memo, I had been at CRS for more than three decades, "taking positions" on a range of issues in CRS products and in outside writings and statements. Dilger concluded: "There is little doubt that the readers of your Report, *National Security Whistleblowers,* who also read the *Government Executive* interview, can conclude that your work cannot be presumed to be balanced. This is an intolerable result, and places in jeopardy your ability to continue to provide service to the Congress on this subject. Such conduct on your part displays a lack of judgment in a matter on which you have been counseled on numerous occasions. Such behavior must not be repeated."[58]

Reading this memo, I understood that any further expression by me on public policy matters would result in efforts to demote or fire me. I could have decided to go quickly, and quietly, to a new place that would support independent and professional analysis. Instead, I chose to defend the right of Congress, expressed in a statute, to receive analytical and expert assistance from CRS. I wrote to Mulhollan about these larger implications. The dispute "concerns the capacity of CRS analysts to function within this organization and outside, without fear of retribution and punishment. It concerns the continued policy of the front office to engage in ad hoc, unprincipled actions and threats, leaving all analysts on guard and anxious as to when the next shoe will drop."[59]

Unable to resolve this issue within the Library—to protect the right of Congress to receive professional analysis, not neutral products—I decided to take the matter outside. I received legal assistance from two highly experienced attorneys at the Government Accountability Project (GAP), Tom Devine and Joanne Royce. Their steady guidance and support sent a strong signal to the Library to get this right. CRS employees had already begun sharing these memos with Hill contacts. Documents were reaching the press, universities, and private organizations in the United States as well as abroad.

58. Memo from Robert Dilger, Assistant Director, Government and Finance Division, "Comments Appearing in Government Executive," to Louis Fisher, Senior Specialist in Separation of Powers, Government and Finance Division, January 13, 2006.

59. Memo from Fisher to Mulhollan, January 18, 2006, at 1.

On February 9, 2006, an article in the *Wall Street Journal* was titled: "Expert on Congress's Power Claims He Was Muzzled for Faulting Bush." The story discussed my situation but raised the broader point that scientists and analysts throughout the executive branch were being silenced when their findings did not promote the agenda of the Bush administration.[60] An article in *Legal Times*, reviewing Dilger's reprimand of me, explained that senior specialists in CRS have "a long tradition of analyzing policy issues and drawing conclusions." It quoted Beth Daley of the Project on Government Oversight (POGO): "The CRS exists entirely to tell Congress the truth."[61] An article in *Roll Call* reported that the CRS policy of neutrality and "taking no positions" was only two years old, and "had been the focus of intensive debate over the past month in division and section meetings, producing no agreement or even an understanding of what the terms mean."[62] The *Christian Science Monitor* added its coverage to the story.[63]

The American Press Institute, with a commitment to the First Amendment and free speech, noted that CRS analysts had built a reputation for fairness and accuracy, drawing grudging respect from partisans on both sides of the aisle in Congress. It now warned: "Inexorably, the sound of silence is spreading throughout the federal government."[64] To Danielle Brian, executive director of POGO: "It is undeniable that unprecedented numbers of government whistleblowers face retaliation with no adequate protections. We are stunned that the Congress is offended to hear the truth about its failures to help whistleblowers and are even punishing their own seasoned researchers for talking about it."[65]

Senator Robert C. Byrd issued a public statement on February 9, 2006. His press statement defended "Library of Congress expert Dr. Louis Fisher, who for 36 years has provided insight and analysis of issues involving Constitutional checks and balances, separation of powers, and Congressional responsibility." The text of his statement:

60. Yochi J. Dreazen, "Expert on Congress's Power Claims He Was Muzzled for Faulting Bush," Wall Street Journal, February 9, 2006, at A6.

61. Tony Mauro, "Veteran Congressional Scholar Under Fire," Legal Times, February 20, 2006, at 3.

62. John McArdle, "CRS Director, Analyst Continue War of Memos," Roll Call, February 21, 2006, at 20.

63. Gail Russell Chaddock, "A Surge in Whistle-blowing . . . and Reprisals," Christian Science Monitor, February 16, 2006, at 1, 10.

64. Paul K. McMasters, "Discouraging Words: The War on Information," American Press Institute, February 23, 2006, at 1.

65. "Manager Censors Analyst at Congressional Research Service," Project on Government Oversight, January 25, 2006, available at http://www.afterdowningstreet.org/?=node/7121/print.

Lou Fisher is a scholar of integrity and insight. He has assisted me on many occasions. Dr. Fisher understands that the Constitution's Framers purposely placed the People's Branch at the front of this government. The Republic needs people who understand the role of the Congress, who share a determination to protect the people's liberties, and who are unafraid to point out when Congress abdicates that role or when another branch of government tries to steal it away. Quite simply, the Congress needs people like Lou Fisher with the brains and the backbone to help us do our work. I only wish that more people, including some who have sworn to protect and defend the Constitution, shared his passion.[66]

Steven Aftergood, author of the online *Secrecy News* for the Federation of American Scientists, remarked that my work "is widely cited and universally respected by his academic colleagues." He observed: "The uncertain premise of the dispute is that Congress desires deep and thoughtful analysis. What complicates matters further is that in many cases, as they say on the Comedy Channel, 'the facts are biased' against the Bush Administration."[67]

To reporter Steve Clemons, in an online story, Director Mulhollan was engaging in "silly, unbecoming, and potentially devastating brinksmanship" against experts in his agency. The dispute made him look "simultaneously small and perhaps a lap dog not of Congress, but of the White House."[68] Kevin Drum of the *Washington Monthly* defended professional analysis over "artificial neutrality" and recommended that newspaper reporters "might well take note of this: objectivity is not neutrality. The fact that there are two sides to a story does not make both sides equally valid." The issue was whether CRS analysts would be fired for finding one side stronger than another.[69]

Scholars Take Notice

These press and Internet stories were picked up around the world. John Hart, political science professor at the Australian National University (ANU), wrote to Dr. James H. Billington, Librarian of Congress, stating he was "horrified" at

66. "Byrd Defends CRS Expert," released by his office on February 9, 2006.

67. Steven Aftergood, "More Turmoil at the Congressional Research Service," Secrecy News, February 12, 2006, available at http://www.fas.org/blog/secrecy/2006/02/more_turmoil_at_the_congressio.html.

68. Steve Clemons, "CRS Separation of Powers Expert Under Attack for Slim-to-No Deference to White House," February 12, 2006,

69. Kevin Drum, "Neutrality vs. Objectivity," Washington Monthly, February 14, 2006.

CRS accusations against its experts. The conduct of CRS made the agency "look quite silly and unprofessional," doing more damage to its reputation than to analysts. Claims that agency standards of impartiality and objectivity had been damaged, he said, were unconvincing. Any effort by CRS to cover up the consequences of research "by attempting to remain 'neutral' would be doing a disservice to scholarship and, in the case of CRS, to the clientele that organization is supposed to be serving." Professor Douglas Craig, also of ANU, advised the Library that if I were an "advocate" of anything "it is for a Congress that fulfills its Constitutional powers and obligations."[70]

From Asia, a professor from China wrote to me in February 2006. He noted with regard to the CRS policy that "even in a country with the reputation of freedom of speech there would be some problems with free speech." He expected at the end of the conflict that "you are right and they (CRS) are totally wrong." In March 2006, I heard from an attorney in South Korea, who explained he had a similar experience with the government there. He had offered his professional judgment about a matter, after he had been advised to be "neutral," and had paid a price. He wished me luck with my situation at CRS.[71]

Dr. Nigel Bowles of Oxford University informed the Library that it was true I had opinions. "How could he not have? His opinions are reasonable, deeply informed, and rational." He inquired whether the Library intended to replace me with an "invertebrate," something incapable of forming expert judgments. Dr. Alan Ware, also of Oxford, explained his objections to the CRS policy of neutrality. No scholar or expert could follow such a guideline, "if what is meant by 'neutrality' is *never* drawing conclusions that support particular positions. . . . [I]ndeed to refuse to draw the appropriate conclusion in such circumstances is the very antithesis of research." For CRS to reprimand experts for expressing professional opinions "is an affront to the entire world of scholarship." The "censorship" imposed on CRS analysts "is, quite simply, disgraceful."[72]

A letter to the Library from Guillaume Parmentier, director of the Federal Center on the United States (CFE) in Paris, said that reports of CRS reprimanding me "shocked" him because I was known in France and in Europe "as one of the foremost, and perhaps the foremost, American experts on the separation of powers under the U.S. Constitution, and that his writings as a scholar

70. Letter from Dr. John Hart to Dr. Billington, February 10, 2006; letter from Professor Craig to Dr. Billington, February 13, 2006.

71. E-mail from a professor in China, February 28, 2006; e-mail from an attorney in South Korea, March 2, 2006.

72. Letter from Dr. Bowles to Dr. Billington, March 3, 2006; letter from Dr. Ware to Dr. Billington, March 16, 2006 (emphasis in original).

are a source of inspiration and sure knowledge for all Europeans who are interested in United States government, policies and politics."[73]

Dr. Nada Mourtada-Sabbah, professor at the American University of Sharjah, United Arab Emirates, and visiting professor at the Institute of Political Studies in Paris, advised the Library that it "is unfortunate indeed for someone of such eminence in representing the very best in American constitutional scholarship to be taken to task for voicing the conclusions that his sound empirical research naturally leads to." To those in the "embryonic democracies" of the Middle East and those in the "long-established democracy of France," who had long held the United States as a benchmark of freedom of expression and discussion, "it is a significant departure of legal and political tradition that Dr. Fisher may have been sanctioned for airing his exemplary scholarship."[74]

In other letters to the Library of Congress, political scientists and law professors in the United States protested CRS efforts to punish its experts and for adopting a "neutrality" standard that enfeebled the agency's capacity to perform analytical work for Congress. Professor Richard M. Pious of Barnard College acknowledged that experts take positions. That is what made them preeminent scholars and commentators in their field. Professor Nancy Kassop of the State University of New York (New Paltz) recalled that during the nomination hearings of Samuel Alito to be Associate Justice, Senator Joe Biden cited my position on war powers "precisely because he *is* so well-respected, after three decades of proving his intellectual credibility and professional expertise." Mark Rozell, political science professor at George Mason University, considered it empty to say I had "taken positions" in *Political Science Quarterly* and in the interview with *Government Executive*. Having read both items, he regarded "the accusation to be so obviously baseless that it is astonishing that anyone would take it seriously."[75]

Academics found the new CRS standard of neutrality to be hollow of meaning. To Professor Cornell Clayton of Washington State University, "honest research should lead on to whatever conclusion the evidence recommends." An effort to punish analysts for positions on various issues "smacks of either partisan censorship or political cowardice." Robert Spitzer, political science professor at the State University of New York (Cortland), asked, "[I]s it proper, or sensible, for a researcher on the holocaust to maintain neutrality regarding the question of whether the holocaust occurred during World War II?" Would a researcher

73. Letter from Mr. Parmentier to Dr. Billington, March 15, 2006.
74. Letter from Dr. Mourtada-Sabbah to Dr. Billington, August 1, 2006.
75. Letter from Professor Pious to Dr. Billington, January 20, 2006; letter from Professor Kassop to Dr. Billington, January 21, 2006 (emphasis in original); letter from Professor Rozell to Dr. Billington, January 20, 2006.

who challenged the Holocaust deniers be "casting neutrality to the winds?" Professor David Gray Adler of Idaho State University defended the need to unearth evidence and identify conclusions that flow from it. Any effort to reprimand analysts for such work "calls into question the professionalism and judgment of those at the helm of CRS."[76]

Other academics were critical of CRS management for failing to defend analytical integrity and its statutory mission to support an independent Congress. Phillip Cooper, political science professor at Portland State University, expressed wonderment that the Library of Congress, "charged with developing the kind of knowledge central to democratic governance," could be seen as a place "where those who have the knowledge the people need can be silenced or punished if they will not be silent." Professor William Weaver of the University of Texas at El Paso, an attorney and political scientist, concluded that CRS had adopted a policy not of "impartiality" but of partiality: "This brand of cowardice is sure to wreck the institution, for it means that CRS analysis is controlled by non-experts who are only interested in navigating a path designed to cause minimum disagreement and discussion. Now *that* is a bonafide example of partiality; *that* jeopardizes the perception and mission of CRS."[77]

Neal Devins, professor at the William and Mary law school, expressed dismay that CRS would accuse me "of acting as a partisan, against the Library's interests. Lou's professionalism and commitment to the Library's mission are beyond reproach." Professor Michael Genovese of Loyola Marymount University at Los Angeles regarded the neutrality standard as repugnant: "Issuing vague or specific warnings to senior researchers 'not' to take public policy positions, or to be strictly neutral makes little sense if what you are after is useful and meaningful information, sound ideas, and useful approaches to public policy problems and issues." Tying the hands of senior researchers amounted to "a form of censorship that is intolerable in a robust democracy."[78]

University scholars defended the need of congressional experts to assist lawmakers in maintaining their status as a coequal branch. James Pfiffner, political science professor at George Mason University, found it "entirely appropriate for scholars in general, and at CRS in particular, to argue in favor of the role of Congress in our constitutional system." To punish analysts for taking professional

76. Letter from Professor Clayton to Dr. Billington, January 23, 2006; letter from Professor Spitzer to Dr. Billington, January 23, 2006; letter from Professor Adler to Dr. Billington, January 24, 2006.

77. Letter from Professor Cooper to Dr. Billington, January 24, 2006; letter from Professor Weaver to Dr. Billington, January 25, 2006 (emphasis in original).

78. Letter from Professor Devins to Dr. Billington, February 1, 2006; letter from Professor Genovese to Dr. Billington, February 5, 2006.

positions "seems to signal to the world of scholars that the claims of unilateral executive power should prevail and that scholars in the congressional branch should censor themselves so as not to irritate the current administration." He applied the word "current" to the Nixon, Ford, Carter, Reagan, Bush I, Clinton, and Bush II presidencies.[79]

Other attorneys and political scientists took the time to send their objections to the Library of Congress. Eugene Fidell, a lawyer in private practice and for nearly two decades president of the nonpartisan National Institute of Military Justice, also taught at the Yale and Harvard law schools and the Washington College of Law at American University. In reading the Dilger admonishment, he concluded that its overall thrust was to penalize experts "for no valid reason, and in so doing to chill [their] future communications." He could think "of no better way to degrade CRS's ability to contribute to public understanding in our democratic society." A similar message came from Professor Gordon Silverstein of the University of California at Berkeley: "Congress requires expertise and analysis. To suggest that 'neutrality' precludes expert analysis is preposterous. If the Library allows this effort to chill and intimidate, it will do a great disservice to scholars as well as to Members of Congress—and therefore to the country as a whole."[80]

Rogers Smith, political science professor at the University of Pennsylvania, voiced his concerns. If CRS scholars are reprimanded for expressing judgments that "may appear unflattering to at least some of those currently in power," not only are the scholars treated unjustly, but such actions also "inevitably send a signal of willingness to use governmental power to suppress scholarship that will have a chilling effect on academic inquiry more generally." Telling scholars to express views only if they do not "take a position" and adhere to "neutrality" on the subject was "simply nonsensical." Scholars naturally express a point of view. "It is foolish, indeed intellectually dishonest, to pretend otherwise."[81]

Several letters from scholars predicted that the new climate within CRS would produce empty and useless reports.[82] Professor Jonathan Entin of the Case Western Reserve University School of Law said that sanctions against me "would

79. Letter from Professor Pfiffner to Dr. Billington, February 8, 2006.
80. Letter from Professor Fidell to Dr. Billington, February 10, 2006; letter from Professor Silverstein to Dr. Billington, February 10, 2006.
81. Letter from Professor Smith to Dr. Billington, February 12, 2006.
82. E.g., letters to Dr. Billington from Professor Mark Rozell of George Mason University, January 30, 2006; Professor Brian Hallett of the University of Hawaii, February 6, 2006; Thomas E. Cronin, Professor Emeritus at Whitman College, February 10, 2006; Professor Susan R. Burgess of Ohio University, February 13, 2006; Professor Leonard Markovitz of Queens College, February 16, 2006; Lawrence R. Velvel, Dean of the Massachusetts School of Law, March 1, 2006.

be a major loss to the nation to have his thoughtful voice muzzled or silenced." The nation would be "much the worse" if scholars are not welcome at CRS. Professor Christopher Kelley of Miami University of Ohio, joined by seven of his colleagues, objected to sanctions against CRS analysts "for violating something as nebulous as institutional 'neutrality' and for 'taking positions.'"[83]

Professor Nancy Baker of New Mexico State University advised the Library that "taking positions" is a natural result of doing research. Reprimands by CRS management implied political interference in the work of scholars. Professor Joel Aberbach, political scientist at UCLA, warned that shutting off free inquiry and the communication of conclusions "throttles something very precious in our society." The immediate victim was the individual researcher, "but our nation is the ultimate victim when it is deprived of the judgments of our leading thinkers on the subjects they know best." Professor Mark Miller of Clark University, an attorney and political scientist, urged the Library "to end such attacks on academic freedom" and the "principles underlying our country's First Amendment."[84]

Repressive policies at CRS reminded some scholars of conditions within the executive branch. Loch Johnson, political science professor at the University of Georgia, advised the Library that senior analysts in CRS had a right to engage in exhaustive research and "lay all the cards on the table." In his judgment, the nation had suffered greatly in recent years by intimidating analysts in the intelligence community, a field he had closely studied. Analysts needed to be free to "do the research and speak the truth." From Middle Tennessee State University, Professor John Vile found it ironic that a scholar "known throughout the world for trumpeting the American system of separation of powers and the concomitant liberties that this system brings might himself fall prey to governmental pressures to conform." Professor Stephen Dycus of the Vermont Law School worried that CRS analysts were being pressured to either reshape their research "to serve a particular political agenda" or quit the agency.[85]

While these letters were arriving at the Library, I learned that CRS Director Mulhollan had visited one of the divisions and was asked about my situation. He responded: "Lou has a great record of accomplishment, but he is an advo-

83. Letter from Professor Entin to Dr. Billington, February 13, 2006; letter from Professor Kelley to Dr. Billington, February 13, 2006.

84. Letter from Professor Baker to Dr. Billington, February 13, 2006; letter from Professor Aberbach to Dr. Billington, February 15, 2006; letter from Professor Miller to Dr. Billington, February 24, 2006.

85. Letter from Professor Johnson to Dr. Billington, February 27, 2006; letter from Professor Vile to Dr. Billington, March 1, 2006; letter from Professor Dycus to Dr. Billington, March 3, 2006.

cate for Congress." It seemed a strange remark to those in the audience, given that I (and they) worked for Congress. He told the analysts I should not favor either Congress or the executive branch. Calling me an "advocate" for Congress implied that I saluted Congress no matter what it did, which was never the case. Frequently I testified against bills that invaded powers of the President (as with Gramm-Rudman in 1985) or threatened the independence of the judiciary (my testimony on the item veto in 1995). In articles and books, I criticized Presidents of both parties. Did I defend congressional powers and the system of checks and balances? Very definitely. I not only performed that function but was expected to. For more than three decades I consistently received the full support and appreciation of CRS management.

CRS vs. Professional Societies

Several prominent institutes and organizations registered their concerns. Ira Katznelson, President of the American Political Science Association, asked the Library to clarify reports that I "might face disciplinary action for his peer reviewed scholarship and his commentary to the press on issues relating to his expertise." Efforts to restrict the public speech of experts "put in question the reputation and merit of the non-partisan Congressional Research Service, which, over the years has commanded the regard of Administrations of both parties, of Congress irrespective of which party was in the majority, and of scholars who have relied on its work."[86]

Demetrious James Caraley, President of the Academy of Political Science, editor of *Political Science Quarterly,* and a faculty member at Columbia University, shared his views with the Library. Senior specialists at CRS "are hired to engage in rigorous academic research and reach objective, non-partisan conclusions based on that research." CRS had an obligation to produce objective analysis without political pressure. Rebukes to analysts for expressing professional judgments represented an attack on "the very essence of the Library of Congress." No one would be able to trust the CRS if it becomes "politicized and analysts' research and conclusions are silenced when they can be construed as not falling into line with the political party in power."[87]

Turning to my article in *Political Science Quarterly,* Professor Caraley observed that I criticized "not only the Executive, but also Congress and not only the Republicans, but also the Democrats." My manuscript "received rave

86. Letter from Dr. Katznelson to Dr. Billington, February 15, 2006.
87. Letter from Professor Caraley to Dr. Billington, February 6, 2006.

referee reports (in a double blind process) from reviewers on our editorial board, which consists of a variety of academics of all stripes." In closing, Caraley examined the new CRS policy of neutrality. Because there was no claim of partisanship about my article, the claim that it lacked "neutrality" apparently meant "he is not neutral in his commitment to our Constitution as the founders established it and as it has developed over the centuries." He asked whether the standard of neutrality would have been satisfied by concluding it would be perfectly legitimate for members of Congress and the President to ignore the Constitution when it doesn't suit their political interests. "May God protect us all from that kind of neutrality."

Additional views came from Malcomb M. Feeley, President of the Law and Society Association and professor at the Boalt Hall School of Law, University of California at Berkeley. He said scholars at the Library of Congress "should be feted rather than sanctioned by officials at the Congressional Research Service." Although the CRS attack on experts was "disturbing enough, what is even more frightening is that this is not an isolated case in government these days." The American system depends on "the free flow of ideas and on policy built on credible information." The Library of Congress and CRS were established "to provide precisely this sort of information to members of Congress." Senior analysts had been fulfilling that responsibility for years. To suddenly sanction them "is outrageous." Feeley urged Dr. Billington to "intervene and to take unambiguous actions to correct this mistake." The reputation of Dr. Billington and the Library were "now at stake."[88]

Nancy Kassop, professor of political science at the State University of New York (New Paltz), wrote to the Library on behalf of the Presidency Research Group, an organization of 450 presidential scholars. She asked the Library to find a "reasonable, swift and satisfactory resolution . . . to guarantee the independence and integrity of CRS and the scholars who work there." George Edwards, professor of political science at Texas A&M University and editor of *Presidential Studies Quarterly,* shared his views with the Library. Offering professional conclusions made CRS analysts valuable to Congress, the academic profession, and the public. Would CRS, he asked, want to hire a legal expert "who could only provide lists of cases and statutes?" Why would members of Congress "value the reports of analysts who synthesize but cannot analyze?" Why would anyone in Congress ask someone to testify "who could not take positions?" The people asked to testify were prominent in their field, with views important to hear. Would the Library of Congress "abandon the field of

88. Letter from Professor Feeley to Dr. Billington, February 15, 2006.

detached analysis and leave Congress at the mercy of interested parties? I hope not."[89]

Transfer to the Law Library

On March 6, 2006, the Library transferred me from CRS to the Law Library, where I recovered in full my intellectual and professional freedom. An e-mail to Law Library staff described my books, teaching, congressional testimony, and foreign speaking engagements. The last line of the announcement touched me greatly: "We are honored to welcome Dr. Louis Fisher to the staff of the National Law Library."

Over a period of almost five years at the Law Library, I testified eleven times before committees on various constitutional issues: presidential item veto, war powers, NSA surveillance, the state secrets privilege, restoring the rule of law, national security whistleblowers, and criminal penalties for Presidents and executive officials who mislead Congress and the public about the need to initiate military operations. On each occasion, I expressed my professional judgments, helping Congress receive the analytical assistance it needs to perform as a coequal branch. In the review process within the Law Library, there was no effort to water down my writing or insist on neutrality. Members of Congress and committees asked for my expert opinions and received them.

Far from being embarrassed or uncomfortable about my expert views, the Law Library in its monthly newsletter included a section called "Outreach by Lou Fisher." It provided convenient links to my talks, testimony, and outside publications. The Law Library placed my congressional testimony and journal articles—always expressing positions on controversial matters of public policy and constitutional law—on two Web sites, one for Congress and the other for the general public. My professional work was therefore within easy reach of congressional offices and citizens, in this country and abroad.

After my transfer to the Law Library, letters continued to reach the Librarian of Congress. Professor Jasmine Farrier of the University of Louisville reported her "shock and disappointment" at the CRS treatment of senior analysts. She voiced her concern "for the future relevance of CRS and its original mission in light of what appears to be political pressure to maintain research 'neutrality.'" Professor James A. Nathan of Auburn University (Montgomery) learned of my transfer from CRS to the Law Library after his return from an appointment at

---

89. Letter from Professor Kassop to Dr. Billington, February 14, 2006; letter from Professor Edwards to Dr. Billington, February 4, 2006.

China's Foreign Affairs University, serving as Distinguished Senior Fulbright. He had been abroad for several years, presenting talks at many State Department events, arguing that "the American process is one that thrives because of the freedom to exchange views." When he discovered "that Dr. Fisher was charged with having an opinion, and thus compromising 'CRS standards of impartiality and objectivity,'" he wrote to the Library that the charge "is quite fantastic."[90]

Douglas Brattebo, with a law degree and a doctorate in political science, observed that my absence "from the CRS roster is a conspicuous reminder of CRS's inability to retain world-class talent for the benefit of Congress, the American public, and the country's future." Analytical objectivity, he pointed out, "does not imply an absence of judgments. Whether driven by large institutional pressures, the whims of small commissars, or both, insistence that the policy analysis of CRS's senior scholars be 'neutral' has brought about the institution's irrelevance." Lawmakers and their staff "now know that they cannot get unvarnished perspectives from senior scholars at CRS who have been ordered to produce 'neutral' (or perhaps 'neutered'?) narratives."[91]

Professor Mitchel Sollenberger of Bowling Green State University wrote to Dr. Billington, commending him for removing me from "such a destructive environment" at CRS. Sollenberger stated that CRS "is legally obligated to advise Congress on legislative and policy outcomes, but certain self-imposed policies have limited its ability to carry out this task." By adopting the "neutrality" standard, Director Mulhollan "has actively worked against the intent of Congress under the Reorganization Act of 1970 by creating a culture of fear among CRS analysts." No other congressional support agency, including CBO and the GAO, "insists on such a rule." When CRS fails to provide Congress with legislative analysis, "the system of checks and balances breaks down."[92]

In November 2009, I learned that Colonel Morris Davis was fired as the new chief of the CRS division of foreign affairs. The charge: he had published an article in the *Wall Street Journal*, explaining why military commissions were not an adequate substitute for prosecuting detainees in federal court. He was responding to an article by former Attorney General Michael Mukasey, who urged that detainees be tried only in military commissions and not in federal court.[93] Colonel Davis came to CRS with impressive credentials, serving 25 years

90. Letter from Professor Farrier to Dr. Billington, April 19, 2006; letter from Professor Nathan to Dr. Billington, June 14, 2006.

91. Letter from Professor Brattebo to Dr. Billington, October 25, 2006.

92. Letter from Professor Sollenberger to Dr. Billington, January 22, 2007.

93. The Davis article is available at http://online.wsj.com/article/SB1000142405274870440 24045745255581723576284.html. The Mukasey article is available at http://www.washington post.com/wp-dyn/content/article/2009/11/05/AR2009110504331.html.

in the Air Force and most recently as chief prosecutor at Guantánamo. He decided to retire from the military after concluding that the procedures in place at the commissions were insufficient to protect the right of detainees to defend themselves. For CRS to fire Davis for expressing expert views was very disturbing. Represented by the ACLU, he went to federal court to secure his right (and others at the Library of Congress) to express expert views. I joined with several colleagues in filing declarations in district court to support his position. Davis became another casualty of the CRS policy of "neutrality." An article in the *Los Angeles Times* on December 6, 2010, recounts the major issues of the Davis litigation.[94]

During House hearings on February 24, 2010, Dennis Roth, head of the CRS union (CREA), testified before the House Appropriations Committee that the firing of Davis "has had an intimidating and chilling effect" within the agency. CRS employees want to participate in their fields of expertise, "but now they are uncertain about possible negative consequences." Roth explained the incoherence and unfairness of this policy. Outside speaking and writing "are a necessary, obligatory part of their duties, i.e., it is a promotion criterion." His prepared statement expressed concern that CRS employees, because of the firing of Davis, "will refrain from outside speaking and writing activities that could enhance their professional reputations and, ultimately, enhance the credibility of the Service." Roth noted that under CRS guidelines, "recognition of the analyst's professional expertise" by "high ranking officials in State governments, public interest groups, the courts, and subject matter experts and policy analysts in the Federal and other professional communities, among others, is a specific ranking factor in evaluation for promotion to higher-level grades in CRS." But in seeking to gain such recognition, CRS employees are at risk of being sanctioned or fired.[95]

On August 27, 2010, I retired from the Library after a career of 40 years. My last product was a 32-page analytical report on national security law for a member of the House who had asked specifically for my personal and professional judgments. I did precisely that, and the Law Library cleared the report for his use. It was a satisfying way to conclude my work for the Library of Congress. However, uncertainty within CRS remains about the rules for outside writing

94. David Zucchino, "Retired Colonel Fights Library of Congress over Firing," Los Angeles Times, December 6, 2010, available at http://www.latimes.com/news/nationworld/nation/la-na-fired-20101206,0,2574412.story.

95. "Legislative Branch Appropriations for 2011, Part 2, Fiscal Year 2011, Legislative Branch Appropriations Requests," hearings before the House Committee on Appropriations, 111th Cong., 2d Sess. 54–55, 58–59 (2010).

and speaking. If CRS continues to prohibit analysts from expressing expert views, both within the organization and outside, they will be prevented from doing the analytical work that Congress requested, authorized, and mandated under the LRA of 1970.

On January 19, 2011, CRS Director Mulhollan announced his plan to retire in April 2011. In a meeting with agency employees, he spoke about joining the Legislative Reference Service in 1969 at a time when the country turned against President Lyndon Johnson because of the Vietnam War. Congress "felt that it must bolster its capacities to govern and assess problems independent of the executive." It passed the Legislative Reorganization Act of 1970 "to bolster its standing as the First Branch of Government" and ensure that specialists in the Library of Congress would provide "independent, objective sources of expertise, analysis and information." Congress insisted that it "have readily available experts whose level of knowledge allows them to provide sophisticated analyses of all issues." With other initiatives, Congress "asserted its prominence within the checks and balances of the American government." Mulhollan recalled several actions in those early years that "seared into my mind the dangers inherent in the centralization of power within the executive branch."

These were remarkable statements. I arrived at the Library of Congress about the same time (September 1970) and also understood those legislative objectives: restoring the institutional capacity of Congress and safeguarding the constitutional system of checks and balances. What I found after 2003, however, was a CRS that eliminated the two levels of expertise (senior specialists and specialists), transferred those titles and salaries to administrators with no capacity for analytical research, and put in place a new policy of "neutrality" that undermined the ability of CRS staff to provide independent and objective assistance to lawmakers.

Congressional Budget Office

CBO was created in 1974 as part of the Congressional Budget and Impoundment Control Act. Congress understood that in the field of budgeting it was at a substantial disadvantage to the executive branch. Presidents had the support of the Office of Management and Budget (OMB) and thousands of experts and policy analysts throughout the agencies. In shoring up legislative expertise, CBO encountered in its early years some opposition from members of Congress who thought its role was too public and independent. Allen Schick's *Congress and Money* (1980) details these early conflicts. CBO Director Alice Rivlin explained in 1975 the multiple roles she anticipated for the agency: "CBO wants to be fair and nonpartisan, and to be perceived as and to be an analytically straightforward professional organization that calls issues as we see them, without any bias in any political direction."[96]

Nonpartisanship is essential for a legislative support agency, but what is the difference between "calling issues as we see them" and avoiding charges of bias? One difference is that an analyst does not start with a conclusion, even though professional values guide the process. Only at the end of objective and analytical work does a conclusion begin to emerge. Schick explored the inherent difficulties of this process: "Although CBO wants to be perceived as nonpartisan, it also wants to remain free to call the shots without inhibition. It cannot have it both ways, professing to be neutral while finding that one option is more costly or less efficient than another." Promises by CBO to avoid policy recommendations "cannot surmount the plain fact that analysis is inseparable from advocacy in Congress."[97]

In a statement issued on June 7, 2002, CBO Director Dan Crippen spoke about another value that guides CBO: its place in the constitutional system: "The U.S. form of government is based on separated powers, and so part of CBO's job is to help the Congress to assert its independence in our constitutional system."[98] Congress "could not remain coequal with the President on budgetary affairs without its own budget and economics experts."[99] The duty of CBO is to provide "objective budgetary and economic information," not neutrality.[100] The work of CBO necessarily reflects its "best judgment."[101]

Members of Congress need reliable information to satisfy their constitutional duties. Executive officials control much of that information. How could lawmakers vote in an informed manner? Crippen noted: "[F]or the Congress to make effective budget policy and protect its powers under the Constitution, it is especially critical that it have a source of reliable budgetary information independent of the Administration."[102] No hedging on that point. CBO supports the coequal status of Congress and has a role in the system of checks and balances. Unlike CRS Director Mulhollan, who worried that agency analysts might become an "advocate" for Congress, Crippen understood that CBO is a support agency for Congress and has a duty to uphold legislative interests.

---

96. Allen Schick, Congress and Money 162 (1980).

97. Id.

98. Dan L. Crippen, Director, Congressional Budget Office, "Informing Legislators About the Budget: The History and Role of the U.S. Congressional Budget Office," June 7, 2002, at 9.

99. Id. at 12.

100. Id. at 2.

101. Id. at 7.

102. Id. at 2.

Toward the end of his statement, Crippen spoke of the need for "an independent cadre of disinterested and dispassionate analysts working exclusively for the Congress."[103] I appreciate why agency heads want to assure potential critics that analysts are "distinterested and dispassionate," implying they are not biased or prejudiced. But the language could be read to favor some kind of standard of neutrality, as though CBO analysts go about their work without any values. That is not so. As Crippen notes in his closing paragraph: "[I]t is important that no single government entity monopolize the information needed in the legislative process. Legislative institutions and the legislative process can only be strengthened when legislators are informed."[104] That is one value. Knowing that Congress created CBO as part of a system of checks and balances is another. Moreover, CBO analysts have their own professional standards that guide their work and their recommendations. Those standards are neither distinterested nor dispassionate.

With a staff of about 250, CBO devotes most of its time in estimating the cost of bills, making revenue estimates and economic forecasts, calculating budget projections, and preparing policy analysis in the program divisions. CBO estimates as best it can, knowing that critics can always point to a different economic model that yields different numbers. During debate on the health bill in 2009, CBO was regularly expected to estimate the cost of the bill and its impact on budget deficits. It made professional judgments and stood by them. It didn't release conflicting numbers and ask congressional offices to puzzle through them.

CBO directors and analysts tackle issues of the budget process that concern the balance of power between Congress and the President. They understand that CBO was created as part of a concerted effort to strengthen congressional capabilities against the executive branch. A recurring issue is item-veto authority. In hearings in 1992, CBO Director Robert D. Reischauer punctured the belief that giving the President an item veto could offer substantial relief for the heavy deficits that began appearing in the early 1980s. He testified that an item veto was "likely to have little effect, either on total spending or on the deficit."[105] Clear, straightforward professional analysis. He did not point to two rival schools of thought and invite lawmakers to pick one or the other, or neither. He gave three reasons to support his judgment: an item veto would not apply to the vast sums of mandatory spending; experience with item vetoes at the state level

103. Id. at 12.
104. Id. at 13.
105. "Legislative Line-Item Veto Proposals," hearings before the House Committee on Rules, 102d Cong., 2d Sess. 257 (1992).

provided scant evidence that they had been an instrument of fiscal restraint; and total discretionary spending has been limited by multiyear spending caps, with little likelihood of reductions below those caps.[106]

Testifying before a joint hearing in 1995, Reischauer again counseled against accepting the item veto as "a powerful tool of spending and the deficit. I urge you to be very skeptical about such claims." Evidence from the states, he said, revealed that an item veto was more likely to be used to favor executive spending over legislative priorities.[107] No one denounced him or the agency for setting forth expert views without equivocation. CBO officials have also testified on other budget reforms that raise substantial questions about the balance between Congress and the President. When asked at a hearing whether a balanced budget amendment could shift powers to the executive branch, so that Congress "would be the lesser of three bodies," Reischauer did not duck or retreat behind obscurity. He agreed with the questioner: "[T]hat is a real danger."[108]

CBO functions as a professional organization when it performs research, knowing that whatever scorekeeping it does or projections it makes, exasperated members of Congress will object that better numbers are available. It is impossible to do analysis without stimulating complaints from some quarters. Research agencies must take comfort that their expert judgments are solidly based and are the best available.

Office of Technology Assessment

Congress created the Office of Technology Assessment (OTA) in 1972 to be "within and responsible to the legislative branch of the Government." It marked another effort by Congress to strengthen itself as a coequal branch and attract the technical support needed to perform its constitutional functions. As Bruce Bimber explains in his study of the agency, members of Congress "were intensely interested in shoring up Congress' independence from the executive."[109] The basic function of OTA was to provide "early indications of the probable beneficial and adverse impacts of the application of technology and to develop other

106. Id. at 258.
107. "Line-Item Veto," joint hearing before the House Committee on Government Reform and Oversight and the Senate Committee on Governmental Affairs, 104th Cong., 1st Sess. 62 (1995).
108. "The Balanced Budget Amendment," vol. 2, hearings before the House Committee on the Budget, 102d Cong., 2d Sess. 490 (1992).
109. Bimber, The Politics of Expertise in Congress, supra note 4, at x.

coordinate information which may assist the Congress."[110] Congress directed it to ascertain cause-and-effect relationships, identify alternative technological methods of implementing specific programs, identify alternative programs for achieving requisite goals, make estimates and comparisons of the impacts of alternative methods and programs, and perform other duties.[111]

As Bimber notes, many lawmakers hoped that CBO would not just be "a means to better policy, but also a lever that might help tilt the balance of power back toward Congress and away from an increasingly hostile administration." Representative Charles Mosher remarked: "Let us face it, Mr. Chairman, we are constantly outmanned and outgunned by the expertise of the executive agencies." This "expertise" was not intended to be neutral. Representative John Wydler observed that "the only real technical witnesses we heard from [in congressional hearings] were administration witnesses whose bias was obvious."[112] Lawmakers wanted their own experts to evaluate claims from the executive branch.

In the early years, OTA received credit for playing the "expert witness" role. It completed important studies on the computer procurement strategy of the Social Security Administration, radioactive and medical waste, acid rain and clear air, offshore oil and gas development, a basing plan for the MX missile, and the Reagan administration Strategic Defense Initiative (SDI).[113] OTA was abolished in 1995, in large part because Republicans in the 1994 elections promised to cut the size of the federal government. Small agencies that lacked important protectors on the Hill were in jeopardy, even if their disappearance would have practically no effect on the size of the federal budget. What made an agency vulnerable? It was well said by Bimber that it is a "conspicuous feature of the political logic of the federal budget that OTA came to an abrupt end not because its budget had grown too large, but precisely because it was so small."[114]

OTA also damaged its usefulness to Congress by hiding behind the "strategy of neutrality."[115] It could have decided to release studies after ensuring their professional integrity, realizing that any recommendations and positions taken would offend some members of Congress and outside groups. If that prospect seemed too risky, the alternative was to issue reports with muddled thinking. Bimber suggests that the concept of neutrality is an attractive one for experts advising Congress: "The traditional ideal of the policy expert is someone who

110. 86 Stat. 797, sec. 3(c) (1972).
111. Id. at 798.
112. Bimber, The Politics of Expertise in Congress, at 41.
113. Id. at 42–47.
114. Id. at x.
115. Id.

brings the neutral authority of science to bear on policy. Indeed, acknowledging the distinction between expert and non-expert requires acceptance of a technical standard in which objectivity is an important part."[116]

Neutrality and objectivity are not the same. Objectivity and the scientific method attempt to analyze evidence for the purpose of understanding what is true. Procedures and attitudes to ensure objectivity are important in this quest for knowledge. Neutrality is too vague and spiritless. Generally it means opposition to taking sides. After its creation, Bimber says that OTA "devised a strategy for asserting neutrality and non-partisanship."[117] Being nonpartisan is essential for a congressional support agency, but has nothing to do with neutrality.

Some argue that Congress "is actually quite successful at producing neutrally competent advisors. In fact it is better equipped than the executive branch to inform policy debates with balanced expert views."[118] It is unclear what "neutrality" means in this context. Nonpartisan? Fine. Experts who cannot decide what to recommend or what results to conclude? If it is a matter of locating reliable facts, neutrality is helpful. Competent advisors and experts reach conclusions, like them or not.

In his study of OTA, Bimber states that experts bring "interests, values, and political views to the policy process, and these limit the fulfillment of the goal of objectivity."[119] That is half true: experts have values. Values are not automatically at war with objectivity. How could experts perform their work devoid of values? If an expert identifies the values that guide a research project, that is all to the good. The danger is the expert who has values but pretends not to. As acknowledged by Bimber: "It is not the case that experts at OTA had no values, no opinions, no position on policies. What is interesting is that the agency chose not to reveal those positions in its work."[120] It should have. Not to do so is dishonest and deceptive. The values that guide a research product should be stated up front. A policy expert who is "neutral" is unlikely to have credibility.

To protect its powers to legislate and conduct oversight, Congress needs the full assistance of its support agencies. Organizations like GAO, CRS, and CBO provide that assistance by following objective and nonpartisan standards. They can-

116. Id. at 4.
117. Id. at 6.
118. Id. at 7.
119. Id. at 14.
120. Id. at 97.

not, however, be "neutral." They exist to defend institutional interests. Presidents (with some regrettable examples) do not tell experts in the executive branch to withhold their expert judgments. Legislative support agencies need to ensure that their senior analysts are available to provide lawmakers and committees with professional and expert counsel. Congress needs to encourage that policy. Statutory titles (specialist and senior specialist) must be reserved for research analysts and not given to nonresearch administrators. The stakes are high: the integrity of statutory policy, the health and independence of the legislative branch, and the system of checks and balances.

CONCLUSIONS

Members of Congress and the public often paint an imaginary picture of an all-wise, all-knowing Supreme Court. Instead of praising the judiciary, with its very shaky record, lawmakers should direct compliments at their own branch. For more than two centuries, Congress has a pattern of defending constitutional values as well as, or better than, the Court. Previous chapters describe legislative accomplishments in many areas, often in the face of judicial opposition and obstruction. As a nation, we are better off with this display of legislative independence. On the downside, Congress has a record of not protecting its key prerogatives over the power of the purse and going to war.

What attitude should members of Congress have about their constitutional duties and oath of office? An understanding of legislative independence and its contributions over history is an essential step. Congress has a good story to tell in defending the Constitution and protecting individual freedoms. Lawmakers need to tell it. At the same time, they can recognize previous legislative mistakes and learn from them. The other branches commit errors also. With the Sedition Act of 1798 and the detention of Japanese Americans after Pearl Harbor, all three branches violated their constitutional duties. Unfortunately, too many lawmakers are inclined to disparage their institution and defer to the supposedly superior talents of the executive and judicial branches. In yielding to other branches, lawmakers fail to represent their constituents, violate their oath of office, and cripple the system the framers counted on to limit the destructive capacity of government: checks and balances.

There is no societal value in believing that the Supreme Court, compared to the other branches, is our best hope for achieving neutral and objective interpretations of the Constitution. Chief Justice Earl Warren once argued that progress in politics "could be made and most often was made by compromising and taking half a loaf where a whole loaf could not be obtained." He insisted that the "opposite is true so far as the judicial process was concerned." Through the process of adjudication, "and particularly in the Supreme Court, the basic ingredient of decision is principle, and it should not be compromised and parceled out a little in one case, a little more in another, until someone receives the full benefit."[1]

1. The Memoirs of Earl Warren 6 (1977).

First, in many cases the Court has stood "on principle" to deny blacks access to public accommodations, women the right to practice law, and to allow children to be exposed to dangerous working conditions. Second, there is nothing intrinsically wrong or deficient about compromise. In a society as complex as the United States, it is often the only way to proceed. Compromise, expediency, and ad hoc actions are no strangers to a multimember Court that seeks, in incremental fashion, a consensus. Different constitutional issues must be balanced before reaching a decision. If there were some bright-line "principle" to guide government, the dispute would have been settled out of court or certainly before the case moved to the Supreme Court.

Would "judicial finality" provide the nation with important closure and definitiveness to legal matters? Would constitutional analysis by all three branches invite confusion about the law? We have managed for more than two centuries to survive all the rethinking and retooling done regularly by federal courts. Stability is less important than finding the correct policy that promotes constitutional government. One of the problems with the Supreme Court, in terms of judicial finality, is the obscurity of its decisions. Excessively long majority opinions now fail to provide clear guidance to lower courts or to the nation. At his confirmation hearing to be Chief Justice, John Roberts said: "I hope we haven't gotten to the point where the Supreme Court's opinions are so abstruse that the educated layperson can't pick them up and read them and understand them." We have reached that point with contemporary decisions.[2]

Inspecting a Famous Quip

Why do we equate the Constitution with what the Court says? In part, it reflects a decision to rely on quips, including this one: "We are under a Constitution, but the Constitution is what the judges say it is."[3] It is often attributed to Charles Evans Hughes when he was Chief Justice, but he actually delivered it while serving as governor of New York. What did he mean? How seriously should we accept his statement? We should first note that his remarks were impromptu. He abandoned his prepared speech to the Elmira Chamber of Commerce because he wanted to respond to critics who opposed giving power to a commission to investigate abuses by railroads.[4] Hughes believed that unless those

2. Adam Liptak, "Justices Long on Words but Short on Guidance," New York Times, November 18, 2010, at A1, A22.
3. Charles Evans Hughes, Addresses and Papers 139 (1908).
4. Id. at 133.

powers were placed in the hands of a commission, highly emotional and divisive issues would be litigated and cause injury to the courts. Far from regarding the courts as a supremely able and powerful body, he wanted their duties carefully circumscribed. Here is the context of his remarks:

> I have the highest regard for the courts. My whole life has been spent in work conditioned upon respect for the courts. I reckon him one of the worst enemies of the community who will talk lightly of the dignity of the bench. We are under a Constitution, but the Constitution is what the judges say it is, and the judiciary is the safeguard of our liberty and of our property under the Constitution. I do not want to see any direct assault upon the courts, nor do I want to see any indirect assault upon the courts. And I tell you, ladies and gentlemen, no more insidious assault could be made upon the independence and esteem of the judiciary than to burden it with these questions of administration,—questions which lie close to the public impatience, and in regard to which the people are going to insist on having administration by officers directly accountable to them.[5]

Hughes warned that any effort to transfer railroad disputes to the judiciary "would swamp your courts with administrative burdens and expose them to the fire of public criticism in connection with matters of this description, from which I hope they will be safeguarded." If courts attempted to decide those questions, "free from that direct accounting to which administrative officers are subject, you will soon find a propaganda advocating a short-term judiciary, and you will turn upon our courts—the final safeguard of our liberties—that hostile and perhaps violent criticism from which they should be shielded and will be shielded if left with the jurisdictions which it was intended they should exercise."[6]

We should not make too much of quips and impromptu remarks or the assertion by Hughes that the judiciary is "the safeguard" or "final safeguard" of our liberties. The courts have never reliably served that cause. Correctly, Hughes recognized that courts are fragile institutions and need to exercise their powers with great care. Otherwise, the public will turn against them and narrow their field of operation.

5. Id. at 139–40.
6. Id. at 141–42. Hughes later reflected on his Elmira address; David J. Danelski and Joseph S. Tulchin, eds., The Autobiographical Notes of Charles Evans Hughes 143–44 (1973).

Independent Branches

The Constitution provides federal judges with lifetime tenure and prohibits reductions in their compensation—measures designed to ensure judicial independence. Certainly judges need to reach their decisions without fear of retribution or penalty, yet they cannot be kept free of political pressure. Judges are part of government and must be aware, at all times, of the public. Their work would not improve if they lived in an ivory tower, free to spin out judicial doctrines without sensitivity to public reactions. Federal judge Richard S. Arnold made the point bluntly: "[W]e work for the people."[7]

The constitutional system is strengthened when lawmakers, Presidents, courts, academics, reporters, and the media treat all three branches as part of a political system, each branch capable of good and bad decisions. There is no need to create heroes or villains. That is why we have a system of checks and balances. Regrettably, lawmakers, academics, and the general public have a custom of placing Presidents and the Supreme Court on pedestals.[8] There is no reason to pretend that the judiciary has the authority or the competence to decide constitutional questions in any final sense. It is equally harmful to believe that Presidents have a unique capacity in national security or any other field to decide public policy and national commitments. Being cynical of government is not helpful. A healthy skepticism is. Lawmakers and citizens need to evaluate judicial and presidential claims and insist on credible evidence. A durable constitutional system cannot coexist with idolatry of the President or the Court. I did not add Congress to that list because I know of no one who idolizes Congress. Adulation of the President and the Court is all too familiar.

Members of Congress take an oath to support the Constitution, not the Court or the President. It is appropriate for them to respect the Court and the President, in the same manner that the Court and the President should respect Congress. All three branches take an oath of office. But the branches are separate for a purpose. They need to preserve their institutional powers while working jointly with the other branches toward national solutions. Respect, yes. Deference, no. Acquiescence, never. Deference and acquiescence are habit forming. Do it once, with perhaps some misgivings, and the next time will feel more comfortable.

7. Robert A. Katzmann, Courts and Congress 113 (1997).
8. Louis Fisher, "Scholarly Support for Presidential Wars," 35 Pres. Stud. Q. 590 (2005), available at http://www.loufisher.org/docs/wp/421.pdf.

Executive Expertise

Broad claims are made about the President's natural expertise and capacity to represent the national interest. The historical record is more sobering. The executive branch may seem more hierarchical and better organized than Congress, but, as political scientist Jasmine Farrier notes, its policy objectives "are no less subject to the accusation of being partisan, narrow, or even flat-out wrong." There is no evidence that the President has the ability "to create objectively better policy."[9] Careful analysis by Richard Pious, political science professor at Barnard College, chronicles the pattern of grave errors and misconceptions by Presidents in both domestic and foreign policy. As to expertise within the executive branch, Pious concludes that "in the past thirty years, there has been a growing gap between what experts claim to be able to discover, describe, and predict, and what they actually deliver."[10] When Presidents fail "with misguided attempts to maintain their authority," they may decide to "lie or dissemble," as Lyndon Johnson did with the Vietnam escalation and Bush II did in claiming the existence of weapons of mass destruction in Iraq.[11]

In a book published in 2008, former Senator Bob Graham wrote: "The tradition has been to trust what the President tells members of Congress as entirely truthful."[12] Actually, as developed in Chapter 9, the tradition has been for Presidents to present misleading information to Congress and the public. No lawmaker should trust that the President will speak truthfully or be adequately informed. That is why we have a separate legislative branch to form an independent judgment. As a ranking member of the Senate Intelligence Committee, Graham attended national security briefings conducted for the Gang of Eight: party leaders in each chamber plus the chairman and ranking members of the intelligence committees. According to Graham: "You have to respond immediately, without the benefit of advice, without access to all the relevant facts, and without the means to independently corroborate the information that is being presented."[13] The intelligence agencies are creatures of Congress. They were created by statute and are regularly authorized and funded by Congress. Lawmakers are elected officials, entrusted to carry out constitutional

9. Jasmine Farrier, Congressional Ambivalence: The Political Burdens of Constitutional Authority 168 (2010).

10. Richard M. Pious, Why Presidents Fail: White House Decision Making from Eisenhower to Bush II 248 (2008).

11. Id. at 264.

12. Bob Graham, Intelligence Matters: The CIA, the FBI, Saudi Arabia, and the Failure of America's War on Terror xiv (2008).

13. Id. at xvi.

duties. They cannot, or should not, be placed in a subordinate status by agency briefers.

After the Bay of Pigs disaster, President Kennedy wondered how he could have accepted the assurances of CIA officials and other executive advisers: "How could I have been so far off base? All my life I have known better than to depend on the experts."[14] Presidents and members of Congress need the advice of experts, but the value of this process does not come from mechanically accepting claims and assertions. Public policy must be grounded in evidence and subject to independent scrutiny by other experts. Experts prevail too often because the policy discussion is narrowed to a select few, without proper vetting. That risk, prevalent throughout government, is especially grave in the field of national security.

How Lawmakers Respond to Judicial Rulings

Just as members of Congress defer far too often to presidential claims and assertions, they similarly find it difficult to criticize judicial rulings. At times, they announce support for a decision after first denouncing its reasoning and persuasive quality. In a floor statement in 2001, Senator Patrick Leahy said he had become "increasingly concerned about some of the recent actions of the U.S. Supreme Court. As a member of the bar of the Court, as a U.S. Senator, as an American, I, of course, respect the decisions of the Supreme Court as being the ultimate decisions of law for our country." Referring to himself again as "an American," he accepted "any of its decisions as the ultimate interpretation of our Constitution, whether I agree or disagree."[15]

What is behind this line of argument? Why not state one's disagreement and leave it at that? If a ruling is unsound and unpersuasive, frank and informed criticism may help the Court rethink its reasoning. Total deference will not. Citizens and members of Congress know that the Court is capable of making errors, and has a long record of doing so. Why the double reference to being an American? Is it patriotic to support the Court, even when one disagrees? Perhaps Senator Leahy equates Court decisions with the rule of law and is concerned that any criticism of the Court might undermine respect for, and confidence in, the legal system.

However, the Court is not equivalent to the rule of law. It is under the Constitution, like the other branches. Blunt criticism is not only acceptable but also reflects support for one's country and the aspiration of self-government. This

14. Ted Sorensen, Counselor: A Life at the Edge of History 317 (2008).
15. 147 Cong. Rec. 2457 (2001).

book has made the point repeatedly that decisions of the Supreme Court are not "the ultimate decisions of law for our country." Our constitutional system is far more complex than that. American liberties have been protected because the Court is not the "ultimate interpreter" of the Constitution.

Senator Leahy noted that judicial activism "can work both ways. It can work to expand protections for all our rights or it can be used to limit our rights."[16] If a Court ruling limits rights, why not say so and explain why? He objected that a recent decision by the Court was "just the latest in a long and ever growing line of 5–4 decisions that second-guess congressional policy judgment[s] to strike down Federal statutes and generally treat Congress as a least favored administrative agency rather than a coequal branch of the Federal Government."[17] An important point, and all the more reason to insist on coequality and not subordinate Congress to the Court as the ultimate interpreter. There is no reason for Congress to defer automatically to the judiciary because of supposed technical skills and political independence.

Leahy concluded with this thought: "Again, as I have said, I have stood on the floor of the Senate defending the Supreme Court as much or more than anybody I know in my 26 years here. I have defended the Supreme Court on decisions even when I disagreed with the Court."[18] Why defend what you disagree with? Robert Katzmann, now a federal judge on the Second Circuit, wrote in 1997 about the need for candid public comments on court rulings: "Reasoned criticism of judicial decisions and of the administration of justice are useful and valuable; but excesses in rhetoric and political attacks can heighten insecurity about legislative intention." Courts need to understand that "not every disagreement is a threat to independence."[19]

Senator Orrin Hatch has had a long career in following and evaluating decisions of the Supreme Court, having chaired the Judiciary Committee, as has Leahy. Hatch knows how much the quality of court rulings can vary. When the Court decided *Boumediene* in 2008, holding that Guantánamo detainees have a right of habeas corpus to federal district courts, Senator Hatch announced his disagreement: "This decision, written by Justice Kennedy, gives terrorists one of the most important rights enjoyed by the people of the United States." (At issue were not the rights of terrorists but of detainees *suspected* of terrorism.) The questions were difficult, Hatch admitted, but "I do not believe that the Supreme Court has provided the correct answer." He understood that it is natural to be

16. Id.
17. Id. at 2458.
18. Id.
19. Katzmann, Courts and Congress, at 112.

concerned about people's rights, "even those of terrorists, but sometimes we have to be practical and pragmatic and do the things that have to be done to protect the American people, and our citizens overseas."[20]

Senator Hatch had every right to express his views about the decision and register his objections. He might have left it there, but, like Leahy, he gave full support to a decision he disagreed with: "There are many who will believe that the Supreme Court made the right decision and others, such as myself, who believe that the Court made a lousy decision. However, I uphold the Supreme Court, even though it was a 5-to-4 decision. Nevertheless, it is a decision by one-third of the separated powers of this country, and must be recognized as such."[21] What is the value of this statement? Hatch decided to "uphold" the Court, but only after he added that the ruling was closely split and reflected the views of only one of the three branches of government.

A third example of legislative deference comes from Representative John Conyers, who has chaired the Judiciary Committee for many years and has a close understanding of legislative-judicial relations. In a floor statement on January 9, 2009, he rebuked the Court for its decision in the Lilly Ledbetter case two years earlier. As explained in Chapter 5, a divided Court held that her effort to file a wage-discrimination complaint failed because she had to file within 180 days of the first discrimination payroll decision. Of course, years elapsed before she became aware of discriminatory actions against her. Conyers urged Congress "to reverse the wrongheaded and discriminatory" decision.[22]

Congress did precisely that in a bill signed into law by President Obama. What makes the Conyers statement unusual is how he characterized the judiciary: "I believe that our courts are our last line of defense when it comes to protecting the fundamental rights enshrined in our Constitution and in our civil rights laws."[23] Yes, courts are supposed to protect fundamental rights, but the performance of the federal judiciary over the last two centuries does not merit unstinting praise. For most of their existence, federal courts were more likely to protect government and corporations than individuals. Courts are not the last line of defense. Often Congress, working with the executive branch, is the last line of defense and has exercised that duty with great frequency over its history. If courts were reliably effective as the last line of defense, when it comes to protecting rights in the Constitution and civil rights statutes, the Court would not

20. 154 Cong. Rec. S5575 (daily ed., June 12, 2008).
21. Id.
22. 155 Cong. Rec. H122 (daily ed., January 9, 2009); Ledbetter v. Goodyear Tire & Rubber Co., 550 U.S. 618 (2007).
23. Id.

have decided as it did in the Ledbetter case. It would not have been necessary for Congress to pass legislation to repair the damage.

Edward R. Becker, former chief judge of the Third Circuit, died in 2006. He served on the bench for almost 36 years. His obituary in the *New York Times* described the extent to which he was admired by colleagues and litigants. One of his former clerks explained that he greeted new clerks on their first day with a single rule: "no deference."[24] The newspaper story does not explain exactly what he meant. I like to think he told clerks no deference, period: to litigants, to authorities, or to him. What made his court function well was a premium on independent, fearless, and principled thinking. It is a good rule for anyone. It is an essential rule for members of Congress.

Constructive Dialogues

The belief that the Supreme Court somehow delivers the final word on the meaning of the Constitution has been challenged throughout this book. The Court is only one of many participants, and often not the primary or dominant one. A recent Supreme Court decision, *United States v. Stevens,* helps illustrate this point. On April 20, 2010, it held that a statute passed by Congress to criminalize the commercial creation, sale, or possession of certain depictions of animal cruelty was substantially overbroad and therefore invalid under the First Amendment. The Court split 8 to 1, with only Justice Alito dissenting. It might appear that at least on this particular constitutional dispute, the Court would have the final word.

In fact, the Court's decision was just one stage of many, and by no means the final stage. The Court explained that the legislative background of this statute focused primarily on the interstate market of "crush videos." These videos feature the intentional torture and killing of helpless animals, including cats, dogs, monkeys, mice, and hamsters. They depict women slowly crushing animals to death with their bare feet or while wearing high-heeled shoes. Persons with a sexual fetish find the depictions sexually arousing and exciting. The problem with the statute, however, is that it was not written specifically for crush videos, even if that was the legislative intent. As a result, the Justice Department prosecuted someone for trafficking in videos of dogfighting. The statute was so broad, as the Court noted, that it could criminalize popular hunting videos and hunting magazines.

How did this come about? In 1999, the House Judiciary Committee reported

24. Tim Weiner, "Edward R. Becker, 73, Judge on Federal Court of Appeals," New York Times, May 20, 2006, at B16.

a bill to punish the depiction of animal cruelty. The committee report expressed concern about "a growing market in videotapes and still photographs depicting insects and small animals being slowly crushed to death." Women in bare feet and high-heeled shoes inflicted the torture. In some videos, the woman's voice could be heard "talking to the animals in a kind of dominatrix patter. The cries and squeals of the animals, obviously in great pain, can be heard in the videos."[25] The bill defined "depiction of animal cruelty" as any visual or auditory depiction (including photographs and video recordings) of conduct "in which a living animal is intentionally maimed, mutilated, tortured, wounded, or killed."[26] That language could apply to hunting and fishing videos. The committee report explained that "depictions of ordinary hunting and fishing activities do not fall within the scope of the statute,"[27] but the bill did not make exceptions for those commercial activities.

The bill passed the House 372 to 42.[28] Like the committee report, floor debate focused on crush videos and stated that "the sale of depictions of legal activities, such as hunting and fishing, would not be illegal under this bill."[29] That was legislative history, not legislative language. By unanimous consent, the Senate passed the bill.[30] In signing the bill into law, President Clinton noted the concern during legislative action that the bill "may violate the First Amendment of the Constitution." In an effort to ensure that the statute did not chill protected speech, he decided to "broadly construe the Act's exception and will interpret it to require a determination of the value of the depiction as part of a work or communication, taken as a whole. So construed, the Act would prohibit the types of depictions, described in the statute's legislative history, of wanton cruelty to animals designed to appeal to a prurient interest in sex. I will direct the Department of Justice to enforce the Act accordingly."[31]

In this manner, Clinton attempted to refocus an overly broad statute and to correct features that should have been fixed during the legislative process. The statute put a stop to the market in crush videos. However, whatever direction Clinton decided to give the Justice Department in the enforcement of the statute would come to an end with his administration. The new administration, under George W. Bush, would not feel bound by his signing statement. Instead of prosecuting someone for trafficking in crush videos, the department brought crim-

---

25. H. Rept. No. 106-397, 106th Cong., 1st Sess. 2 (1999).
26. Id.
27. Id. at 8.
28. 145 Cong. Rec. 25901-02 (1999).
29. Id. at 25894.
30. Id. at 31216–17.
31. Public Papers of the Presidents, 1999, II, at 2245; P.L. 106-152, 113 Stat. 1732 (1999).

inal charges against an individual who sold dogfighting videos. When the Third Circuit struck down the statute in 2008 as facially unconstitutional,[32] the market for crush videos quickly revived.

Animals were once again being tortured to satisfy customers who asked for videos tailor-made for their tastes. Congress needed to act promptly. One month after the Court decided *Stevens,* a House subcommittee heard testimony from constitutional scholars and practitioners. They agreed that a new law, focusing exclusively on crush videos, would be constitutional.[33] Although the House Judiciary Committee is often highly partisan and polarized, the bill was reported unanimously, 23 to 0.[34] The legislative language expressly states that the bill does not apply to hunting, trapping, or fishing.[35] The bill passed the House on July 20. Although the contemporary Congress has a well-deserved reputation for partisanship and gridlock, the vote in the House was 416 to 3.[36] After the Senate Judiciary Committee held a hearing, the Senate passed an amended bill by unanimous consent.[37] The two chambers agreed on common language and sent the bill to President Obama, who signed it into law on December 9, 2010.[38]

The Supreme Court played an important role in finding the 1999 statute to be overbroad. The more significant responsibility, however, fell to the elected branches. They were the driving force in identifying the problem, to hear from those in the private sector who wanted to put an end to crush videos, and to pursue whatever legislative language was needed to achieve the legislative purpose.

Executive Accountability

In recent years, federal courts have accepted arguments by the executive branch that a particular lawsuit cannot move forward without jeopardizing national security. The reason: the case implicates "state secrets" and must be closed down before damage to the nation occurs. Judges receive executive affidavits making those assertions. Sometimes the statements are classified for reasons of national security, to be read only by the judge. But it is not sufficient for judges to defer to those claims. They need to insist on examining actual documents and evidence,

32. United States v. Stevens, 533 F.3d 218 (3d Cir. 2008).
33. H. Rept. No. 111-549, 111th Cong., 2d Sess. 4 (2010).
34. Id. at 6.
35. Id. at 12.
36. 156 Cong. Rec. H5892–93 (daily ed., July 21, 2001). See House debate at H5788–91.
37. Id. at S7653–54 (daily ed., September 28, 2010).
38. Id. at H7403–04 (daily ed., November 15, 2010); S8202–04 (daily ed., November 19, 2010); P.L. 111-294.

in the privacy of their own chambers. Otherwise, they surrender judicial independence and become an arm, willing or not, of the executive branch.

This pattern of judicial subservience to executive claims is evident in *United States v. Reynolds* (1953), involving the crash of a B-29 bomber. The Supreme Court accepted the argument of the executive branch that the official accident report contained confidential information. We now know that claim was false. As explained in Chapter 9, the report contained no state secrets. This is not the only time that federal courts have been deceived by executive branch claims. To automatically accept executive claims degrades the judiciary, undermines the rights of private litigants to bring a case charging the government with illegality, and sends a green light to the executive branch that it may violate statutes, treaties, and the Constitution without any accountability. Congress has drafted legislation in recent years to strengthen judicial independence in state secrets cases. It needs to enact the legislation.

Another invitation to lawlessness is the concept of official immunity for executive officials. A level of qualified immunity is needed for otherwise they will be reluctant to make any decisions for fear of prosecution. The Supreme Court in 1971 created a "*Bivens* action" to find damages against federal agents who commit constitutional violations, but lawsuits against government officials are nearly always unsuccessful, for one technicality or another.[39] The last time top officials in the executive branch paid a price was the Watergate affair, which sent Attorney General John Mitchell and other senior executive officials to prison. A decade later, with the Iran-Contra affair, many top officials were headed in the same direction, but a December 1992 action by President George H. W. Bush, issuing pardons to six officials (three of them from the CIA), put an end to successful prosecutions.[40]

A similar pattern occurred with the multiple statutory and constitutional violations during the administration of George W. Bush. The telecoms that assisted the NSA in conducting surveillance operations, acting in plain violation of the Foreign Intelligence Surveillance Act (FISA), gained immunity from Congress in 2008. The message from Congress was extraordinary: "We passed FISA in 1978 to prohibit these actions, but now that you decided to violate the law we will give you immunity." How can lawmakers square that action with their oath to support and defend the Constitution? Other federal officials and private contractors, also acting in violation of law, were protected by federal court rulings pursuant to the state secrets privilege. The same privilege was extended to fed-

39. James E. Pfander and David Baltmanis, "Rethinking *Bivens:* Legitimacy and Constitutional Adjudication," 98 Geo. L. J. 117 (2009); Fisher, Constitutional Conflicts Between Congress and the President, at 169–72.

40. Lawrence E. Walsh, Firewall: The Iran-Contra Conspiracy and Cover-up (1997).

eral officials involved in the extraordinary rendition program that sent individuals to foreign countries for interrogation and torture.[41]

In a 2009 case involving former Attorney General John Ashcroft, the Supreme Court continued to extend immunity to executive officials accused of violating law.[42] The Court has accepted another lawsuit against Ashcroft. This one is from Abdullah al-Kidd, who was detained as a "material witness" to testify in court, never used for that purpose, and imprisoned for weeks under harsh conditions.[43] The Justice Department carried out a multiyear investigation into the professional conduct of two Office of Legal Counsel (OLC) attorneys (John Yoo and Jay Bybee) who wrote what are properly called torture memos. Did their work constitute professional misconduct? The department concluded that their legal advice was merely an exercise of "poor judgment."[44] From Watergate to the present time, we have a consistent pattern of executive violations without executive accountability. It is time for Congress to revisit the state secrets privilege, executive immunity, and the practical availability of remedies against executive officials who violate the law and professional standards.

Campaign Spending

What other steps might be taken to improve the ability of lawmakers to protect their institutional powers and strengthen the checks and balances that safeguard individual rights? Part of the answer lies in placing limits on the amount of money that can be spent in political campaigns. Otherwise, lawmakers must devote precious time to raising vast sums of money instead of concentrating on legislation and oversight. It is estimated that members of Congress spend about 25 percent of their time raising money for themselves and their party.[45] Legislative dependence on outside money creates an ethical cloud about how much lawmakers rely on private contributions and to what degree their decisions about national policy are corrupted by seeking money.

41. Louis Fisher, The Constitution and 9/11: Recurring Threats to America's Freedoms 333–60 (2008).

42. Ashcroft v. Iqbal, 556 U.S. ___ (2009).

43. Adam Liptak, "Justices Will Decide Whether Ashcroft May Be Sued in 2003 Detention Case," New York Times, October 19, 2010, at A19; Robert Barnes, "Supreme Court to Consider Ashcroft Bid for Immunity," Washington Post, October 19, 2010, at A2.

44. Nancy Baker, "Who Was John Yoo's Client?: The Torture Memos and Professional Conduct," 40 Pres. Stud. Q. 750 (2010); David Cole, "The Sacrificial Yoo: Accounting for Torture in the OPR Report," 4 J. Nat'l Sec. L. & Pol'y 455 (2010).

45. 156 Cong. Rec. S5174 (daily ed., June 21, 2010) (statement by Senator Specter).

Placing limits on expenditures would require Congress to reject opinions by the Supreme Court in such cases as *Buckley v. Valeo* (1976) and more recently *Citizens United v. FEC* (2010). The Court made a highly strained argument in *Buckley* that it is permissible to limit campaign contributions by individuals but unconstitutional to limit overall expenditures. Justices have been deeply divided over that issue ever since. In 1978, Justice Byron White correctly stated that in the area of campaign financing "the expertise of legislators is at its peak and that of judges is at its very lowest."[46] I doubt if anyone reading *Citizens United* could call it a model of persuasive reasoning. It is built upon two legal fictions: corporations are "persons," and money is "speech." Congressional hearings should be held to seek expert testimony on the corrupting influence of money on democratic institutions and procedures.

In his concurrence in *Citizens United,* Chief Justice Roberts explained that "we must keep in mind that stare decisis is not an end in itself." Borrowing language from a 1986 Court decision, he said that it is the means we use to ensure that the law "will develop in a principled and intelligible fashion." When fidelity to a particular ruling "does more to damage" a constitutional ideal than to advance it, he advised that "we must be more willing to depart from that precedent."[47] Roberts identified other guidelines that call for fresh thinking. When a precedent's validity "is so hotly contested that it cannot reliably function as a basis for decision in future cases," it is necessary to alter a Court ruling. When a precedent's "underlying reasoning has become so discredited that the Court cannot keep the precedent alive without jury-rigging new and different justifications to shore up the original mistake," it is time to rethink. Information developed at congressional hearings can document why it is necessary to depart from *Buckley* and *Citizens United.*[48]

In the field of campaign finance, the legislative branch has equal, if not superior, competence, authority, and legitimacy. Instead of trying to analyze case law and ensure that legislative language is perfectly consistent with past rulings, Congress should start from scratch. It needs to produce a coherent, principled, evidence-based, and intelligible law on campaign finance. For more than three decades, the Court has demonstrated overwhelmingly that it is incapable of doing that. Careful and persuasive analysis by Congress can send this message to the Court: "With all respect, you got it wrong. We are passing new legislation to regulate money in political campaigns. The level of spending is corrupt-

---

46. First National Bank of Boston v. Bellotti, 435 U.S. 765, 804 (1978) (White, J., dissenting).

47. Citizens United v. FEC, 130 S.Ct. 876, 921–22 (2010) (Robert, C.J., concurring).

48. These comments come from my article, "Saying What the Law Is: On Campaign Finance, It's Not Just for the Court; Congress Has a Co-equal Say," *National Law Journal*, February 22, 2010, at 38, available at http://www.loufisher.org/docs/ci/415.pdf.

ing our political system, draining power from the people, and weakening Congress as an independent branch."

Would the Court invalidate congressional efforts that conflict with *Buckley* and *Citizens United*? It depends on how well Congress assembles evidence, develops outside support, and acts with some bipartisan agreement. Faced with such a statute, it would be intellectually and institutionally foolish for the Court to strike it down by sticking dogmatically to its artificial doctrines of corporations being persons and money being speech. With some grace and prudence, the Court can announce: "Congress has persuaded us that unlimited campaign spending inflicts too much damage on our democratic and constitutional system."

Campaign finance reform would not, by itself, put Congress where it needs to be to carry out its constitutional duties. Members are not in town for a sufficient number of days to attend to legislation and oversight. Generally arriving on Tuesday and leaving early on Thursday places Congress, constituents, and the Constitution at too great a risk. Congress is not, like some state legislatures, a part-time institution. To be coequal requires a commitment to remain in town to do what is necessary. Shortcuts do not work.

Confirming Justices

Confirmation hearings for Supreme Court Justices should be an ideal opportunity to help lawmakers and citizens understand how the Court functions in a constitutional democracy. Instead, observers are regularly treated to sophomoric, erroneous, and dishonest statements. A familiar theme: "Judges don't make law; they apply it." Whoever says that, or hears that, must know it is false. In applying law, judges inevitably make law, especially at the level of the Supreme Court when it announces new rules and standards. Another popular message: judges are like baseball umpires, calling balls and strikes. Who believes that judges basically stand behind the catcher and monitor a strike zone with the width of the plate and a height between a batter's knees and shoulders? What is the strike zone for such constitutional values as due process, equal protection, free speech, religious liberty, and cruel and unusual punishment?

There is no reason to conduct hearings in this manner. I do not believe judicial nominees will be rejected if they speak intelligently, thoughtfully, and avoid platitudes. If nominees are reluctant to speak straight, committee members need to ensure that the hearings do not continue to be vapid and bland. It is a disservice to Congress, the public, and the Constitution. Chris Edelson, who teaches at American University after earlier practicing law, recently offered helpful suggestions on how these hearings should be run. The Elena Kagan hearings, he says, were a missed opportunity for the Judiciary Committee to explain how the Court actually decides constitutional law. Senators "should ask questions aimed at unveiling the reality that justices must often exercise judgment when deciding constitutional cases, and that this often means making choices. . . . [J]ustices must choose; they must, not surprisingly, exercise judgment." Edelson offers a constructive dialogue on the kind of thoughtful discussion that senators and nominees could, and should, have.[49]

In carrying out public duties, all three branches respond to pressure from private citizens. Without that sense of urgency, public policy is likely to continue without change. The Constitution is protected when society at large is actively engaged. It is an error to depend on supposed experts within government to get it right, regardless of which branch they belong to. William Howard Taft, who served as a federal appellate judge before becoming President, appreciated the important link between judicial rulings and the public. Nothing made judges "more careful in their decisions and anxiously solicitous to do exact justice than the consciousness that every act of theirs is to be subjected to the intelligent scrutiny of their fellow-men, and to their candid criticism." Some evaluations are from specialists within the legal community, but Taft placed special weight on attitudes from the general public: "If the law is but the essence of common sense, the protest of many average men may evidence a defect in a judicial conclusion though based on the nicest legal reasoning and profoundest learning."[50]

Judicial Independence

Readers will not miss in this book the battering ram against the pretense that courts can be the final arbiters of the Constitution. Quite true. But I have always regarded judicial independence as an essential part of the Constitution. When I testified against the item veto in 1995, I protested that the bill undermined judicial independence by empowering the President to cancel judicial items (Chapter 8). As an advocate of checks and balances, I have consistently supported independence for all three branches. In this chapter and Chapter 9, I urged courts to independently scrutinize executive assertions of state secrets. I worked closely with both judiciary committees to strengthen independent court review.

49. Chris Edelson, "Missed Opportunity: What We Should Have Learned from the Kagan Hearings," D.C. Bar, October 2010, available at http://www.dcbar.org/for_lawyers/resources/publications/washington_lawyer/october_2010/stand.cfm.
50. William Howard Taft, "Criticisms of the Federal Judiciary," 29 Am. L. Rev. 641, 642 (1895).

Courts regularly review legislation passed by Congress to ensure that it has a rational basis. The same standard needs to be applied to judicial rulings and presidential statements. In *Korematsu v. United States* (1944), the Court deferred to claims by the Roosevelt administration that it was necessary to transfer 110,000 Japanese Americans (two-thirds of them U.S. citizens) to detention camps. Writing for the Court, Justice Black deferred to military experts: "[W]e are unable to conclude that it was beyond the war power of Congress and the Executive to exclude those of Japanese ancestry from the West Coast war area at the time they did."[51] "We are unable to conclude"! Frequently we hear that phrase when courts are about to bow to unconstitutional actions, especially in the field of national security. In one of three dissents, Justice Jackson wrote: "[T]he Court, having no real evidence before it, has no choice but to accept General DeWitt's own unsworn, self-serving statement, untested by any cross-examination, that what he did was reasonable. And thus it will always be when courts try to look into the reasonableness of a military order."[52]

Look at the language: no real evidence; an unsworn, self-serving statement; no cross-examination; and the extent to which the Court "has no choice." But the Court *did* have a choice. It should have said: "We decide cases based on evidence. You have provided none and on that ground we invalidate the exclusion order." In his dissent, Justice Murphy identified an effective way to challenge executive statements: "Justification for the exclusion is sought, instead, mainly upon questionable racial and sociological grounds not ordinarily within the realm of expert military judgment."[53] There was no reason to defer to DeWitt's personal beliefs about race and sociology.[54]

Judges and lawmakers should not accept untested assertions by administration officials, especially in areas where executive agents cannot possibly claim expertise. The same can be said of untested assertions by judges. Law has to be something more than ipse dixits. If that is the standard, government is purely arbitrary and capricious, and the constitutional system does not exist. Officials in power must always be asked: "On what authority do you act? What evidence do you have? Why is your argument reasonable?" That type of independent spirit was present when American colonists questioned the authority and actions of a distant monarch. With that attitude, democratic government and the system of checks and balances have a reasonable chance to succeed.

51. Korematsu v. United States, 323 U.S. 214, 217–18 (1944).
52. Id. at 245 (Jackson, J., dissenting).
53. Id. at 236–37 (Murphy, J., dissenting).
54. For analysis of the executive branch deceptions to the judiciary on these cases, see Peter Irons, Justice at War: The Story of the Japanese American Internment Cases (1983).

SELECTIVE BIBLIOGRAPHY

Acheson, Dean. Present at the Creation (New York: Norton, 1969).

Ackerman, Bruce. The Failure of the Founding Fathers: Jefferson, Marshall, and the Rise of Presidential Democracy (Cambridge: Harvard University Press, 2007 ed.).

Adams, John. The Works of John Adams (Charles Francis Adams, ed., Boston: Little, Brown, 1856).

Adler, David Gray. "Presidential Power and Foreign Affairs in the Bush Administration: The Use and Abuse of Alexander Hamilton," 40 Pres. Stud. Q. 531 (2010).

———. "Foreign Policy and the Separation of Powers: The Influence of the Judiciary," in Judging the Constitution: Critical Essays on Judicial Lawmaking (Michael W. McCann and Gerald L. Houseman, eds., Glenview, Ill.: Scott, Foresman, 1989).

Agresto, John. The Supreme Court and Constitutional Democracy (Ithaca, N.Y.: Cornell University Press, 1984).

Ahlstrom, Sydney E. A Religious History of the American People (New Haven: Yale University Press, 1972).

Alexander, Larry, and Frederick Schauer. "On Extrajudicial Constitutional Interpretation," 110 Harv. L. Rev. 1359 (1997).

Allen, Thomas B. "Remember the *Maine?*," National Geographic, February 1998.

———. "A Special Report: What Really Sank the *Maine?*," Naval History, March–April 1998.

Amar, Akhil Reed. "*Marbury*, Section 13, and the Original Jurisdiction of the Supreme Court," 56 U. Chi. L. Rev. 443 (1985).

Andrews, William G. Coordinate Magistrates: Constitutional Law by Congress and President (New York: Van Nostrand, 1969).

Baker, Nancy V. "Who Was John Yoo's Client? The Torture Memos and Professional Misconduct," 40 Pres. Stud. Q. 750 (2010).

Barilleaux, Ryan J., and Christopher S. Kelley, eds. The Unitary Executive and the Modern Presidency (College Station: Texas A&M University Press, 2010).

Bernstein, Richard B. Amending America (New York: Random House, 1993).

Beveridge, Albert J. The Life of John Marshall (Boston: Houghton Mifflin, 1919).

Bickel, Alexander M. The Unpublished Opinions of Mr. Justice Brandeis (Cambridge: Harvard University Press, 1957).

Bimber, Bruce. The Politics of Expertise in Congress: The Rise and Fall of the Office of Technology Assessment (Albany: State University of New York Press).

Bloch, Susan Low, and Maeva Marcus. "John Marshall's Selective Use of History in *Marbury v. Madison*," 1986 Wis. L. Rev. 301 (1986).

Boudin, L. B. "Government by Judiciary," 26 Pol. Sci. Q. 238 (1911).

Bradley, Gerald V. Church–State Relationships in America (Westport: Greenwood Press, 1987).

Brest, Paul. "The Conscientious Legislator's Guide to Constitutional Interpretation," 27 Stan. L. Rev. 585 (1975).

Burger, Warren E. "The Doctrine of Judicial Review: Mr. Marshall, Mr. Jefferson, and Mr. Marbury," in Judges on Judging: Views from the Bench 14 (David M. O'Brien, ed., Washington, D.C.: CQ Press, 2004).

Burgess, Susan R. Contest for Constitutional Authority: The Abortion and War Powers Debates (Lawrence: University Press of Kansas, 1992).

Burton, Harold M. "The Cornerstone of Constitutional Law: The Extraordinary Case of Marbury v. Madison," 36 Am. Bar Ass'n J. 805 (1950).

Butts, R. Freeman. The American Tradition in Religion and Education (Boston: Beacon Press, 1950).

Calabresi, Stephen G., and Christopher S. Yoo. The Unitary Executive: Presidential Power from Washington to Bush (New Haven: Yale University Press, 2008).

Campbell, Colton C., and John H. Stack Jr. Congress Confronts the Court: The Struggle for Legitimacy and Authority in Lawmaking (Lanham, Md.: Rowman & Littlefield, 2001).

Cannon, Joseph G. "The National Budget," H. Doc. No. 264, 66th Cong., 1st Sess. (1919).

Casper, Gerhard. Separating Power: Essays on the Founding Period (Cambridge: Harvard University Press, 1997).

Chalou, George C. "St. Clair's Defeat, 1792," in Congress Investigates, 1792–1974 (Arthur M. Schlesinger Jr. and Roger Bruns, eds., New York: Chelsea House, 1975).

Chayes, Abram, and Antonia Handler Chayes. "Testing and Development of 'Exotic' Systems Under the ABM Treaty: The Great Reinterpretation Caper," 99 Harv. L. Rev. 1956 (1986).

Choper, Jesse H. Judicial Review and the National Political Process (Chicago: University of Chicago Press, 1980).

Clark, Mary L. "The First Women Members of the Supreme Court Bar, 1879–1900," 36 San Diego L. Rev. 87 (1999).

Clinton, Robert Lowry. Marbury v. Madison and Judicial Review (Lawrence: University Press of Kansas, 1989).

Cohen, William S., and George J. Mitchell. Men of Zeal: A Candid Inside Story of the Iran-Contra Hearings (New York: Viking, 1988).

Cole, David D. "The Sacrificial Yoo: Accounting for Torture in the OPR Report," 4 J. Nat'l Sec. Law & Pol'y 455 (2010).

Collins, Charles Wallace. "Constitutional Aspects of a National Budget System," 25 Yale L. J. 376 (1916).

Commager, Henry Steele. Majority Rule and Minority Rights (New York: Oxford University Press, 1953).

Corbett, Michael, and Julia Mitchell Corbett. Politics and Religion in the United States (New York: Garland Publishers, 1999).

Corwin, Edward S. "What Kind of Judicial Review Did the Framers Have in Mind?," 86 Pittsburgh L. J. 4 (1938).

———. John Marshall and the Constitution (New Haven: Yale University Press, 1919).

———. The Doctrine of Judicial Review (Princeton: Princeton University Press, 1914).

———. "Marbury v. Madison and the Doctrine of Judicial Review," 12 Mich. L. Rev. 538 (1914).

Danzig, Richard. "Justice Frankfurter's Opinion in the Flag Salute Cases: Blending Logic and Psychologic in Constitution Decisionmaking," 36 Stan. L. Rev. 675 (1984).

Dellinger, Walter, and H. Jefferson Powell. "The Constitutionality of the Bank Bill: The Attorney General's First Constitutional Law Opinions," 44 Duke L. J. 110 (1994).

Denvir, John. Democracy's Constitution: Claiming the Privileges of American Citizenship (Urbana: University of Illinois Press, 2011).

Devins, Neal. "How Not to Challenge the Court," 39 Wm. & Mary L. Rev. 645 (1998).

———. Shaping Constitutional Values: Elected Government, the Supreme Court, and the Abortion Debate (Baltimore: Johns Hopkins University Press, 1996).

———, ed. "Elected Branch Influences in Constitution Decisionmaking," 56 Law & Contemp. Prob. 1 (Autumn 1993).

Devins, Neal, and Louis Fisher. The Democratic Constitution (New York: Oxford University Press, 2004).

————. "Judicial Exclusivity and Political Instability," 84 Va. L. Rev. 83 (1998).

Devins, Neal, and Keith E. Whittington, eds. Congress and the Constitution (Durham: Duke University Press, 2005).

Divine, Robert A. "The Case of the Smuggled Bombers," in Quarrels That Have Shaped the Constitution (John A. Garraty, ed., New York: Harper & Row, 1966 ed.).

Donald, David Herbert. Lincoln (London: Jonathan Cape, 1995).

Douglas, William O. The Court Years, 1939–75 (New York: Viking Books, 1981).

Dworkin, Ronald. Freedom's Law: The Moral Reading of the American Constitution (Cambridge: Harvard University Press, 1996).

————. "The 'Devastating' Decision," N.Y. Rev. of Books, February 25, 2010, at 39.

————. "The 'Devastating' Decision: An Exchange," N.Y. Rev. of Books, April 29, 2010, at 65.

————. "The Decision That Threatens Democracy," N.Y. Rev. of Books, May 13, 2010, at 63–64, 66–67.

Dumbauld, Edward. The Bill of Rights and What It Means Today (Norman: University of Oklahoma Press, 1957).

Ebersole, Luke Eugene. Church Lobbying in the Nation's Capital (New York: Macmillan, 1951).

Eckenrode, H. J. Separation of Church and State in Virginia (Richmond, Va.: Davis Bottom, Superintendent of Public Printing, 1910).

Edgerton, Henry W. "The Incidence of Judicial Control over Congress," 22 Corn. L. Q. 299 (1937).

Einzig, Paul. The Control of the Purse: Progress and Decline of Parliament's Financial Control (London: Secker & Warburg, 1959).

Epps, Garrett. "To an Unknown God: The Hidden History of Employment Division v. Smith," 30 Ariz. St. L. J. 953 (1998).

Farrier, Jasmine. Congressional Ambivalence: The Political Burdens of Constitutional Authority (Lexington: University Press of Kentucky, 2010).

————. Passing the Buck: Congress, the Budget, and Deficits (Lexington: University Press of Kentucky, 2004).

Fehrenbacher, Don E. The Dred Scott Case: Its Significance in American Law and Politics (New York: Oxford University Press, 1978).

Finkelman, Paul. Dred Scott v. Sandford (Boston: Bedford Books, 1997).

Fisher, Louis. "Crush Videos: A Constructive Dialogue," National Law Journal, February 21, 2011, at 38.

————. "John Yoo and the Republic," 41 Pres. Stud. Q. 177 (2011).

————. "The Unitary Executive and Inherent Executive Power," 12 U. Pa. J. Const. L. 569 (2010).

————. "The Unitary Executive: Ideology Versus the Constitution," in The Unitary Executive and the Modern Presidency (Ryan J. Barilleaux and Christopher S. Kelley, eds., College Station: Texas A&M University Press, 2010).

————. "National Security Law: The Judicial Role," in Freedom and the Rule of Law (Anthony Peacock, ed., Lanham, Md.: Lexington Books, 2010).

————. "When Wars Begin: Misleading Statements by Presidents," 40 Pres. Stud. Q. 171 (2010).

————. "Saying What the Law Is: On Campaign Finance, It's Not Just for the Court; Congress Has a Co-equal Say," Nat'l L. J., February 22, 2010, at 38.

————. "Congress, Don't Cede Budgetary Power to the President," Roll Call, January 19, 2010, at 4.

————. "Abraham Lincoln: Preserving the Union and the Constitution," 3 Albany Gov't L. Rev. 503 (2010).

————. The Supreme Court and Congress: Rival Interpretations (Washington, D.C.: CQ Press, 2009).

————. "Judicial Interpretations of *Egan*," Law Library of Congress, November 13, 2009.

————. "The Mexican War and Lincoln's 'Spot Resolutions.'" Law Library of Congress, August 18, 2009.

————. "Destruction of the *Maine*," Law Library of Congress, August 4, 2009.

————. "Congressional Access to National Security Information: Precedents from the Washington Administration," Law Library of Congress, May 22, 2009.

————. "The Baker–Christopher War Powers Commission," 39 Pres. Stud. Q. 128 (2009).

————. The Constitution and 9/11: Recurring Threats to America's Freedoms (Lawrence: University Press of Kansas, 2008).

————. "Domestic Commander in Chief: Early Checks by Other Branches," 29 Cardozo L. Rev. 961 (2008).

————. "When the Shooting Starts," Legal Times, July 28, 2008, at 44.

————. Thomas F. Eagleton: A Model of Integrity," 52 St. Louis U. L. J. 97 (2008).

————. "Congressional Access to National Security Information," 45 Harv. J. on Legis. 219 (2008).

————. Constitutional Conflicts Between Congress and the President (Lawrence: University Press of Kansas, 5th ed., 2007).

————. "Invoking Inherent Powers: A Primer," 37 Pres. Stud. Q. 1 (2007).

————. "Presidential Inherent Power: The 'Sole Organ' Doctrine," 37 Pres. Stud. Q. 139 (2007).

————. In the Name of National Security: Unchecked Presidential Power and the *Reynolds* Case (Lawrence: University Press of Kansas, 2006).

————. "Lost Constitutional Moorings: Recovering the War Power," 81 Ind. L. Rev. 1199 (2006).

————. "Justifying War Against Iraq," in Rivals for Power (James A. Thurber, ed., Lanham, Md.: Rowman & Littlefield, 2006).

————. "The 'Sole Organ' Doctrine," Law Library of Congress, August 2006.

————. "State Your Secrets," Legal Times, June 26, 2006, at 66–67.

————. "Constitutional Analysis by Congressional Staff Agencies," in Congress and the Constitution (Neal Devins and Keith E. Whittington, eds., Durham: Duke University Press, 2005).

————. "Scholarly Support for Presidential Wars," 35 Pres. Stud. Q. 590 (2005).

————. "Judicial Review of the War Power," 35 Pres. Stud. Q. 466 (2005).

————. The Politics of Executive Privilege (Durham: Carolina Academic Press, 2004).

————. "Deciding on War Against Iraq: Institutional Failures," 118 Pol. Sci. Q. 389 (2003).

————. Religious Liberty in America (Lawrence: University Press of Kansas, 2002).

————. "Congressional Access to Information: Using Legislative Will and Leverage," 52 Duke L. J. 323 (2002)

————. Congressional Abdication on War and Spending (College Station: Texas A&M University Press, 2000).

———— (with David Gray Adler). "The War Powers Resolution: Time to Say Goodbye," 113 Pol. Sci. Q. 1 (1998).

————. "Sidestepping Congress: Presidents Acting Under the U.N., and NATO," 47 Case W. Res. L. Rev. 1237 (1997).

————. "Biennial Budgeting in the Federal Government," 17 Public Budgeting & Finance 87 (1997).

————. "White House Aides Testifying Before Congress," 27 Pres. Stud. Q. 139 (1997).

————. "The Korean War: On What Legal Basis Did Truman Act?," 89 Am. J. Int'l L. 21 (1995).

————. "The Legislative Veto: Invalidated, It Survives," 56 Law & Contemp. Prob. 273 (August 1993).

————. "The Effects of a Balanced Budget Amendment on Political Institutions," 9 J. Law & Pol. 89 (1992).

————. "Separation of Powers: Interpretation Outside the Courts," 18 Pepp. L. Rev. 57 (1990).

————. "Congressional Participation in the Treaty Process," 137 U. Pa. L. Rev. 1511 (1989).

————. Constitutional Dialogues: Interpretation as Political Process (Princeton: Princeton University Press, 1988).

————. "The Administrative World of *Chadha* and *Bowsher*," 47 Public Admin. Rev. 213 (1987).

————. "Constitutional Interpretation by Members of Congress," 63 N.C. L. Rev. 707 (1985).

————. Presidential Spending Power (Princeton: Princeton University Press, 1975).

————. "Congress, the Executive and the Budget," 411 The Annals 102 (1974).

————. President and Congress (New York: The Free Press, 1972).

————. "Efficiency Side of Separated Powers," 5 J. Am. Stud. 113 (1971).

————. "The Politics of Impounded Funds," 15 Admin. Sci. Q. 361 (1970).

————. "Funds Impounded by the President: The Constitutional Issue," 38 G.W. L. Rev. 124 (1969).

Fisher, Louis, and Neal Devins. Political Dynamics of Constitutional Law (St. Paul, Minn.: Thomson West, 5th ed., 2011).

Fisher, Louis, and Katy J. Harriger. American Constitutional Law (Durham: Carolina Academic Press, 9th ed., 2011).

Fitzgerald, John J. "Budget Systems," Municipal Research, No. 62 (June 1915), at 312.

Fowler, Robert Booth, and Allen D. Hertzke. Religion and Politics in America: Faith, Culture, and Strategic Choices (Boulder, Colo.: Westview Press, 1995).

Fox, Harrison W., Jr., and Susan Webb Hammond. Congressional Staffs: The Invisible Force in American Lawmaking (New York: The Free Press, 1977).

Friedman, Barry. The Will of the People: How Public Opinion Has Influenced the Supreme Court and Shaped the Meaning of the Constitution (New York: Farrar, Straus and Giroux, 2009).

Frost, J. William. A Perfect Freedom: Religious Liberty in Pennsylvania (University Park: Pennsylvania State University Press, 1990).

Fulbright, J. William. "American Foreign Policy in the 20th Century Under an 18th-Century Constitution," 47 Corn. L. Q. 1 (1961).

Glennon, Michael J. "Two Views of Presidential Foreign Affairs Power: *Little v. Barreme* or *Curtiss-Wright?*," 13 Yale J. Int'l L. 5 (1988).

Goldstein, Leslie Friedman. "The ERA and the U.S. Supreme Court," 1 Law & Policy Stud. 145 (1987).

Gould, Lewis L. The Spanish-American War and President McKinley (Lawrence: University Press of Kansas, 1982).

Goulden, Joseph C. Truth Is the First Casualty: The Gulf of Tonkin Affairs—Illusion and Reality (New York: Rand McNally, 1969).

Graham, Bob. Intelligence Matters: The CIA, the FBI, Saudi Arabia, and the Failure of America's War on Terror (Lawrence: University Press of Kansas, 2008).

Grant, J. A. C. "Marbury v. Madison Today," 23 Am. Pol. Sci. Rev. 673 (1929).

Grant, Ulysses S. Memoirs and Selected Letters (New York: Library of America, 1990).

Greenberg, Karen J., and Joshua L. Dratel, eds. The Torture Papers: The Road to Abu Ghraib (New York: Cambridge University Press, 2005).

Grimes, Alan P. Democracy and the Amendments to the Constitution (Lexington, Mass.: Lexington Books, 1978).

Groves, Leslie R. Now It Can Be Told: The Story of the Manhattan Project (New York: Harper, 1962).

Gunther, Gerald, ed. John Marshall's Defense of *McCulloch v. Maryland* (Stanford: Stanford University Press, 1969).

Haines, Charles Grove. The American Doctrine of Judicial Supremacy (Berkeley: University of California Press, 1932).

Hamilton, Walton, and George Braden. "The Supreme Court Today," The New Republic, vol. 103, at 180, August 5, 1940.

Hanyok, Robert J. "Skunks, Bogies, Silent Hounds, and the Flying Fish: The Gulf of Tonkin Mystery, 2–4 August 1964," Cryptologic Quarterly, declassified by the National Security Agency, November 3, 2005.

Haskell, Thomas L. Objectivity Is Not Neutrality: Explanatory Schemes in History (Baltimore: Johns Hopkins University Press, 1998).

Havemann, Joel. Congress and the Budget (Bloomington: Indiana University Press, 1978).

Hayden, Ralston. The Senate and Treaties, 1789–1817 (New York: Macmillan, 1920).

Heller, Francis H. "A Turning Point for Religious Liberty," 29 Va. L. Rev. 440 (1943).

Hinkley, Barbara. Less Than Meets the Eye: Foreign Policy Making and the Myth of an Assertive Congress (Chicago: University of Chicago Press, 1994).

Hirsch, H. N. The Enigma of Felix Frankfurter (New York: Basic Books, 1981).

Hobson, Charles F. The Great Chief Justice: John Marshall and the Rule of Law (Lawrence: University Press of Kansas, 1996).

Holmes, Oliver Wendell, Jr. Collected Legal Papers (New York: Harcourt, Brace and Howe, 1920).

Hoopes, Townsend, and Douglas Brinkley. FDR and the Creation of the U.N. (New Haven: Yale University Press, 1997).

Howard, J. Woodford, Jr. Mr. Justice Murphy: A Political Biography (Princeton: Princeton University Press, 1968).

Hoyt, Edwin C. "The United States Reaction to the Korean Attack: A Study of the Principles of the United States Charter as a Factor in American Policy-Making," 55 Am. J. Int'l L. 45 (1961).

Hughes, Charles Evans. The Supreme Court of the United States (New York: Columbia University Press, 1928).

Hyman, Harold M. A More Perfect Union (Boston: Houghton Mifflin, 1975).

Irons, Peter. Justice at War: The Story of the Japanese American Internment Cases (New York: Oxford University Press, 1983).

Jackson, Robert H. "Maintaining Our Freedoms: The Role of the Judiciary," delivered to the American Bar Association, Boston, Mass., August 1953; reprinted in Vital Speeches, No. 24, Vol. XIX, at 761 (October 1, 1953).

Johnson, John D., Jr., and Charles L. Knapp. "Sex Discrimination by Law: A Study in Judicial Perspective," 46 N.Y.U. L. Rev. 675 (1971).

Kaczorowski, Robert J. The Politics of Judicial Interpretation: The Federal Courts, Department of Justice, and Civil Rights, 1866–1876 (New York: Fordham University Press, 2005).

Katzmann, Robert A. Courts and Congress (Washington, D.C.: Brookings Institution Press, 1996).

Keeffe, Arthur John, and John Harry Jorgenson. "Solicitor General Pocket Vetoes the Pocket Veto," 61 Am. Bar Ass'n J. 755 (1975).

Ketcham, Ralph, ed. The Anti-Federalist Papers (New York: Signet Classics, 2003).

Keynes, Edward, with Randolph K. Miller. The Court vs. Congress: Prayer, Busing, and Abortion (Durham: Duke University Press, 1989).

Kliman, Albert J., and Louis Fisher. "Budget Reform Proposals in the NPR Report," 15 Public Budgeting & Finance 27 (1995).

Kofmehl, Kenneth. Professional Staffs of Congress (West Lafayette: Purdue University Press, 1977 ed.).

Korn, Bertrum Wallace. American Jewry and the Civil War (Philadelphia: Jewish Publication Society of America, 1951).

Kutler, Stanley I. The Dred Scott Decision: Law or Politics? (Boston: Houghton Mifflin, 1967).

Kyvig, David E. Explicit and Authentic Acts: Amending the U.S. Constitution, 1776–1995 (Lawrence: University Press of Kansas, 1996).

Levinson, Sandford. "Why I Do Not Teach Marbury (Except to Eastern Europeans) and Why You Shouldn't Either," 38 Wake Forest L. Rev. 553 (2003).

Levitan, David M. "The Foreign Relations Powers: An Analysis of Mr. Justice Sutherland's Theory," 55 Yale L. J. 467 (1946).

Levy, Leonard W. The Establishment Clause: Religion and the First Amendment (Chapel Hill: University of North Carolina Press, rev. ed., 1994).

Licht, Robert A., ed. Is the Supreme Court the Guardian of the Constitution? (Washington, D.C.: The AEI Press, 1993).

Linford, Orma. "The Mormons and the Law: The Polygamy Cases" (Part II), 9 Utah L. Rev. 543 (1965).

Longaker, Richard P. "Andrew Jackson and the Judiciary," 71 Pol. Sci. Q. 341 (1956).

Lund, Nelson. "Resolved, Presidential Signing Statements Threaten to Undermine the Rule of Law and the Separation of Powers (Con)," in Debating the Presidency: Conflicting Perspectives on the American Executive (Richard J. Ellis and Michael Nelson, eds., Washington, D.C.: CQ Press, 2010).

Malbin, Michael J. Unelected Representatives: Congressional Staff and the Future of Representative Government (New York: Basic Books, 1979).

Mansfield, Harvey C. "The Legislative Veto and the Deportation of Aliens," 1 Public Admin. Rev. 281 (1940).

Mansfield, Jane S. Why We Lost the ERA (Chicago: University of Chicago Press, 1986).

Manwaring, David R. Render unto Caesar: The Flag-Salute Controversy (Chicago: University of Chicago Press, 1962).

Marcy, Carl. "A Note on Treaty Ratification," 47 Am. Pol. Sci. Rev. 1130 (1953).

Marshall, Lynn L. "The Authorship of Jackson's Bank Veto Message," 50 Miss. Valley Hist. Rev. 466 (1965).

Martin, Joe. My First Fifty Years in Politics (New York: McGraw-Hill, 1960).

Mason, Alpheus Thomas. Harlan Fiske Stone: Pillar of the Law (New York: Viking Press, 1956).

McConnell, Michael W. "The Story of Marbury v. Madison," in Constitutional Law Stories (Michael C. Dorf, ed., New York: Foundation Press, 2004).

———. "Institutions and Interpretation: A Critique of City of Boerne v. Flores," 111 Harv. L. Rev. 153 (1997).

McLaughlin, Andrew C. "Marbury v. Madison Again," 14 Am. Bar Ass'n J. 155 (1928).

McMaster, John Bach, and Frederick D. Stone, eds. Pennsylvania and the Federal Constitution (Philadelphia, 1888).

McMurtry, Virginia A. "Legislative Vetoes Relating to Public Works and Buildings," in Studies on the Legislative Veto, House Committee on Rules, 96th Cong., 2d Sess. (1980), at 432–514.

Mikva, Abner J. "How Well Does Congress Support and Defend the Constitution?," 61 N.C. L. Rev. 587 (1983).

———, and Joseph R. Lundy. "The 91st Congress and the Constitution," 38 U. Chi. L. Rev. 449 (1971).

Miller, David Hunter. Secret Statutes of the United States (Washington, D.C.: Government Printing Office, 1918).

Miller, Mark C. The View of the Courts from the Hill: Interaction Between Congress and the Federal Judiciary (Charlottesville: University of Virginia Press, 2009).

————, and Jeb Barnes, eds. Making Policy, Making Law: An Interbranch Perspective (Washington, D.C.: Georgetown University Press, 2004).

Mishler, William, and Reginald S. Sheehan. "The Supreme Court as a Countermajoritarian Institution? The Impact of Public Opinion on Supreme Court Decisions," 87 Am. Pol. Sci. Rev. 87 (1993).

Moïse, Edwin E. Tonkin Gulf and the Escalation of the Vietnam War (Chapel Hill: University of North Carolina Press, 1996).

Monaghan, Henry P. "Foreword: Constitutional Common Law," 89 Harv. L. Rev. 1 (1975).

Moore, John Norton. "The National Executive and the Use of the Armed Forces Abroad," 21 Naval War College Rev. 28 (1969).

Naval Documents Related to the United States Wars with the Barbary Pirate (Washington, D.C.: Government Printing Office, 1939).

Neuborne, Burt. "The Role of the Legislative and Executive Branches in Interpreting the Constitution," 73 Corn. L. Rev. 375 (1988).

Newcomb, Thomas. "In from the Cold: The Intelligence Community Whistleblower Protection Act," 53 Admin. L. Rev. 1235 (2001).

Noonan, John T., Jr. The Believer and the Powers That Are (New York: Macmillan, 1987).

O'Brien, David M. Judges on Judging: Views from the Bench (Washington, D.C.: CQ Press, 2d ed., 2004).

O'Connor, Sandra Day. The Majesty of the Law: Reflections of a Supreme Court Justice (New York: Random House, 2003).

O'Donnell, Alice L. "Women and Other Strangers Before the Bar," Yearbook 1977, Sup. Ct. Hist. Soc., at 59–61, 114.

O'Fallon, James M. "Marbury," 44 Stan. L. Rev. 219 (1992).

Offner, John. An Unwanted War: The Diplomacy of the United States and Spain over Cuba, 1895–1898 (Chapel Hill: University of North Carolina Press, 1992).

Ohaegbulam, F. Ugboaja. A Culture of Deference: Congress, the President and the Course of the U.S.-Led Invasion and Occupation of Iraq (New York: Peter Lang, 2007).

Paige, Glenn D. The Korean Decision, June 24–30, 1950 (New York: The Free Press, 1968).

Patterson, C. Perry. "In Re The United States v. The Curtiss-Wright Corporation," 22 Tex. L. Rev. 286 (1944).

Penner, Rudolph G. "An Appraisal of the Congressional Budget Process," in Crisis in the Budget Process (Allen Schick, ed., Washington, D.C.: American Enterprise Institute, 1986).

Peters, Shawn Francis. Judging Jehovah's Witnesses: Religious Persecution and the Dawn of the Rights Revolution (Lawrence: University Press of Kansas, 2000).

Pfander, James E., and David Baltmanis. "Rethinking Bivens: Legitimacy and Constitutional Adjudication," 98 Geo. L. J. 117 (2009).

Pfiffner, James P. The President, the Budget, and Congress: Impoundment and the 1974 Budget Act (Boulder: Westview Press, 1979).

Phillips, Jerry I. "Marbury v. Madison and Section 13 of the 1789 Judiciary Act," 60 Tenn. L. Rev. 51 (1992).

Pickerill, J. Mitchell. Constitutional Deliberation in Congress: The Impact of Judicial Review in a Separated System (Durham: Duke University Press, 2004).

Pierson, William Whatley, Jr. "The Committee on the Conduct of the War," 23 Am. Hist. Rev. 550 (1918).

Pious, Richard M. Why Presidents Fail: White House Decision Making from Eisenhower to Bush II (Lanham, Md.: Rowman & Littlefield, 2008).

Pois, Joseph. Watchdog on the Potomac: A Study of the Comptroller General of the United States (Washington, D.C.: University Press of America).

Powell, H. Jefferson. "The Story of Curtiss-Wright Export Corporation," in Presidential Power

Stories (Christopher H. Schroeder and Curtis A. Bradley, eds., New York: Foundation Press, 2009).

Powell, Talcott. Tattered Banners (New York: Harcourt, Brace, and Co., 1933).

Reed, Thomas B. "Spending Public Money: Appropriations for the Nation," 424 North Am. Rev. 319 (1892).

Relyea, Harold. "Across the Hill: The Congressional Research Service and Providing Research to Congress—A Retrospective on Origins," 27 Gov't Info. Q. 414 (2010).

Renick, E. I. "The Power of the President to Sign Bills After the Adjournment of Congress," 32 Am. U. L. Rev. 208 (1898).

Rhodes, Irwin S. "Marbury Versus Madison Revisited," 33 U. Cinc. L. Rev. 23 (1964).

Rickover, H. G. How the Battleship *Maine* Was Destroyed (Annapolis, Md.: Naval Institute Press, 2d rev. ed., 1995).

Rosen, Jeffrey. The Most Democratic Branch: How the Courts Serve America (New York: Oxford University Press, 2006).

Rosenberg, Morton. When Congress Comes Calling: A Primer on the Principles, Practices, and Pragmatics of Legislative Inquiry (Washington, D.C.: The Constitution Project, 2009).

Rossiter, Clinton. Constitutional Dictatorship: Crisis Government in the Modern Democracies (New York: Harcourt, Brace & World, 1963 ed.).

Rotnem, Victor W., and F. G. Folsom Jr. "Recent Restrictions upon Religious Liberty," 36 Am. Pol. Sci. Rev. 1053 (1942).

Salokar, Rebecca Mae. "Legal Counsel for Congress: Protecting Institutional Interests," 20 Cong. & the Presidency 131 (1993).

Sarna, Jonathan D., and David G. Dalin. Religion and State in the American Jewish Tradition (Notre Dame: University of Notre Dame Press, 1997).

Schick, Allen. The Capacity to Budget (Washington, D.C.: Urban Institute Press, 1990).

———. "How the Budget Was Won and Lost," in President and Congress: Assessing Reagan's First Year (Norman J. Ornstein, ed., Washington, D.C.: American Enterprise Institute, 1982).

———. Congress and Money: Budgeting, Spending, and Taxing (Washington, D.C.: Urban Institute, 1980).

Schliessel, Lillian, ed. Conscience in America: A Documentary History of Conscientious Objection in America, 1757–1967 (New York: E. P. Dutton & Co., 1968).

Schuwerk, Robert P. "The Philadelphia Plan: A Study in the Dynamics of Executive Power," 39 U. Chi. L. Rev. 723 (1972).

Siegel, Barry. Claim of Privilege: A Mysterious Plane Crash, a Landmark Supreme Court Case, and the Rise of State Secrets (New York: Harper, 2008).

Sirica, John J. To Set the Record Straight (New York: Norton, 1979).

Sloan, Cliff, and David McLean. The Great Decision: Jefferson, Adams, and Marshall and the Battle for the Supreme Court (New York: PublicAffairs, 2009).

Slomovitz, Albert Isaac. The Fighting Rabbis: Jewish Military Chaplains and American History (New York: New York University Press, 2001 paper ed.).

Smith, Jean Edward. John Marshall: Definer of a Nation (New York: Holt Paperbacks, 1998).

Snell, Ronald K. "Annual v. Biennial Budgeting: No Clear Winner," 68 Spectrum 23 (1995).

Sofaer, Abraham D. "The ABM Treaty and the Strategic Defense Initiative," 99 Harv. L. Rev. 1972 (1986).

———. War, Foreign Affairs, and Constitutional Power: The Origins (Cambridge, Mass.: Ballinger Publishing Co., 1976).

Sollenberger, Mitchel A. Judicial Appointments and Democratic Controls (Durham: Carolina Academic Press, 2011).

———. The President Shall Nominate: How Congress Trumps Executive Power (Lawrence: University Press of Kansas, 2008).

————. "Must the Senate Take a Floor Vote on a Presidential Judicial Nominee?," 34 Pres. Stud. Q. 420 (2004).

Sorauf, Frank J. The Wall of Separation: The Constitutional Politics of Church and States (Princeton: Princeton University Press, 1976).

Sorensen, Ted. Counselor: A Life at the Edge of History (New York: Harper Perennial, 2008).

Spitzer, Robert J. Saving the Constitution from Lawyers: How Legal Training and Law Reviews Distort Constitutional Meaning (New York: Cambridge University Press, 2008).

————. "The 'Protective Return' Pocket Veto: Presidential Aggrandizement of Constitutional Power," 31 Pres. Stud. Q. 720 (2001).

————. The Presidential Veto: Touchstone of the American Presidency (Albany: State University of New York Press, 1988).

Stathis, Stephen W. "Civil Rights Act of 1875," in Landmark Debates in Congress (Washington, D.C.: CQ Press, 2009), at 193–202, 487.

Stern, Theodore. The Klamath Tribe: A People and Their Reservation (Seattle: University of Washington Press, 1965).

Stockman, David A. The Triumph of Politics: How the Reagan Revolution Failed (New York: Harper & Row, 1986).

Story, Joseph. Commentaries on the Constitution of the United States (Littleton, Colo.: Fred B. Rothman & Co., 1991 issue; originally published in 1833).

Sutherland, George. Constitutional Power and World Affairs (New York: Columbia University Press, 1919).

Taft, William Howard. Popular Government: Its Essence, Its Permanence, and Its Perils (New Haven, Conn.: Yale University Press, 1913).

Tap, Bruce. Over Lincoln's Shoulder: The Committee on the Conduct of the War (Lawrence: University of Kansas Press, 1998).

Thelwell, Raphael. "Gramm-Rudman-Hollings Four Years Later: A Dangerous Illusion," 50 Public Admin. Rev. 190 (1990).

Tiefer, Charles. "The Senate and House Counsel: Dilemmas of Representing in Court the Institutional Congressional Client," 61 Law & Contemp. Prob. 47 (1998).

Tocqueville, Alexis de. Democracy in America (Phillips Bradley, ed., New York: Vintage Books, 1945).

Treanor, William Michael. "Fame, the Founding, and the Power to Declare War," 82 Corn. L. Rev. 695 (1997).

Trefousse, Hans L. "The Joint Committee on the Conduct of the War," 10 Civil War Hist. 4 (1964).

Tribe, Laurence H. God Save This Honorable Court (New York: Random House, 1985).

Tushnet, Mark. "Why the Supreme Court Overruled National League of Cities," 47 Vand. L. Rev. 1623 (1994).

U.S. Congress. "Reining in the Imperial Presidency: Lessons and Recommendations Relating to the Presidency of George W. Bush," House Committee on the Judiciary, Majority Staff, Final Report to Chairman John Conyers Jr., March 2009.

Van Alstyne, William W. "A Critical Guide to Marbury v. Madison," 1969 Duke L. J. 1 (1969).

Vile, John R. Encyclopedia of Constitutional Amendments, Proposed Amendments, and Amending Issues, 1789–2002 (Santa Barbara: ABC-CLIO, 2d ed., 2003).

Vile, M. J. C. Constitutionalism and the Separation of Powers (London: Oxford University Press, 1967).

Wallace, Clifford J. "The Jurisprudence of Judicial Restraint: A Return to the Moorings," 50 G.W. L. Rev. 1 (1981).

Walsh, Lawrence B. Firewall: The Iran-Contra Conspiracy and Cover-up (New York: Norton, 1997).

Warren, Charles. The Supreme Court in United States History (Boston: Little, Brown, 1937).

Warren, Earl. "The Bill of Rights and the Military," 37 N.Y.U. L. Rev. 181 (1962).

Weber, Paul J., and W. Landis Jones. U.S. Religious Interest Groups: Institutional Profiles (Westport, Conn.: Greenwood Press, 1994).

Webster, Daniel. The Great Speeches and Orations of Daniel Webster (Edwin P. Whipple, ed., Boston: Little, Brown & Co., 1879).

Weinberg, Louise. "Our *Marbury*," 89 Va. L. Rev. 1235 (2003).

Weisberg, D. Kelly. "Barred from the Bar: Women and Legal Education in the United States, 1870–1890," 28 J. Leg. Ed. 485 (1977).

Weissman, Stephen R. A Culture of Deference: Congress's Failure of Leadership in Foreign Policy (New York: Basic Books, 1995).

Wiecek, William M. The Sources of Antislavery Constitutionalism in America, 1760–1848 (Ithaca, N.Y.: Cornell University Press, 1977).

Wilson, Theodore. "The Truman Committee, 1941," in Congress Investigates, 1792–1974 (Arthur M. Schlesinger Jr. and Roger Bruns, ed., New York: Chelsea House Publishers, 1975).

Wilson, Woodrow. Constitutional Government in the United States (New York: Columbia University Press, 1964 paper ed., originally published 1908).

Witte, John, Jr. Religion and the American Constitutional Experiment (Boulder, Colo.: Westview Press, 2000).

Wood, Gordon S. The Radicalism of the American Revolution (New York: Vintage Books, 1993).

Wright, Edward Needles. Conscientious Objectors in the Civil War (Philadelphia: University of Pennsylvania Press, 1931).

Wright, Jim. Balance of Power: Presidents and Congress from the Era of McCarthy to the Age of Gingrich (Atlanta, Ga.: Turner Publishing Co., 1996).

Wyatt-Brown, Bertram. "The Civil Rights Act of 1875," 18 West. Pol. Q. 763 (1965).

Yoo, John. "An Executive Without Much Privilege," New York Times, May 26, 2010, at A23.

———. Crisis and Command: The History of Executive Power from George Washington to George W. Bush (New York: Kaplan Publishing, 2009).

———. The Powers of War and Peace: The Constitution and Foreign Affairs After 9/11 (Chicago: University of Chicago Press, 2005).

———. "The Continuation of Politics by Other Means: The Original Understanding of War Powers," 84 Cal. L. Rev. 167 (1996).

Young, Ernest A. "Just Blowing Smoke? Politics, Doctrine, and the Federalist Revival After Gonzales v. Raich," 2005 Sup. Ct. Rev. 1.

ABOUT THE AUTHOR

Louis Fisher is Scholar in Residence at the Constitution Project and worked for four decades at the Library of Congress as Senior Specialist in Separation of Powers (Congressional Research Service, 1970–2006) and Specialist in Constitutional Law (the Law Library, 2006–2010). During his service with CRS he was research director of the House Iran-Contra Committee in 1987, writing major sections of the final report. Many of his articles and congressional testimony are available on his personal Web site at www.loufisher.org.

From 1972 to the present, he has written 20 books, listed in the front of this book. He is the author of more than 400 articles for law reviews, political science journals, encyclopedias, books, magazines, and newspapers. His writings cover a range of legal and political topics, from separation-of-power disputes to national security law to constitutional law in general. He has twice won the Louis Brownlow Book Award (for *Presidential Spending Power* and *Constitutional Dialogues*). The encyclopedia of the presidency he coedited with Leonard W. Levy was awarded the Dartmouth Medal. In 1995, Fisher received the Aaron B. Wildavsky Award "for Lifetime Scholarly Achievement in Public Budgeting" from the Association for Budgeting and Financial Management. In 2006 he received the Neustadt Book Award for *Military Tribunals and Presidential Power*. Three of his books have been selected by Choice as "Outstanding Academic Title": *On Appreciating Congress: The People's Branch* (2010), *Nazi Saboteurs on Trial* (2004), and *Congressional Abdication on War and Spending* (2000).

Fisher received his doctorate in political science from the New School for Social Research (1967) and has taught at Queens College, Georgetown University, American University, Catholic University, Indiana University, Johns Hopkins University, the College of William and Mary law school, and the Catholic University law school.

Dr. Fisher has been invited to testify before Congress about 50 times on such issues as war powers, state secrets privilege, NSA surveillance, executive spending discretion, presidential reorganization authority, Congress and the Constitution, the legislative veto, the item veto, the Gramm-Rudman deficit control act, executive privilege, executive lobbying, CIA whistleblowing, covert spending, the pocket veto, recess appointments, the budget process, the balanced budget amendment, biennial budgeting, and presidential impoundment powers.

He has been active with CEELI (Central and East European Law Initiative) of the American Bar Association, traveling to Bulgaria, Albania, and Hungary to assist constitution writers; participating in CEELI conferences in Washington, D.C., with delegations from Bosnia-Herzegovina, Lithuania, Romania, and Russia; serving in CEELI working groups on Armenia and Belarus; and assisting in constitutional amendments for the Kyrgyz Republic. As part of CRS delegations, he traveled to Russia and Ukraine to assist on constitutional questions. For the International Bar Association, he helped analyze the draft constitutions for Swaziland and Zimbabwe.

Dr. Fisher's specialties include constitutional law, war powers, budget policy, executive–legislative relations, and judicial–congressional relations. He has been invited to speak in Albania, Australia, Belgium, Bulgaria, Canada, China, the Czech Republic, Denmark, England, France, Germany, Greece, Israel, Japan, Macedonia, Malaysia, Mexico, the Netherlands, Oman, the Philippines, Poland, Romania, Russia, Slovenia, South Korea, Sweden, Taiwan, Ukraine, and the United Arab Emirates.

INDEX OF CASES

INDEX OF SUBJECTS